The Foreground of *Leaves of Grass*

The Foreground of
Leaves of Grass

by Floyd Stovall

University Press of Virginia
Charlottesville

The University Press of Virginia
Copyright © 1974 by the Rector and Visitors
of the University of Virginia

First published 1974

ISBN: 0–8139–0523–0
Library of Congress Catalog Card Number: 73–87861
Printed in the United States of America

In Memory of
M. L. S.
Who was my best and kindest
critic
from first to last

Contents

Preface

IN THE following pages I attempt to tell, within the limits of the information available to me, the story of Walt Whitman's intellectual and cultural development, especially during the years preceding the first two or three editions of *Leaves of Grass*. At times I have suggested that a writer or a book had or did not have a significant influence on the writing of *Leaves of Grass*, but almost every influence, significant or not, was indirect; that is, its impact was on the poet's mind and character and became integral with them before it was reflected in his poems.

As originally planned this story was to have been an introduction to a detailed critical study of the poems themselves. As an ambitious young "scholar" I began to work, and over the years have continued to work, assiduously among my own books and in libraries across the country, gathering materials for such a critical study and for the proposed introduction to it. In the course of time I filled more than ten thousand cards with notes and purchased metal filing cases to keep them in. I enjoyed the note taking, but I could never convince myself that I knew enough to justify my undertaking the task of responsible composition. From time to time I found it necessary to put aside my Whitman notes and turn to other tasks that offered greater promise of early completion. After each task was completed, I would turn again hopefully to Whitman, take from the closet my files of notes, and read them all over to condition my mind for composition. This reading, which usually consumed three or four weeks, was a pleasant activity, but invariably, by the time I had finished the last file, some other project would turn up to require my immediate attention. So back to the files and the closet would go my ten thousand cards for another period, as it were, of hibernation. Thus the years went by until the cards were yellow and my hair white with age.

Eventually all other unfinished projects that I had cherished were finished, and I was retired from my professional duties. At last, I thought, I am free to write my long-postponed critical study of *Leaves of Grass*. But then I discovered for very truth what for years I had suspected, that I had lost my zeal to instruct other people in the true meaning of *Leaves of Grass*. Whether from crabbed age or too much thinking on it, I had become disillusioned with literary criticism and was now content to let every reader form his own opinion and interpretation of the poems. On the other hand, my interest in the ways in which Whitman's life experiences prepared the way for the writing of his poems had so grown that they were more important to me than my original purpose. I was convinced that his enthusiasm for the theater in youth and early manhood and his planned self-education through the reading of books, reviews, and magazines during the late 1840's and early 1850's were of great significance in his intellectual and cultural development, and that they had not been sufficiently evaluated as foreground to the poems. Thus what at first was intended as the introduction to the book became the book itself.

Perhaps my title needs a brief comment. I could think of no more appropriate one than, borrowing words from Emerson's letter to Whitman, "The Foreground of *Leaves of Grass.*" Because of the length to which the book has grown, readers may think I should have incorporated Emerson's adjective in the title and called it "The Long Foreground." Indeed, it is long; but I tried to make the picture reasonably complete, and I found that to cut any considerable part would seriously distort it.

It would serve no purpose to try to acknowledge here all the debts I owe in connection with my many years of Whitman studies, since most of what I gathered from these studies pertained to the book I did not write, and only indirectly to this one. The actual writing was done in my study here in the Alderman Library of the University of Virginia, which I found remarkably adequate for general research, and I am grateful to the Librarian and all the staff for the many privileges I have enjoyed. Not least among those privileges has been the freedom to use the magnificent collections of C. Waller Barrett, now a part of Alderman. I have found indispensable the Trent Collection of the Duke University Library, where many years ago I was allowed to make extensive notes on many Whitman manuscripts and annotated clippings from books and magazines. To the Library of Congress I owe a great deal, as every serious student of Whitman must, and especially to the unrivalled collection of Whitman materials recently acquired from Charles E. Feinberg, who generously permitted me to examine them long before they passed from his hands. All my many benefactors not here named are nonetheless remembered gratefully, and my greatest concern is that this book may not prove worthy in their eyes.

Charlottesville, Virginia
November 1972

The Foreground of *Leaves of Grass*

I. *The Enigma of Genius*

IN HIS letter to Whitman of July 21, 1855, acknowledging receipt of a complimentary copy of the first edition of *Leaves of Grass*, Emerson praised the poems for their extraordinary "wit and wisdom," for their "great power," for their "free and brave thought," and for their "incomparable things said incomparably well," and added: "I greet you at the beginning of a great career, which yet must have had a long foreground somewhere, for such a start." This was the voice of authority, and it confirmed the new poet's self-confidence. Bronson Alcott and Henry Thoreau also read the book, were impressed, and visited the author in Brooklyn. All three men undoubtedly recognized in the poems, despite their uncouth form and occasional vulgarity, the essence of transcendentalism. Another New Englander, Charles Eliot Norton, reviewed the book in *Putnam's Magazine* for September 1855 and described the poems as "a mixture of Yankee transcendentalism and New York rowdyism." This was not unjust, but outside New England, Yankee transcendentalism was hardly more acceptable than New York rowdyism.

Only a few reviews were published, and most of these charged that the poems were not only crude but indecent and condemned the poet as worse than a rowdy, a villain. Sales of the book were also disappointing, and for a while Whitman had a notion to address the people from the lecture platform, as Emerson had done, but he gave that up after preparing rough drafts of a number of lectures that were never delivered. In a belated acknowledgment of Emerson's letter, which Emerson did not see until he read it in the appendix to the 1856 edition of *Leaves of Grass*, Whitman addressed him as "master," and promised that the work of his life would be "the making of poems," and that he would keep on until he had made "a hundred, and then several hundred—perhaps a thousand." He had reason eventually to regret this public letter, both for its brashness and for its allusion to Emerson as "master," which was inconsistent with the claims of originality he had made in the poems, in the Preface to this first edition, and in three anonymous reviews he wrote himself to stimulate interest in his book.

Whitman had the disadvantage of knowing few influential people in literary circles. Although Emerson had lectured in New York a number of times, and Whitman may have heard him, the two had not met personally. Whitman had been respected in journalistic circles in Brooklyn and New York during the 1840's, but even there he was not so well known in 1855 as he had been in 1848. As a creative writer he was virtually unknown. He had published undistinguished rhymed verses in newspapers and a few magazines, and a few sketches and stories, but the editors were obviously not impressed by his talents. At one time he had been known to William Cullen Bryant as a fellow newspaper editor and a pleasant companion on walks into the country, and Edgar A. Poe had published and approved a short contribution to the *Broadway Journal* in 1845; but Poe did not live to read *Leaves of Grass*, and Bryant, meanwhile, had lost touch with Whitman and did not care for the book. Even Emerson's first enthusiasm cooled somewhat after a time, although he never publicly retracted his approval of the poems.

In his Preface, Whitman called for American poets with the largeness of nature who should be spokesmen for democracy and address the people in a language transcendent and new. He made no specific claims for himself, but in the poems he boldly proffered himself as the first of a new kind of poet, a natural man yet also a seer, qualified to say for his fellow Americans what they would but cannot say for themselves. This was bold indeed, since the very last sentence of his Preface asserted, "The proof of a poet is that his country absorbs him as affectionately as he has absorbed it." But the country needed some reminders that its poet had appeared and was ready to be absorbed, and since favorable reviews by the critics were few, Whitman wrote several himself and published them anonymously in friendly periodicals.

The first of these to appear in print was published in the September issue of the *United States Review*.[1] Whitman begins by announcing, "An American bard at last!" He goes on to characterize this bard as one of the roughs, self-reliant, "talking like a man unaware that there was ever hitherto such a production as a book." He says little of the style of the poems except that it is new; nature may have given the author a hint, but no book could have influenced him. The sec-

---

[1] This was in effect the same magazine as the *Democratic Review*. The first issue with the new title appeared in January 1853. In 1856 the new magazine was reunited with the old. The editor in 1855 was D. W. Holly. (See Luther N. Mott, *A History of American Magazines* [Cambridge, Mass., 1928], I, 678 note.) I presume Holly was a friend of Whitman's, but I cannot document the point. The review is not printed among the literary notices but like an essay, with the title "Walt Whitman and His Poems."

ond review, which appeared in the Brooklyn *Daily Times* on September 29, is somewhat less excessive in its praise and more personal, describing the poet's appearance and habits, as if the reviewer appealed particularly to the people of Brooklyn who might know him. He is "a person singularly beloved and looked toward, especially by young men and the illiterate."[2] The third review, which embraced a commentary on Tennyson's poems in comparison with *Leaves of Grass*, was called "An English and an American Poet." It was published in the *American Phrenological Journal* in October 1855 and reprinted in the 1856 edition.[3] The most significant passage in this review is a quotation of nineteen lines from the English poet Alexander Smith containing a prophecy of the coming of a "mighty poet" who shall be the spokesman of this age to all coming times, whose love shall "sphere the world" as the air, and who will reflect humanity as the lake reflects the heaven. How carefully Whitman read Smith's poems I cannot say, but in a manuscript note dated 1854, obviously made while reading them, he wrote: "There is one electric passage in this poetry, where the announcement is made of a great forthcoming Poet, and the illustration given of a king who, about dying, plunges his sword into his favorite attendant, to send him on before." Whitman surely here refers to the lines he quoted in the review and their context. The lines about the dying king are just below the lines about the coming poet.[4] The insertion of this long quotation, together with

2 The *Times* was owned by George C. Bennett, an advocate of Free-Soil principles, as was Whitman. Apparently, however, Charles Gayler was editor at the time. He was Whitman's immediate predecessor in the editorial chair and later was not very friendly. (See Emory Holloway and Vernolian Schwarz, eds., *I Sit and Look Out* [New York, 1932], p. 10). At this time, however, they probably had no ill feelings. On Dec. 17, 1856, before Whitman became editor, the *Times* printed a rather discriminating review of the 1856 edition. The style is unlike Whitman's and I doubt that he wrote it, but who did write it, whether Gayler, or Bennett, or someone else, it is impossible to say. On Dec. 24, 1859, the *Times* carried a brief notice of the appearance that day in the *Saturday Press* of "A Child's Reminiscence." (See Holloway and Schwarz, pp. 186–88). Gayler soon turned to playwriting and became popular. He was one of the patrons of Pfaff's restaurant and continued to be long after most of the Bohemians had dispersed. When Whitman was at home in Brooklyn for a visit in August 1870, he went to Wallack's Theater to see Gayler's play *Fritz, Our German Cousin*, which he called "a miserable, sickish piece." (See his letter to Peter Doyle in *The Correspondence of Walt Whitman* [hereafter cited as *Correspondence*], ed. Edwin H. Miller, 5 vols. [New York, 1961–69], II, 107–8.)

3 Fowler and Wells, who published this journal, were the agents through whom Whitman sold the 1855 and 1856 editions.

4 The passage is from Scene ii of *A Life-Drama*, which he probably read in *Poems*, by Alexander Smith (Boston, 1853; reprinted in 1854). The note is in *Complete Writings*, ed. Horace L. Traubel, Richard Maurice Bucke, and Thomas

the adjective "electric" in his note, can mean nothing less than that Whitman hoped to be recognized as that poet. The doubtful note with which the review concludes indicates that it was written somewhat later than the other two: "His is to prove either the most lamentable of failures or the most glorious of triumphs, in the known history of literature. And after all we have written we confess our brain-felt and heart-felt inability to decide which we think it is likely to be."[5]

The third edition of *Leaves of Grass* (Boston, 1860) was better received by the critics and sold better than the first two, but the poet still felt it necessary to boost his book whenever he had the chance. He was given the chance by his friend Henry Clapp in the pages of the New York *Saturday Press*, which had printed his "A Child's Reminiscence" (later titled "Out of the Cradle Endlessly Rocking") on December 24, 1859. In the issue of the Cincinnati *Daily Commercial* for December 28, a professed admirer of the *Saturday Press*, which he called "that prince of literary weeklies," took its editor to task for printing such "hopeless drivel" as "A Child's Reminiscence," by "the laureate of the empty deep." On January 7, 1860, the *Saturday Press* reprinted the *Daily Commercial* article and also an anonymous prose piece, usually considered a reply, under the title "All About a Mocking-Bird." On May 19 the *Saturday Press* published an anonymous review of the third edition of *Leaves of Grass*, on June 9 a two-page advertisement of the book, and on June 30 still another advertisement accompanied by a review by "January Searle" (George Searle Phillips) reprinted from the issue of the New York *Illustrated News* for May 26.[6] Both "All About a Mocking-Bird" and the anonymous review have been attributed to Whitman on stylistic grounds.[7]

B. Harned, 10 vols. (New York, 1902), IX, 156. Whitman adds in the same note a comment on Smith, who he thinks "is imbued with the nature of Tennyson," and who "seems to be neither better nor worse than the high average." This appraisal was perhaps better than Smith deserved.

[5] These reviews are all reprinted in *In Re Walt Whitman* (hereafter cited as *In Re*), ed. Horace L. Traubel, Richard Maurice Bucke, and Thomas B. Harned (Philadelphia, 1893), pp. 13–21, 23–26, 27–32.

[6] The poem and all the prose pieces named were reprinted in a thin quarto volume bearing the title *A Child's Reminiscence* (Seattle, 1930), by Thomas O. Mabbott and Rollo G. Silver, with an introduction and notes. For more on Phillips's support of *Leaves of Grass* see Charles I. Glicksberg, "Walt Whitman and 'January Searle,' " in *American Notes and Queries*, VI (July 1946), 51–53.

[7] By Mabbott and Silver in the notes to *A Child's Reminiscence* and by William White in his bibliography published in the *Walt Whitman Review*, Sept. 1968, p. 130. Gay Wilson Allen attributes "All about a Mocking-bird" to Whitman but thinks Clapp wrote the review. (See *The Solitary Singer: A Critical Biography of Walt Whitman* [New York, 1955], pp. 232, 260, and 569, note 3.)

My own opinion is that "All About a Mocking-Bird" was a work of collaboration between Clapp and Whitman, or of Whitman with revisions and additions by Clapp. It is not properly speaking a "reply" to the *Daily Commercial* article; nor is it a defense of Whitman's poetry in general, since it relates specifically to "A Child's Reminiscence." Brief as it is, it may be divided into three parts of approximately equal length, each serving a separate and distinct purpose. In the first part we are promised a new edition of *Leaves of Grass* with many new and superior poems, all arranged with more attention to the structure of "the ensemble" than in the two earlier editions. He did not then know for certain who would publish the book, for the offer of Thayer and Eldridge came several weeks later, in a letter dated February 10. The language of this letter indicates that Whitman had not directly applied to them to publish his poems, but it is probable that a mutual acquaintance had been instrumental in convincing them that the new book was worth a risk. Gay Allen suggests that Whitman had sent Emerson proof sheets of some of the new poems and that Emerson showed them to Thayer and Eldridge and induced them to offer publication.[8] Whitman's friend Col. Richard J. Hinton told W. S. Kennedy in 1894: "The Thayer and Eldridge edition was made through me."[9] Hinton was a close associate of James Redpath, who was also a friend of Whitman. Both men were ardent abolitionists and had been active supporters of John Brown's activities in Kansas during the 1850's. Both also were contributors to the New York *Tribune*, where Whitman had several friends, including the managing editor, Charles A. Dana. Within a month after the execution of Brown on December 2, 1859, Redpath, then residing in or near Boston, completed *The Public Life of Capt. John Brown*, which was one of the first books published by Thayer and Eldridge.[10]

[8] P. 237. Allen's reasoning is that Whitman must have sent Emerson copies of some of the "Children of Adam" poems in advance since these poems "were still in manuscript" and yet Emerson urged him, soon after his arrival in Boston on March 15, 1860, to withhold them from publication. As a matter of fact three of the poems had been published in previous editions, and for frankness on sexual matters the language of these was much more objectionable than that of the poems first published in 1860. These were (to use later titles) "I Sing the Body Electric" (1855), "A Woman Waits for Me" (1856), and "Spontaneous Me" (1856).

[9] W. S. Kennedy, *The Fight of a Book for the World* (West Yarmouth, Mass., 1926), p. 242. See also *Correspondence*, II, 30, note 85. Hinton had first met Whitman in 1855. He was working as a clerk in the editorial office of the *Knickerbocker Magazine* when Whitman dropped by to leave a copy of the first edition of *Leaves of Grass* for the editor, Lewis Gaylord Clark. He says it was June, but it must have been later since the *Leaves* was not out in June. Hinton relates this incident in "Walt Whitman at Home," in the New York *World*, April 14, 1889.

[10] C. F. Horner, *The Life of James Redpath* (New York, 1926), pp. 66–68. Horner

Since Redpath and Hinton had collaborated in writing the *Hand-book to Kansas Territory and the Rocky Mountains' Gold Region* (New York, 1859), they might both have had a hand in introducing Whitman's poems to the publishers. William D. O'Connor might also have recommended *Leaves of Grass,* for although he did not meet Whitman before March or April, he had read the first and second editions.[11] Another possible intermediary was Edward H. House, also a member of the *Tribune* staff of writers, through whom Whitman submitted the manuscript of "Bardic Symbols" to James Russell Lowell, editor of the *Atlantic Monthly,* in December 1859 or early January 1860.[12] Whitman knew House as a frequenter of Pfaff's cellar restaurant under Broadway, where Henry Clapp reigned as the Prince of Bohemia and received the homage of many young writers, artists, and actors of the time. Edmund C. Stedman came to New York in the late fifties and on October 18, 1859, published in the *Tribune* the first of several poems that attracted the attention of the literary fraternity. Edward House, accompanied by Fitz-James O'Brien, called on him, and Stedman many years later remembered seeing him at Pfaff's.[13] In 1862 Greeley sent House as a special correspondent to report activities of the Federal Armies in Virginia, where Whitman might have seen him again. On May 5, 1867, Whitman wrote to William D. O'Connor from Brooklyn that he had met Henry Clapp and Edward H. House

---

states that the publishers asked Redpath to write the story of John Brown and that the proceeds of the sale of the book went to Brown's family. Just when Thayer and Eldridge began publishing I cannot be sure. In *Imprints on History: Book Publishers and American Frontiers* (Bloomington, Ind., 1956), Madeleine B. Stern says (p. 410): "The firm of Thayer & Eldridge is listed as booksellers and publishers in the *Boston Almanac* of 1860 and 1861." Redpath's book was reviewed in *Frank Leslie's Illustrated Newspaper,* Feb. 25, 1860.

11 See Ellen M. Calder, "Personal Recollections of Walt Whitman," *Atlantic Monthly,* XCIX (June 1907), 825–34. O'Connor's vehement abolitionist novel *Harrington* was being printed by Thayer and Eldridge at the same time as *Leaves of Grass.* O'Connor's wife Ellen, who became Mrs. Calder after O'Connor's death in 1889, might have read the 1855 *Leaves* before he did. On Emerson's recommendation her brother-in-law, William F. Channing, bought a copy in Boston and later presented it to her before her marriage in 1856. (See Bliss Perry, *Walt Whitman, His Life and Work* [Boston, 1906], p. 98, note 1.)

12 See Whitman's letters to Lowell, Jan. 20 and March 2, 1860 (*Correspondence,* I, 47–48). The poem was published in the April issue of the *Atlantic* and reprinted without title in the 1860 edition of *Leaves of Grass.* Later it was given the title "As I Ebb'd with the Ocean of Life."

13 *Life and Letters of Edmund Clarence Stedman,* ed. Laura Stedman and George M. Gould, 2 vols. (New York, 1910), I, 207.

in Broadway—"also other of my young men friends."[14] It seems probable that Edward House knew Lowell well enough to believe he could influence him in Whitman's favor, for Lowell was not an admirer of the early editions.[15] He might also have met either Thayer or Eldridge, or both, during the years he was on the staff of the *Courier*, but I have no evidence of such an acquaintance.

In the second part of "All About a Mocking-Bird" the writer explains that Whitman's poems—"these mystic leaves"—are hard for the ordinary critic to understand because they appeal to the soul, not to the intellect. He compares the situation of the new reader of *Leaves of Grass* to that of the man accustomed to popular music who hears Italian operatic music for the first time. "Walt Whitman's method in the construction of his songs," he declares, "is strictly the method of Italian Opera, which, when heard, confounds the new person aforesaid, and, as far as he can then see, showing no purport for him, nor on the surface, nor any analogy to his previous-accustomed tunes, impresses him as if all the sounds of earth and hell were tumbled promiscuously together."[16] He then advises his readers to persevere and they may in time come to appreciate both Italian opera and *Leaves of Grass*.

This implied praise of Italian opera as suited to America is inconsistent with the call in the third part of the essay on the "bold American" to receive all foreign poetry only as "studies, exercises" and to listen "with accumulated eagerness" for those native voices that shall

[14] *Correspondence*, I, 328. Clapp was four or five years older than Whitman but House was seventeen years younger. House had gone to Boston in 1854, at the age of eighteen, to be music and dramatic critic for the Boston *Daily Courier*. At that time it supported the Whigs, but in the 1850's it became more conservative, even proslavery in tone. That may have been one reason why House left it in 1858 to become music and dramatic critic for the New York *Tribune*. In late October 1859 Greeley sent him as a special correspondent to cover the trial of John Brown for insurrection at Harper's Ferry. After Brown's execution on Dec. 2, House followed the body to Ohio, where it was buried. His final story appeared in the *Tribune* on Dec. 13. House was a man of varied talents. He is said to have collaborated with Dion Boucicault in writing the very popular play *The Colleen Bawn*, first presented on March 29, 1860. This play was based on Gerald Griffin's novel *The Collegians*, first published in 1829. (See Harry Emerson Wildes, *Social Currents in Japan* [Chicago, 1927], pp. 266–68; also the same author's article on House in the *Dictionary of American Biography*.)

[15] He wrote to C. E. Norton from Dresden Oct. 12, 1855, to disagree with his favorable review of *Leaves of Grass* in the September issue of *Putnam's Monthly*. (See *The Letters of James Russell Lowell*, ed. Charles Eliot Norton, 2 vols. [New York, 1894], I, 242–43.)

[16] The careless structure of this sentence is more likely to be Whitman's than Henry Clapp's, but the facetious tone of the article suggests Clapp's manner.

"make the vaults of America ring here to-day" with our own song, our own music, "broad with the broad continental scale of the New World." Then, becoming more personal, he adds: "Ah, if this Walt Whitman, as he keeps on, should ever succeed in presenting *such* music, *such* a poem, an identity, emblematic, in the regions of creative art, of the wondrous all—America, material and moral, he would indeed do something." The implication is clear that Walt Whitman will do no less than that!

Philips's review of the 1860 edition of *Leaves of Grass* is a rhapsody of praise which Whitman would have been unwilling to write, but he was doubtless pleased to have someone else do it. Phillips says that, although Whitman "often speaks for the race when he appears to be speaking for himself," the book as a whole is "as genuine a piece of autobiography as that of Augustine, or Gibbon, or the Confessions of Rousseau." He had read the 1855 *Leaves* soon after the book came out, and he evidently knew Whitman personally, but whether he knew him well enough to make that statement on his own authority is doubtful. He was apparently not one of Clapp's Bohemian fraternity, for he calls them "flippant young gentlemen of the French school," but he had been associated with Charles A. Dana on the *Tribune*. He was a great admirer of Emerson, whom he first met in England in 1847 while Emerson was lecturing there. His book, *Emerson: His Life and Writings*, was published in England in 1855. This enthusiasm for Emerson was doubtless a common interest that improved acquaintance.[17]

It is clear that Whitman had many friends among the New York literary fraternity even before the publication of the third edition, and that with the appearance of that volume his career was well launched. Many new difficulties lay ahead, but with time and patience they would be overcome. Neither Whitman nor his friends as yet claimed for *Leaves of Grass* more than what might reasonably be expected of a man of literary gifts, high moral purpose, ambition, and devotion to his art. He was a man of the people, a democrat, an artist,

[17] George Searle Phillips (1816–89) was born in England and educated at Trinity College, Cambridge. He came to New York in 1836 and remained about a year working with New York newspapers and then went back to England. He returned to New York about 1855, or soon afterward. How long he remained with the *Tribune* I do not know, but he became the first editor of the New York *Illustrated News* in November 1859. He became insane in 1873 and died in a New Jersey asylum. (Information drawn chiefly from the *Dictionary of National Biography* and *Modern English Biography*, ed. Frederic Boase, 1965 edition, supplemented by *The Correspondence of Emerson and Carlyle*, ed. Joseph Slater [New York, 1964].)

and a philosopher. Whitman doubtless believed in his genius, but the egotism manifested in the poems is not altogether a personal idiosyncracy. It is rather an expression of poetic faith in the potential greatness of the human spirit, for which he assumes to speak in the person of the generic "I" of *Leaves of Grass.* In his personal relationships he showed relatively little of that boastful pride which in the *persona* of his poems is unbounded. There was a quality in his personality that attracted many people, though by no means all; Whitman liked to think of this quality as "personal magnetism," concerning which much was written in the pseudo-scientific literature of the middle nineteenth century. In *The Good Gray Poet* W. D. O'Connor speaks of something "which is felt upon his approach like magnetism." Though in the context he attributes it to Whitman's "unexcluding friendliness and goodness," the eulogistic tone and much of the language of the pamphlet are calculated to persuade the reader that the actual Walt Whitman is identical with the "I" of the poems and that as a person he is far superior to ordinary man.[18]

The first biographical study of Whitman was *Notes on Walt Whitman as Poet and Person,* by John Burroughs (New York, 1867; new edition, expanded, 1871). Here the legend set afloat by O'Connor gathers momentum. In his preface Burroughs says that in history at wide intervals there appear special developments of individuals who "mark and make new eras, plant the standard again ahead, and in one man personify vast races or sweeping revolutions. I consider Walt Whitman such an individual." Speaking of the 1855 edition and Emerson's remark about "the long foreground" to it, he comments: "But that foreground, that vast previous ante-dating requirement of physical, moral, and emotional experiences, will forever remain untold."[19] Much of that foreground has now been told, of course, but much more has been conjectured, or rumored, without documentary proof. It was necessary to the life of the legend that Whitman's life before 1855 should remain a closed book. However O'Connor, Bur-

18 *The Good Gray Poet. A Vindication,* New York, 1866. This pamphlet was written during the autumn of 1865. It is now rare, but was reprinted by Richard Maurice Bucke in his biography *Walt Whitman* (Philadelphia, 1883), pp. 99–130. The passage cited is on p. 103. The "vindication" was provoked by Secretary Harlan's firing Whitman from his job in the Interior Department in the summer of 1865. The claim has been made that Whitman had a hand in writing *The Good Gray Poet* (see Nathan Resnick's pamphlet, *Walt Whitman and the Authorship of The Good Gray Poet* [Brooklyn, 1948], but it seems unlikely that he did more than supply O'Connor with needed information, probably in the form of notes. O'Connor was a skilled controversialist and needed no help in the art of composition.

19 Burroughs, p. 83.

roughs, and Bucke contrived to foster it, the legend was Whitman's creation.[20] Not content with the efforts of others, even such champions as these friends, to speak for him, he continued throughout his life to write anonymously about himself and his poems.[21]

Dr. Bucke went further than O'Connor and Burroughs in trying to obscure the "foreground" of *Leaves of Grass* and explain the transformation of Walter Whitman the journalist into Walt Whitman the poet on the theory that about 1850 he underwent some mysterious experience that endowed him with "cosmic consciousness." With Whitman's knowledge and approval he argued that the poet of *Leaves of Grass* had, like Gautama, Confucius, and Mohammed, attained a higher spiritual and moral stature than others of his time and place, and that *Leaves of Grass* was the bible of democracy and destined to become for future Americans what the Vedas were to Brahminism, the books of the Prophets to Judaism, and the Gospels to Christians.[22] Bucke was the head of a hospital for the insane in Canada, but he was also something of a mystic. A few years later he developed his theory of "cosmic consciousness," which he described as a level of consciousness as far above the ordinary person's "self-consciousness" as that is above "simple consciousness" in the animals. He believed Whitman to be one of the latest in a long line of superior persons endowed with this higher consciousness, including Jesus and the other founders of religions and also a few literary geniuses such as Dante, Shakespeare, and even Balzac.[23] Whitman's English biographer, H. B. Binns, who was acquainted with Bucke's theory, af-

[20] There is no doubt that Whitman wrote a large part of the *Notes* published as the work of Burroughs. He admitted the fact to Traubel in old age, and Burroughs himself is on record as saying that Whitman wrote at least half of the book and revised the rest. (See Frederick P. Hier, Jr., "The End of a Literary Mystery," *American Mercury*, I [April 1924], 471–78. See especially the letter of Burroughs to Hier, p. 476.)

[21] See Emory Holloway, "Whitman as His Own Press-Agent," *American Mercury*, XVIII (Dec. 1929), 462–83. Holloway quotes from an article in the Washington *Chronicle*, Sunday, May 9, 1869, which describes Whitman as "possessing singular personal magnetism." He thinks the poet had a hand in writing *Notes*.

[22] *Walt Whitman*, pp. 178–85.

[23] Bucke outlined his theory in a paper read before the American Medico-Psychological Association in Philadelphia on May 18, 1894, and published in the *Conservator* the same year (V, 37–51). He later developed and published it in the book *Cosmic Consciousness* (Philadelphia, 1901). This idea was often reasserted, though not by disciplined scholars. One of Whitman's Lancashire friends, J. W. Wallace, repeated it in a lecture at Bolton, England, March 28, 1915. The lecture was not published, but I have seen typewritten copies of it in the Henry S. Saunders collection at Brown University.

firmed that Whitman had undergone an experience that ended in an "illumination" of a kind that belongs only to "the highest of the stages of consciousness the race has yet attained," and he believed that this experience was precipitated by a "romance" Whitman had with a New Orleans woman in the spring of 1848, while he was working on a newspaper in that city.[24] Bucke and Binns wrote without having seen the surviving early notebooks in which, probably about 1853–54, Whitman had begun to write down rough drafts of a new kind of verse suggesting the form of *Leaves of Grass*, but Emory Holloway did see them and printed portions of them in 1921 in his *Uncollected Poetry and Prose of Walt Whitman*. Nevertheless, in his biography, published in 1926, he allowed the reader to suspect, if not to believe, that a New Orleans romance, though different from that supposed by Binns, had had something to do with the emergence of Whitman's poetic genius.[25] Some years later John Erskine wrote a novel, based on hints taken from Holloway, in which he represented Whitman as deriving ideas for both the form and the content of *Leaves of Grass* from a highly cultivated octaroon returned from several years of residence in Paris.[26]

Later biographers have discarded the legend of a New Orleans romance, but not always the idea that there was a sudden change in Whitman's life that enabled him to write better poetry than he would have been capable of writing had his development progressed normally. Jean Catel, a Freudian critic, concluded that the poetic genius was born in Whitman about 1845, after an unhappy love affair which led him to associate love and death, but that circumstances delayed the expression of his new power for about ten years.[27] He described Whitman as a maladjusted and autoerotic person suffering from suppressed desires who, having been unsuccessful as a young man, had turned his back on real life to embrace an imaginative self more flattering to his ego than his real self and to project this self into his new poetry. He defined the "I" of *Leaves of Grass* as "le projection de l'inconscient."[28] Another European critic, Frederik Schyberg, believed that Whitman's genius was evoked by a perpetual conflict between his homosexual impulse, which he did not clearly understand, and his ambition to write a new and American bible. The key to all this, according to Schyberg, is the Calamus group of poems, and the

---

[24] *A Life of Walt Whitman* (London, 1905), pp. 69–70.
[25] *Whitman: An Interpretation in Narrative* (New York, 1926), pp. 65–66.
[26] *The Start of the Road*, New York, 1938.
[27] *Walt Whitman: La naissance du poète* (Paris, 1929), pp. 190–91.
[28] *Ibid.*, pp. 232, 400, and *passim*.

critical years were from 1858 to 1860, when he experienced a passionate homosexual love that was not returned. Schyberg was nearer than
Catel to the earlier biographers in accepting Section 5 of "Song of
Myself" as a true account of a genuine mystical experience comparable to the "enlightenment" of Jacob Böhme and the "illumination"
of Swedenborg.[29] More recently Roger Asselineau seemed in his biographical study to accept Catel's theory of the birth of the poet in
Whitman, but to date it in 1854 instead of 1845, and he also agreed
that the "I" in *Leaves of Grass* was a projection of the unconscious.
Asselineau's main concern, however, was with Whitman's poetic development after 1855.[30] Most European biographers believed that
Whitman was homosexual by tendency and that he had a homosexual
"romance" either before 1855 or between 1855 and 1860, and that
the evidence for this belief exists chiefly in the Calamus poems, but
also in some other poems, in his letters, and in his affectionate friend-
ships with young workingmen and soldiers. It is sometimes argued
that the Calamus poems were composed in an effort to sublimate an
abnormal love into healthy comradeship and to make it essential in
a democratic society. The most recent and most authoritative biography, that of Gay Wilson Allen, was strongly influenced by the
Europeans, especially Schyberg, but Allen did not explicitly agree
with them as to Whitman's homosexuality and did not stress the idea
that he had a mystical experience which precipitated the writing of
Leaves of Grass.[31]

Esther Shephard dismisses the theory of Whitman's illumination
through a mystical experience and finds the source of *Leaves of Grass*
in the epilogue of George Sand's *Countess of Rudolstadt.* There he
came across a poet-prophet dressed in laborer's garb who goes into a
trance and composes a great poem. This, she thinks, gave Whitman
the idea that by imitating this character he might pass for a poet-
prophet and win fame. Actually, she argues, he was merely an artificer
posing as a seer, and so he had to conceal the secret of his source. Her
proof of this theory is not very convincing, but it is interesting. There
can be little doubt that Whitman read *The Countess of Rudolstadt,*
and it is probable that he was somewhat influenced by it, as well as
by other books by George Sand, but it could not have been so impor-

[29] *Walt Whitman* (Copenhagen, 1933; translated from the Danish by Evie Alli-
son Allen and published in New York, 1951), pp. 55–60, 161–64, and *passim.*
[30] *L'évolution de Walt Whitman après la première édition des Feuilles d'herbe*
(Paris, 1954), pp. 55–61 and *passim.* This has been translated into English (New
York, 1960).
[31] *The Solitary Singer,* pp. 187, 218–28, 421–25, and *passim.* See also Allen's *A
Reader's Guide to Walt Whitman* (New York, 1970), pp. 63–64, 69, 71–72, 136.

tant as Mrs. Shephard believes.[32] As a matter of fact, on the page immediately preceding the announcement of her discovery she quotes Thomas Donaldson's statement that Whitman told him, "I have just done my work because I believed in it ... there is no secret about it, or in it."[33] Whitman is known to have owned Francis G. Shaw's translation of *Consuelo* and its sequel *The Countess of Rudolstadt*, altogether five volumes, published in 1847, and he probably read it soon afterward, not in the fifties, as Mrs. Shephard conjectures. There is a sense in which Whitman was a poseur: he created an ideal character suited to the role of poet of democracy and tried to conform his own life to that ideal. But he could not have created such a character and made him convincing in the poems unless he possessed already much of the moral and intellectual quality with which he endowed him. It is simply impossible to accept Mrs. Shephard's contention that "Walt Whitman's pose as a poet is responsible for his beautiful poems as well as for his long catalogues of materials scattered about the old and the new world and his empty verbiage and platitudes and meaningless optimism."[34] How could "Out of the Cradle Endlessly Rocking" and "When Lilacs Last in the Dooryard Bloom'd" have been created by a poseur, without original genius, borrowing his substance and manner from such prose fiction as *The Countess of Rudolstadt*?

There is no accounting for genius, of course, and yet there is nothing occult about it. History is rich with the stories of ordinary men who have proved to have genius when the right occasion called for it. As a matter of fact there was nothing sudden or very remarkable about the transition between 1845 and 1855 from Walter Whitman, the first-rate journalist but third-rate poet and fictionist, to Walt Whitman, the original genius and accomplished poet of *Leaves of Grass*. There was change, to be sure, but no such revolutionary change as to be called a new birth, and no illumination that cannot be accounted for by a normal, if unusual, intellectual and spiritual growth. His family observed no sudden change, nor did his friends so far as we know. Bucke quotes a statement, perhaps from Andrew Rome, who printed the 1855 volume and had known its author intimately since about 1849, indicating that to his friends there was no apparent change in Whitman in 1855 and later. Long before he published his

---

[32] Esther Shephard, *Walt Whitman's Pose* (New York, 1936), pp. 140–42. Mrs. Shephard devotes the first 40 pages of her book to a survey of Whitman's reading during his early years, and this part is very helpful. But then she seems to turn her back on all else and concentrate on one book, *The Countess of Rudolstadt*.

[33] *Ibid.*, p. 139. See also Donaldson's *Walt Whitman, the Man* (New York, 1896), p. 265.

[34] Shephard, p. 244.

first edition the Rome family "looked upon him as a man who was to make a mark for himself in the world."[35] His brother George, ten years younger, told Traubel in 1893: "I was in Brooklyn in the early fifties, when Walt came back from New Orleans. We all lived together. No change seemed to come over him: he was the same man he had been, grown older and wiser."[36] His family recognized that Walt was different from the rest of the family during the years when he was preparing his first edition of *Leaves of Grass*, but if there was no change in him we must suppose this difference to have been largely one of temperament and taste. Like most other people who attempted to read *Leaves of Grass*, they did not understand it, for it grew from that part of him that was different. They did not recognize the poet of the *Leaves* as the son and brother they knew. This is not to say that Whitman was a poseur, for the qualities with which he endowed his poet were latent if not active in himself, and indeed, as he believed, in every man.

The only mystery in the composition of *Leaves of Grass* was the mystery of the poetic imagination. In Whitman it flowered late, but it must have been innate. The perceptive reader may see signs of it in his early prose. The flowering, in my opinion, was not the result of an "illumination" or a love affair of whatever kind. It was more probably the gradual opening of latent faculties under the stimulation of his reading combined with a growing confidence in himself. Circumstances, of course, played a part. He was a genuine believer in democracy, and he had participated as fully as he could as a journalist in the movement working for the development of a national literature. Along with these factors, he had grown weary of political bickering among the newspaper editors, had felt no enthusiasm for the business of house building, and was soon to find association with the literary and artistic Bohemians who gathered about Henry Clapp at Pfaff's restaurant stimulating. His frequent attendance at the theater and opera also excited his aesthetic sense. It was natural that a young and ambitious literary man of that time should ask himself what kind of poetry would be appropriate in a native American bard. He was familiar with the heroic characters created by Homer and Shakespeare as typical representatives of their time, and he had given some attention to the early poetry of Europe, including the legendary Ossian.

[35] Bucke, *Walt Whitman*, p. 25. In a letter dated Aug. 23, 1867, Whitman named Andrew Rome as the printer of the 1855 edition. J. Johnston believed that Andrew Rome was "the friend in Brooklyn referred to on page 25 of Dr. Bucke's book." (See *Visits to Walt Whitman in 1890–91* by J. Johnston, M.D., and J. W. Wallace, Whitman's two Lancashire friends, p. 63).

[36] *In Re*, p. 35.

He had become interested in language and its development, although he was technically ill-equipped for such a study. So when he was ready to try his own hand at an American poem he had formed definite ideas about the character and speech of the person who would be its hero. That person must somehow represent the actual American of the nineteenth century and the ideal which he conceived to be latent in each person. He knew that if it was to be authentic, he must begin with himself, both as he was and as he would like to become as a type of the democratic American at his best. So he created the "I" of *Leaves of Grass* and tried to conform his outward life to that pattern. He was utterly sincere, and yet he did not deceive himself. Neither did he claim, except possibly under the flattery of intimates in old age, that the Walt Whitman of *Leaves of Grass* was a true image in all particulars of the actual man. When Mrs. Anne Gilchrist, a woman of literary taste, the widow of the biographer of Blake, read *Leaves of Grass* in 1869, she fell in love with the image of the poet as she supposed it was represented in the poems, wrote him passionate letters, proposed marriage, and made plans a year or two later to come to the United States to effect her purpose. When Whitman became aware of this purpose, he was distressed, knowing that he was not actually the man she visualized. So he wrote her as tactfully as he could on November 3, 1871, that his book was his best letter; but when she persisted, he wrote on March 20, 1872: "Dear friend, let me warn you somewhat about myself—& yourself also. You must not construct such an unauthorized & imaginary ideal Figure, & call it W. W. and so devotedly invest your loving nature in it. The actual W. W. is a very plain personage, & entirely unworthy such devotion."[37] This is a clear distinction between the imaginary figure in *Leaves of Grass* and the real man that a woman would have to live with if she married him. It was obviously made in complete sincerity, an explanation he felt morally bound to make.

The ideal must, nevertheless, have evolved from the real. True, the one must be latent in the other, but how is the latent power realized? The old proverb, *poeta nascitur non fit*, is a fine sentiment and it appeals strongly to young and romantic would-be poets, but few great poets or critics have accepted it without qualification. Sir Philip Sidney said it must be validated by "Art, Imitation, and Exercise,"[38] and

[37] *Correspondence*, II, pp. 140, 170. For more on the subject of the distinction between the actual Walt Whitman and the *persona* of *Leaves of Grass*, see my essay "Whitman and the Poet in *Leaves of Grass*," in *Essays Mostly on Periodical Publishing in America*, a collection in Honor of Clarence Gohdes, ed. James Woodress (Durham, N.C., 1973), pp. 3–21.

[38] *An Apology for Poetry*, ed. Geoffrey Shepherd (New York, 1965), pp. 132–33.

Ben Jonson would not give nature all the credit even for the genius of Shakespeare, for, he said, "a good Poet's made, as well as born."[39] Even Coleridge, the fountainhead of English Romantic theory, agreed essentially with Jonson: "But the sense of musical delight, with the power of producing it, is a gift of imagination; and this together with the power of reducing multitude into unity of effect, and modifying a series of thoughts by some one predominant thought or feeling, may be cultivated and improved, but can never be learned. It is in these that "poeta nascitur non fit.' "[40] It is only the sensibility to beauty and form that is born and not made; the rest, even by Coleridge's definition, comes from art, from cultivation, from education. In Whitman the sense of beauty, both physical and moral, was strong from the beginning, and even the sense of form was stronger than one might suppose who mistakenly thinks the verse of *Leaves of Grass* is formless. We can discover these innate qualities only in their effects, but the process of education we fortunately have the means of discovering in the materials he used and preserved.

[39] "To the Memory of My Beloved, the Author, Mr. William Shakespeare," in *Poems of Ben Jonson,* ed. George Burke Johnston (London, 1954), p. 287.
[40] *Biographia Literaria,* ed. J. Shawcross, 2 vols. (Oxford, 1907), II, 14.

II. *Family and Early Environment*

LITTLE is known of Whitman's genealogy except the information he himself collected and printed in *Specimen Days*.[1] Even if more facts were available it would be impossible to deduce from them with certainty his hereditary traits and separate them from the traits he acquired in childhood and youth. His father was of English stock; his immediate ancestors were farmers who settled in the western part of Suffolk County, Long Island, in the seventeenth century. His mother was of Dutch stock on the side of her father, Major Cornelius Van Velsor, but on the side of her mother, Amy (Naomi) Williams, she was probably Welsh, at least in part. The Van Velsors were also farmers and had been settled for several generations in the eastern part of what was then Queens County, only a few miles from the Whitmans. The Williamses, said to have come originally from Wales, were followers of the sea, or some of them were.[2] It is tempting, though fruitless of course, to look for the sources of Whitman's temperament in the presumed national characteristics of his ancestors; for example, to trace to the English his practical realism, to the Dutch his prudence and geniality, and to the Welsh his imagination. William Sloane Kennedy saw many Dutch traits in Whitman, but he thought he discerned one quality that he attributed to the Welsh. That was his imagination, which he suggests may have come through a "Welsh crevice." "After all," he concludes, "Walt Whitman may be a Celtic geyser bursting through a Flemish mead."[3]

Walter Whitman, Jr., the second of the Whitman children, had ample opportunity to know the families of his mother and father during his most impressionable years. He was born on the farm near his grandparents on both sides, for although his father had earlier adopted the carpenter's trade in New York City he moved to the

[1] *Prose Works 1892*, ed. Floyd Stovall, 2 vols. (Vol. I, *Specimen Days*; Vol. II, *Collect and Other Prose*; New York, 1963–64), I, 1–10.

[2] For an account of the Williamses, see Henry Bryan Binns, *A Life of Walt Whitman*, pp. 8 and 347–48.

[3] "Dutch Traits of Walt Whitman," *In Re*, p. 199. Yet Kennedy quotes Whitman's letter to him, Aug. 2, 1890: "Don't know of Williams having mark'd Welsh blood—never heard ab't that." (*Reminiscences of Walt Whitman* [London, 1896], p. 65.)

country after his marriage, where, it seems, he combined farming with carpentry work in the neighborhood. In May, 1823, near young Walter's fourth birthday, he moved his family to Brooklyn, then a small but growing city of seven or eight thousand inhabitants, where he busied himself building and selling houses. There Walter grew up, although he made frequent and extended visits to the Van Velsor farm throughout his boyhood. He also must frequently have crossed the East River, via Fulton Ferry, to the city of New York, already one of the largest cities of the western world. His grandfather Jesse Whitman died long before Walt was born, but he remembered his grandmother (Hannah Brush), who lived until 1834. He described her in *Specimen Days* as "a natural lady" of "great solidity of mind," who had in early life been a schoolmistress.[4] His grandmother Van Velsor (Amy Williams) died when Walt was only seven years old, but he seems to have remembered her very well. He recalled that she "was a Friend, or Quakeress, of sweet, sensible character, housewifely proclivities, and deeply intuitive and spiritual."[5] Since Cornelius Van Velsor lived until 1837, Walt remembered him particularly well. He had spent many vacations as a boy in his household, of which he gives the following picture in *Specimen Days* after revisiting the cemetery and the neighborhood in the summer of 1881: "The whole scene, with what it arous'd, memories of my young days there half a century ago, the vast kitchen and ample fireplace and sitting-room adjoining, the plain furniture, the meals, the house full of merry people, my grandmother Amy's sweet old face in its Quaker cap, my grandfather 'the Major,' jovial, red, stout, with sonorous voice and characteristic physiognomy, with the actual sights themselves, made the most pronounc'd half-day's experience of my whole jaunt."[6]

In Whitman's published writings there are few direct references to his father, who died in 1855, a few days after the publication of the first edition of *Leaves of Grass*. On the basis of some lines from "There Was a Child Went Forth" ("The father, strong, self-sufficient, manly, mean, anger'd, unjust, / The blow, the quick loud word, the tight bargain, the crafty lure") and a few secondhand reports, Walter Whitman, Sr., it is generally supposed, was a moody, silent, and discontented man, hot-tempered, and often in conflict with Walt. The

---

[4] *Prose Works 1892*, I, 10 (quoted from *Notes on Walt Whitman as Poet and Person*, by John Burroughs, who of course had received his information directly from the poet).

[5] *Ibid.*, p. 9 (also quoted from Burroughs's *Notes*).

[6] *Ibid.*, pp. 7–8. If the picture of the Van Velsor household is a genuine recollection, it must go back more than fifty years since his grandmother died in 1826. She could have been no more than fifty-five at the time.

biographical introduction to the *Complete Writings*, edited by his literary executors R. H. Bucke, Thomas Harned, and Horace Traubel, states that Walt's father was "a quiet, kind, industrious man," but, "when aroused, capable of memorable vehemence." Walt is said to have had some "stormy scenes" with his father, who, it seems, "sometimes strove to exert an undue parentalism which Walt had, out of self-respect, to resent."[7] On the other hand, Walt's brother George said, "His relations with his father were always friendly, always good."[8] He was beyond doubt an unusually silent man, slow, and rather moody. Walt wrote his mother on September 15, 1863, describing a soldier he had met and liked, "he is a large, slow, good natured man (somehow made me often think of father), shrewd, very little to say—wouldn't talk to any body but me. . . ."[9] In December, 1865, after the war was over and George was at home, Mrs. Whitman wrote to Walt, then in Washington, complaining that George had been moody and would hardly speak to her, and adding the significant comment: "what has made him act so god only knows but i believe it runs in the Whitman family to have such spells."[10] It is well known that Walt himself sometimes had similar moody and contrary spells.

Another characteristic of Walter Whitman, Sr., that may have been passed on to his son was an independent, not to say stubborn, will, and a tendency to sympathize with radical and reformist movements. He had known and "had been an acceptor of" Thomas Paine in New York City during Paine's last years, and he had been a subscriber to the *Free Enquirer*, established in New York in January 1829 by Frances Wright, who was later assisted by Robert Dale Owen. Walt himself said he had heard her lecture in the antislavery halls of New York and also in "the old Tammany Hall there, every Sunday, about all sorts of reforms."[11] Frances Wright lectured in New York in 1829, but it is doubtful that Whitman heard her then. She returned, after several years in Europe, and after marrying Phiquepal D'Arusmont, she spoke in New York in 1836 in support of the Democratic candidate for the Presidency, Martin Van Buren, and again in the fall and

[7] *Complete Writings*, I, xvi.

[8] Horace L. Traubel, "Notes from Conversations with George W. Whitman, 1893: Mostly in His Own Words," *In Re*, p. 34.

[9] *Correspondence*, I, 147.

[10] Quoted by Gay Wilson Allen in *The Solitary Singer* (New York, 1955), p. 362 crediting the Trent Collection.

[11] *With Walt Whitman in Camden* (hereafter cited as *WWC*), ed. Horace Traubel, I, 79; II, 204–5. This work, now consisting of five published volumes dated at intervals from 1906 to 1964, is a collection of notes made by Traubel in 1888–89 on conversations with Whitman.

winter of 1838–39. It was probably in 1836 and 1838 that Whitman heard her. She sailed for Europe on June 16, 1839, not to return.[12] On January 28, 1877, on the occasion of the 140th anniversary of Paine's birth, Whitman read a short paper in Lincoln Hall, Philadelphia, "In Memory of Thomas Paine." In this speech he praised Paine for his "noble personality" and service to American independence and defended him against the "foul and foolish fictions yet told about the circumstances of his decease." He had learned much about Paine from one of his friends and followers, Colonel Fellows, a minor official who was very much about Tammany Hall in the early 1840's.[13]

Whitman's love and admiration for his mother are too well known to need documentation. He was particularly attentive to her after the death of his father, when he became the responsible head of the family. Bucke wrote, apparently with Whitman's approval: "There is no doubt that both Walt Whitman's personality and writings are to be credited very largely to their Holland origin through his mother's side. . . . From his mother also he derived his extraordinary affective nature, spirituality and human sympathy."[14] There is no doubt that Whitman was proud of his Dutch ancestry and was inclined to exaggerate its importance in the formation of his own physical and spiritual characteristics. He admired the Dutch, particularly those who settled in New York and Long Island: "A grand race, those Dutch! those forefathers of this Island, and of Manhattan Island! full as grand as any of the antique races." And he resented the burlesque treatment of them, "full of clown's wit," in Irving's Knickerbocker "history."[15] It is just possible, however, that his pride in his Dutch characteristics was stimulated as much by the image of himself he projected in *Leaves of Grass* as by the real self which he attributed to a Dutch heritage. In any case, I find in his published writings no praise of the Dutch before 1857 and no mention of them before 1851. Earlier, he seemed to admire Irving. Holloway quotes the following sentence from his review of Irving's *Life and Voyages of Christopher Columbus*, March 12, 1847: "Our poor commendation is not needed

12 See *Frances Wright, Free Enquirer*, by A. J. G. Perkins and Theresa Wolfson (New York, 1939), pp. 249–51, 329–39.

13 *Prose Works 1892*, I, 140–42.

14 Bucke, *Walt Whitman* (Philadelphia, 1883), p. 17. Mrs. Whitman's mother was described by Whitman as "deeply intuitive and spiritual."

15 From the Brooklyn *Daily Times*, June 3, 1857 (reprinted in *Uncollected Poetry and Prose of Walt Whitman* [hereafter cited as *UPP*], edited by Emory Holloway, 2 vols. [Garden City, N.Y., 1921], II, 1–5). See also numerous passages in *Brooklyniana*, first published serially in the Brooklyn *Standard* in 1861–62 (reprinted in *UPP*, II, 221–321).

for any writings of such a man as Irving."[16] In the 1840's, his political and journalistic years, the rationalism of the English and French eighteenth century, coming to him through his father and through the Jeffersonian tradition, was a predominant influence. By 1855, when he was much more closely associated with his mother, and had also acquired strong romantic sentiments from Emerson, Carlyle, and others, he may have felt the need to balance rationalism with the practical yet "terribly transcendental and cloudy" characteristics which he associated with his Dutch forebears.[17]

In view of Whitman's own statements in his later years, it is not surprising that biographers and critics have been disposed to stress the influence of his mother. Sometimes they have distorted the relationship. Binns says, "His mother was the great link with his boyhood. . . ."[18] Speaking of Whitman's feelings after the death of his mother, he says: "It seemed as though in her life his mother had given to her son something that was essential to that soul-consciousness in which he had lived, and that her death had broken his own life asunder, so that it was no longer harmonious and triumphant."[19] It may have seemed so, but it surely was not. Whitman, at the time of his mother's death, had recently suffered a severe paralytic stroke, and for many months it was uncertain whether he would recover or not. Naturally his mother's death at such a time affected him more than it would have done if he had been in perfect health. There is no real evidence that Whitman as a boy and young man felt a more than normal or usual attachment to his mother. When his family moved from Brooklyn back to the country in 1833, Whitman, although only fourteen years old, stayed behind, and did not live regularly with his family again for a dozen years. His letters from Washington from 1863 to 1873 show nearly as much affection for his brothers and sisters, and even his sisters-in-law, as they do for his mother. In short, he was very close to all his family and felt a responsibility for their welfare, but he also preferred to live away from them. Even when he went home

[16] *UPP*, I, 133; from the Brooklyn *Daily Eagle*. Also in the *Eagle*, Sept. 22, 1846, Whitman notes that Irving "reached New York City last Friday evening, and, on the following morning proceeded to his residence at Tarrytown." (Reprinted in *The Gathering of the Forces* [hereafter cited as *GF*], ed. Cleveland Rodgers and John Black, 2 vols. [New York, 1920], II, 275.)

[17] W. S. Kennedy, in "Dutch Traits of Walt Whitman," *In Re*, p. 198, quotes Whitman as having written him that though the Dutch are practical and materialistic, they are "terribly transcendental and cloudy too." (See also Kennedy's *Reminscences of Walt Whitman* [London, 1896], p. 90.)

[18] *A Life of Walt Whitman*, p. 223.

[19] *Ibid.*, p. 250.

on visits from Washington he usually rented a room in the house of their neighbors and friends, Mrs. Abby Price and her husband. Sometimes his mother's house was crowded, but this was not, I suspect, his main reason for rooming out. A British biographer, Hugh I'Anson Fausset, reflecting a Freudian bias, said: "His was no normal filial attachment. Psychologically the umbilical cord which attached him to his mother had never been cut." [20] Schyberg said, "To Whitman the family meant primarily the mother. . . . The mother completely dominated his concept of the female." [21] Fausset's statement, in view of known facts, is absurd, and Schyberg's is much exaggerated. It is true that Whitman exalted motherhood in *Leaves of Grass,* but it is also true that he admired noble womanhood, as he conceived it, whether in mothers or childless women. Frances Wright captured his fancy as a youth, and even in old age he remembered her as "a woman of the noblest make-up." She had always been to him "one of the sweetest of sweet memories; we all loved her." He told Traubel that he still had her picture.[22] The greatest compliment he ever paid, or could pay, Fanny Wright was in comparing her to his beloved friend, Mrs. Anne Gilchrist. Mrs. Gilchrist was a mother, but Fanny Wright was not during the years when she most appealed to him. The picture may be the same one mentioned by Whitman in a manuscript note published by Bucke in *Notes and Fragments* (1899), where he said: "I like much her portrait-engraving—where she is represented seated." [23] It is said that of his two sisters, Hannah, who had no children, was his favorite rather than Mary, who had several. Instances could be multiplied to show that in actual life motherhood, much as he honored it, meant less to Whitman than has been supposed by those who base their biographical interpretations on *Leaves of Grass.*

The seeds that fell from Whitman's ancestral tree found a fertile soil in the social and political environment in which he grew up. He was born in the forty-third year of American independence, but only the fourth after it was made secure by the Treaty of Ghent ending the second war with Great Britain. James Monroe was President, and the next few years have been called by historians the "Era of Good Feelings." There followed four decades of westward expansion, national pride, and general prosperity. The atmosphere of peace and contentment was marred only by the money panic of 1837, the Mexican War,

---

[20] *Walt Whitman; Poet of Democracy* (New Haven, 1942), p. 243.

[21] *Walt Whitman,* p. 38.

[22] *WWC,* II, 204–5; III, 513.

[23] Reprinted in *Complete Writings,* IX, 130. I believe this is the portrait which forms the frontispiece of Amos Gilbert's *Memoir of Frances Wright* (Cincinnati, 1855).

and the increasingly divisive question of slavery. While the vast terri-
tories of the middle west and beyond the Mississippi drew millions of
settlers from the eastern states, their places were quickly filled by
floods of immigrants from Europe, who contributed by their cheap
labor to the rapid industrialization of New England towns and the
cities of Boston, New York, and Philadelphia. As a consequence of
these and other changes the old political alignment of Federalists
versus Jeffersonian Republicans broke up into Whigs of various loy-
alties—Eastern, Southern, and Western—and Democrats of almost
equal diversity. In religion the rationalism of the eighteenth century
was giving way everywhere, except possibly in Boston, before the
emotional push of evangelical Protestantism. In the cities the influx
of Irish Catholics disturbed the equanimity of the dominant social
groups. With the spread of Jacksonian principles of democratic government, a wider educational base was needed to prepare voters for
their responsibilities. There was a growing demand for more and better public schools, and the more readers the schools turned out the
more demand there was for newspapers, most of which were politically oriented.

It would be difficult to imagine a person more completely representative of nineteenth-century America than Walt Whitman. Of
mixed ancestry long settled in this country, he grew up partly in the
country and partly in a semirural small city, attended the public
schools until his thirteenth or fourteenth year, learned the printing
trade and worked in Brooklyn and New York for a while as a printer,
taught for several years in the country schools of Long Island, and
then embarked upon a career of big city journalism. Biographers
sometimes assume that Whitman's formal schooling ended at the age
of eleven, when he became office boy in the employ of the Brooklyn
lawyers James B. Clarke and his son Edward.[24] It is not certain, however, that this and his first jobs in newspaper offices in 1831 and 1832
occupied all his time throughout the year. There were two or three
school terms during the year, each usually lasting only three or four
months. It seems probable that Whitman continued to attend school
in Brooklyn for a few months each year until the summer of 1833,
when his family moved back to the country.[25] It is generally supposed
that after his family left Brooklyn Walt continued his apprenticeship
there and in New York until 1835, and yet he says in *Specimen Days*
that during the years 1833–35 he was "down Long Island more or

[24] See Allen, p. 17. Allen spells the name "Clark" but Whitman spelled it
"Clarke" (see *Prose Works 1892*, I, 13; also *UPP*, II, 86, 294, 296).
[25] See Whitman's notebook, *UPP*, II, 86.

less every summer, now east, now west, sometimes months at a stretch. . . ."[26] It does not seem probable that an apprentice would be free to leave his work for such long intervals. Bucke says: "He was quite popular at Jamaica, in Queen's County. (He had been a student at the Academy there when a big lad.)"[27] Binns says that he taught at Jamaica Academy, but he never did; he may have lived in Jamaica during the winter of 1839–40, but the school he taught was in the country between Jamaica and Flushing.[28] The academy Bucke referred to must have been Union Hall Academy, which was founded in 1792; in 1833–34, when Whitman probably attended if Bucke's statement is correct, it had separate buildings in different parts of the village for boys and girls. In the late 1830's it had a library of five hundred volumes. The village of Jamaica had a population of about fifteen hundred.[29] Apparently there was then no comparable school in Brooklyn. Jamaica was ten miles east of Brooklyn and on the road weekly traveled by Whitman's grandfather Van Velsor on his way to and from Brooklyn in his market wagon.[30]

His religious training was not rigorous, but it was not entirely neglected. There were Quakers on both sides of his family, and his mother, though not a Quaker, was a pious woman. He seems to have attended two or three different Sunday schools in Brooklyn, including that of the Episcopal church, St. Ann's, where, as a boy, in a "long edifice for Sunday school," he had "a pupil's desk." To this church, according to Allen, the Clarkes belonged.[31] We have Whitman's own statement that he went to Sunday school in the Dutch Reformed Church in Joralemon Street.[32] He also remembered in old age that when he was an apprentice and "devil" in the office of S. E. Clements, proprietor of the *Long Island Patriot* in 1831, the "boss," presumably Clements, took him and the other boys to the Dutch Reformed Church in Joralemon Street, but whether to Sunday school or regular church services he does not specify.[33] If it was customary for an em-

---

26 *Prose Works 1892,* I, 15.

27 *Walt Whitman,* p. 22.

28 See Binns, p. 33. See also *UPP,* II, 87.

29 See Benjamin F. Thompson, *History of Long Island* (New York, 1839), pp. 397–99.

30 *Faint Clews & Indirections,* ed. Clarence Gohdes and Rollo G. Silver (Durham, N.C., 1949), p. 45.

31 See *Walt Whitman's Diary in Canada,* ed. W. S. Kennedy (Boston, 1904), p. 5. Allen (p. 17) suggests that the Clarkes might have taken him to St. Ann's.

32 See *Brooklyniana (UPP,* II, 262).

33 *Prose Works 1892,* I, 14. Allen interprets the "boss" to mean William Hartshorne, who probably was Clements's foreman of the printing shop. In reminis-

ployer to take his apprentices to church, Whitman might also have attended the Presbyterian Sunday school or church in 1832 or 1833, while he worked for Alden Spooner, who seems to have been a member of that church.[34] Many churches maintained secular Sunday schools at this period, schools where pupils were taught reading, writing, and other subjects much as in the district schools.[35] Usually the pupils attended these Sunday schools several hours each Sunday before and after the regular church services. It is quite possible, even probable, that Whitman got part of his secular education in one or more of these schools.

Many years later Whitman remembered with some detail the meetings of the Methodist Church in Sands Street, and especially the singing and the revival meetings. He must have attended services there more than once, but whether he went to Sunday school there he does not say. The tone of this reminiscence is ambiguous; he might have been a boy at the time but it is more probable that he was a young man, since he did not live regularly in Brooklyn between 1834 and 1845. He says: "A third of the young men in Brooklyn, particularly the mechanics and apprentices, the young women of the same class in life, (and O, what pretty girls some of them were!) 'experienced religion,' as it is still called."[36] He also saw and heard the Quaker preacher, Elias Hicks, both in Brooklyn and in Queens and Suffolk Counties, and was evidently much impressed, although he could have been no more than ten years old. He makes two specific references to Hicks, one in *Specimen Days* and one in his "Notes" on Hicks in *Collect*. In the former he says he accompanied his parents "to hear Hicks preach in a ballroom on Brooklyn heights" about 1829 or 1830.[37] In the latter, which obviously refers to the same occasion, he says the time was November or December 1829 and that the ballroom

cences of Brooklyn that Whitman wrote for the Brooklyn *Daily Times*, June 3, 1857 (*UPP*, II, 3–4), he describes Clements as a Quaker and admirer of Elias Hicks. One is left to wonder why, being a Quaker, he attended the Dutch Reformed Church, unless it was to take some of the boys there because their parents were members of that church and requested it. In this same article, however, Whitman states explicitly, "Of a Sunday he used to go to the old Dutch Church." Here Whitman does not say whether he went alone or with the boys.

34 Allen (p. 20) says that Spooner was one of the most prominent members of the Presbyterian Church on Cranberry Street, citing as authority Ralph Foster Weld's *Brooklyn Village, 1816–1834* (New York, 1838), p. 78.

35 See Edgar W. Knight, *Education in the United States*, 3rd rev. ed. (Boston, 1951), pp. 167–70.

36 *Brooklyniana* (*UPP*, p. 293).

37 *Prose Works 1892*, I, 13.

was the "second story of 'Morrison's Hotel,' used for the most genteel concerts, balls, and assemblies," and that "the principal dignitaries of the town" were present.[38]

It is possible that Clements, in addition to taking Whitman to a Dutch Reformed Church, had encouraged his interest in Hicks and Quakerism, but if so Whitman does not mention the fact. Although his father was an admirer of Thomas Paine and Frances Wright and knew the former as a young man in New York, it is likely that by the time Walt was old enough to take notice he had begun to feel counteracting influences, particularly the transcendental Quakerism of Elias Hicks. Many another rationalist about that time was turning away from deism, and some went far in the opposite direction. Hicksite Quakerism after 1826, although a far cry from evangelical Methodism, was definitely an aspect of the romantic trend of the time.[39]

Other religious influences may have reached Whitman through his mother, who seems to have been closer to evangelican Protestantism than her husband. At least that was the case at the time of his death in 1855, for she engaged a Baptist minister to conduct his funeral.[40] After Whitman's death his brother George told Traubel that their mother "pretended to be a Baptist," but went to other church services as well, and that Walt and their father did not go to church at all. He also said, "They all leaned towards the Quakers."[41] During his years as a newspaper editor Walt went to church at intervals, in New York and in Brooklyn, but his going then was probably more in the line of duty to gather material for his editorials than for devotional purposes.

If Whitman did attend an academy in Jamaica it probably was not for many months. The remaining time between 1833 and 1835 he pretty certainly continued his service as an apprentice printer, which

---

38 *Ibid.*, II, 636–37. Hicks died near the end of February 1830.

39 Allen (p. 7) states that Elias Hicks was a friend of Thomas Paine, was kind to him in his last days, and that this was partly responsible for the schism in the Quaker Church in 1826, citing Moncure Conway's *Life of Thomas Paine* (New York, 1892), II, 422, as his authority. But Conway does not say that Elias Hicks knew Paine. The Hicks who did know him and was kind to him was Elias's cousin, Willett Hicks, also a Quaker preacher. This is confirmed in other biographies of Paine, including the most recent, Alfred Owen Aldridge's *Man of Reason, the Life of Thomas Paine* (Philadelphia, 1959), p. 315. Paine, whose father had been a Quaker, wished to be buried in the cemetery controlled by Willett Hicks's society. Willett Hicks was willing, but the committee responsible for the cemetery objected on the ground only that Paine's friends would wish to erect a monument in his memory, which would be contrary to Quaker principles.

40 Allen, p. 151.

41 *In Re*, p. 38.

he must have completed in 1835. In *Specimen Days* he says he "work'd as a compositor in printing offices in New York city" in 1836–37.[42] This must be an error for 1835–36, for in his notebook he recorded, probably in the early fifties and so likely to be more accurate than his recollection in 1882, the fact that he left New York to rejoin his family at Hempstead, Long Island, May 1, 1836.[43] Although he may then have been a journeyman printer, he was still relatively inexperienced. Because of the financial panic of 1836 and the resulting effect on all kinds of business in New York, it is probable that many printers lost their jobs. As he was still very young, not quite seventeen, Whitman would naturally have been one of the first to go. Whether he secured a teaching position before he left is doubtful, but at any rate the following June he began teaching the school at Norwich, near his grandfather Van Velsor's farm. The old man, though in the last year of his life, was doubtless still a person of influence, and may have helped his grandson obtain this job. Teaching was about all he could do in the country, since he did not like farming.[44] After Norwich he taught in a school west of Babylon in the winter of 1836–37, at Long Swamp in the spring of 1837, at Smithtown two terms in the fall and winter of 1837–38, at a school between Jamaica and Flushing in the winter of 1839–40, at Triming Square, near West Hills, in the spring of 1840, at Woodbury in the summer of 1840, and at Whitestone, apparently two terms, in the winter and spring of 1840–41. Some of these places are in Queens County and some in Suffolk, but all are near his birthplace.[45]

Schools were few and of poor quality everywhere in the 1830's, but they were better in New York State than anywhere else in the country except in New England. State law required that in each district "a qualified teacher shall be annually employed for three months" in order that the district might receive state funds. But the inhabitants could tax themselves for an equal amount in addition, or even twice as much, for the purchase or lease of a schoolhouse, books, and other equipment. However, the tax for purchasing books was limited to twenty dollars for the first year and ten dollars per annum thereafter. If the state funds and money raised from local taxes were insufficient, the balance required was raised by "rate-bills," which provided that parents should pay according to the number of days each child had attended school. Indigent families might be exempted from paying

---

[42] *Prose Works 1892*, I, 15.

[43] See *UPP*, II, 86.

[44] His brother George told Traubel, "Walt would not do farm work." (See *In Re*, p. 39).

[45] See Whitman's manuscript notebook (*UPP*, II, 86–87).

the rate-bills. In an effort to improve the quality of school teachers, the Regents of New York University were authorized in 1834 to establish regional academies where for three years the prospective teacher would prepare himself for his profession.[46] Each term lasted about three months, and there were usually three terms, sometimes four if a summer term was added, during the year. Each school had a single teacher, and the number of his pupils might range from a very few up to a hundred or more. Men were engaged for the fall and winter terms, which were attended by large and small children, but women were sought for the summer terms, as a rule, when only small children attended.[47] All teachers were poorly paid, but men received much more than women. In New York, even as late as 1846, the average for men was about $15.00 per month and for women less than half that amount.[48] There were more than 625,000 children between the ages of five and sixteen in New York State, outside New York City, but only 4,128 attended the whole year, and 2,626 attended less than two months. There were 11,000 districts and presumably almost an equal number of teachers, of whom only 1,261 were above thirty years of age, and 1,522 were under eighteen—chiefly women. The highest wages paid any man that year was $26.00 per month, and the highest paid any woman was $11.00.[49] Under such conditions, teaching could hardly be called a profession. It was merely a temporary job that young men turned to while they waited for something better.

According to a school report discovered by Katherine Molinoff, Whitman had eighty-five pupils at Smithtown ranging in age from five to fifteen years, and he received $72.00 for a little more than five months of teaching.[50] Whitman's salary was about average for the period. If he did attend the Academy in Jamaica as Bucke states, un-

[46] Much of this information about the common schools of New York is drawn from a volume with the cumbersome title *A Digest of M. Victor Cousin's Report on the State of Public Instruction in Prussia: also the Organization and Administration of the School System of the State of New-York, Taken from the Report of the Superintendent of Common Schools in 1836,* ed. J. Orville Taylor, Professor of Popular Education in New York University (Albany, 1836). See especially pp. 62–87 and 123–25.

[47] Edward H. Reisner, *The Evolution of the Common School* (New York, 1930; reprinted 1941), pp, 286, 295, and 311–12.

[48] *Cyclopedia of Education,* ed. Paul Monroe (New York, 1911), V, 509, quoted from Horace Mann's report of 1847.

[49] Brooklyn *Daily Eagle,* Feb. 11, 1847, giving a synopsis of the State Superintendent's report for 1846. (Reprinted in *Walt Whitman Looks at the Schools,* ed. Florence Bernstein Freedman [New York, 1950], pp. 165–66.)

[50] *Whitman's Teaching at Smithtown, 1837–1838,* No. 3 in a series of monographs presenting previously unprinted materials on Whitman (Brooklyn, 1942). This information is reprinted in *Walt Whitman Looks at the Schools,* p. 27.

doubtedly on the authority of Whitman himself, he was better prepared to teach than has hitherto been supposed. He was not wholly
occupied with teaching during these years. Between the spring of
1838 and the summer of 1839 he edited the *Long Islander* at Huntington; from August to December 1839 he worked as a printer for
James J. Brenton on his *Long Island Democrat*, at Jamaica, and in the
fall of 1840 he worked as a political electioneer in Queens County.
During the same period he did a good deal of writing. He published
ten poems in the *Long Island Democrat* before the end of 1840, as
well as several installments of the sentimental sequence he called *Sun-
Down Papers—From the Desk of a Schoolmaster*, and it is likely that
some of the short stories later published in the *Democratic Review*
were written while he was teaching. The recollections of two or three
of Whitman's pupils have been recorded, but they do not agree as to
his effectiveness as a teacher. One said he was effective, engaging the
pupils in conversation and playing games with them; another said
he was not because he was always musing and writing instead of attending to his duties.[51] It is hard to see how he found much time for
idleness, yet Mrs. Brenton remembered him as "inordinately indolent
and lazy." [52] During these "indolent" periods Whitman was probably
mentally busy on ideas for poems, essays, and tales, but Mrs. Brenton,
a New Englander, was unable to appreciate such activities in a young
man. He did not dislike country life. In the second paragraph of the
tale "The Tomb-Blossoms," which was probably written before he
left the country, he describes the joys of village life, where men are
not "racked with notes due, or the fluctuations of prices, or the break-
ing of banks. . . ." [53] Though he enjoyed country life and teaching, he
liked the city and the printer's trade better, and so in the spring of
1841 he gave up teaching for good and resumed his trade in New
York City, where jobs were again plentiful.

He did not lose his interest in schools and school teaching, however. He was employed as a visitor of the public schools in Manhattan twice, on September 3, 1841, and January 12, 1842, and examined
the pupils in both grammar and arithmetic. Between 1845 and 1848
he frequently visited the schools of Brooklyn and wrote numerous
editorials and articles in the *Evening Star* and the *Daily Eagle* in
which he explained his philosophy of education, discussed school
libraries and the preparation of teachers, and offered many sug-

[51] See Allen, pp. 35–37.

[52] As reported to Holloway by her daughter-in-law. (See *UPP*, p. xxxiii.)

[53] See *The Early Poems and the Fiction*, ed. Thomas L. Brasher (New York,
1963), pp. 88–94. This is a volume in the *Collected Writings of Walt Whitman*.
This story was first published in the *Democratic Review*, Jan. 1842.

gestions for the improvement of public education. Many times he strongly condemned the use of corporal punishment as a discipline and he advocated normal schools for the preparation of teachers. Among other principles which he advocated in the *Eagle* are the following maxims for teachers: "Govern more by the law of kindness than authority. . . . Lead your scholars to act from principle rather than from feeling. . . . Teach the child ideas rather than words. . . . Teach children to govern themselves. When your scholars fail of doing a duty, let your first inquiry be, if you yourself are not in the wrong."[54] When, ten years later, he was editor of the Brooklyn *Daily Times*, he continued to advocate normal schools for the education of teachers and he urged the elimination of whipping, more care for the pupils' health and recreation, and the teaching of music as a required subject.[55] This interest in public schools remained lively throughout his life. On October 31, 1874, he appeared at the ceremonies inaugurating a new school in Camden, New Jersey, and read "An Old Man's Thought of School," a poem composed for the occasion.

[54] Freedman, *Walt Whitman Looks at the Schools*, p. 126. See also pp. 106, 112, 119, 134, 138, 139, 159, 169, 180, and elsewhere. These maxims were perhaps not original with Whitman, but he subscribed to them.

[55] See *I Sit and Look Out*, ed. Emory Holloway and Vernolian Schwarz (New York, 1932), pp. 53–56.

III. *Journalist and Politician*

W HITMAN was immersed in journalism, and consequently also in politics, from the time he was twelve years old until he was thirty, and during the last ten years of that period he was active in the Democratic Party. The *Long Island Patriot* was an organ of the Democratic Party in Brooklyn, and its editorial offices were often the gathering place of influential politicians. One of its contributors and a frequent visitor in these offices was Henry C. Murphy, who later became one of the political "bosses" of the party in Brooklyn; in 1831 he was a youth of twenty or twenty-one, just out of college and as much interested in literature as in politics. In the reminiscent article Whitman wrote for the *Daily Times* of June 3, 1857, meant as a complimentary notice of Murphy's appointment as minister to the Netherlands, he comments: "Does he not recollect the 'carrying-on,' the cigar-smoking, the animated political discussions, and the canvassing pro and con of some manuscript article intended for the 'Pat'? The writer of this was then a 'devil,' only twelve or thirteen years old himself—and Henry Murphy, though not very much older, treated him with great indulgence, good-humoredly overlooking a great many boyish capers." [1]

Although Whitman left no record of his interest in politics between this time and 1840, the fact that in the fall of that year he was "electioneering" in an official capacity in Queens County for Van Buren in the presidential campaign against Harrison, the Whig candidate, shows that he had kept in touch with political affairs during the intervening years. In the spring of 1838, possibly with financial backing by friends in Smithtown, he estabished and conducted for a year *The Long Islander*, a weekly, serving the town of Huntington and neighboring communities, including Smithtown. [2] After giving up this paper he returned to New York briefly, but was back in the

---

[1] *UPP*, II, 4. Murphy assisted Isaac Van Anden in the founding of the Brooklyn *Daily Eagle* and probably had a hand in the appointment, and possibly in the dismissal, of Whitman, who was the editor from 1846 to 1848.

[2] In *Specimen Days* (*Prose Works 1892*, I, 287), he says this was 1839, but we know from various sources, including the recent book of the Smithtown Debating Society, that it was 1838. See also *UPP*, I, 1, note 1.

country and teaching again by late 1839, probably because work for inexperienced compositors was still scarce in New York. It may be, however, that he was attracted by the opportunity to work with James J. Brenton, Democratic functionary and proprietor of the local Democratic organ, The *Long Island Democrat*, published in Jamaica. This was but a part-time job, for he also taught in nearby schools during the winter and spring terms, 1839–40, and at Woodbury, also close by, the following summer.

It was probably through Brenton's influence that he was appointed electioneer for the Van Buren campaign. How much speaking and writing he did in this capacity there is no way of knowing, but we do have the record of one occasion when he defended the Democratic cause against a Whig advocate by the name of John Gunn. This was early in October 1840 and produced an exchange of newspaper statements on October 6. In the weekly *Long Island Farmer*, the Whig paper, of that date Whitman was accused of "a most indecent and ungentlemanly attack" on Charles King, editor of the New York *American* and later president of Columbia College. King had spoken at a Whig rally in Jamaica on September 24, at which Webster was the principal speaker. Whitman was warned by the anonymous writer in the *Long Island Farmer* that if he made "another such encroachment on the decencies of life" he would be chastised. Whitman replied in the *Democrat* of the same date and repeated his charge that Charles King "uttered a lie" in saying Van Buren and the Democratic Party upheld the doctrine of a "community of goods, wives, and children."[3] The only other political speech of which at present we have a record was delivered in New York City on July 29, 1841, at a mass meeting of Democrats concerned lest President Tyler (who succeeded to the Presidency after the death of President William Henry Harrison on April 4, 1841) should approve a movement in Congress to recharter the Bank of the United States, which Jackson had vetoed earlier. Whitman reprinted this report in the *Eagle* on April 6, 1847, to refute a charge by another paper that he had been a Whig in the summer of 1841.[4] Whitman, of course, had never been a Whig, although as a boy of thirteen he had worked for Alden Spooner, whose *Long Island Star* was then a Whig paper in Brooklyn.

The charge that Whitman had been a Whig in 1841 might have been based, though with a confusion of dates, on his connection for about two months in the spring of 1842 with the New York *Aurora*.

---

[3] This exchange was discovered by Joseph Jay Rubin and published with annotations in *American Literature*, IX (May 1937), 239–42.

[4] *GF*, II, 3–7. See also *UPP*, I, 51.

After Whitman left the *Aurora* in late April, and possibly before he became editor, the *Aurora* supported the administration of President Tyler. But Tyler was himself disapproved by the more conservative Whigs, followers of Clay, because of his suspected leaning toward the Democrats. When the *Aurora* was new, in November 1841 its editor declared that it would be independent, neither Whig nor Democrat, but democratic in the broadest sense.[5] The tone of the editorials during Whitman's connection with the paper leaves no doubt that he supported the Democratic Party, although he sometimes took issue with the leadership in Tammany Hall. Some of the most vehement of these editorials were provoked by Tammany's compromise with the Catholics, led by Bishop John Hughes, on the question of state support of parochial schools. Having been a teacher in the public schools of Long Island, he felt a peculiar interest in the question. Besides, as a Jeffersonian democrat he was bound to uphold the principle of the separation of church and state. He was not opposed to the Catholics on religious grounds or because they were predominantly Irish immigrants. He made this clear on April 18, in an editorial repudiating the "Native American" party, which a year or two later became powerful in New York.[6]

As a matter of fact, the *Aurora*, while Whitman was in charge of it, was not politically motivated. The editor's interest was obviously in the nonpolitical life about him in the city—the people in the streets, public occasions, lectures, and the theater. The same may be said probably of some of his later ventures in newspaper editing. In his notebook is the record: "Edited *Tattler* in summer of '42. Edited *Statesman* in the Spring of '43. Edited *Democrat* in Summer of '44."[7] In *Specimen Days* he says he "wrote regularly" for the *Tattler* but does not mention the *Statesman* and *Democrat*.[8] Whitman's connection with these last two was obviously of brief duration. He probably refers to the *Democrat* in the *Eagle* editorial of April 6, 1847, where he says he was "one of the instruments" in the latter part of July 1844 "through a Democratic daily" in bringing about the nomination

[5] Quoted in *Walt Whitman of the New York* Aurora, ed. Joseph Jay Rubin and Charles H. Brown (State College, Pa., 1950), p. 1. Whitman later wrote for the Brooklyn *Evening Star*, also a Whig paper, successor to the *Long Island Star*, from August 1845 to March 1846, while it was edited by E. B. Spooner, son of Alden Spooner.

[6] *Walt Whitman of the New York* Aurora, pp. 82–85. Although it cannot always be proved that these editorials were written by Whitman, those reprinted by the editors were selected on the basis of evidence that seems to be sound.

[7] *UPP*, II, 88.

[8] *Prose Works 1892*, I, 287.

of Silas Wright in defiance of party leaders (doubtless the conservative "Hunkers," who were said to have prevented his reelection in
1846).[9] Wright was a close friend of Van Buren, and perhaps not
particularly liked by the Democratic leaders of the Polk administration. I can find nothing about the *Statesman* beyond Holloway's statement that it was a semiweekly paper with more than one editor.[10]
The *Evening Tattler* had been established in July 1839 by Park
Benjamin and R. W. Griswold. It was printed at noon and sold by
newsboys on the streets at a penny a copy. The first issue, dated July 8,
contained the following statement of policy: "The *Tattler* will be
strictly *Neutral* in politics—espousing the causes of no party in church
and state; and while it will fearlessly expose the humbugs of the day
—while it will steadily hold up to merited scorn and ridicule the unprincipled and corrupt of all classes who may come within its *tell-tale*
investigations; it will strive to circulate good morals, and correct
principles, and will contain nothing that will provoke the parents'
frown, or put a blush upon the cheek of beauty. It will aim to be
witty without vulgarity, and to be lively without licentiousness." The
editors promised to present the public with "the sublimest songs of
the great poets—the eloquence of the most renowned orators—the
heart-entrancing legends of love and chivalry—the laughter-loving
jests of all lands."[11]

A week later the publishers of the *Tattler* announced their weekly,
Brother Jonathan, a mammoth folio, which would contain in each
number all the matter of the daily *Evening Tattler* for the week and
much more, original and selected. A few months later Benjamin and
Griswold quarrelled with the publisher, J. Gregg Wilson, and set up
rival papers, the *Evening Signal*, a daily, and the *New World*, like
Brother Jonathan a mammoth weekly. Their new publisher was J.
Winchester & Co. Soon after that, Griswold departed and Benjamin
continued with the editorial assistance of various persons. The rivalry
between Benjamin and his former publisher was keen for two or three
years, and Whitman seems to have been involved with both parties.
When he had come to New York in May 1841, he had worked for
several months as a compositor in the office of the *New World* and
made occasional contributions to that paper, including both verse
and fiction.[12] He may still have been working there when on January
29, 1842, he published the poem "Ambition" in *Brother Jonathan*,

[9] *GF*, II, 6.
[10] *UPP*, II, 88, note 2.
[11] Quoted by Joy Bayless in *Rufus Wilmot Griswold* (Nashville, Tenn., 1943), p. 29.
[12] See *The Early Poems and the Fiction*, pp. 16, 18, 68, and 124.

and even when he wrote his defense of Dickens, "Boz and Democracy," although by the date of its publication in *Brother Jonathan*, February 26, 1842, he had probably begun writing for the *Aurora*.[13] The bitterness between the *New World* and *Brother Jonathan* was at its height in March 1842, while Whitman was editing the *Aurora*. Some of the articles published during his editorship contained sharp criticism and ridicule of Park Benjamin. Allen assumes that Whitman wrote these articles and suspects that they induced the proprietor of the *Tattler* to ask him to edit that daily.[14] It is probable, however, that Whitman was not chiefly responsible for the editorial policy of the *Aurora* and that Benjamin was aware of the fact, for he had been attacked in that paper before Whitman began to write for it.[15] Moreover, Benjamin must have known Whitman in 1841 when he was a compositor for the *New World* and an occasional contributor to it. His asking Whitman to write *Franklin Evans*, a temperance novel, which he published as an extra of the *New World* on November 26, 1842, suggests that they were then on good terms.

Concerning *Franklin Evans* Whitman remarked to Horace Traubel on May 2, 1888: "Parke Godwin and another somebody (who was it?) came to see me about writing it. Their offer of cash payment was tempting—I was so hard up at the time—that I set to work at once ardently on it."[16] But he must have confused the names of Parke Godwin and Park Benjamin, or, as is perhaps more likely, Traubel did in his notes, for only the editor of the *New World* would have had the authority to make an offer of "cash payment." The other "somebody" who came with Benjamin to see Whitman was probably a member of the Washingtonian Total Abstinence Society of New York, and might have been James Burns, editor of the New York *Washingtonian*, which was established March 19, 1842, by the proprietors of the *Aurora*, but survived only about two months.[17]

The year 1842 was marked by tremendous enthusiasm for temperance reform. In hundreds of towns and cities throughout the country there were festivals on Washington's birthday, with banquets, songs,

[13] An article on "Dickens and Democracy," dated April 2, 1842 (reprinted in *Walt Whitman of the New York* Aurora, pp. 114–16), is similar in theme to "Boz and Democracy," but different in detail.

[14] *The Solitary Singer*, p. 54.

[15] *Walt Whitman of the New York* Aurora, p. 145, note 6.

[16] *WWC*, I, 93. A few months later Whitman told Traubel he was paid seventy-five dollars cash and later an additional fifty dollars because the book sold so well. (*WWC*, II, 322–23.)

[17] See *Walt Whitman of the New York* Aurora, pp. 5 and 139, note 19. The *Washingtonian* was succeeded by the *Washingtonian and Organ*, but that too was short lived.

speeches, and testimonials by those who had pledged themselves to give up drinking altogether. "But the festival at New York surpassed all others in its extent, beauty, and appropriateness," according to one of the more important lecturers of the period. It was held at Centre Market Hall, with "an immense crowd of people," with "temperance odes sung by thousands of voices," with dinner at eight and testimonials afterward until eleven. Between February 22 and July 4, when even greater celebrations were held, "many of the most notorious rum-sellers in the land gave up the business from sincere convictions of duty. In Brooklyn, N. Y., four shops were closed in one week." On April 1, the *Journal* of the American Temperance Union reported the founding, since February 22, of a great many new temperance papers, and named about a score in the East, including "the New York *Washingtonian,* edited by E. Burns, a handsome and well-furnished sheet, weekly," and the *Essex County Washingtonian,* of Salem and Lynn, Massachusetts, also a weekly.[18] The initial "E" of the editor of the *New York Washingtonian* may be a mistake made by Hawkins, the reporter, or a printing error, for surely he is the same person as the "James" Burns represented as editor in *Walt Whitman of the New York* Aurora. The likelihood that Whitman knew him is strengthened by the fact that he published a short story, "Reuben's Last Wish," in the *Washingtonian* on May 21, 1842, and that Burns or his successor published the first installment of Whitman's *The Madman* in the *Washingtonian and Organ* on January 28, 1843. *The Madman* may have been intended for a novelette which was never completed, since short chapter divisions are indicated in the part printed.[19]

The editor of the *Essex County Washingtonian* was none other than Henry Clapp, who later went to New York by way of Paris and became the leader of the bohemian group there and an intimate

---

[18] This information is drawn from *The Life of John H. W. Hawkins,* compiled by his son, the Rev. William George Hawkins (New York, 1859), pp. 187–89, 197, and 215. John Hawkins, a reformed drunkard, was a crusader for temperance, traveled widely, and spoke at many of the meetings on which he reports. In New York on July 4, 1842, he reports "a mass meeting of the Chelsea Temperance Society, at the foot of 49th Street, in a beautiful grove." There were fifty societies in New York alone, and meetings were held weekly, attended by large crowds.

[19] Both stories were discovered by Emory Holloway and announced but not reprinted in his article "More Temperance Tales by Whitman," in *American Literature,* XXVII (June 1956), 577–78. They are reprinted by Thomas L. Brasher in *The Early Poems and Fiction* (New York, 1963), 110–14 and 240–43. If further installments of *The Madman* were published the issues containing them have not been found. I do not know whether James Burns continued as editor of the *Washingtonian and Organ* or not.

friend of Walt Whitman. Despite Whitman's own period of bohemianism in the late 1850's and his tendency in old age to disclaim interest in *Franklin Evans* and temperance generally, he was in all probability, like Clapp, an honest promoter of temperance in the early 1840's, though doubtless drawn as much by the excitement of the times as by devotion to the principle of reform. There is little doubt that his editorials in the *Aurora* were sincere or that he undertook the writing of *Franklin Evans* for a somewhat better reason than to earn seventy-five dollars, however much he needed it.[20]

During the years 1841 and 1842 the publishers of *Brother Jonathan*, of which H. Hastings Weld was chief editor, also published the *Dollar Magazine*, a monthly, edited by Weld and Nathaniel P. Willis. It was here, very likely, that Whitman met Willis for the first time, though he saw him often afterward, and for a few weeks in the fall of 1844 may have worked in the office of the *New Mirror*, edited by Willis and George P. Morris.[21] About 1855 or 1856 he knew Willis's sister, Sara Payson Willis, who wrote under the pen name of "Fanny Fern" and who in 1856 married James Parton, also known to Whitman then and later. He told Traubel in 1888: "I knew Willis—met and talked with him often. . . . He was agreeable—we got on well together; but God help me what a contrast we must have presented!" Later he said Willis was the "horror of photographers"; he "had his topknot; this had to be got into the pictures." Still later he said: "I

[20] Henry Clapp was born in Nantucket, in 1814, and as a young man was a merchant in Boston, a church member and even a Sunday School teacher. About 1840 he entered journalism by way of the *New Bedford Bulletin*, edited by Charles T. Congdon, but soon afterward turned to lecturing on temperance and slavery. All this was before he edited the *Essex County Washingtonian*. In 1846 he published *The Pioneer; or Leaves from an Editor's Portfolio*, which consists mainly of editorials from the *Essex County Washingtonian* and its successor, the *Pioneer*, which he also edited. Charles T. Congdon was a well-known newspaper man, going from New Bedford to Boston, and in 1857 to New York to join Greeley on the *Tribune*. He knew Clapp very well, and reports that Clapp was sent to "some World's Temperance Convention, or World's Antislavery Convention, in London" after leaving the *Pioneer*. Clapp lived in Paris for a while and met Horace Greeley there and apparently was engaged to write for the *Tribune*, though if he published anything there it has not been identified. Coming to New York, he assisted Albert Brisbane in translating some of the works of Charles Fourier, and later established the *Saturday Press*, a sophisticated paper, which, as we have seen, strongly supported Whitman and *Leaves of Grass*. (Much of this information is drawn from Charles T. Congdon's *Reminiscences of a Journalist* [Boston, 1880], pp. 338–42.)

[21] *UPP*, II, 86. In *Specimen Days* (*Prose Works 1892*, I, 287), he recalled that in 1832, when he was thirteen, he "had a piece or two in George P. Morris's then celebrated and fashionable 'Mirror,' of New York city." So far as I know, no one has yet identified any "piece" of his in the *Mirror*.

knew an artist, a painter, who had portraitized N. P. Willis; can you imagine what that meant? It was fix this, fix that: it was a curl wrong here, a curl wrong there. . . ."[22] The topknot and the curls can be seen in all the early pictures of Willis, before he grew a beard. The best known portrait, however, is that of Samuel Lawrence, the English portrait painter (sometimes spelled Laurence), dated 1837. It was used by H. A. Beers as the frontispiece of his biography of Willis in 1885. Since Willis left England in May 1836 and did not return for three years, he must have sat for the portrait before that date. Lawrence was in New York from 1855, and Whitman might well have known him then. Most likely he visited Pfaff's restaurant at one time or another. Another painter Whitman may have had in mind was George Goffe Rand, born in New Hampshire, but resident in London in 1834 and 1835 and in New York most of the time after 1840, living in Roslyn, Long Island. I have not seen the portrait by Rand unless his is the one appearing as the frontispiece of the 1844 edition of Willis's *Poems, Sacred, Passionate, and Humorous,* and also of the revised edition of 1850. As printed in these volumes, the portrait is endorsed in Willis's well-known hand: "Yours always, my dear Laurence. N. P. Willis." Presumably this copy was presented to the English painter. This portrait resembles Lawrence's, though the pose is different, and the two appear to have been made during the same period in the life of their subject. Another portrait in *Graham's Magazine* for April 1844 shows him without the topknot. Whitman remembered Hastings Weld also in 1888, for on April 18 of that year he described to Traubel a British visitor as "a striking counterpart of Hastings Weld, a literary minister from Washington, who comes to see me and whom I like."[23]

As I have already noted, Whitman edited the *Statesman* for a while in 1843 and the *Democrat* for a while in 1844, but for how long and with what degree of responsibility I do not know. He also wrote for the New York *Sun* and perhaps other papers during this time. The frequency with which he changed his boarding house may indicate a corresponding frequency in changes in the place of his employment. He published but little fiction in 1843, but some of the nine tales, including the novelette "Arrow-Tip" (later "The Half-Breed"), that he published between March 1844 and July 1845, may have been

[22] *WWC,* I, 531; III, 554; IV, 105.

[23] *WWC,* I, 47. He spoke of Weld again on Sept. 13, shortly after he learned of his death. Weld gave up journalism in 1845 to become a minister. He later lived in Philadelphia and New Jersey, and apparently also in Washington. I cannot tell from Whitman's remarks whether he remembered him from the time he was editor of *Brother Jonathan* or only from later acquaintance.

written in 1843. In 1844, through the *Democrat*, he supported the candidacy of Silas Wright for governor, and so continued political activity. To be a newspaper editor at that time was of necessity to be embroiled in politics. Whitman possibly believed that, like Bryant, he could combine a literary career with newspaper editing, which was more remunerative, but there are signs that by 1844 he was beginning to lose interest in party politics and that he continued newspaper work only because he could not make a living by creative writing alone. In his notebook he had this record: "From the middle to the latter part of Oct. 1844 I was in *New Mirror*." Whether he was employed there in the literary magazine or in the daily newspaper cannot be determined.[24] He was probably employed as a temporary editorial assistant.

There is no way of knowing precisely how Whitman occupied his time between October 1844 and August 1845. The composition of "Arrow-Tip," published in the *Aristidean* in March 1845, the first issue of its short career, might have kept him busy for several weeks, but the two or three other items he might have written then are very brief. I believe that it was during the year 1845 that he began the intensive self-education through reading serious books, magazines, and quarterlies that suggests his first resolute effort to prepare himself for a literary career.[25] In August 1845 he moved his place of residence from Manhattan back to Brooklyn. At about the same time his parents and the younger children also returned to Brooklyn from the country, where they had lived at Dix Hills since 1840. Whether the family's move induced Whitman's is a matter for speculation, for Walt apparently had only part-time work on the Brooklyn *Evening Star* from September 1845 until March 1846, when he became editor of the Brooklyn *Daily Eagle*.[26] He is said to have been making only four or five dollars a week on the *Star*, but the only authority for this is Whitman's successor as editor of the *Eagle*, some years later, who may have understated the amount.[27] Mrs. Florence Bernstein Freed-

[24] See *UPP*, II, 86. According to Luther N. Mott's *History of American Magazines* (I, 327–30 and 320, note 1), George P. Morris, with Willis as chief editor, established the *New Mirror* as a weekly on April 8, 1843, but discontinued it on Sept. 28, 1844. The first issue of its successor, the *Weekly Mirror*, was dated Oct. 12, 1844. Gregory's *American Newspapers, 1821–1936* dates the first issue of the *Evening Mirror* Oct. 7, 1844.

[25] Whitman's reading will be discussed in detail in later chapters.

[26] Whitman's connection with the *Star* was discovered by Emory Holloway and announced in his article "More Light on Whitman," in the *American Mercury*, I (Feb. 1924), 183–89. Holloway says he was "more nearly a reporter than an editor."

[27] See Emory Holloway's Introduction to *I Sit and Look Out* (New York, 1932), pp. 4–5.

man, who had the opportunity to examine carefully a complete file of the *Evening Star* for the period concerned, identified to her own satisfaction a total of forty-two articles as Whitman's, thirty-three of which are signed "W" and nine are unsigned.[28] She reprints eleven of the signed articles and the nine unsigned ones, all of which are on the subject of schools. The remaining twenty-two articles, which she briefly summarizes in an appendix, are mostly on such subjects as books, the theater, music, and city improvements. None of them have anything to do with party politics. One article, dated October 2, 1845, with the title "The Cause and a Man," is summarized by Mrs. Freedman as follows: "W. comments on the alleged intoxication of a temperance leader named Gough, concluding that this does not detract from 'the great principle of temperance,' but presents another argument in its favor."[29]

Much as he may have desired to break away from party politics, Whitman was not able to do so at this time. When the editor of the Brooklyn *Daily Eagle*, William B. Marsh, died on February 26, 1846, and he was invited to be his sucessor, he could not afford to decline. The *Eagle* was owned by Isaac Van Anden, a prominent resident of Brooklyn Heights and one of the political "bosses" of the Democratic

[28] *Walt Whitman Looks at the Schools*, pp. 10–12. Mrs. Freedman reports that all the articles signed "W" appeared between Sept. 22, 1845, and Jan. 31, 1846. One of the unsigned articles is dated Sept. 15, 1845; the remaining eight are dated from Feb. 3 to March 6, 1846. She argues that the articles were unsigned because Whitman had become an assistant editor about a month before he left the *Star* to go to the *Eagle*.

[29] John B. Gough, born in England in 1817, came to America as a boy, became an actor and singer of comic songs, then a bookbinder in Worcester, Massachusetts. In his young manhood he became a confirmed drunkard and remained so for several years. He was induced to attend a temperance meeting in Worcester in October 1842, where he publicly signed the total abstinence pledge, and afterwards became a famous lecturer. His first lecture in New York City was delivered in Broadway Tabernacle on May 9, 1844. He returned to New York and Brooklyn the following autumn and lectured a number of times, including one lecture given to the inmates of the penitentiary on Blackwell's Island. He stayed with friends in Brooklyn, one of whom was George C. Ripley. He returned to New York for more lectures on Sept. 5, 1845, but was tricked, it appears, into taking a drink in the guise of "soda" and became thoroughly intoxicated and ill, coming to his full senses a week later to find himself in a house reputed to be of ill fame. He was rescued by friends from Brooklyn. The story of this episode was in the papers through most of September, and on Sept. 22, Gough published his own account, which is reprinted in his *Autobiography and Personal Recollections* (Chicago, 1869), pp. 201–5. When he recovered, after a severe illness, he resumed his lecturing. He had published a much briefer autobiography in 1845, before the unhappy events of September. There is a fair chance that Whitman had attended one or more of the lectures in the spring or fall of 1844.

Party in Brooklyn. He was rather conservative, but there was no serious difference between him and his editor for nearly two years. Whitman accepted his responsibility as the spokesman of the Democrats in opposition to the Whigs, who were represented in the city by two papers, the old and conservative *Star*, founded by Alden Spooner and now edited by his son, and the new and more boisterous *Advertiser*, edited by Henry A. Lees. Whitman carried the Democratic banner loyally through the state election of November 1846 and the local election of April 1847, and the Democrats lost both. Except just before and after each election he was not aggressively partisan. Of three hundred and fifty items reprinted from the *Eagle* in *The Gathering of the Forces*, only twenty-six are classified by the editors as strictly political. Perhaps a hundred more, on subjects like slavery, the war with Mexico, the Oregon boundary, free trade, and political personalities such as Jackson, Webster, Clay, and Calhoun, might be classified as related to politics. The rest, more than two-thirds of all in the two volumes, are definitely nonpolitical, being devoted to such subjects as education, civic improvements, travel and diversions, health, literature, the theater, and art. Emory Holloway, in his *Uncollected Poetry and Prose*, reprints a number of nonpolitical items omitted from *The Gathering of the Forces*, and lists about a hundred book reviews or notices not reprinted in either collection. In the area of reform, Whitman's chief interest becomes the improvement of labor conditions, especially for women and children, the abolition of capital punishment, and, eventually, antislavery. Toward the end of 1847 the Democratic Party began to split into two factions, one supporting the Wilmot Proviso governing the extension of slavery into new states, the other opposing it. Whitman found himself more and more in the camp of the opponents of slavery and eventually moved into the Free-Soil camp. Isaac Van Anden, on the contrary, aligned himself with the more conservative group opposing the Wilmot Proviso. This difference is thought to have been the chief reason why Whitman lost his position in January, 1848.[30]

Whitman tried, honestly I think, to fulfill his responsibilities as editor of a party newspaper, but he was never quite in agreement with the party bosses at Tammany Hall. He early came under the influence of William Leggett, who during the early 1830's was an asso-

[30] In the conventions of 1848, the conservative branch nominated Lewis P. Cass as their candidate for President, and the supporters of the Wilmot Proviso joined with the Free-Soil advocates, both Democratic and Whig, to nominate Martin Van Buren. (For a summary of these events, see Cleveland Rodgers's Introduction to *GF*, I, xvii–xxxii; see also Thomas L. Brasher, *Whitman as Editor of the Brooklyn* Daily Eagle [Detroit, 1970], pp. 103–6.

ciate of William Cullen Bryant on the New York *Evening Post.* He was also a minor literary figure at the time. By temperament he was hotheaded, radical, and an activist. After he left the *Post* he established his own paper, the *Plaindealer,* in 1837, and became a strong advocate of free trade, direct taxation, and the right of workingmen to organize. Before his death in 1839, at the age of thirty-eight, he had come to sympathize with the abolitionists. In 1840 *Political Writings* were published in two volumes. Since this was the year when Whitman first became active in politics, it is more than probable that he read portions, at least, of these volumes. The Locofoco element in the Democratic Party adopted many of Leggett's principles. Whitman thought of Leggett as the spokesman of Jeffersonian ideas in his generation, and in an editorial November 3, 1847, he linked the two together as "the great Jefferson and the glorious Leggett."[31]

He admired Jackson for his honesty and force of character, but it was Jefferson's idealistic democracy that he embraced as a religion and that, for a time, became the dominant force of his intellectual life. In the *Eagle* he called Jefferson "the Columbus of our political faith."[32] When the first edition of the *Writings of Thomas Jefferson,* in nine volumes, edited by H. A. Washington, was published in 1853–54, Whitman became the owner of a set and kept it until 1857, when he offered it, valued at nine dollars, as partial payment of a debt he owed James Parton.[33] In "Poetry To-day in America" he wrote: "Jefferson's verdict on the Waverley novels was that they turn'd and condens'd brilliant but entirely false lights and glamours over the lords, ladies, and aristocratic institutes of Europe, with all their measureless infamies, and then left the bulk of the suffering, downtrodden people contemptuously in the shade."[34] For Whitman the

[31] *GF,* I, 218.

[32] *GF,* I, 8.

[33] See *WWC,* III, 239.

[34] *Prose Works 1892,* II, 476–77. Substantially the same statement exists in a manuscript fragment now published in *Faint Clews & Indirections,* ed. Clarence Gohdes and Rollo G. Silver (Durham, N.C., 1949), p. 33. I have searched for this criticism of Scott's novels both in the edition Whitman owned and in later editions, but I have been unable to locate it as Whitman records it. In a letter to H. Burwell, March 14, 1818 (*Writings of Thomas Jefferson,* 9 vols. [New York, 1853–55], VII, 102), Jefferson said that reading novels was time lost and a great obstacle to good education, but he did not mention Scott. Perhaps Whitman got the general idea from James Parton's *Life of Thomas Jefferson* (1874). Parton said on page 713 that Jefferson "could not relish Scott's novels, because they concealed, as he thought, the ugly truth of the past under an alluring guise of the romantic and picturesque." Parton does not mention his source. Whitman, of course, had formed the same opinion of Scott's novels long before. (See *GF,* II, 264–66, and *UPP,* I, 163–64.)

Declaration of Independence was a greater statement of democratic idealism than the more legalistic Constitution. It may have been through Jefferson's writings that he was led to the reading of Rousseau's *Social Contract*, on which he made some summary notes that survive, though it is equally likely that his friend William Swinton introduced him to Rousseau's work.[35]

For a few weeks after Whitman left the *Eagle* there was talk of establishing in Brooklyn a liberal Democratic, or "Barnburner," paper with Whitman as editor, but nothing came of it. On February 9, 1848, he met J. E. McClure who, with A. H. Hayes as partner, was planning to establish a new newspaper in New Orleans, and he offered Whitman employment, even advancing him two hundred dollars to pay his expenses to New Orleans. Whether or not the bargain provided that Walt's fifteen-year-old brother Jeff was also to be employed, Jeff accompanied him and was actually employed. Whitman's first contributions (the first issue was dated March 5) were articles describing his voyage by rail, coach, and river boat, and his later contributions, in the main, were of a literary nature. Even when he did ordinary reporting, such as writing up the happenings of the police courts, he managed to stress their aspect of human interest rather than the mere facts. There was no regular editorial page, yet Whitman in his notebook memoranda speaks of editorials, written chiefly by a Mr. Larue. There is evidence that Whitman wrote some articles that might be called editorials, although they dealt with general ideas rather than specific issues. He states categorically that a Mr. Reeder was the "city news" man.

Whitman may have welcomed this opportunity to escape from the bothersome political wrangling between conservative and liberal Democrats he had experienced as editor of the *Eagle* and at the same time to travel and see more of the country, especially the romantic city near the mouth of the Mississippi. All the evidence points to the fact that by this time he was more concerned with his own literary career than with public affairs. It is not clear what he planned to do after returning to Brooklyn, but he probably had no intention of starting another newspaper. In a note added to Jeff's letter to the family on March 27, he wrote: "My prospects in the money line are bright. O how I long for the day when we can have our quiet little farm, and be together again—and have Mary and her children to pay us long visits." And on April 23, Jeff wrote: "Walter is trying to save up all the money he can get, and allready he has quite a sum, as soon

[35] Whitman's notes on the *Social Contract* are in the Trent Collection at Duke University and are published in *Faint Clews & Indirections*, pp. 33–41. For more on Whitman and Rousseau, see Chapter XII.

as he gets a thousand dollars he is comeing north, And I too am save-
ing all I can get." Whether because his employers suspected Whitman
was not deeply interested in the paper or for some other reason, after
a few weeks he noticed that they were not as friendly as they had been,
and so he and Jeff gave up their jobs and departed, on May 27, evidently much sooner than they had planned.[36]

Whitman did not buy a farm on his return to New York, of course,
and for several weeks after he and Jeff arrived in Brooklyn on June 15,
he had no regular job and probably spent a good deal of time in writing. It was to be expected that in the election year of 1848 a man of
Whitman's ability and experience in political journalism would be
called on for service. On August 5 he was one of the delegates elected
to represent Kings County at the state convention of the Free-Soil
faction in Buffalo a few days later, and on his return he was selected
to be a member of the Free-Soil General Committee for Brooklyn. Already a Free-Soil paper had been arranged for, and of course Whitman became its editor. It was a weekly, called the *Freeman*. The first
issue appeared on September 9, but the following day the building in
which he had set up his press was burned to the ground, and he was
not able to resume publication for two months. In the meantime, the
presidential election had been completed, and the Free-Soil candidate
had lost. The *Freeman* struggled on until September, 1849, and then
expired.

During the winter of 1848–49 Whitman built a three-story house on
a lot on Myrtle Avenue, moved the family into the upper floors, and
used the ground floor for his printing shop. In connection with the
printing shop he also opened a bookstore.[37] This was his home and
place of business until May, 1852. Apparently the bookstore was given
up with the house, or perhaps earlier. For two or three years after
that, he joined his father and brothers in the building and selling of
frame houses in Brooklyn. In 1850 and 1851 he contributed a few
human interest sketches to the Brooklyn *Daily Advertiser* and to Bry-

[36] In addition to more general biographical sources, see William Kerman Dart,
"Whitman in New Orleans," *Publications of the Louisiana Historical Society*,
VII (1915), 97–112, and Emory Holloway, "Walt Whitman in New Orleans," *Yale
Review*, V (Oct. 1915), 172 ff. For Whitman's notebook memoranda, see *UPP*,
II, 77–79. For the letters, see *Correspondence*, I, 33–34.

[37] A picture of this house appears in *GF*, II, opposite p. 242. See also *UPP*, II,
88. For more on Whitman's bookstore, see Charles E. Feinberg, "A Whitman Collector Destroys a Whitman Myth," *Papers of the Bibliographical Society of
America*, LII (1958), 81–82. See also Madeleine B. Stern, *Heads & Headlines*
(Norman, Okla., 1971), pp. 105–6.

ant's New York *Evening Post*. To all intents and purposes his career as a political journalist had ended in 1849, although he did not lose interest in public affairs. The revolutionary disturbances in Europe in 1848 had aroused his sympathies, and his feeling against slavery was intensified. The revolution in France inspired a poem which he published on June 21, 1850, in the *Daily Tribune* under the title "Resurgemus," and in the summer of 1854 he wrote a satiric ballad condemning the arrest and trial of the fugitive slave Anthony Burns. Both of these poems appeared in the 1855 edition of *Leaves of Grass*. By 1856 he was so completely disillusioned with party politics that he wrote and printed in proof sheets, though he did not publish, an intemperate speech attacking both parties and government officials in general and calling on all young men, farmers and mechanics, to unite against them.[38]

It seems fairly certain that he accepted the position of editor of the Brooklyn *Daily Times* in May 1857 only because he needed money to tide him over until he could get a third edition of *Leaves of Grass* published, which he hoped would be more successful than the first two editions. The *Times* was politically independent, although it opposed President Buchanan's proslavery policy and supported in general the position of Stephen A. Douglas in 1858. As editor of this paper Whitman showed little interest in political controversy on either the local or national level, but more interest in literature than any previous editor had shown. During his editorship, Whitman seemed to become less radical, taking the position of a moderate not only in politics but in most other matters as well. There are editorials ridiculing reformers of various types, including temperance reformers, and even the question of capital punishment is dealt with realistically.[39] This change of temper can also be detected in some of the poems written in the late fifties. The title which Holloway gave to his collection of editorials from the *Times, I Sit and Look Out*, very well expresses the tone of Whitman's contributions to the paper. It is the title of a short poem written in the late fifties and first published in the 1860 edition. The poet represents himself as sitting and looking out on all the evils and sorrows of the world but remaining silent, evidently because there is no remedy for them which he can command. The activist has become an observer, the reformer a philoso-

[38] This was "The Eighteenth Presidency," first published in 1928; in this country in Clifton Joseph Furness's *Walt Whitman's Workshop* (Cambridge, Mass., 1928), pp. 92–113, and as a pamphlet in Montpelier, France, by Jean Catel.

[39] See *I Sit and Look Out*, pp. 42–50.

pher, the journalist a poet. The exact date of his leaving the *Times* is not known, but it probably was in June 1859. Why he left is also undetermined, but it was pretty certainly because he had accomplished the purpose for which he had taken the job and now wished to be free to devote all his energies to the preparation of the third edition of the poems.

IV. *Early Reading: Popular Literature*

EMERSON once said to Whitman, "You surprise me in one way Mr. Whitman: surprise me greatly: yet do not surprise me either: for I might have assumed as much: that is, I find you a copious book man —a readier knower of conventional things in literature than I had thought you to be."[1] This remark was probably made between 1855 and 1860 on one of Emerson's visits to the New York area to lecture. Whitman told Traubel he had met Emerson "twenty and more times."[2] The first time was probably December 11, 1855, when Emerson lectured in New York; the second, January 8, 1857, when he lectured in Patterson, New Jersey, and the third January 15, 1858, when he lectured in Brooklyn. Emerson's biographer says, "It may have been on December 11, 1855, that Emerson first had Whitman to dinner at a New York hotel."[3] Edward Carpenter said that Emerson told him in 1877, speaking of Whitman, "I saw him in New York, and asked him to dine at my hotel. He shouted for a 'tin mug' for his beer."[4] This must have been the first of their meetings. They also met at the Astor House on January 8, 1857, but apparently not for dinner. Traubel reported Whitman as saying Emerson visited him at his home after dinner and they walked together three miles to the ferry. When they arrived at the Astor House, where Emerson had a room, they had, at Emerson's invitation, "some drink," though he could not remember what. Perhaps it was beer; if so, one is inclined to wonder if this was not the occasion when Whitman called for a "tin mug," and not at the dinner, which presumably had been on their first meeting.[5] On another occasion Whitman told Traubel that A. B. Alcott came to see him in Brooklyn just before Emerson.[6] From this I assume that Emerson did not go to Whitman's house in Decem-

---

[1] As reported by Horace Traubel in *WWC*, III, 401–2.

[2] *WWC*, II, 230.

[3] Ralph L. Rusk, *The Life of Ralph Waldo Emerson* (New York, 1949), p. 374.

[4] Edward Carpenter, *Days with Walt Whitman* (London, 1906), pp. 166–67.

[5] *WWC*, II, 504–5. Whitman said Emerson was to lecture that night in Newark, but doubtless it was in Paterson, as indicated in the Emerson manuscripts consulted by Rusk. The approximate date is made certain by Whitman's statement that Emerson's *English Traits* had just been published; that was in August 1856.

[6] *WWC*, I, 130.

ber 1855. Alcott visited Whitman alone on October 4, 1856, returned
with Thoreau on November 10, and later made other visits before the
end of the year. On December 28 Alcott took Whitman for an evening
of conversation with several other invited friends at the home of
Samuel Longfellow, then minister of the Second Unitarian Church
in Brooklyn, where the author of *Leaves of Grass* was somewhat ill
at ease.[7]

   Whitman saw a good deal of Emerson during the weeks he spent
in Boston in 1860 and 1881 in connection with the publication of
Leaves of Grass, but by 1860 there could have been no question in
Emerson's mind about the extent to which Whitman was a bookman.
As we have seen, Whitman was careful to leave the impression in his
reviews of the 1855 *Leaves of Grass* that the poems were the work of
a relatively uneducated workman unacquainted with literature. After
1860 he seems to have abandoned this pretense, although he always
protested that he was not a studious reader. During the 1880's, the
years of his enforced idleness, he read a great deal both in contemporary writing and in old books, some of them his own, but most of
them procured for him by Traubel, Thomas Harned, and other
friends of Camden and Philadelphia. His brother George said, doubtless speaking of the years 1845–62, that Walt was not a book collector
and had few books, though he "spent a good many hours in the libraries of New York."[8] Yet most of the books he had in 1885 were
acquired during those New York years. Among these books were
volumes of the Bible, Homer, Shakespeare, Aeschylus, Epictetus, Marcus Aurelius, Horace, and Virgil; Volney's travel books, Voltaire's
Dictionary, and the poems of Ossian, Omar Khayyám, Hafiz, and
Saadi; C. C. Felton's *Greece, Ancient and Modern* (2 vols., 1851–52),
George Grote's monumental *History of Greece* (12 vols., 1846–56), and

   [7] See *The Journals of Bronson Alcott,* selected and edited by Odell Shepard
(Boston, 1938), pp. 286–94. The Rev. Samuel Longfellow was the brother and
biographer of Henry Wadsworth Longfellow. He was minister of the Brooklyn
church from 1853 to 1860. Later, 1878 to 1882 he was minister of the Unitarian
Church of Germantown, Pa. Whitman told Traubel that he heard Samuel Longfellow preach in Brooklyn and had been told that Longfellow admired *Leaves of
Grass*—called it modern Greek. However, he had apparently not seen him during
his Germantown residency. Whitman admitted he "was not au fait" in Longfellow
circles and preferred not to "push" himself. (*WWC,* II, 502–3.) Yet Samuel Longfellow was a Transcendentalist, an admirer of Emerson, and a contributor to the
Boston *Radical* (1865–72), in which Mrs. Gilchrist's "A Woman's Estimate of
Walt Whitman" appeared in May 1870, and in which *Drum-Taps* had been
favorably reviewed and one of the poems published (*WWC,* IV, 495).

   [8] Horace L. Traubel, "Notes from Conversations with George W. Whitman,
1893," *In Re,* p. 39.

J. A. Symonds's *Studies of the Greek Poets* (2 vols., 1880); George Ellis's *Specimens of Early English Metrical Romances* (probably the Bohn Library edition of 1848), Scott's *Minstrelsy of the Scottish Border* (an edition published in the 1830's), and C. C. Fauriel's *Histoire de la poésie provençale* (Paris, 1846) in the English translation of 1860; John Carlyle's translation of Dante's *Inferno*, George Ticknor's *History of Spanish Literature* (3 vols., 1849), and F. H. Hedge's *Prose Writers of Germany* (1847); E. C. Stedman's *Library of American Literature* (11 vols., 1888); the novels of George Sand, including *Consuelo* (3 vols.) and *The Countess of Rudolstadt* (2 vols.) in Shaw's translation of 1847 which he had owned since that date; Heine's *Reisebilder* in Charles Leland's translation, the poetical works of Scott in an edition of the 1830's and most of his novels, some of the novels of Cooper, Dickens, and Bulwer-Lytton, the poems of Blake, Burns, Moore, and Tennyson; Elias Hicks's *Journal* (1832), and the essays and other volumes of Emerson's works. These were by no means all, as one can discover by reading carefully in the five volumes of *With Walt Whitman in Camden*, but they are evidence that Whitman had kept many of the books acquired earlier. Among the books acquired in later years two examples will suffice to indicate the variety of his interests. In 1888 Traubel discovered him reading the *Memoir of Thomas Bewick, Written by Himself, 1822–1828*, probably in the edition of 1862, since he says he had had the book for years.[9] In a letter to Peter Doyle, February 6, 1874, Whitman says, "I have been reading a book *Merrie England in the Olden Time*, a London book, with pictures, full of fun and humor—I have enjoyed it much."[10]

It is not possible to determine what exactly were Whitman's reading habits as a young man. The evidence is often contradictory. Even Bucke, who surely got his information directly from Whitman, is inconsistent. In one place he said, "Reading did not go for so very much in Walt Whitman's education," but in another he said he usually read a couple of hours every day, and that "if he sat in the library an hour, he would have half a dozen to a dozen volumes about him."[11] This habit of having many books about him in the library suggests an eager rather than a desultory reader—a man looking for information and ideas rather than a casual reader for pleasure. Trau-

[9] *WWC*, II, 492. Traubel calls it "Memoirs," but the word is singular. Bewick was famous for his engravings, especially of birds and animals.

[10] *Correspondence*, II, 274–75. This book, written by George Daniel, was first published in 1842, but Whitman probably had the edition of 1873. Miller's note mentions only the 1842 edition.

[11] *Walt Whitman* (Philadelphia, 1883), pp. 21 and 52.

bel, who knew more of his reading habits than anyone else, said that "books have had not a little to do with his initiative as well as with the growths of later years." [12]

As a child he had access to such books as were to be found in the public school libraries of Brooklyn, and we know that although his father was not an educated man he had a few books, including Volney's *Ruins*, Frances Wright's *A Few Days in Athens*, and probably some of the works of Thomas Paine, Jefferson, and other deistic writers. He said it was his good fortune at the age of eleven to receive from his lawyer-employer a gift subscription to a good circulating library. No doubt young Edward Clarke had already noticed that the boy was fond of reading. In *Specimen Days* he referred to this as the "signal event" of his life up to that time. "For a time," he remembered, "I now revel'd in romance-reading of all kinds; first, the 'Arabian Nights,' all the volumes, an amazing treat. Then, with sorties in very many other directions, took in Walter Scott's novels, one after another, and his poetry, (and continue to enjoy novels and poetry to this day.)" [13] Habits and tastes are formed early, and a child who loves to read is likely to grow into a man who loves books and chooses a profession, if opportunity permits, that will allow him to indulge his literary taste. It was probably by his own choice that he was a little later apprenticed to a printer.

A bookish child will usually turn to fiction before any other type of literature. Whitman was no exception. In 1888 Traubel asked him if he had read many novels. He replied: "Cartloads of 'em—cartloads—when I was younger: indeed, that was a most important formative element in my education, nurture." [14] He told Traubel at another time, "If you could reduce the Leaves to their elements you would see Scott unmistakably active at the roots." [15] This influence of Scott included both the poems and the novels, perhaps the novels more than the poems. In the circulating library he undoubtedly found many novels then popular which were inferior to Scott's, or even to the early romances of Bulwer, and he must have read many such inferior novels then and later. One very good novel then popular but now forgotten was *The Collegians*, by the Irish writer Gerald Griffin, published in 1829. Whitman said, "It is a beautiful study of Irish life, Irish character—a little uncanny, but very important for some of the things it discloses. I am not a voracious novel reader—never was—but some of the few novels I have read stick to me like gum arabic—won't let go.

12 "Walt Whitman to Date," *In Re,* p. 112.
13 *Prose Works 1892,* I, 13.
14 *WWC,* II, 553.
15 *WWC,* I, 96–97.

The Collegians was one of them." [16] It is likely that he read the novel in the early 1830's. It was the type of book that circulating libraries would acquire soon after publication. It was popular because it was a highly moral, somewhat sentimental, yet moving story of love, betrayal, remorse, and the tragic consequences of ungoverned passion, pride, and selfishness. These were very likely the aspects also that pleased the youthful Whitman, although in old age he remembered it for its vivid pictures of Irish life and character. Even now it is an interesting novel and does not deserve to be forgotten. In his foreword to the handsome 1898 edition in the series called *The World's Great Books*, James, Cardinal Gibbons calls Griffin "Ireland's Sir Walter Scott." Although *The Collegians* is unlike Scott's novels, Griffin wrote two or three later novels in which he is said to have tried to do for Ireland what Scott had done for England in the Waverley novels.[17]

If Whitman had commented on *The Collegians* in the 1840's he would probably have been less complimentary than he was in the 1880's. The contemporaries of Griffin whom he commented on, Lady (Marguerite) Blessington, Edward Bulwer, Captain (Frederick) Marryat, William Harrison Ainsworth, and G. P. R. James, produced "cataracts of trash," he declared in the essay "Home Literature" in the *Eagle,* July 11, 1846. Specifically, he referred to the "tinsel sentimentality" of Bulwer, the "inflated, unnatural, high-life-below-stairs" of Ainsworth, the "dish-water senility" of Lady Blessington, and the "vulgar coarseness" of Marryat.[18] In a review of Fredrika Bremer's novels he alludes to the "verbose weakness" of James.[19] In the essay "Home Literature" Whitman voiced the literary nationalism of the times and so may have spoken more harshly of some British writers than he really felt. There is evidence that he rated Bulwer-Lytton's

---

[16] *WWC,* I, 376. This statement seems to contradict his other statement that he had read cartloads of novels. I think he meant that though actually he read many novels, they were few in proportion to his total reading.

[17] *The Collegians* was dramatized and presented on the New York stage a number of times in 1842–43. Whitman probably revived his memory of the story by seeing the play at that time. He also probably saw Dion Boucicault's 1860 dramatic version under the title *The Colleen Bawn.* Griffin wrote a number of plays, but none has survived except *Gisippus.* It was presented on stage for the first time by William Macready in 1842 before an enthusiastic London audience. He saw the play as a possible vehicle for reviving interest in classical drama. Whitman saw *Gisippus,* perhaps several times, during the 1840's with an English actor named James R. Anderson in the leading part. (See Floyd Stovall, "Walt Whitman and the Dramatic Stage in New York," *Studies in Philology,* L [July 1953], 520–21.)

[18] Reprinted in *GF,* II, 242–45 and *UPP,* I, 121–23.

[19] Reprinted in *GF,* II, p. 268.

novels rather high, though well below those of Scott, and I have no
doubt that he read his early novels, published before he became Lord
Lytton, especially the historical romances, with almost as much pleasure as he read Scott's. However, this love of medieval history had
pretty much run its course by 1846, and by 1870 it was only a pleasant
memory. In his letter to Charles Eldridge June 23, 1873, he said he
had been reading Bulwer-Lytton's *Kenelm Chillingly* and liked it—
"the story is good, and the style a master's—Like Cervantes, Bulwer's
old age productions are incomparably his best."[20] He told Traubel
that Bulwer was a gifted story teller but not of the first class. He was
reading *What Will He Do with It?* (1858) in January, 1873, when he
suffered his first severe paralytic stroke. A year later he resumed his
reading at the point where he had left off.[21] In the 1870's and 1880's
he liked Bulwer-Lytton's later novels better than the early ones presumably because they were more realistic and critical of social conditions. He seems never to have cared for stories of romantic love. As
early as 1841, in one of his "Sun-Down Papers," he condemned the
"puerile, moping love, painted by such trashy writers as Byron and
Bulwer, and their more trashy imitators."[22] Among the English novel-
ists whom he read for the first time in his early maturity he rated
Dickens highest. He told Traubel in 1889 that he was a reader of
Dickens "from the first." Certainly, he had read all the Dickens novels
published before February 26, 1842, when his essay "Boz and Democracy" appeared in *Brother Jonathan.*[23] In this essay Whitman defends
Dickens against the charge that his scenes of cruelty and vice in these
novels disqualify them for the title "Literature of Democracy." He
would like Dickens to know "how much I love and esteem him for
what he has taught me through his writings." In 1846–47 he wrote
three short notices of *Dombey and Son* while it was still appearing
serially. He thought in his first notice, on November 5, 1846, that it
promised "something of the *real* Dickens sort—the Nickleby and
Twist style;—something much better than his later larger works." But
in the third notice, July 20, 1847, he was less enthusiastic, saying,
"The only real *characters* in 'Dombey and Son' are little Paul and
Edith. The rest are all imitations,—second-hand affairs."[24] I presume

20 Quoted by Clara Barrus in *Whitman and Burroughs—Comrades* (Boston,
1931), p. 84. *Kenelm Chillingly,* published in 1873, was Bulwer-Lytton's last completed novel.

21 *WWC,* III, 220–22.

22 This was No. 9 of the series published in the *Long Island Democrat* July 6,
1841 (reprinted in *UPP,* I, 46–48).

23 *WWC,* V, 395. "Boz and Democracy" was reprinted in *UPP,* I, 67–72.

24 Reprinted from the *Eagle* in *GF,* II, 285–96.

he meant that they are imitations of earlier Dickens characters. Yet he remembered *Dombey and Son* in old age as "a fine, almost great, book." He admitted that he no longer read Dickens. He also came to feel that Dickens was sometimes "false to human nature" in depicting character.[25] Dickens's harsh criticism of America in his *American Notes* (1842) may have disillusioned Whitman. In 1846 he wrote: "There are few things that ever filled us with more regret than Dickens' book on America. It is so hard to be misjudged and misunderstood by one you love! It is so hard that a man high above his fellows in the impulses of Literary Democracy (if we may use that phrase) should fail in seeing the *whole* truth about us, and not merely a few of the evil points alone! But we are inclined to think that Dickens himself is now sorry for writing that book."[26] Two further references to Dickens may be mentioned. In the Brooklyn *Daily Times*, May 6, 1857, he agrees with a critic in *Blackwood's Magazine* that Dickens's later works have degenerated from the "high standard" of his earlier novels. Yet Whitman adds that there is enough excellence in *Dombey and Son* and *Bleak House* "to show that none but a good novelist" could have written them.[27] In some fragmentary notes printed by Bucke there is a statement inserted in parentheses: "(Bring in a sockdolager on the Dickens fawners.)"[28] The date of this note is not known, but the context proves that Whitman was not disparaging the novels of Dickens, but scolding his countrymen for reading British literature to the neglect of American.

Whitman grew more critical as he grew older and acquired fame, but he never took a supercilious attitude toward popular literature. In a marginal note on a clipping from the *American Whig Review* (May 1845) apropos of a critic's complaint on the poor quality of so much popular literature, Whitman wrote: "Still all kinds of light reading, novels, newspapers, gossip etc., serve as manure for the few *great productions* and are indispensable or perhaps are premises to something better."[29] Obviously Whitman left no record of most of his "light reading" during his early years and did not remember authors or titles in old age. In Holloway's list of reviews contributed to the *Eagle* but not reprinted are the following authors and books, as he gave them: Ainsworth's *The Miser's Daughter*, Bulwer's *Lucretia; or*

---

[25] *WWC*, II, 552–53; V, 21–22.

[26] "Boz and His New Paper," from the *Eagle* of March 10, 1846, was reprinted in *GF*, II, 256–57.

[27] Reprinted in *I Sit and Look Out*, ed. Emory Holloway and Vernolian Schwarz (New York, 1932), p. 62.

[28] *Complete Writings*, IX, 197.

[29] *Ibid.*, IX, 161. This clipping is in the Trent Collection at Duke University.

The Children of the Night, Lydia Maria Child's *Fact and Fiction*, a volume of shorter fiction by Dickens, Dumas's *The Duke of Burgundy*, Mrs. E. F. Ellet's *Rambles about the Country*, Mrs. Gore's *The Courtier of the Days of Charles II*, a story called *Jack Long, or Shot in the Eye*, Mary J. McIntosh's *Two Lives, or To Seem and To Be*, Mrs. Phelps's *The Fireside Friend, or Female Student*, Mrs. Sigourney's *Water-Drops*, W. G. Simms's *Guy Rivers: A Tale of Georgia*, Eugene Sue's *The Wandering Jew*. These are a fair sample of more than half of the 100 books in Holloway's list. The remaining titles were of serious, standard works.[30] This light reading, as I have already indicated, continued even in his later years. Usually he gave the books away, presumably after reading them himself. In November 1866 he sent his sister Hannah Heyde *Lady Audley's Secret*, a popular novel by Mary Elizabeth Braddon, first published in 1862; and in December he sent her Florence Percy's *Poems*, then just published.[31] Peter Doyle told Traubel in an interview in 1895 that Whitman often gave him and other soldier friends "papers, books, and other such articles."[32] Thomas A. Gere wrote in an article published in the New York *World*, June 4, 1882, that about thirty years before, when he was an employee on the East River ferry, Whitman "would pass entire afternoons and even nights" with him and his fellow ferrymen discoursing "upon politics, literature, art, music or the drama, from a seemingly endless storing of knowledge."[33] One surprising enthusiasm of Whitman's later years was for the writing of Mrs. Amelia E. Barr. He told Traubel in 1888: "She is a worthy woman: she has written a great deal: I read all her writings I light upon: I came across her first years ago in a magazine: she wrote about Robert Burns—Bobby: wrote well: wrote in a way to attract me. She is best in sketchy reminiscence—things of that sort."[34] Mrs. Barr began to write about 1870, chiefly feature articles for the *Christian Union* and other religious papers although she contributed also to Robert Bonner's *Ledger*, the *Independent, Harper's Weekly* and other journals. I do not know where Whitman saw her article on Burns. Her first novel, *Cluny MacPherson*, was published in 1883, when she was fifty-two years old, but she lived to write sixty before she died in 1919.[35]

30 *UPP*, I, 127–29.

31 *Correspondence*, I, 296–97, 303. Florence Percy was the pen name of Elizabeth Chase Allen. The volume included the famous song, "Rock Me to Sleep."

32 R. M. Bucke, Introduction to *Calamus* (Boston, 1897), p. 24.

33 Reprinted by Bucke in *Walt Whitman*, p. 33. There is a clipping of this article in a large bound volume of clippings in the Duke University Library.

34 *WWC*, III, 154–55.

35 See Mrs. Barr's autobiography, *All the Days of My Life* (New York, 1913),

At one time or another Whitman must have read many other popular books and articles which in the course of time were forgotten. Most of the books he discussed with Traubel were recalled to his mind by some contemporary event or some interest of his friends. But all this "light reading" was incidental to his more serious reading, which must have begun early. He must have read a good deal during his years of teaching in the country. School libraries were small, but I suspect he found some books in them worth reading. There was also a circulating library in the village of Jamaica which contained four hundred volumes in 1838. There can be little doubt that Whitman made good use of these books. He lived with the Brentons in Jamaica while working on the *Long Island Democrat*. Mrs. Brenton, who disapproved of his habits, told her daughter-in-law later that he "spent most of the time off duty reading by the fire in winter or out of doors dreaming in the summer."[36] He probably had access also to the 500 volumes of the library of Jamaica Academy.[37]

Good books were available to him in the New York libraries, some of them free, others open to readers for a small fee. The New York Society Library, which had 36,000 volumes in 1857, was expensive for regular members, but temporary subscribers were accepted at ten dollars for a year. The Mercantile Library, established in 1821 with 700 volumes, prospered so well that it had 6,000 volumes by 1826 and 40,000 in 1857. Clerks could belong by paying an initiation fee of $1.00 and $2.00 a year and have full use of the reading room and the

---

especially pp. 300–373. Whitman had somewhere picked up some misinformation about Amelia E. Barr. He told Traubel that she went to Holland at one time and furnished a house in things all Dutch and tried to saturate herself with Hollandish customs. Of course she was never in Holland. Whoever invented this story must have related it to the composition of her novel *The Bow of Orange Ribbon* (1886), which is about the Dutch, but the Dutch of eighteenth-century New York, not Holland. Whitman also supposed that she was "a Southern woman." He said he liked Southern women; "they draw me close: there is something a bit mobile about them." (*WWC*, III, 154–55.) Actually she was born in Lancashire, England, in 1836, at nineteen married Robert Barr, a Scotsman, came with him to America in 1853, and went soon afterward to Texas. The family lived in Austin and Galveston until 1867, when her husband and two sons died. The next year she went with her three daughters to New York. She was the friend of several New York men who might have constituted a link with Whitman. Henry Ward Beecher first met her in Glasgow, and in New York helped her to get a start as a writer. J. H. Johnston, Whitman's jeweler friend, bought the jewels from her wedding ring when she was in need, and remained a staunch friend for many years following 1868, when she became more prosperous. The Astor Library provided her with a special alcove, where she worked eight or nine hours every day for fifteen years.

36 See Holloway's Introduction to *UPP*, I, xxxii, note 8, and xxxiii, note 1.

37 See p. 24.

library. Others paid $5.00 a year—some patron members much more.[38]
Between 1830 and 1854 this library was housed in Clinton Hall, at the
corner of Nassau and Beekman Streets, not far from Whitman's
boarding houses during the years 1842–44.[39] The Apprentices' Library had 14,000 volumes in 1857 and was reserved for the exclusive
use of apprentices. It was a little farther away, but still within easy
reach.[40] The Astor Library, richly endowed by John Jacob Astor at
his death in 1848, opened its doors in February 1854. It was the best
research library in New York at the time, and by 1864 contained
100,000 volumes.[41] How much Whitman used these libraries during
the 1840's it is impossible to say, but he certainly used them during
the 1850's.

There is abundant evidence that Whitman was familiar with the
Bible both as a young man and later. His pious mother would surely
have encouraged his reading of it; and his varied experiences in
Brooklyn Sunday Schools would have furthered his acquaintance
with the New Testament. His known love of history would have made
the reading of the Old Testament a pleasure. It may have been from
his early reading of the Old Testament that he derived his later love
of primitive poetry in general. Not much later than his introduction
to the Bible as literature he must have become an interested, though
not a critical, reader of Shakespeare. He would have found volumes
of the plays in all public libraries, and he might even have introduced
some of them into his schoolroom discipline. If he had not read the
plays before, he certainly did read them at the age of thirteen or fourteen in connection with his theater experience. There is in fact a close
connection between his reading not only of Shakespeare's plays, but
also of the novels of Scott, Bulwer-Lytton, and Dickens, and his love
of the stage.

---

38 Philip Hone was a member of the Mercantile Library Association and doubtless a patron. Other members and friends of Hone placed a marble bust of him in
the principal room of the Library in 1846. (See *The Diary of Philip Hone*, ed.
Allan Nevins, new 1-vol. ed. [New York, 1936], pp. 781–82.) By January 1848,
the library contained 27,000 volumes. (*Ibid.*, p. 834.)

39 *UPP*, II, 87. John and Vesey Streets, where he lived in 1843, were in easy
walking distance of the library, and Duane Street was not much farther.

40 Most of the information about libraries is drawn from *Francis's New Guide
to the Cities of New-York and Brooklyn, and the Vicinity* (New York, 1857), pp.
73–74.

41 Daniel Van Pelt, in *Leslie's History of the Greater New York*, I, 367.

V. Whitman and the Dramatic Stage in New York

EXT to books, magazines, and newspapers, the most important
cultural influence on the development of Walt Whitman during his residence in Brooklyn and New York was the theater, especially, during the 1830's and 1840's, the dramatic theater.[1] There was,
in fact, a close connection between his reading and his interest in the
theater. With the exception of the plays of Shakespeare, most of the
dramatic performances he saw were on the literary level of the popular novel. His knowledge of Shakespeare's plays, which eventually
became considerable, was initially derived more from seeing them
presented on the stage than from reading them independently.

Whitman's attendance on the dramatic stage occurred chiefly during two distinct periods of his boyhood and young manhood: from
1832 to 1836 and from 1841 to 1848. In addition, he may have seen
plays during his brief visits to New York in the spring of 1838 and
the summer of 1839. In *Specimen Days* he says that in 1839 (his error
for 1838) he was encouraged to start a paper in Huntington and went
to New York to buy a press and hire help.[2] In his autobiographical
data recorded in the early 1850's he says: "Came down to New York
(after selling Nina) in the summer of 39." In other journal entries he
says he went to Jamaica in the latter part of the summer of 1839 and
to New York in May 1841. He was in New York and Brooklyn until
he left for New Orleans February 11, 1848. After 1848 he continued
to see plays occasionally, but by that time he had developed a greater
interest in the opera.[3] He says he spent much time in the country
during the summers of 1833–35 and that he left the city in May 1836

[1] For some details not included in this chapter, the reader is referred to my
essay "Walt Whitman and the Dramatic Stage in New York," *Studies in Philology*,
L (July 1953), 515–39. Additional particulars may be found in two other essays
of mine: "Whitman's Knowledge of Shakespeare," *ibid.*, XLIX (Oct. 1952), 643–69,
and "Whitman, Shakespeare, and Democracy," *Journal of English and Germanic
Philology*, LI (Oct. 1952), 457–72. The footnotes in these articles contain information about related works by other scholars that may also be helpful.

[2] *Prose Works 1892*, I, 287. The paper was the *Long Islander*, which he continued until May 1839.

[3] *UPP*, II, 87–88. See also Chapters II and III. Nina was the horse which he
used for delivering the *Long Islander* to country subscribers.

for several years of teaching in the country schools of Long Island.[4] The principal sources for the names of plays and actors remembered by Whitman are *Specimen Days* ("Plays and Operas Too"), *November Boughs* ("The Old Bowery"), and *Good-Bye My Fancy* ("Old Actors, Singers, Shows, &c., in New York").[5] Other sources are chiefly reprints of early newspaper articles.[6] The plays he saw as a boy seem to have made a much more lasting impression on him than those he saw in the 1840's and later.

It is not possible to determine exactly the date of Whitman's first attendance at the New York theaters, but it can be established that it was not later than April 1833. It might possibly have been as early as September 1832. A good deal can be learned by comparing his recollection of the plays and players he saw with the casts and dates of these plays recorded in Ireland's *Records of the New York Stage* and Odell's more detailed *Annals of the New York Stage*.[7] The theaters Whitman knew best were the Park and the Bowery. The Park was the more elite, importing British actors as a rule and imitating the style of the Drury Lane of London. In *November Boughs* he wrote: "The Park held a large part in my boyhood's and young manhood's life."[8] His memory of plays and actors is usually so accurate as to suggest that he had preserved many playbills and had them before him when he wrote the articles published in *Specimen Days, November Boughs,* and *Good-Bye My Fancy.* His identification of plays and actors in these late writings was more accurate than the recollections in the articles contributed to the New York *Leader* in 1862.[9] If he did have

4 *Prose Works 1892*, I, 15; *UPP*, II, 86.

5 *Prose Works 1892*, I, 19–21; II, 591–97, 693–99.

6 See *UPP*, I, 141–58; II, 97–101; and *GF*, II, 309–59. See also *Walt Whitman of the New York Aurora*, ed. Joseph Jay Rubin and Charles H. Brown (State College, Pa., 1950), pp. 9, 18, 110, 118; *Walt Whitman Looks at the Schools,* ed. Florence B. Freedman (New York, 1950), pp. 214–16; *New York Dissected*, ed. Emory Holloway and Ralph Adimari (New York, 1936), pp. 18–23; *Walt Whitman and the Civil War*, ed. Charles I. Glicksberg (Philadelphia, 1933), pp. 52–58; and *Faint Clews & Indirections*, ed. Clarence Gohdes and Rollo G. Silver (Durham, N.C., 1949), pp. 13, 18–19.

7 Joseph N. Ireland, *Records of the New York Stage from 1750 to 1860* (hereafter cited as *Records*), 2 vols. (New York, 1867); George C. D. Odell, *Annals of the New York Stage* (hereafter cited as *Annals*), 15 vols. (New York, 1927). Most of my information about stage performances is drawn from Odell's work, which is so well indexed that volumes and page references will not in every case be cited. References to Ireland's volumes will be made as the need occurs. Other annalists and historians have also been consulted.

8 *Prose Works 1892*, II, 592.

9 These were reprinted by Glicksberg in *Walt Whitman and the Civil War*. See especially pp. 52–58.

playbills when he wrote in old age he did not mention them, and presumably they have not been preserved. ,

Among the actors and actresses who impressed him most as a boy, his first love was Fanny Kemble, who came to New York in September 1832 with her father, Charles, younger brother of the more famous John Kemble and Mrs. Siddons. Whitman said, "It was my good luck to see her nearly every night she played at the old Park—certainly in all her principal characters." He remembered her most vividly in the parts of Bianca in H. H. Milman's *Fazio, or the Italian Wife*, Lady Townly in Cibber's *The Provoked Husband*, and Marianna in Sheridan Knowles's *The Wife*.[10] She appeared as Bianca five times: September 18 and November 8, 1832, March 25 and May 20, 1833, and (for her last appearance in New York) June 9, 1834; as Lady Townly only twice: April 4 and 6, 1833; and as Marianna four times: October 4 and December 2, 1833, April 24 and June 13, 1834. Whitman's "nearly every night" might mean that he had missed her performances in the fall of 1832 because he had not begun attending the theater in New York at that time. On the other hand, it seems that Fanny Kemble made her greatest impression on the New York audience as Bianca, in *Fazio*, on September 18, 1832. Philip Hone wrote in his diary of this performance and of Fanny Kemble's part in it: "I have never witnessed an audience so moved, astonished, and delighted. Her display of strong feelings which belong to the part was great beyond description. . . . The fifth act was such an exhibition of female powers as we have never before witnessed, and the curtain fell amid the deafening shouts and plaudits of an astonished audience."[11] One would like to think that the thirteen-year-old Whitman was present at this performance of *Fazio*. Of the three plays mentioned, he was obviously most impressed by this one. In a paragraph telling his experience of it in *Good-Bye My Fancy* he wrote: "One of the finest characters was a great court lady, Aldabella, enacted by Mrs. Sharpe. O how it all entranced us, and knock'd us about, as the scenes swept on like a cyclone!"[12]

Another great occasion at the Park was the benefit performance of *Brutus, or The Fall of Tarquin* for its author, John Howard Payne, on November 19, 1832, with Edwin Forrest in the title role. Seats in the pit, as well as in the boxes, were five dollars, but in the gallery

[10] *Prose Works 1892*, I, 20.

[11] *The Diary of Philip Hone*: 1828–51, ed. with an introduction by Allan Nevins, 2 vols. (New York, 1927), I, 77.

[12] *Prose Works 1892*, II, 695. Mrs. Sharpe, a member of the regular company then playing in the Park Theater, played the part of Aldabella on Sept. 18, and presumably in each of the later performances of *Fazio*.

they were offered at one dollar to accommodate the less prosperous patrons. Gabriel Harrison, a boy of fourteen, like Whitman interested in amateur theatricals, witnessed the performance and remembered it many years afterward as a great occasion.[13] It is possible that Whitman was also in the Park that night. In *November Boughs* he said: "It was at the Bowery I first saw Edwin Forrest (the play was John Howard Payne's 'Brutus, or the Fall of Tarquin,' and it affected me for weeks; or rather I might say permanently filter'd into my whole nature,) then in the zenith of his fame and ability." I cannot identify this performance at the Bowery, where Forrest appeared on November 27, 1833, for the first time in four years. But the play was not *Brutus*, nor can I find by a careful search in all the annals and biographies available any record of Forrest's playing the part of Brutus in Payne's play in any theater between November 29, 1832, and October 3, 1837. He was in England and Europe from the summer of 1834 until the autumn of 1837 except for a brief season in the early fall of 1836. Whitman could have seen him for the first time in 1832 in this play at the Park or at the Bowery in 1833 but not in this play. His description of the play's effect on him suggests that the performance was a great occasion. I am inclined to believe, improbable as it seems, that Whitman really remembered the Payne benefit performance at the Park, but confused the place, recording it as the Bowery. During the years he remembered most vividly as a theatergoer, 1833–35, Forrest did not appear at the Park, but frequently played at the Bowery. He could not have seen Forrest in 1836–37 because he was teaching in the country.

As noted earlier, Whitman certainly attended the Park Theater on at least one of Fanny Kemble's two appearances as Lady Townly, April 4 and 6. Other proof that he frequented the Park in 1833–34 are his references to the singing of Mrs. Austin and Mrs. Joseph Wood in English operas. He remembered Mrs. Austin especially for her singing in the part of Ariel in *The Tempest*, which he might have heard in the spring and autumn of 1833, the summer of 1834, and in her farewell engagements at the Park on March 20 and April 6, 1835.[14] He probably remembered her best from the spring of 1833,

[13] Gabriel Harrison, *John Howard Payne, Dramatist, Poet, Actor* (Philadelphia, 1885), p. 16. Harrison moved from New York to Brooklyn in 1848, became a photographer for several years, and made Whitman's most famous picture, the one that appeared as frontispiece in the 1855 edition of *Leaves of Grass*. He and Whitman were friends, but when they first met I do not know.

[14] This was the D'Avenant-Dryden version, or a variation of it. *The Tempest* had been one of the most popular English operas for more than a century. Mrs. Austin's first name is never given in the *Annals*.

for he also remarked on the drunken song of Caliban, sung by Peter Richings, whose farewell benefit performance occurred on June 13, 1833, after which he returned to England.[15] He remembered Mrs. Wood best as Cinderella in the famous English opera of that title. She appeared in this role frequently between September 9, 1833 and September 1835. The music of this opera was by Rossini. Whitman also speaks of seeing the "inimitable Power in 'Born to Good Luck.' " So far as I can learn Tyrone Power appeared in that play at the Park for the first time September 2, 1833, and repeated it in May or June, 1834, and in April, 1835, which would have been Whitman's last chance to see him. In *Good-Bye My Fancy* he said he had seen James H. Hackett at the Park many times, including his first performance there as Rip Van Winkle in the revised version of the play by Bayle Bernard. This was on September 4, 1833. He also saw Hackett as Falstaff in *Henry IV, Part I*, a role in which he attained considerable fame. Whitman remembered a number of other actors and singers he saw at the Park, including Mrs. Sharpe, Henry Placide, and T. D. Rice, whose song "Jim Crow" he loved to sing even as an old man.[16] It seems odd that Whitman associated Rice's "Jim Crow" song with the Park, since it was first sung by him at the Bowery on November 12, 1832, and continued there most of the time through August 1833.[17] I can find no specific mention of his singing it at the Park except at Peter Richings's benefit on June 13, 1833, though doubtless he did sing it several times during his engagement there. The fact that he remembered Rice in connection with the Park instead of with the Bowery is strong evidence that he had not begun going to the Bowery until after the summer of 1833.

In the article on the Bowery in the New York *Leader* he says he had his first knowledge of that theater when he was fifteen years old, although it is obvious that he was really only fourteen. Perhaps he meant he was in his fifteenth year. He says it was just after the theater had raised its fortunes by bringing out the melodrama *Jonathan Bradford, or the Murder at the Roadside Inn*. The play began September 23, 1833, and was repeated often through the spring of 1834,

15 *Annals*, III, 623; *Records*, II, 51.

16 Logan Pearsall Smith, "Walt Whitman," in *Unforgotten Years* (Boston, 1939), pp. 96–97, says that Whitman, who visited in their home in Philadelphia, "had the habit of singing 'Old Jim Crow' when not occupied in conversation, and his loud and cheerful voice could be heard echoing every morning from the bathroom or the water closet."

17 *Annals*, III, 675. Odell says that in 1834 Rice became popular in other roles, particularly in the play "Oh! Hush!" Apparently "Jim Crow" was sung less frequently after 1833.

but not again until 1840. He does not say that he saw the play, but I suspect he did. He saw George Gale in the title role of *Mazeppa*, which was first presented at the Bowery on July 22, 1833, and repeated from time to time, but not after October 1834, with Gale as Mazeppa.[18] It is certain, therefore, that his first attendance at the Bowery was during the 1833–34 season, probably during the fall of 1833.

Thomas Hamblin, at that time manager of the Bowery Theater, was perhaps not a great actor, but he was popular in certain plays, and Whitman called him "great" as Arbaces, the Egyptian, in *The Last Days of Pompeii*, which was first produced February 19, 1835. It was repeated in the fall, but no longer with Hamblin as Arbaces. He was evidently a good manager, though, since the Bowery became a serious rival of the Park for the first time under his management. The success of the Bowery for several years beginning in 1833 was undoubtedly due to the fact that Edwin Forrest and Junius Brutus Booth left the Park and played there exclusively for a time. There were also several other players who impressed Whitman. One of these was John R. Scott, long associated with the Bowery, whom he particularly remembered in the role of Tom Cringle in *Tom Cringle's Log*. This was first presented on October 2, 1834. Others in the cast were David Ingersoll and W. F. Gates ("Old Gates," Whitman called him), both favorites. Odell says this play "gave Scott a great reputation." [19] In Whitman's *Leader* article he compared him favorably with Forrest.[20] Hamblin, Scott, Ingersoll, Mr. and Mrs. Thomas Flynn, Mrs. Herring, and Mrs. C. F. McClure often appeared in plays with Booth in 1834–35, and doubtless were the better remembered for that reason. Henry and J. W. Wallack appeared with him occasionally, but usually were themselves stars and separately cast.

There is no doubt that Junius Brutus Booth was the actor who most impressed Whitman, especially during the years 1833–35. In his article on "The Old Bowery," in *November Boughs*, he wrote: "As is well known to old play-goers, Booth's most effective part was Richard III. Either that, or Iago, or Shylock, or Pescara in 'The Apostate,' was sure to draw a crowded house. (Remember heavy pieces were much more in demand those days than now.) He was also unapproachably grand in Sir Giles Overreach, in 'A New Way to Pay Old Debts,' and the principal character in 'The Iron Chest.' "[21] Ireland confirms Whitman's judgment of Booth's best parts. He writes: "In *Richard*,

18 *Ibid.*, IV, 28 and 34.
19 *Ibid.*, IV, 27.
20 *Walt Whitman and the Civil War*, p. 57.
21 *Prose Works 1892*, II, 593.

Shylock, Iago, Lear, Sir Giles Overreach, Sir Edward Mortimer and *Pescara*, he was allowed, by universal suffrage, to have been unrivaled here for near a quarter of a century." [22] Whitman evidently saw Booth as Richard many times, but one performance especially stood out in his memory as his greatest, one which apparently others had commented upon. Again in "The Old Bowery" article he said:

I happen'd to see what has been reckon'd by experts one of the most marvelous pieces of histrionism ever known. It must have been about 1834 or '35. A favorite comedian and actress at the Bowery, Thomas Flynn and his wife, were to have a joint benefit, and securing Booth for Richard, advertised the fact many days before-hand. The house fill'd early from top to bottom. There was some uneasiness behind the scenes, for the afternoon arrived, and Booth had not come from down in Maryland, where he lived. However, a few minutes before ringing-up time he made his appearance in lively condition.

After a one-act farce over, as contrast and prelude, the curtain rising for the tragedy, I can, from my good seat in the pit, pretty well front, see again Booth's quiet entrance from the side, as, with head bent, he slowly walks down the stage to the footlights with that peculiar and abstracted gesture, musingly kicking his sword, which he holds off from him by its sash. Though fifty years have passed since then, I can hear the clank, and feel the perfect following hush of perhaps three thousand people waiting.[23]

Whitman remembered in this article that the part of Richmond was played by "a stalwart young fellow named Ingersoll." This was obviously the same performance recalled in the article on the Bowery Theater in the New York *Leader*, May 3, 1862. There he says, more accurately than in the *Tribune* article, quoted above, that it was a benefit performance for Thomas Flynn.[24] There also he remembered a third actor, Charles Thorne, who played the part of Tressel. With these bits of information it is possible to identify the exact date of the performance.

David Ingersoll made his debut in New York at the Bowery on December 27, 1833, having previously played in Philadelphia. Near the

[22] *Records*, I, 393. It has occurred to me that Whitman might have consulted this work before writing his articles, but I have no objective grounds for believing that he did.

[23] *Prose Works 1892*, II, 596. This article was first published in the New York *Tribune*, Aug. 16, 1885, with the title "Booth and 'The Bowery.'" There also he says it was fifty years ago. Elsewhere Whitman compared the effect on him of this performance to the preaching of Father Taylor, the singing of Alboni in *Norma*, and the sight of Niagara Falls. (See, respectively, *Prose Works 1892*, II, 550; II, 694; and I, 236.) He also, at times, included Fanny Kemble and the tenor Bettini in the comparison.

[24] Mrs. Flynn's benefit performance had come a few days earlier.

end of September 1835 he broke his contract with Hamblin, the manager, and did not play there again until June 30, 1836, after Whitman had gone to the country. He died in St. Louis in 1837.[25] It is certain, therefore, that Booth's *Richard III* that impressed Whitman so much was presented between January 1, 1834, and September 1835. I can find a record of only six performances between those dates in which Booth played in *Richard III*: April 21, and October 8 and 17, 1834, and June 8 and July 9 and 13, 1835. The only one of these performances listed as a benefit is that of June 8, 1835, and that was for Thomas Flynn. Charles R. Thorne appeared at the Bowery February 2, 1835, for the first time in five years. Thomas Flynn and his wife played there regularly since he was stage manager. The farce that preceded the tragedy on the program on June 8 was *The Siamese Twins*, then popular, starring Thomas Flynn and W. F. Gates.[26] I feel reasonably certain, in the light of these facts, that Booth's great performance in *Richard III* occurred June 8, 1835.[27]

I have remarked on the accuracy of Whitman's memory in old age of the plays and actors he saw as a boy and young man. He did make mistakes, however. In *Good-Bye My Fancy* he speaks of having seen William and John Sefton at the Chatham Theatre. He might have seen John Sefton there, but not William. The Chatham, or the New Chatham as it was called for a while, was not opened until the fall of 1839, a year after the death of William Sefton.[28] In 1862 his memory was better. In the New York *Leader* article he says, following the statement about his first acquaintance with the Bowery: " 'The Golden Farmer' was another very successful piece, a season or two afterwards. (But this last drew better at the little Franklin Theater down in the square—on account of the real genius of the acting in it of William and John Sefton.)"[29] The Franklin, a small theater seating only 600, was opened September 7, 1835, and *The Golden Farmer*, with the Sefton brothers as chief characters, was first presented there October 5. It was repeated many times throughout the fall and winter. Presumably Whitman saw it while it was still something of a sensation, but when and how often there is no way of knowing. The Franklin flourished for three or four years, but was evidently ruined

25 *Records*, II, 88–89. See also *Annals*, IV, 85, 91, and 103.

26 *Annals*, IV, 35. There was also a feminine part of some importance, not mentioned by Odell, which was doubtless the one remembered by Whitman.

27 This corrects my error in "Walt Whitman and the Dramatic Stage in New York," where I failed to take all the facts into account and conjectured the date of Oct. 8, 1834.

28 See *Annals*, IV, 305, 375.

29 *Walt Whitman and the Civil War*, p. 53.

by the building, in 1839, of the New Chatham, a large theater seating 2,200, in the same neighborhood.

It is my opinion, on the basis of a careful consideration of the available facts, that Whitman attended the theater infrequently, if at all, during the winter of 1835–36 and the spring of 1836. If he did not, it was probably because he was irregularly employed during this period. As I have suggested earlier, he probably had the use of a newspaperman's pass during his Brooklyn apprenticeship in 1833 and 1834, but as a journeyman printer in New York he would naturally have to buy his tickets. Although the money panic, growing out of Jackson's war with the United States Bank, did not strike until 1837 or the latter part of 1836, times became difficult among laborers and craftsmen in New York City several months earlier. Inflation raised prices faster than wages, and in the general unrest, there was trouble between laborers and employers because of the formation of labor unions. Crops were poor in 1835, and the farmers could not pay their debts to the merchants, and the merchants could not meet their obligations to the banks; hence people began to feel already the hard times which reached their crisis in the money panic of 1836–37.[30] To make matters worse, New York suffered a devastating fire on the nights of December 16 and 17, with the destruction of about 600 buildings and a property loss estimated at from fifteen to twenty million dollars. Philip Hone recorded many hardships, including the destruction of "a large number" of printing offices.[31] Rioting was worse than ever, and there were frequent conflicts between the immigrant Irish and the native population. "One firm after another failed. It was a winter of distress."[32] Under these circumstances it is not unlikely that Whitman, a very young and inexperienced printer, would be one of the first to be laid off when jobs became scarce. Besides, his family on Long Island may also have begun to feel hard times. A job as a schoolmaster, though the pay was small, would help all around.

Emory Holloway has suggested that Whitman may have turned to teaching because he could not find more remunerative employment, and calls attention to the parallel case of Archie Dean in the story "The Shadow and the Light of a Young Man's Soul."[33] Holloway does not mention the parallel circumstance of the fire, which seems

[30] A good brief account of these matters can be found in *The Age of Jackson*, by Arthur M. Schlesinger, Jr. (Boston, 1945), pp. 128 f., 192–99, and 217.

[31] See *The Diary of Philip Hone*, ed. by Allan Nevins (New and enlarged edition, New York, 1936), p. 192.

[32] *History of the City of New York*, by Mrs. Martha J. Lamb and Mrs. Burton Harrison (New York, 1896), III, 727.

[33] *UPP*, I, xxx.

to have been the immediate cause of Archie's unemployment. "And poverty compelled Archie Dean; for when the destructive New-York fire of '35 happened, ruining so many property owners and erewhile rich merchants, it ruined the insurance offices, which of course ruined those whose little wealth had been invested in their stock."[34] After having "ransacked every part of the city for employment as a clerk," and "happening accidentally to hear of a country district where, for poor pay and coarse fare, a school teacher was required," he left the city to become a teacher.[35] The two cases are not identical, of course, but the parallels are suggestive.

It is not likely that Whitman had many opportunities to see plays in New York between May 1836 and May 1841, since most of that time he was fully engaged in teaching and newspaper work in the country. But he did visit New York twice. In *Specimen Days* he says that before starting his newspaper in Huntington, *The Long Islander,* he went to New York during the summer of 1838 to purchase supplies.[36] In *November Boughs* he recalls "the fine comedietta of 'The Youth that Never Saw a Woman,' and the jolly acting in it of Mrs. Herring and old Gates."[37] Unless the annalists have overlooked some performances, Gates and Mrs. Herring appeared in this play only once, and that was at Vauxhall Gardens on July 31, 1838.[38] There is no way of determining just when Whitman was in New York during the summer of 1838 unless his reference to this play and these actors in it constitutes evidence.

There is also uncertainty about the period of Whitman's residence in New York in 1839. In his notebook autobiographical data he says: "Came down to New York (after selling Nina) in the summer of 39. . . . In Jamaica first time in the latter part of the summer of 1839."[39] Allen says he went to Jamaica in August 1839 to work for James J. Brenton on the *Long Island Democrat,* after a summer spent in New York City, but he does not cite his authority for that date.[40] I am inclined to doubt that he spent all the summer of 1839 in the city; if he did, I can find no evidence that he saw his usual quota of plays for so long a period. More likely he was there only in the latter part

34 *UPP,* I, 229–30. The story is reprinted on pp. 229–34 from the *Union Magazine of Literature and Art* for June 1848. It was undoubtedly written much earlier.

35 *Ibid.,* I, 230–31.

36 *Prose Works 1892,* I, 287. Whitman said it was 1839, but we know from other sources that it was really 1838.

37 *Ibid.,* II, 594.

38 *Annals,* IV, 267.

39 *UPP,* I, 87.

40 *The Solitary Singer,* p. 34

of the summer. In *November Boughs* he said he remembered "an actor named Ranger, who appeared in America forty years ago in genre characters"; and in *Good-Bye My Fancy* he says: "There was a series of plays and dramatic *genre* characters by a gentleman bill'd as Ranger—very fine, better than merely technical, full of exquisite shades, like the light touches of the violin in the hands of a master."[41] Ranger's first appearance on the New York stage was at the Park on August 27, 1839, and he had a return engagement in late December that lasted into January. He was at the Bowery in March and May 1840, at the Olympic the following June, and at Niblo's Garden in late August and early September 1840. He played again at the Olympic on May 19, 1841, and, according to Odell, on January 13, 1842, though Ireland says he returned to England in 1841.[42] It is possible that Whitman saw him on August 27, 1839, and again in 1841 or 1842. He seemed to remember his acting so well that one suspects he saw him more than once. It is also just possible that between the end of his summer school session in 1840 and the beginning of his electioneering in the fall he went to New York and saw Ranger at Niblo's Garden.

We learn from Whitman's autobiographical data in a notebook that he returned to New York in May 1841 and was employed as a printer in the office of the *New World*; that he was an editor on the *Aurora* in the spring of 1842, on the *Tattler* the following summer, on the *Statesman* in the spring of 1843, and on the *Democrat* in the summer of 1844; and that he became editor of the Brooklyn *Eagle* in February 1846 and retained that post until January 1848.[43] From other sources we know that he wrote more or less regularly for the Brooklyn *Evening Star* from about September 1844 until he became editor of the *Eagle*.[44] As a printer he probably did not have a pass to theaters, but for much, perhaps most, of the time between March 1842 and February 1848 he probably did have one. I have expressed the opinion that the plays he saw in 1833–35 left a deeper impression upon his mind than those he saw later. One may assume that, after

[41] *Prose Works 1892*, II, 592 and 697. This was W. Ranger, whose real name, Odell says, was Codwise, and he was an American educated in England. In the *November Boughs* article, first published in 1885, Whitman says it was forty years ago, that is, about 1845. In *Good-Bye My Fancy* he says it was fifty years ago. The article was there printed partly from manuscript and partly from proof sheets, presumably dating from about 1890.

[42] *Annals*, IV, 577; *Records*, II, 296.

[43] *UPP*, II, 87–88.

[44] Emory Holloway, "More Light on Whitman," *American Mercury* I (Feb. 1924), 183–89. See also *Walt Whitman Looks at the Schools*, p. 37 and p. 221, note 4.

his return to the city, he continued to see the plays and actors he had liked best during the earlier period, if they were still current, but there were some actors and plays mentioned in old age that he could not have seen before the late spring or summer of 1841. His favorite actor, J. B. Booth, did not appear in the role of Shylock, so far as I can determine, between 1831 and June 1843, but between the latter date and November 1847 he played the part several times, although it was not one of his favorites. Another Booth play mentioned by Whitman was *The Iron Chest*, in which Booth is listed by the annalists only once when Whitman might have seen him during 1833–36, and that was on January 8, 1833. However, between 1842 and 1848 he appeared as Sir Edward Mortimer in that play at least half a dozen times. Odell lists Booth as Sir Giles Overreach in *A New Way to Pay Old Debts* on November 21, 1832, but not again until December 5, 1835, and after that not until July 8, 1841.

Whitman's favorite actress in his mature years was Charlotte Cushman. In *Specimen Days* he remembered her as Lady Gay Spanker in *London Assurance*, and in *Good-Bye My Fancy* he said she "had a superbly enacted part" in "All is not Gold that Glitters." He says she "was great in such pieces; I think better than in the heavy popular roles."[45] This opinion is in accordance with his statement to Traubel that he found her representation of Meg Merrilies, in the dramatic version of Scott's *Guy Mannering*, too horrible for his taste; and he added, "Much of Charlotte Cushman's great acting was done in her earlier days before she was famous."[46] I am not certain what he meant by "her earlier days," but since he says that was before she became famous, I presume he meant before 1845. In several articles in the Brooklyn *Daily Eagle* in 1846 he had praised Charlotte Cushman extravagantly, not just accepting the opinion of the London critics that she was better than Ellen Tree, but asserting that she "is ahead of any player that ever yet trod the stage," man or woman. Her great quality, he thought, was her ability to identify herself completely with the character she played, and particularly that character's mental peculiarities. He does not mention Meg Merrilies, but he praises her in two other melodramatic parts. "Ah," he exclaims, "who has seen her appalling Nancy Sykes (the most intense acting ever *felt* on the Park boards,)—who has seen her Evadne, in *The Bridal*, but acknowledged the towering grandeur of her genius! In the simple utterance of her shrieking 'yes! yes! yes!' as she swings down to her

---

45 *Prose Works 1892*, II, 694. The correct title of the last-named play is *All that Glitters Is Not Gold.*

46 *WWC*, IV, 189–90.

brother's feet, was one of the greatest triumphs of the histrionic art, ever achieved! In the twinkling of an eye—in the utterance of a word— was developed the total revolution of a mighty and guilty mind—from pride, defiance, anger, and rioting guilt, to an utterly crushed state of fear, remorse, and conscious vileness! Never shall we forget the surpassing beauty of that performance!"[47] The only other of Charlotte Cushman's roles mentioned in these articles was that of the Widow Melnotte in *The Lady of Lyons*, which he praised, but less enthusiastically.

After her debut in Boston and minor engagements in New Orleans and other cities, Charlotte Cushman first appeared in New York at the National Theater in May 1837 and on May 13 appeared there as Meg Merrilies. Later she was engaged by the manager of the Park and appeared there regularly from August 26, 1837, until August 12, 1840, when she went to Philadelphia. She returned for a while to the Park in 1841, then went again to Philadelphia, this time as manager of the Walnut Street Theater, but was induced to return to the Park in 1843 to support Charles Macready as the star there during the season of 1843–44. Macready returned to England at the end of September 1844, and she also, at his suggestion, went there not long afterward. When she returned to her native country in 1849, she had acquired fame and fortune. She was now, Odell says, "indisputably at the head of American tragic actresses—a position she never lost."[48] After 1851 she appeared on the stage less frequently, and spent much time in Europe. Her final engagement in New York began October 1871, and she died in Boston February 18, 1876.

It is not likely that Whitman saw Charlotte Cushman in the role of Meg Merrilies before writing the 1846 articles in the *Eagle*. She appeared in New York in that role only four times during her three years at the Park, 1837–40, and these were at times when it would have been difficult for Whitman to be present; that is, on January 25, September 27, October 3, and October 5, 1839. His earliest opportunity, after that, to see her as Meg came in 1849. On the other hand, it is very probable that he saw her in the role of Nancy Sykes several times during the summer of 1839, when we know he was in New York. She appeared in that role thirteen times in 1839 and four times in 1840. Her appearances in the summer of 1839 came on June 25, July 10, August 1, and August 24. The tone of his *Eagle* articles suggests that he had seen her several times, conceivably on all four of these

---

47 *GF*, II, 325–26. *The Bridal* was Sheridan Knowles's adaptation of *The Maid's Tragedy* by Beaumont and Fletcher. Nancy Sykes (so spelled in the playbills) was a character in the dramatic version of Dickens's *Oliver Twist*.

48 *Annals*, V, 514.

dates. One of her biographers says of these performances: "Nancy
Sykes brought our actress close to the people, and she was hailed as
'Our Charlotte' long before the professional critics were ready to con-
cede her superiority. The newspapers contain a line or two of commendation of Nancy Sykes, nothing of Meg. The latter character was
developed in later years: the former was not played again by Miss
Cushman for twenty years after she left the Park; but the performance
is commonly said to have established her in popular favor."[49] His
impression of *Oliver Twist* might have been somewhat dulled after
six or seven years, but he had seen *The Bridal* more recently. So far
as I can determine, he could have seen Charlotte as Evadne in this
play only four times before 1846: twice in December 1843, once on
June 3, 1844, and for the last time on September 23, 1844. Charles
Macready was Melantius in each case.

His comment in the *Eagle* on *The Lady of Lyons* is interesting and
worth repeating here. "We don't know how others may think; but we
consider it a shame that such a woman as Charlotte Cushman, should
ever have been allowed to be superseded by the fifth rate artistic?
trash that comes over to us from the Old World! We have seen C. C.
throw more genius into a representation of the Widow Melnotte, in
'The Lady of Lyons,' than the much-puffed Claude and Pauline
('from the Theatre Royal,' etc., etc.,) evinced in their whole most
popular and profitable star engagement!"[50] It is necessary to know
the play to appreciate Whitman's comment. The Widow Melnotte,
mother of Claude, appears only briefly and speaks only a few lines,
whereas the role of Claude is the principal one in the play. By his own
efforts, Claude has educated himself so well as to be mistaken for a
born aristocrat, whereas his mother has remained a simple peasant
woman, the widow of a gardener. Charlotte Cushman played the role
of the Widow Melnotte only three times when Whitman might have
seen her: June 10, June 15, and August 4, 1838, during his summer
visit to the city. So far as I can discover, she never played that part
afterward. Later when she had a part in this play it was that of
Claude, which she did for the first time June 23, 1838. Doubtless
Whitman had seen one or more of these appearances. Her more distinguished roles, other than Nancy Sykes and Meg Merrilies, were
those of Lady Macbeth, Emilia in *Othello*, and the Queen in *Hamlet*.

49 W. T. Price, *A Life of Charlotte Cushman* (New York, 1894), pp. 38–39. Price
lists all of her plays (pp. 23–34) during her 1837–40 engagement at the Park, and
Odell is in agreement with his statistics. Joseph Leach's recent biography, *Bright
Particular Star* (New Haven, 1970), provides a more detailed account of her
career, and especially of her personal life.

50 *GF*, II, 326–27.

In male parts, besides Claude Melnotte, she was successful in the part of Romeo and in that of Oberon in *A Midsummer Night's Dream*.

In Whitman's tribute to her in accepting the minor part of the Widow Melnotte, he suggests a comparison with a famous episode in the theatrical career of J. B. Booth. In 1831 Booth was temporarily the manager of a theater in Baltimore, and one night he presented *Hamlet* with Charles Kean in the title role, John Sefton as Osric, Thomas Flynn as the First Grave Digger, and Mrs. Flynn as Ophelia. In order, apparently, to fill out his cast with as much strength as possible, he himself took the part of the Second Actor, who had only half a dozen lines to speak, though they were strong ones. These he delivered "with great beauty and effect, commanding round upon round of applause, thus proving how much more depends upon the ability of the actor, than upon the importance of the part."[51] Whitman undoubtedly refers to this incident in *November Boughs* in the following remark about Booth: "He knew all stage points thoroughly, and curiously ignored the mere dignities. I once talk'd with a man who had seen him do the Second Actor in the mock play to Charles Kean's Hamlet in Baltimore." Whitman may have talked with a man who saw this performance, but it is also possible that he read about it in one or more of the books on Booth.[52]

Although she was noted as a tragic actress, Charlotte Cushman was often seen in comedies. She made her debut at the Park on August 26, 1837, in the part of Patrick in John O'Keefe's musical farce "The Poor Soldier." She played the part of Lady Gay Spanker for the first time on October 11, 1841, with Henry Placide as Sir Harcourt Courtly, when Dion Boucicault's version of *London Assurance* was first presented in this country at the Park Theater. She played the part many times thereafter both in this country and in England. *All that Glitters is Not Gold* came later, probably the first time in 1854. Whitman calls it an "old" play "quite unknown to today's current audiences," yet it was presented in New York during the 1870's and

[51] The earliest reference I have found to this incident, and the one related on pp. 59–60, is a small book published anonymously in 1846 in New York, with the title *The Actor; or, A Peep behind the Curtain*. It is related also in Thomas R. Gould's *The Tragedian; an Essay on the Histrionic Genius of Junius Brutus Booth* (New York, 1858), pp. 63–64, and in Asa Booth Clarke's *The Elder and the Younger Booth* (Boston, 1882), p. 81.

[52] See note 51. I think it is more than probable that he read Asa Booth Clarke's book about her father and brother, and he might have known T. R. Gould's book, which, according to William Winter, contains "the most minute and instructive account that exists of Booth's acting." (See *Vagrant Memories* [New York, 1915], p. 163.) The anonymous author of the book published in 1846 might have been the man Whitman talked to.

1880's and in Brooklyn as late as 1881.[53] It was not a popular play and her part in it was not one of her best.

Whitman's taste in dramatic art did not change essentially between his "hobbledehoy" period of the early 1830's and the period of his dramatic criticism in the Brooklyn *Eagle*, but, as might be expected, it developed considerably. Edwin Forrest, the darling of the Bowery Theater, was, next to Booth, his favorite actor in the early period. He had no opportunity to see the English perfectionist Charles Macready until 1843, and barely mentions him among lesser men in the articles written in old age. He was less aware of Forrest's finer qualities then than later. Like others, he was impressed by his stentorian voice, his magnificent physique, and his forceful personality. Both Forrest and Booth were best in tragedy. As he says in *November Boughs*, "the heavy tragedy business prevail'd more decidedly at the Bowery, where Booth and Forrest were frequently to be heard." Forrest was most liked as Othello, Lear, Shylock, and the non-Shakespearean characters Metamora, Spartacus, and Brutus (in Payne's play). Booth was most famous as Richard III, in which he was preëminent, as Lear, and as Iago, and in such non-Shakespearean characters as Pescara and Sir Giles Overreach. Such roles were by no means unknown at the Park, but there the tradition of English comedy was continued, and there Whitman saw many fine English actors, including Henry Placide, Thomas Cooper, and John H. Clarke. As we have seen, he knew and liked the polished stagecraft at the Park before he began going to the Bowery. There Frances Kemble, with her rich voice, her young beauty, and her finished art, captured his imagination, and there he first saw Charlotte Cushman as Lady Gay Spanker and Lady Teazle, James Hackett as Falstaff, and Tyrone Power in his brilliant Irish comedies, and there he first heard T. D. Rice sing the unforgettable "Jim Crow."

Macready returned to the Park in September 1843, after an absence of seventeen years, and, according to Odell, "drew back to the Park Theatre the fashion and intelligence that had recently all but deserted it."[54] Charlotte Cushman was still in Philadelphia, but she returned to the Park for his second engagement, beginning December 6, 1843, and became his leading lady, though she had not yet reached that degree of mastery of her art which afterward, in New York and in England, pleased his severe standards. Doubtless Whitman saw them a number of times in the same plays, including *Macbeth, Ham-*

let, Othello, and *King Lear.* Macready returned to England in September 1844 and did not reappear in New York until September 4, 1848. During the next several months he appeared a number of times at the Astor Place Opera (the Park being no longer in existence), and there on May 7 and May 10, 1849, ended his American career on the occasion of the famous riots incited by zealots for Forrest and a native American theater. When Miss Cushman returned from England, in September 1849, she had become a star and brought Charles W. Couldock with her to the Broadway Theater as her leading man.

It is surprising that Whitman had nothing to say about Macready in his reminiscences, for he must have seen him a number of times in 1843–44. When in 1846 he undertook to give advice to young aspiring actors, he cited Macready as the exemplar of the best style of acting—the mental, which adheres to nature and works from within outward, as distinguished from the boisterous physical style, which is altogether outward and is repugnant to both truth and taste. He remembered the awe inspired in the crowded theater when Macready "merely appeared, walking down the stage, a king. He was a king—not because he had a tinsel-gilded crown, and the counterfeit robe, but because he then dilated his heart with the attributes of majesty, and they looked forth from his eyes, and appeared in his walk. Such power was worth a thousand vociferous plaudits for giving words of anger or defiance in tones to split the very roof!"[55] The "tones to split the very roof" suggest the voice of Edwin Forrest. In another article Whitman agrees that Forrest has high talent and deserves to be America's favorite actor, but he warns of the danger of producing "vapid imitators," with all his faults but without his talent, who may "tickle the ears of the groundlings," but will appear to men of taste merely ridiculous.[56]

By 1845 Whitman had joined wholeheartedly in the movement for an independent native American literature and art. One of the articles in the Brooklyn *Evening Star* signed "W" and presumed to have been written by Whitman, calls for a reform in the plays, acting, and actors of the American stage, which he declares "has worn the tinselled threadbare robes of foreign fashion long enough." They should be more original than those at the Park and more dignified and artistic than those at the Chatham and Bowery. The Park, he charges, is

[55] Quoted from "Dramatics; and the True Secret of Acting," published in the *Eagle*, Aug. 20, 1846 (reprinted in *GF*, II, 321–25).

[56] From " 'The Gladiator'—Mr. Forrest—Acting," published in the *Eagle*, Dec. 26, 1846 (reprinted in *GF*, II, 330–34).

"a bringer-out of English plays imbued with anti-republican incident and feeling—an usherer before us of second-rate foreign performers, and the castings-off of London and Liverpool."[57] He urged reform more vigorously as editor of the *Eagle,* and continued to complain of American subserviance to British opinion. He admits that, so far, American art seems crude, chaotic, and unformed, but he believes things will improve. "The drama *must* rise: the reign of English managers and English local plays must have its end."[58] He does not charge the Park Theater with vulgarity, but he calls it a "third-rate imitation of the best London theatres," and he objects to the "*star* system" maintained there. He then calls for some bold man to "take the theatre in hand in this country . . . look above merely the gratification of the vulgar and of those who love glittering scenery," and give us American plays with "matter fitted to American opinions and institutions."[59] Though he had never acted on the stage, Whitman boasts in 1846, "we consider ourselves no 'chicken' about stage matters."[60] Evidently he believed himself fully qualified by 1846, on the basis of his threatrical experience, to instruct his readers on all matters of dramatic values and the histrionic art. It must be remembered, however, that his readers were mostly unsophisticated small-city dwellers and probably prejudiced in respect to things British.

Whitman was not always consistent in his judgment of English actors and actresses. In the *Eagle* on September 1, 1846, he noted that "The morning *News* appears angry because we do not applaud Mrs. and Mr. Kean." The *News* must have had reference to Whitman's article of August 14, in which he had praised Charlotte Cushman above all other actors. But Whitman now goes much further, charging that some New York newspapers are suborned to praise Kean every day, despite his defects of manner and voice, and his lack of the "divine fire" that all real artists have. He thinks he owes his reputation largely to the fact that he is Edmund Kean's son. He proposes to be more generous with Mrs. Kean because she is a lady, and because she was once better than she is now. "She *was* a young woman of genius—she is *merely* the frame and thews of that time, with none of

[57] "A Suggestion—Brooklyn Amusements," dated Oct. 27, 1845. (Portions of this article are reprinted in Emory Holloway's "More Light on Whitman," pp. 183–89. See also *Walt Whitman Looks at the Schools,* p. 214.)

[58] "Dramatic Affairs, and Actors," in the *Eagle,* April 19, 1847 (reprinted in *GF,* II, 334–37).

[59] "Miserable State of the Stage," in the *Eagle,* Feb. 8, 1847 (reprinted in *GF,* II, 310–14). Edmund Simpson, who had been manager of the Park for 38 years, retired in June 1848 and died a month or two later. The theater was destroyed by fire on Dec. 15, 1848. (See *Annals,* V, 328, 417.)

[60] See *GF,* II, 322, 325.

its pliant grace, its smoothness, its voluptuous swell." He names several stock company performers who are better than the Keans in his
opinion.[61] Two or three months later he is in a more generous mood.
After describing Kean's elaborate and historically accurate presentation of *King John*, he praises Kean as King John and Mrs. Kean as
Queen Constance. "We are not given to superlatives in these things—
but if there be any *perfection* in acting, Mrs. K. evinces it in her portrayal of that widowed and crownless Queen!" And he confesses that,
though he is no admirer of Mr. Kean, his representation of King John
"left little to be asked for more, by the reasonable spectator." He
mentions only two others in the cast. "Mr. Vanderhoof's [sic] Falcon-
bridge was acting of the liveliest, heartiest, most refreshing sort, and
gave a light grace to the massiveness of the rest. The young creature
who played Arthur took the sympathies of the whole house; she
played with quiet, grace, and modesty."[62] This was George Vandenhoff's last engagement at the Park, and the playbills state that he was
expressly engaged to represent the character of Faulconbridge.[63]

Whitman had not lost his love of the noisy action and pageantry of
English historical plays, and he must have liked *King John* for these
and also for the authenticity which Charles Kean, who was something
of an antiquary, had so lavishly provided in the scenery and equipment. He described it in some detail both in *November Boughs* and
in *Good-Bye My Fancy*. He was impressed by the part of Faulconbridge, and yet, strangely enough, he later erroneously attributed the
part to Thomas Hamblin. In *November Boughs* he says he thought
"Tom Hamblin's best acting was in the comparatively minor part of
Faulconbridge in 'King John'—he himself evidently revell'd in the
part, and took away the house's applause from young Kean (the King)
and Ellen Tree (Constance,) and everybody else on the stage."[64] In
Good-Bye My Fancy he says, "Must have been in 1844 (or '5) I saw
Charles Kean and Mrs. Kean (Ellen Tree)—saw them in the Park in
Shakspere's 'King John.' Tom Hamblin was *Faulconbridge,* and
probably the best ever on the stage. . . . the delicious acting of Prince

[61] "Acting . . . The Keans" (reprinted in *GF*, II, 327–30).

[62] "Matters Which were Seen and Done in an Afternoon Ramble," published
in the *Eagle*, Nov. 19, 1846 (reprinted in *UPP*, I, 141–44). This engagement began
on Nov. 16 and continued for eighteen successive performances, according to both
Ireland (*Records*, II, 467) and Odell (*Annals*, V, 252 ff.). Whitman saw the play on
Nov. 17, after an afternoon ramble in Brooklyn and New York.

[63] George Vandenhoff, *Leaves from an Actor's Note-Book* (New York, 1860),
pp. 237–40. Vandenhoff states that the play ran three weeks, but that the house
was never full and the best night's attendance yielded less than $800. Since
$12,000 was invested in the production, it probably lost money.

[64] *Prose Works 1892*, II, 594.

Arthur (Mrs. Richardson, I think)—and the fine *blare* and court pomp —I remember to this hour. The death-scene of the King in the orchard of Swinstead Abbey, was very effective. Kean rush'd in, gray-pale and yellow, and threw himself on a lounge in the open. His pangs were horribly realistic. (He must have taken lessons in some hospital.)" [65] Whitman had seen George Vandenhoff in other plays during the 1840's, but apparently he did not remember him very well. Hamblin he remembered best from the 1830's. I suspect Whitman saw J. B. Booth's *King John* at the Bowery April 30, 1834, in which Hamblin played the part of Faulconbridge, and that his recollection of this performance became confused in his memory with Kean's *King John*. [66] Whitman remembered John Vandenhoff, George's father, better than George. He told Traubel that he had seen the elder Vandenhoff several times when he was "almost a boy." [67] John Vandenhoff played in New York, according to Odell, only between September 11, 1837 and March 5, 1841. [68] Odell does not record any performances in New York, if he made any, during the summers of 1838 and 1839, but he records one on September 23, 1839. It may be that John Vandenhoff appeared in New York one time or more during these summers and Odell failed to make note of it.

There can be no doubt that the New York dramatic stage exercised a great influence on Whitman's life. I think his return to New York in the summer of 1839 was motivated as much by a yearning for the theater as by a desire to find employment. He may have been stimulated to write and publish his reminiscences of the stage by reading Fleeming Jenkins's article, "Mrs. Siddons as Lady Macbeth. From Contemporary Notes by George Joseph Bell," published in *The*

---

[65] *Ibid.*, pp. 694–95. The actress who played the part of Prince Arthur was a girl named Susan Denin, then quite young. Mrs. Richardson, whom Whitman had admired in the 1830's, would in 1846 have been past forty. She was then Mrs. Fisher and apparently retired from the stage.

[66] *Annals*, III, 684; see also *Records*, II, 92. Mrs. Flynn was Prince Arthur. Odell says this engagement of Booth lasted until May 17, but *King John* was not repeated. Hamblin also played the part of Faulconbridge with John Vandenhoff as King John on March 4, 1841, with Thomas Barry as King John on May 17 and 24, 1841, and with John Gilbert as King John on June 16, 1842. George Vandenhoff played Faulconbridge to Hamblin's King John on Nov. 12, 1842. Under these circumstances it would be easy to become confused after forty years. Certainly he appreciated the importance of George Vandenhoff in 1846, for in the *Eagle* on July 2 of that year he mentions seeing his photograph among those of other notables in the galleries of Plumbe's daguerreotype establishment. See *GF*, II, p. 115.)

[67] *WWC*, IV, 476.

[68] *Annals*, IV, 213, 337–38, 466–67.

Nineteenth Century for February 1878.[69] One sentence in this essay bears a striking resemblance to a sentiment expressed in the *Eagle* a third of a century earlier: "The actor must go direct to nature and his own heart for the tones and action by which he is to move his audience; these the author cannot give him, and in creating these, if he be a great actor, his art may be supremely great."[70] Whether he had access to books on the New York theater to refresh his memory, it is not possible to say with certainty. There are several books he might have seen, including the three already mentioned.[71] One of these, *The Elder and the Younger Booth,* was sent to Whitman by Edwin Booth in 1884 in reply to the poet's request for a picture of his father. The frontispiece of this book is from a daguerreotype made in 1848. There is also a picture of Booth as Richard III, made about 1820, but not many details that Whitman could have used to refresh his memory of Booth's acting. Such details he could have found in T. R. Gould's *The Tragedian,* and he would have found in Gould an admirer of the elder Booth even more enthusiastic than himself if that were possible.[72] If he had taken the trouble to look for it in the libraries of Philadelphia, or to ask for it at bookstores, he could easily have seen Ireland's *Records of the New York Stage.* But there is no evidence that he saw it, or, if he did see it, that he checked it closely; otherwise he would have corrected some of the mistakes he made, such as attributing the part of Faulconbridge in Kean's *King John* to Thomas Hamblin.

Whitman had seen and admired many actors and actresses, both as a boy and as a man, and all of them must be taken into account if we would estimate the total impact of the theater on his life and work. But Booth undoubtedly impressed him most and had the greatest influence upon him. He admired the exquisite technical perfection and polish of Macready's style, and he also appreciated the sheer force of Forrest and his commanding presence. But Booth, at his best, combined the fine qualities of both—the delicacy of Macready and the power of Forrest. "All my ideals," he told Traubel, "have been made up by long study of the elder Booth." And again he said, "I

[69] III, 296–313.

[70] III, pp. 297–98.

[71] See notes 51 and 52.

[72] It is a little surprising to read in Gould's book (p. 51) that "Hamlet was Booth's favorite part." He certainly did not present "Hamlet" as often as several other plays in New York. It is equally surprising that Whitman, as he told Traubel (*WWC,* IV, 476), had never seen Booth in "Hamlet," though he had seen others, and praised E. L. Davenport's portrayal of the Prince, preferring it to Edwin Booth's, which he had also seen.

attach a great deal of importance to Booth . . . he had much to do with shaping me in those earlier years."[73] Though Whitman's dramatic experience surely had a part in the making of *Leaves of Grass*, it is naturally difficult to point out specific evidence in the poems. The reader is often conscious of a dramatic attitude on the part of the poet, when he seems to be addressing an audience either as orator or as actor, sometimes exhorting and sometimes enacting a part. There are many scenes which suggest the immediacy and reality of the stage scenes of the street, the shop, and the countryside. As he said of Booth in *November Boughs*: "his genius was to me one of the grandest revelations of my life, a lesson of artistic expression."[74] In due proportion, he might have said the same of many other actors and actresses who were the teachers of his youth night after night.

[73] See *WWC*, I, 456; III, 520; IV, 286.
[74] *Prose Works 1892*, II, 597.

VI. *Whitman and the Opera in New York*

A s Whitman's interest in the dramatic stage was a development from his love of reading, so his interest in opera was probably an outgrowth of his early experience as a playgoer and began during the same period, 1833 to 1835. Writers on Whitman and opera sometimes assume that the only opera he cared for was the Italian. For example, Robert D. Faner, who has made the fullest study of the subject, says almost nothing of Whitman's experience of opera in English.[1] In his excellent biography, Gay Wilson Allen barely mentions the English opera and seems to accept Faner's study as definitive.[2] Yet Whitman heard and loved opera in English perhaps ten years before he heard his first opera sung in Italian. I have already mentioned his praise of Mrs. Austin's singing, as Ariel, in the D'Avenant-Dryden version of Shakespeare's *The Tempest,* and of Mrs. Wood's in the title role of the English opera *Cinderella.*[3] There had been a season or two of excellent opera in New York in 1825–26, and for two seasons, in a house built for the purpose, Italian opera was offered beginning in November 1833. After that, "Italian opera went into exile for 10 years."[4] During those two years seats for the opera ranged in price from two dollars to fifty cents, but even if Whitman could have afforded to buy his ticket he probably was not then interested. In fact, few people were, and the Italian company was not successful. As Krehbiel noted, the people of New York were not ready for Italian opera.[5] English opera, on the other hand, was very popular and continued to be for twelve or fifteen years afterward.

[1] Robert D. Faner, *Walt Whitman and Opera* (Philadelphia, 1951). See especially pp. 9 and 19, where perhaps a dozen lines are devoted to operas in English. Among shorter studies, the following may be mentioned: Louise Pound, "Walt Whitman and Italian Music," *American Mercury,* VI (Sept. 1925), 58–63; Julia Spiegelman, "Walt Whitman and Music," *South Atlantic Quarterly,* XLI (April 1942), 167–76; and Alice Lovelace Cooke, "Notes on Whitman's Musical Background," *New England Quarterly,* XIX (June 1946), 224–25.

[2] *The Solitary Singer* (New York, 1955); see especially pp. 112–15 and p. 557, note 34.

[3] In Chapter V; see pp. 60–61.

[4] Henry E. Krehbiel, *Chapters of Opera* (New York, 1908), pp. 16 and 24.

[5] *Ibid.,* p. 23.

Although he remembered Mrs. Austin best in the part of Ariel, he might well have heard her in other roles, for in 1833 she appeared in *T. e Magic Flute, The Barber of Seville, Der Freischütz,* and *Fra Diavolo,* and in 1835 she appeared in *The Beggar's Opera* and *Masaniello.* He might have heard Mrs. Wood also in other operas, including *The Barber of Seville, Fra Diavolo,* and *Masaniello* in November 1833, and *Der Freischütz* and *Fra Diavolo* in January 1834. Mrs. Austin did not sing in New York after the spring of 1835, and Mrs. Wood did not sing after about 1840. But during the 1840's Whitman heard other favorite singers in English opera, notably Edward Seguin and his wife and Mary Taylor. Edward Seguin was a basso, and Odell reports that Mrs. Seguin had "a contralto voice of superb quality."[6] The Seguins appeared in many operas at the Park theater. There on April 25, 1842, *Norma* was presented with Mrs. Seguin as Norma and Mary Taylor as Clotilda. This was repeated many times, and there is little doubt that Whitman heard it at least once. Possibly Mrs. Seguin's contralto prepared him for that of Marietta Alboni, which, of course, was more highly rated by the critics. On April 29 *La Sonnambula* was presented, with Mrs. Seguin as Amina, and it was repeated the next November. At that time the Seguins also sang in *The Barber of Seville* and other operas in English. Mrs. Seguin is said to have attained a great triumph in Balfe's *The Bohemian Girl* on November 25, 1844.[7] He might have heard the Seguins in a number of other operas in English, including *Don Pasquale* on March 9, 1846, and three favorites in November 1849: *The Bohemian Girl, Don Giovanni,* and *Norma,* besides concerts at various times from 1842 through 1849. Mary Taylor also sang in English operas and concerts through the same period.

Many plays besides *The Tempest* contained lyrics that required the services of good singers, and there were also light comedies and farces that involved singing. It was a convenience, especially during the 1830's and 1840's, to have good actors who could also sing. Among the actors and actresses named by Whitman in his late prose works, several appeared in the English operas and other singing parts, notably J. H. Clarke, Henry Placide, Peter Richings, and Mrs. Vernon, a sister of Charlotte Cushman. Charlotte herself, who had been a professional singer before she turned to the dramatic stage, sometimes had singing parts. In addition there were Mrs. Richardson (formerly Mrs. Chapman), Mrs. Clara Fisher, and Mrs. Thomas Flynn, among the women, and W. F. Gates and William Edwin among the men. It

[6] *Annals,* IV, 297.
[7] *Ibid.,* V, 92.

must have been William Edwin of whom Whitman wrote in *Good-Bye My Fancy*: "Every theatre had some superior voice, and it was common to give a favorite song between the acts. 'The Sea' at the bijou Olympic (Broadway near Grand,) was always welcome from the little Englishman named Edwin, a good balladist." And of course there were the popular Negro minstrels. He said, "I often saw [T. D.] Rice the original 'Jim Crow' at the old Park Theatre filling up the gap in some short bill.[8]

Whitman occasionally commented on the opera in his newspaper writing, but less frequently than on plays. Among the articles reprinted from the New York *Aurora* there is one, entitled "Italian Opera in New Orleans," in which the author, presumably Whitman, castigates James Gordon Bennett, of the New York *Herald*, for puffing La Signora Fatoni Sutton, whom he judges to be a second-rate singer, recalling her previous failure in *Norma* at the Park. He points out, however, that New York had some "real" musical talent in Mr. and Mrs. Seguin and a man named Manvers, who were then (April 15, 1842) wanting an engagement at the Park.[9] They got the engagement ten days later, and during it they presented *Norma* and other operas with great success. Whitman's opinion of Mrs. Sutton and of the *Herald's* support of her is corroborated by Odell, who said, "Mme. Sutton, I apprehend, was more appreciated by the critic of the Herald than by any one else. . . . Every time Mme. Sutton sang, the Herald indulged in superlatives."[10] Mary Taylor was very popular both as an actress and as a singer. Odell says that in 1847 the English version of "Fra Diavolo," with her as Zerlina, "was given nine times in succession, from April 12th to April 21st; verily, Mary's acclaim was mounting to the stars.'" He adds, "She has certainly brought the breath of life into a languid season."[11] Whitman, apparently, did not wholly agree, though he liked Mary Taylor's singing. In the article "Dramatic Affairs, and Actors," in the *Eagle* of April 19, 1847, he wrote: "At the Olympic theatre, they are giving a run, after the old sort, of the popular operas, very neatly got up on a small scale; Miss Taylor appears to-night as Zorlina [Zerlina] in 'Fra Diavolo'; (the best played parts of this theatre are Diavolo's two fellow robbers)."[12] The part of one of these robbers was sung by Mrs. H. C. Timm, who sometimes took male parts, and who often sang with Mary Taylor.

8 *Prose Works 1892*, II, 696.

9 *Walt Whitman of the New York* Aurora, ed. Joseph Jay Rubin and Charles H. Brown (State College, Pa., 1950), p. 118.

10 *Annals*, IV, 681.

11 *Ibid.*, V, 295.

12 Reprinted in *UPP*, I, 157. "Zorlina" is evidently a printer's error.

Odell quotes from *The Spirit of the Times* for March 30, 1844, a comparison of Mrs. Timm's popularity with that of Mary Taylor, then appearing in *Cinderella* with Mrs. Timm as the Prince: "If Timm wins the hearts of the pittites, Taylor has the white gloves and boxes in her favor."[13] It would appear that Whitman's taste was a little closer to the pittites than to the white gloves. Another popular singer whom Whitman heard in English opera was Mrs. Anna Bishop, wife of the English composer Henry R. Bishop. She made her debut at the Park on August 4, 1847, as Linda in the English version of Donizetti's *Linda di Chamounix*. Odell says that she created a sensation, and quotes the *Albion* for August 7, where her voice is described as "a very high soprano, neither powerful nor metallic . . . but sweet and pure. . . . Its flexibility is remarkable, her scales, diatonic and chromatic, are executed with lightning rapidity, and at the same time are beautifully emphasized and articulated."[14] In the *Eagle* of August 5, 1847, Whitman comments very favorably on Mrs. Bishop's singing as Linda: "Her voice is the purest soprano—and of as silvery clearness as ever came from the human throat—rich, but not massive—and of such flexibility that one is almost appalled at the way the most difficult passages are not only gone over with ease, but actually dallied with, and their difficulty redoubled. They put one in mind of the gyrations of a bird in the air."[15] His language is less technical than that of the critic of *The Spirit of the Times* but his critical opinion is similar. Since Whitman's article was written immediately after the first appearance of Mrs. Bishop in New York, he could not have had much benefit from the printed reviews of the professional critics. By this time, apparently, he felt confident of his own ability to judge musical performances. Of the operas he mentioned in old age he could have heard, in addition to those already discussed, and probably had heard in English, the following: *The Puritans, The Huguenots, Fille du Regiment, La Favorita, La Gazza Ladra,* and *William Tell.*

By 1848 the English opera had declined in popularity and the Italian opera was preferred, especially by the more sophisticated music lovers of New York. Whitman was not among the sophisticated as yet, although he was by no means unacquainted with Italian opera. It cannot be determined when he first heard opera in Italian. Assuming that he had not gone to the Italian Opera House in 1833–35, his first opportunity would have been during the brief season at Niblo's

13 *Annals,* V, 47.

14 *Ibid.,* V, 321. She repeated this opera nightly through Aug. 10; she sang Amina in *La Sonnambula* on Aug. 12 and for several succeeding nights, and on Aug. 17 she sang portions of three operas. Her engagement ended Aug. 18.

15 *GF,* II, 351–52.

Garden from September 15 to October 23, 1842. Both *Lucia di Lam-mermoor* and *Norma* were presented several times. But apparently New York was still not ready for Italian opera. If Whitman attended any of the performances it was probably more from curiosity than genuine interest. On February 3, 1844, Palmo's Opera House was opened with the performance of *I Puritani*, with the very capable Signora Eufrasia Borghese as Elvira. A little later a tenor named Antognini joined the company. He was hailed by the critics as a great singer and fine actor. Whitman did not mention either Borghese or Antognini. On November 18, 1844, Signora Rosina Pico made her first appearance on Palmo's stage, and sang there and in concerts frequently for several years. Richard Grant White called her voice a "rich, creamy contralto." She was well received in spite of competition with the more popular Seguins in *The Bohemian Girl* at the Park.[16] Odell quotes the New York *Herald* as saying of Pico that she had "extraordinary personal attractions" and a "manner singularly fasci-nating."[17] Whitman mentions her in the *Eagle* on December 4, 1846, but not to praise. In an article called "Music That Is Music" he praises rather the "music of feeling—heart music as distinguished from art music" as exemplified in the singing of the Hutchinson family and several other bands of American vocalists. He wonders why these American singers "do not *entirely* supplant the stale, sec-ond hand, foreign method, with its flourishes, its ridiculous sentimen-tality, its anti-republican spirit, and its sycophantic tainting the young taste of the nation!" The "elegant simplicity" of the American singers, he adds, "is more judicious than the dancing school bows and curtsies, and inane smiles, and kissing of the tips of a kid glove a la Pico."[18] This essay was a revision of a briefer one called "Art-Singing and Heart-Singing" which Poe published in the *Broadway Journal* on November 29, 1845, after Whitman heard a similar group, the Cheney family, in a concert. In the earlier essay he was less vehe-mently critical of the "foreign method" of singing, but he had evi-dently heard Italian singers either in concert or in opera, although he did not mention Pico or any other.[19] He might have heard her at Castle Garden in May 1845 for fifty cents. She sang there several times

---

[16] Richard Grant White, "Opera in New York," *Century Magazine*, XXIII (April 1882), 876. This quotation is from the second in a series of four articles by White. The first is in the issue of March 1882, the third in May, and the fourth in June. White was the very competent music critic of the New York *Courier and Enquirer*. These articles are based largely on reviews of the opera which he wrote for his paper during the 1840's and 1850's.

[17] *Annals*, V, 131.

[18] Reprinted in *GF*, II, 347–49.

[19] "Art-Singing and Heart-Singing" is reprinted in *UPP*, I, 104–6.

in operas presented in concert form, including *Semiramide* and *The Barber of Seville.* She also sang there a number of times in July.[20] If he did see her in opera, he was probably more impressed by her poor acting than by her good singing. Ireland says she had no equal among her contemporaries as a contralto and "ranks with the best who appeared between the days of Malibran and Alboni."[21]

The opera company that began a new season at Palmo's Opera House on January 4, 1847, included, besides Rosina Pico, the tenor Benedetti, the basso Beneventano, both excellent, the buffo Sanquirico, Salvatore Patti, also a tenor, and the soprano Clotilda Barili, Patti's stepdaughter. She was young and not yet fully developed, but her voice was generally praised. Other members of the company were less notable. Whitman must have heard these singers several times before the end of the season, June 7. On March 20 he inserted the following paragraph in the *Eagle*: "Since 'all the papers' are giving testimony in reference to the way in which the Italian opera at Palmo's treats the press, B. E. thinks proper to bear witness to their uniform courtesy and blandness toward *his* folks."[22] A few days later, March 23, he printed a review of *The Barber of Seville*, which had been presented at Palmo's on March 19. S. Patti sang the tenor role of Almaviva and was regarded by the critics as inadequate. Sanquirico was Bartolo, Beneventano was Figaro, and Pico was Rosina. Whitman's criticism sounds knowledgeable, but it is possible that he wrote after he had read reviews in other papers. He suggests that Benedetti should have had the role that Patti attempted, adding: "it would gratify all, and probably ensure a second attendance." Then he goes on confidently:

Beneventano as the barber does very well—better than might be expected from one with so heavy a voice and manner. His opening song is the gem of the performance, and is given with ease and spirit; moreover, his voice improves on acquaintance, and when singing in chorus, comes in like some high toned instrument filling out and sustaining the different parts. . . . Sanquirico, as usual, is full of fun, and submits to the shaving operation to the infinite gratification of all concerned, while Pico does every thing in her own attractive manner so that one could easily sympathize with her guardian in his chagrin at her loss.[23]

Admitting that the reporter often pretends to know more than he does, I think we may assume nevertheless that Whitman had already

---

20 See *Annals,* V, 159–60.
21 *Records,* II, 444. That would be between 1836 and 1852 approximately.
22 *GF,* II, 359.
23 *GF,* II, 349–51.

seen a good many operas and opera singers before writing this article. Probably he had read many reviews of operas by such excellent critics as Richard Grant White in the *Courier and Enquirer,* and the critics of the *Albion* and the *Tribune.*

In the *Eagle* on April 19, 1847, he remarks that at Palmo's they are presenting "a narrow few—those not even the second best—of the Italian operas; tonight, 'Lucrezia Borgia.' On Wednesday night, it will be pleasanter to go, for then they give 'Lombardi.' "[24] This preference for Verdi's *I Lombardi* over Donizetti's *Lucrezia Borgia* is interesting in view of the fact that, according to Odell, the critics had not yet come to like Verdi's music.[25] Was Whitman's taste then in advance of that of the professional music critics? It is surprising to learn that he considered *Lucrezia Borgia* less than a "second-best" opera. It had been popular years before in Europe, but it was offered in New York for the first time at Palmo's on November 25, 1844, and not again until it was presented at the same place on April 7, 1847. Presumably it was less popular in Europe in the 1840's than it had been earlier and Whitman was aware of the fact. A few years later, when it was presented by Marty's Havana Company, it was one of Whitman's favorite operas. Both Pico and Borghese were in the cast of the earlier presentation, which he might have seen.[26] In the same *Eagle* article Whitman says: "Nor must we overlook the new musical corps, late from Havana, now giving operas at the Park, two evenings a week: after the next representation by this corps, our readers will get a plain man's opinions of them." As a matter of fact, the Havana Company appeared at this time for only two nights, April 15 and 16, after which they left, not to return until June 9.[27] He could have heard them during their month's stay at the Park, beginning June 9, or later during their month's engagement at Castle Garden, beginning August 18, 1847, but if he did he did not report the fact in the *Eagle.* I suspect that his failure to review a performance was due less to his own lack of interest than to the fact that he knew his Brooklyn readers were not much interested.[28] There really can be little

---

[24] "Dramatic Affairs, and Actors" (reprinted in *UPP*, I, 157–58).

[25] *Annals*, V, 301. *I Lombardi* had been given first on March 3 and repeated several times. Odell does not give the dates. Ireland (*Records*, II, 481) says that *Lucrezia Borgia* was given April 9 and followed by repetitions of *I Lombardi* and *Lucia*, but he too omits some of the dates.

[26] *Annals*, V, 131.

[27] *Ibid.*, V, 263.

[28] After quoting Whitman's statement about the Havana troupe, Faner comments: "Though it is certain that Whitman saw the productions by the great Havana company, for he later mentioned several of the great singers of the organization, he never fulfilled his promise to review them." I suspect Faner con-

doubt that Whitman was interested in Italian opera in 1847, and yet he probably still preferred opera in the English language. At any rate, he continued to call for a native music as he had called for a native drama. In the *Eagle* on September 8, 1847, he announced that Americans had long enough "followed obedient and child-like in the track of the Old World. We have received her tenors and her buffos, her operatic troupes and her vocalists," and applauded songs made to please royal ears. It is time, he declared, that this should cease. "The subtlest spirit of a nation is expressed through its music—and the music acts reciprocally upon the nation's very soul." [29] He was less nationalistic in his attitude toward instrumental music, and welcomed foreign musicians, such as Ole Bull and Camillo Sivori, though he was even more enthusiastic about the playing of the American violinist, Joseph Burke. Yet, he added, "heavenly genius belongs to no country, and we scorn the common cant which would sneer at such genius' highest development, merely because its birthplace was in a distant land!" [30]

Whitman loved good church music and went occasionally to hear special programs in New York churches, where frequently famous opera stars, as well as good amateur singers, could be heard. He also heard and wrote about two oratorios composed by Mendelssohn. The first was *The Oratorio of St. Paul*, which he wrote about in the Brooklyn *Star* on November 28, 1845, saying: "It is utterly impossible to describe in words the effect produced by this fine composition—for music, more subtle than words, laughs to scorn the lame attempts of an every day medium." [31] The other was the oratorio *Elijah*, which he heard at the New York Tabernacle on November 8, 1847, and wrote about the next day in the *Eagle*. Obviously his musical education had made great progress in two years, for he is now rather critical. He says it is "too heavy in its general character, and wants the relief of a proper proportion of lightness and melody. . . . Some of the choruses are characterized by all the grandeur and sublimity of the best of Handel's productions, but these do not compensate for defects in

---

fused the 1847 performances of the Havana company in New York with their far more important visit of 1850. None of the singers mentioned by Whitmban in his late prose were with the Havana Company in 1847 in New York.

[29] "A Thought of Ours about Music in the United States" (reprinted in *GF*, II, 345–46).

[30] See "Mr. Burke, the Violinist," and "The New Violinist," in the *Eagle* (reprinted in *GF*, II, 352–53, 354–55).

[31] Quoted from Emory Holloway "More Light on Whitman," *American Mercury*, I (Feb. 1924), 186. See also *Walt Whitman Looks at the Schools*, ed. Florence Bernstein Freedman (New York, 1950), Appendix A p. 215.

other respects."[32] This last sentence suggests that he was not unfamiliar with Handel's oratorios. In "Proud Music of the Storm" he mentions both Handel and Haydn, and says: "The *Creation* in billows of godhood laves me." However, since in the same passage he says, "I hear the singing of the children of St. Paul's cathedral," which obviously he had not heard, we cannot be sure that he had heard Haydn's *Creation*, or, if he had, when. Although he himself seemed to appreciate the music of *Elijah*, he said it was "too elaborately scientific for the popular ear," and he thought it was evident that the audience derived little pleasure from it.

Even the singing of Jenny Lind, which enthralled many who heard her in 1850 and 1851, failed to please Whitman at first. On September 11, 1850, under the expert management of P. T. Barnum, she made her first appearance in New York, and gave seven concerts at Castle Garden that month. In late October and November, she gave fifteen more concerts, this time at Tripler Hall. Then she left New York on tour and did not return until May 1851, when she gave several concerts at Castle Garden and others at Tripler Hall. After that she did not sing again in New York for nearly a year. Her farewell concert was given at Castle Garden on May 24, 1852. Whitman thought he had heard her in 1850, probably in her first series of concerts, and he may have heard her in May 1851, before he published his opinion of her singing. This opinion appears in the third of his "Letters from Paumanok," which was published in the New York *Evening Post*, August 14, 1851. He had just been praising the "manly voice" (as exemplified especially in Bettini) as superior to the female voice. Then he inserts this paragraph on Jenny Lind: "The Swedish Swan, with all her blandishments, never touched my heart in the least. I wondered at so much vocal dexterity; and indeed they were all very pretty, those leaps and double somersets. But even in the grandest religious airs, genuine masterpieces as they are, of the German composers, executed by this strangly over-praised woman in perfect scientific style, let critics say what they like, it was a failure; for there was a vacuum in the head of the performance. Beauty pervaded it no doubt, and that of a high order. It was the beauty of Adam before God breathed into his nostrils."[33] Some of the critics expressed views not unlike Whitman's. For example, Odell quotes the critic of the *Albion* for September 21, 1850, as saying: "The tones of her voice are strong and brilliant in the extreme; they ring through the vast area, and vibrate in our ears, but they do not touch the heart, nor give the

---

[32] Reprinted in *GF*, II, 353–54.
[33] Reprinted in *UPP*, I, 257.

thrill which is ever the result of a pure musical sensation."[34] Whitman's comment in *Good-Bye My Fancy*, nearly forty years after the *Evening Post* review previously quoted, is not essentially different. He wrote there: "I remember Jenny Lind and heard her (1850 I think) several times. She had the most brilliant, captivating, popular musical style and expression of any one known; (the canary, and several other sweet birds are wondrous fine—but there is something in song that goes deeper—isn't there?)" In *Specimen Days* he said he had heard her at Castle Garden.[35]

As I have noted, Whitman was acquainted with Italian opera in 1847 and probably in 1845 or earlier, and in the season of 1848–49 he must have gone a number of times to the Astor Place Opera House, where E. R. Fry was manager at first. Fry was later succeeded by Max Maretzek with a first-rate group of singers. Madame Laborde, whom he remembered in *Good-Bye My Fancy*, sang with this troupe but did not appear on the operatic stage in New York after the spring of 1849. It may be assumed that he went a number of times during Maretzek's 1849–50 season, also at the Astor Place Opera House, where he might have heard again such good but not great singers as Borghese, Beneventano, Benedetti, and Sanquirico, as well as Teresa Truffi, who later, if not then, was among the great. But his enthusiasm for Italian opera dates, I feel sure, from the year 1850, and the singers who excited this enthusiasm belonged to the Havana Company, organized in Havana by Don Francisco Marty y Torrens. One group of these singers, as I have already mentioned, came to New York for brief engagements in 1847, but most of the great singers remembered by Whitman were not in this group. Marty's troupe returned to New York in April 1850, "greatly augmented," as Odell notes, "and forming as a whole one of the finest aggregations of singers ever heard in New York." They began on April 11 at Niblo's Opera House. Among the singers remembered by Whitman who were in the group at this time were Balbina Steffanone, soprano, Ignazio Marini, basso, Angiolina Bosio, soprano, who first appeared on April 18, and Cesare Badiali, baritone, who first appeared on April 22. On June 10, Tedesco, another soprano, joined this company. On July 8 they moved to Castle Garden and reduced the admission price to fifty cents.[36] After

34 *Annals*, VI, 88. A full account of Jenny Lind's performances in New York may be found in this volume, pp. 87–90, 95–96, 185, and *passim*.

35 See *Prose Works 1892*, I, 21; II, 696.

36 *Annals*, V, 479–81, 563–64, 575, 590. Tedesco had been in New York with the Havana Company in 1847, and she sang there again in 1849, though not with the Havana Company, but her name is not among those remembered by Whitman in later years.

Marty's Havana troupe had completed their summer engagements at Castle Garden on September 7, 1850, the enterprising Max Maretzek began recruiting them for his own New York company, and during the succeeding months managed to induce most of them to return to New York after the expiration of their next season in Havana. He himself says he "succeeded in securing all of them, with the single exception of Tedesco."[37]

In the three essays published in his prose works in the 1880's and 1890's, the following opera singers in Italian were named: Laborde, Steffanone, Bosio, Truffi, Parodi, Bertucca, Alboni, Grisi, Vestvali, Gazzaniga, and La Grange, among the women; and Beneventano, Marini, Badiali, Bettini, Mario, Amodio, and Brignoli among the men. He says there were others whose names he did not recall. Among those he certainly had heard but did not remember were Pico, Clotilda Barili, S. Patti, Benedetti, and Sanquirico, whom he heard before 1850 and named in the *Eagle*. Laborde is the only singer he did not hear after 1849 whom he remembered. It is strange that he did not remember Tedesco, whom he surely heard in the summer of 1850 and possibly earlier but could not have heard after 1850. It is perhaps more strange that he forgot Salvi, one of the Havana Company, whom the critics rated superior to Bettini. Vestvali, Gazzaniga, La Grange, Amodio, and Brignoli belong to the late fifties. Felicita Vestvali, the "sumptuous Vestvali," as Odell calls her, made her New York debut in February 1855 in *La Favorita*. The *Albion* of March 3 is cited as saying it was suicidal for her to begin with Leonora after Tedesco, Steffanone, Alboni, and Grisi. Pasquale Brignoli, having proved himself with the Paris opera, first sang in New York on March 12, 1855, as Edgardo in *Lucia di Lammermoor*, and soon established himself as the most popular of tenors. Amodio (first name not known) made his debut in New York as the Conte di Luna in *Il Trovatore* in its first performance in America, on May 2, 1855, and was acclaimed.[38]

All the others belong to the period 1850–55; although he might have heard Teresa Truffi during Maretzek's season of 1849–50, he doubtless remembered her best during the seasons of 1850–51 and 1851–52. Bertucca first appeared on November 19, 1849, in Maretzek's performance of Rossini's *Otello*. She afterward married Maretzek. Alboni was heard in opera in New York only between December

---

[37] Max Maretzek, *Crotchets and Quavers* (New York, 1855), p. 158. He gives an amusing account of his troubles with this aggregation, who quarrelled among themselves and with Maretzek because of their idiosyncrasies, their jealousies, and their unbounded egotism.

[38] *Annals*, VI, 387, 393, 394. All remained in New York or returned often; Brignoli died there and was buried Nov. 3, 1884.

27, 1852, and May 1853, although she sang in concerts as late as November 1853. Grisi and her husband Mario first appeared on September 4, 1854, at Castle Garden, and closed their engagement in New York February 20, 1855. The remaining singers named by Whitman belonged to the Havana troupe. Badiali, Marini, Bosio, and Steffanone all came to New York in the spring of 1850 with Marty's second and augmented company. Bettini came a few months later. Bosio, Bettini, and Badiali left Maretzek with some others in January 1852 to form the Artists' Union Opera Company. This lasted only a few weeks. They left in February, and Bosio and Bettini never returned to New York.[39]

The two singers in Italian opera who most influenced Whitman were, first, Alessandro Bettini, and, later, Marietta Alboni. He was, probably for the first time, completely won over to the love of the Italian opera by the singing of Bettini in the summer of 1851. Bettini had first appeared at the Astor Place Opera House on December 5, 1850, in the role of Edgardo in *Lucia di Lammermoor,* but he was hoarse and could not continue after the first act. Apparently he did not sing again in New York until the following June. On June 5, he appeared again at the Astor Place Opera House as Edgardo, with Bosio taking the title role, in *Lucia.* The next night he sang the title role of *Ernani,* with Truffi, Beneventano, and Marini. During that month he also appeared as Fernando in *La Favorita,* with Truffi as Leonora. These were the three operas in which Whitman best remembered Bettini, who appeared in each of them two or three times during the summer of 1851.[40] In the third of his "Letters from Paumanok," dated August 11, 1851, he pays high tribute to the singing of Bettini, especially in *La Favorita,* which he summarizes in part; he also praises Maretzek's orchestra.[41] Several passages in this letter deserve quotation.

Have not you, too, . . . while listening to the well-played music of some band like Maretzek's, felt an overwhelming desire for measureless sound—a sublime orchestra of a myriad orchestras—a colossal volume of harmony, in which the thunder might roll in its proper place; and above it, the vast, pure Tenor,—identity of the Creative Power itself—rising through the universe, until the boundless and unspeakable capacities of that mystery, the human soul, should be filled to the uttermost, and the problem of human cravingness be satisfied and destroyed? . . . Those fresh vigorous tones of Bettini!—I

39 *Ibid.,* VI, 165. See also Maretzek, p. 200.

40 See *Annals,* VI, 65–66, 97–98.

41 Published originally in the New York *Evening Post* for Aug. 14, 1851 (reprinted in *UPP,* I, 255–59). In a footnote Holloway says *La Favorita* was produced on Aug. 8. Doubtless Whitman remembered several performances.

have often wished to know this man, for a minute, that I might tell him how much of the highest order of pleasure he has conferred upon me. His voice has often affected me to tears. Its clear, firm, wonderfully exalting notes, filling and expanding away; dwelling like a poised lark up in heaven; have made my very soul tremble.—Critics talk of others who are more perfectly artistical—yes, as the well-shaped marble is artistical. But the singing of this man has breathing blood within it; the living soul, of which the lower stage they call art, is but the shell and sham. . . . Pure and vast, that voice now rises, as on clouds, to the heaven where it claims audience. Now, firm and unbroken, it spreads like an ocean around us. Ah, welcome that I know not the mere language of the earthly words in which the melody is embodied; as all words are mean before the language of true music.

A passage vaguely similar occurs in a Whitman notebook (Holloway's No. 3), evidently written before 1855. One paragraph in this notebook begins, "I want that tenor, large and fresh as the creation," and includes the sentence, "I want an infinite chorus and orchestrium, wide as the orbit of Uranus, true as the hours of the day, and filling my capacities to receive as thoroughly as the sea fills its scooped out sands . . . stabbing my heart with myriads of forked distractions more furious than hail or lightning—lulling me drowsily with honeyed morphine—tightening the fakes of death about my throat, and awakening me again to know by that comparison, the most positive wonder in the world, and that's what we call life."[42]

This may be compared with some lines from Section 26 of "Song of Myself":

A tenor large and fresh as creation fills me,
The orbic flex of his mouth is pouring and filling me full.

.   .   .   .

The orchestra whirls me wider than Uranus flies,
It wrenches such ardors from me I did not know I possess'd them,
It sails me, I dab with bare feet, they are lick'd by the indolent waves,
I am cut by bitter and angry hail, I lose my breath,
Steep'd amid honey'd morphine, my windpipe throttled in fakes of death,
At length let up again to feel the puzzle of puzzles,
And that we call Being.[43]

There are other passages in *Leaves of Grass*, especially in "Song of Myself" and in "Proud Music of the Storm," based on his recollection of Bettini's singing.

It is evident that in 1851 Bettini had made a greater impression on Whitman than any other singer he had heard. He held to his admira-

[42] *UPP*, I, 85.
[43] I quote the final text, but the text of 1855 is essentially the same.

tion of Bettini although, as he admitted, the critics did not agree with him, and rated Lorenzo Salvi much higher. Salvi, also of the Havana troupe, was more mature. Whitman must have heard him, though his name is not recalled. Krehbiel says, "If we are to believe the testimony of contemporaneous critics he was the greatest tenor of his time, with the exception of Mario." He quotes from Richard Grant White's essays in the *Century Magazine* that critic's statement that Salvi "gave to multitudes who would otherwise have had no such opportunity that education in art which is to be had only from the performances of a great artist." [44] Clearly Whitman heard values in great music that went far beyond the limits of mere art, something that touched the heart and elevated the spirit. Bettini's youthful vigor appealed to him, and it may be he was more nearly right in his judgment of the young tenor than the critics. Maretzek reported in 1855 that since he left New York early in 1852 and returned to Italy he had "been everywhere acknowledged in Italy as its first tenor." [45] Whitman kept track of him and his career as well as he could. Writing of a performance of "Ernani" in 1855, in which Brignoli sang the title role, Whitman said: "The young and manly Ernani used to be well played by Bettini, now at the Grand Opera in Paris. Bettini was a beautiful, large, robust, friendly, young man—a fine tenor.[46]

At the time he wrote of Bettini in 1851 he had heard many fine sopranos whom he remembered in later years, notably Truffi, Steffanone, and Bosio, but he preferred "the *manly* voice," compared to which "the female organ, however, curious and high, is but as the pleasant moonlight." But he had not yet heard the contralto Marietta Alboni. When he did hear her, he set her above all other opera singers, even Bettini. His enthusiasm, in fact, was unbounded. He said in *Specimen Days* that he heard her every time she sang in New York and vicinity, and he told Helen Price just a few years after she left that he had heard her twenty times.[47] I am unable to say just how

44 Krehbiel, pp. 62–63.

45 Maretzek, p. 156. Bettini had achieved no reputation before coming to New York. The English critic Henry F. Chorley, writing of the performance of a Rossini opera in which Bettini appeared in London in 1847, calls him "a very bad tenor" who "had never learned his art." (See Chorley's *Thirty Years' Musical Recollections* [New York, 1926; originally published in London in 1862], p. 204.)

46 "The Opera," first published in *Life Illustrated*, Nov. 10, 1855; reprinted in *New York Dissected*, ed. Emory Holloway and Ralph Adimari (New York, 1936), p. 22.

47 See the memoranda of Helen Price, written in 1881 and published in Bucke's *Walt Whitman* (Philadelphia, 1883), p. 29. Bucke says the supreme enjoyment "of Whitman's young maturity was the Italian opera, and the climax of opera for him was the singing of Alboni." (*Ibid.*, p. 22.)

many times Alboni sang in New York, but it was certainly more than twenty. She sang in opera at least fifteen times during her first engagement at the Broadway Theater, beginning December 27, 1852, and ending January 28, 1853. During her engagement at Niblo's Garden from March 28 to about May 6, she appeared in seven different operas, in some of them more than once. She also appeared in concerts at various intervals and places more than a dozen times, the first two or three in the summer of 1852 and the last in November 1853. Among the operas in which she appeared were *Norma, La Cenerentola, La Figlia del Reggimento, La Favorita, La Sonnambula, Don Pasquale, The Barber of Seville, La Gazza Ladra, Lucrezia Borgia, Don Giovanni*, and *Fra Diavolo*.[48] Some of the critics thought she was not a good actress and did best in concerts, and some thought she was too large for her part in *La Cenerentola, La Figlia del Reggimento*, and *La Sonnambula*, but Whitman thought she was a good actress and was not troubled by her size. In one of his manuscript notes for an article on Italian music, apparently intended for the Brooklyn *Daily Times*, but not published, he wrote:

The best songstress ever in America was Alboni.—Her voice is a contralto of large compass, high and low—and probably sweeter tones never issued from human lips. The mere sound of that voice was pleasure enough.—All persons appreciated Alboni—the common crowd quite as well as the connoisseurs.—We used to go in the upper tiers of the theatre, (the Broadway,) on the nights of her performance, and remember seeing that part of the auditorium packed full of New York young men, mechanics, "roughs," &c., entirely oblivious of all except Alboni, from the time the great songstress came on the stage, till she left it again.—Alboni is a fully developed woman, with perfect-shaped feet, arms, and hands.—Some thought her fat—*we* always thought her beautiful.—Her face is regular and pleasant—her forehead low—plentiful black hair, cut short, like a boy's—a slow and graceful style of walk—attitudes of inimitable beauty, and large black eyes.—We have seen her in pathetic scenes, (as in Norma plann'g the death of her children,) with real tears, like rain, coursing each other down her cheeks.—Alboni is now in Paris, singing at the Grand Opera there.[49]

Whitman remembered Alboni's "real tears" in 1891 in conversations with an English visitor, J. W. Wallace. Wallace reports Whitman as

48 Ireland, *Records*, II, 614.

49 *Faint Clews & Indirections*, ed. Clarence Gohdes and Rollo G. Silver (Durham, N.C., 1949), p. 19. This manuscript can be dated approximately by a reference to Piccolomini earlier in Whitman's note, who made her debut in New York on Oct. 20, 1858, and her final appearance Dec. 7. Whitman said he did not think much of her, although she was then the "rage." Whitman was then editor of the *Daily Times*.

saying that Alboni had two children in Italy and that she was probably thinking of them. But Alboni presumably had no children then,
for she was still unmarried. It may be that this confused account is
the result of Wallace's faulty reporting, not of Whitman's uncertain
memory.[50]

So far as I can discover, Alboni sang the role of Norma only twice
in New York: January 27 and 28, 1853, at the Broadway Theater. At
that time Norma was considered the greatest tragic character in opera, but the music made great demands on the singer, especially on a
contralto voice. Alboni, for some reason, was determined to attempt
it, although advised not to, and indeed she had sung many soprano
roles successfully. On her first night there was not even standing room
in the theater, and as much as five dollars was offered for a seat. Her
performance proved her faith in her ability to meet the high notes,
usually not expected of a contralto, and also demonstrated that she
was a better actress than had been supposed. Odell reports that "to
every one's surprise, the matchless singer acted with authority and
power." The critics fully corroborated Whitman's judgment of Alboni's singing, as they had not of Bettini's. On January 1, 1853, after
Alboni's first opera, the *Albion* declared that she was "queen of con-
tralti, perhaps *the* great contralto, who is destined never to be rivalled
or eclipsed—soul of melody—glorious flood of song."[51] Even Richard
Grant White, who was not easy to please, said that "in her style, her
singing is as purely and absolutely beautiful as it is possible for anything earthly to be." Remembering afterward how he felt, he said
"one was tempted to go and kneel down before her and do something
abject in grateful acknowledgment of this manifestation of supreme
musical divinity." Although he thought she was no actress, and that
her voice was unsuited to the requirements of *Norma*, he admitted
that "she not only sang the music with passion and with fervor, but in
her action showed intuitions of dramatic power which I had never
before remarked in her. . . . She must have brooded over the part until
it took complete possession of her."[52]

[50] J. Johnston and J. W. Wallace, *Visits to Walt Whitman in 1890–1891* (London, 1917), p. 161. Wallace has Whitman saying the children's scene was in *Lucia*,
a mistake he certainly would not have made. Alboni married the Count A. Pepoli
in 1853 and thereafter lived in Paris.

[51] As quoted by Odell, *Annals*, VI, 201.

[52] *Century Magazine*, XXIV (May 1882), 38–39. White says he found no record
of Alboni's having repeated the role of Norma in Europe. Henry F. Chorley, who
perhaps heard her after she left New York, said (p. 207) that though she succeeded
in extending her voice upward, its texture was eventually injured; "its luscious
quality, and some of its power, were inevitably lost."

Next to Bettini's tenor and Alboni's contralto, Whitman seems to have been most impressed by "the trumpet notes of Badiali's baritone" and by "Marini's bass in 'Faliero.'" Badiali is named along with Alboni and Bettini among singers, and J. B. Booth, Edwin Forrest, and J. H. Clarke among actors as the "best dramatic and lyric artists" he saw during his New York experience of the stage.[53] Maretzek, who heard him in England, said that Marini was known in London as "the greatest Italian *basso* who had ever sung there, with the solitary exception of Lablache."[54] Whitman was probably thinking of him when he told Traubel he had known but one or two good bass voices.[55] He also told Traubel, "Badiali was the superbest of all superb baritones in my time—my singing years." He remembered him particularly in *The Puritans*.[56] The phrase "my singing years" is significant in relation to the career of Badiali in New York, for he was the principal baritone there between 1850 and 1855. Odell remarks of one performance, "on the 8th [of December 1851], the great quartette—Bosio, Bettini, Badiali, and Marini—glorified I Puritani."[57]

Whitman was very sensitive to sounds of all kinds, but especially to the sound of the human voice. There is something, he felt, in the "quality and power" of the best human voice that "touches the soul, the abysms." Such a voice had Alboni, as did also Bettini, Fanny Kemble, Booth, Elias Hicks, and the preacher Father Taylor. But it was not found exclusively in singers, actors, and public speakers; he had noticed it often, he said, in ordinary people, frequently women.[58] He heard this quality usually in strong male voices of the lower range. The soprano voices of Bosio, Steffanone, and Truffi pleased him, but they did not excite him like Alboni's contralto. In the original manuscript of a paragraph printed in *Specimen Days* with the title "A Contralto Voice," appears the following passage, deleted before publication: "(This kind of voice has always to me the sense of young maternity—the last art-sense of all. Alboni was its fruition and apex. I wonder if the lady will ever know that her singing, her method, gave the foundation, the start, thirty years ago to all my poetic literary effort since?)"[59] One must suppose that Alboni, whose figure was more

[53] *Prose Works 1892*, II, 591–92.

[54] Maretzek, p. 157.

[55] *WWC*, II, 123.

[56] *WWC*, II, 173–74.

[57] *Annals*, VI, 158.

[58] "The Perfect Human Voice," in *Good-Bye My Fancy*, (*Prose Works 1892*, II, 673–74).

[59] *Prose Works 1892*, I, 235, note. The passage may have been deleted because, on reflection, he decided it attributed too much to Alboni; he may, on the other

mature than her years in 1852, became for Whitman the ideal woman of *Leaves of Grass*. Doubtless the "children's scene in Norma," which he compared in its effect on him to Booth's "Richard III" and the sight of Niagara Falls,[60] was the more affecting if, indeed, he believed her "real tears" were shed for the children he imagined she had left in Italy. So she became, despite her youth when he saw her, the mother figure of *Leaves of Grass*.

> (The teeming lady comes,
> The lustrous orb, Venus contralto, the blooming mother,
> Sister of loftiest gods, Alboni's self I hear.)[61]

Although the climactic experience of his "singing years" was hearing Alboni in operas and concerts, hers was only the best of many fine voices. Doubtless he heard and liked many singers whose names he did not remember. One of these was Henrietta Sontag, whose concerts and opera performances occurred chiefly, like Alboni's, during the winter of 1852–53; sometimes the two singers appeared on the same nights. Sontag had a great reputation in Europe before she came to New York. She and Alboni, says Odell, were "two of the greatest operatic artists the world has ever known."[62] It is odd that Whitman did not remember her; one must believe that, great as she was, she was eclipsed, in his experience, by Alboni, in whose brilliance all other stars became invisible. The same thing had happened in the case of the tenor Salvi, who was eclipsed by Bettini. Two other great singers, Giuseppi Mario and Giula Grisi, came to New York in late August 1854 and remained until the following February. He was thirty-eight, she forty-two, both famous all over Europe. He was still in his prime as a singer, but she had grown matronly and her voice was past its prime. White reported, after hearing Mario as Edgardo in *Lucia*, "Signor Mario has the sweetest tenor voice in the world, and is supreme master of all the delicate mysteries of *nuance*; he is the prince of romance singers." However, he thought his acting deficient. He thought Grisi was perhaps at her best in *Norma*, where her ma-

---

hand, have deleted it because it was not germane to the paragraph as printed, which concerns a church hymn he heard one evening while sitting outside a friend's house in New York. Some of the materials used here may be found also in my essay "Whitman and the Poet in *Leaves of Grass*," published in *Essays Mostly on Periodical Publishing in America*, a collection in honor of Clarence Gohdes, ed James Woodress (Durham, N.C., 1973), pp. 3–21.

60 "Seeing Niagara to Advantage," *Specimen Days* (*Prose Works 1892*, I, 236).
61 "Proud Music of the Storm," lines 92–94.
62 *Annals*, VI, 241.

tronly figure was suited to the part, as it was not in some other roles.[63] Whitman remembered them well. He mentioned hearing them in *Specimen Days*. In *November Boughs* he wrote: "I also heard Mario many times, and at his best. In such parts as Gennaro, in 'Lucrezia Borgia,' he was inimitable—the sweetest of voices, a pure tenor, of considerable compass and respectable power. His wife, Grisi, was with him, no longer first-class or young—a fine Norma, though, to the last."[64] He heard Mario in a concert in Washington in 1873 and wrote his mother that Mario, though an old man, "sings first rate yet."[65]

In 1855 Whitman heard for the first time four singers whose names he later recalled. These were Anna de la Grange, a soprano, Felicita Vestvali, a contralto, Pasquale Brignoli, a tenor, and Amodio, a baritone. Vestvali is only a name listed among others by Whitman in *Good-Bye My Fancy*, and so we do not know what he thought of her; yet the fact that he remembered her at all suggests that he thought her good. She first appeared with Mario and Grisi in "Semiramide" on February 17, 1855. Richard Grant White is quoted as saying Vestvali was the hit of the evening. She had a "radiant face" and a "tall, magnificent figure," but her voice was imperfect.[66] La Grange made her debut in New York on April 21, 1855, and became the leading soprano at the Academy of Music for the season beginning October 1, 1855. White says she had a voice of great compass and pleasing quality and that she sang with "delicately perfect execution."[67] Amodio made his debut as the Conte di Luna in *Il Trovatore* on May 2, 1855, its first performance in America. Steffanone was Leonore, Vestvali Azucena, and Brignoli Manrico. Odell says both Brignoli and Amodio were "acclaimed."[68] White was not complimentary, saying that Brignoli's voice was "like the bleating of a sheep made musical" and his acting poor; yet his method was good, and he was such a "nice" young man that all the women admired him. "His high and long-continued favor is one of those puzzling popular freaks not uncommon in dramatic annals."[69] Whitman liked him, though with moderation, and

[63] *Century Magazine*, XXIV (June 1882), 193–94. See also *Annals*, VI, 390–92.

[64] In a manuscript note with items listed in the Trent catalogue, pp. 33–34, but not listed there, this note in ink is written on a separate strip of paper: "Grisi and Mario arrived in N. Y. Aug. 19, 1854.—I heard them that winter & in 1855." In red ink at the top: "Specimen Days." This seems to indicate that Whitman referred back to this note when writing that book.

[65] *Correspondence*, II, 191.

[66] *Annals*, VI, 388.

[67] *Century Magazine*, XXIV (June 1882), 200.

[68] *Annals*, VI, 393–94.

[69] *Century Magazine*, XXIV (June 1882), 199.

heard him from time to time in after years.[70] When he died, on October 30, 1884, Whitman wrote his poem "The Dead Tenor" as a memorial.[71] In the poem he called Brignoli's "the perfect singing voice," firm, but "liquid-soft" and "tremulous." The roles he named were those of Fernando, in *La Favorita*, Manrico, in *Il Trovatore*, Gennaro, in *Lucrezia Borgia*, and Ernani. W. S. Kennedy says the poem was written "on the occasion of the death of his old friend Brignoli," but I have found no other evidence that he was acquainted with Brignoli.[72]

There can be no doubt that the opera, as well as the dramatic stage, was an important part of the foreground of *Leaves of Grass*. In *Good-Bye My Fancy*, in what may be considered his final word, he sums up the matter as follows: "Seems to me I ought acknowledge my debt to actors, singers, public speakers, conventions, and the Stage in New York, in my youthful days, from 1835 onward—say to '60 or '61—and to plays and operas generally. (Which nudges a pretty big disquisition: of course it should be all elaborated and penetrated more deeply —but I will here give only some flitting mentionings of my youth.) Seems to me now when I look back, the Italian contralto Marietta Alboni (she is living yet, in Paris, 1891, in good condition, good voice yet, considering) with the then prominent histrions Booth, Edwin Forrest, and Fanny Kemble and the Italian singer Bettini, have had the deepest and most lasting effect upon me." The only composer he mentions is Verdi, but he might equally well, of course, have named Rossini, Bellini, Donizetti, and Meyerbeer, whose works he heard before he heard Verdi's. Some of his friends, he added, "claim that the new Wagner and his pieces belong far more truly to me, and I to them. Very likely. But I was fed and bred under the Italian dispensation, and absorb'd it, and doubtless show it."[73] The date 1835, as we have seen, is slightly inaccurate, since he is known to have seen plays and heard English opera in 1833. The other date, 1860 or 1861, is close enough, but I have tried to show that the first half of the decade 1850–1860 is more significant than the second half. Whitman was

[70] In a letter to his mother April 16, 1867, he said he had heard Brignoli with Parepa in concert the night before. His laconic comment was, "nothing very great." (*Correspondence*, I, 324.) He wrote Peter Doyle from Brooklyn March 15, 1872, that he had heard Brignoli in "Il Trovatore" and "Robert le Diable," "both good." (*Correspondence*, II, 169.)

[71] See his letter to John H. Johnston, Nov. 18, 1884, and the editor's note 75, *Correspondence*, III, p. 382.

[72] See W. S. Kennedy, *The Fight of a Book for the World* (West Yarmouth, Mass., 1926), p. 267.

[73] *Prose Works 1892*, II, 693–94.

pleased that his friends should say the Wagnerian operas were like
Leaves of Grass, but of course there was no possibility of influence
either way. He had heard bits of Wagnerian music in concerts, but he
recognized no resemblance to *Leaves of Grass.* It was rather "like the
discovery of a new world.[74] In "Poetry To-Day in America" he said
the poetry of the future aims at the "free expression of emotion . . .
and to arouse and imitate, more than to define and finish." He seems
to think that Gounod and Verdi tend away from the "splendid roul-
ades" of Rossini and the "suave melodies" of Bellini toward the freer
expression of emotion of the new Wagnerian school.[75] There is no
logical reason why he should not have liked Wagner as well as Bellini,
as, for comparison, he liked Longfellow and Tennyson as well as
Shakespeare's stormy historical plays and the songs of Ossian. He
liked the lyrical ballads of early English poetry as well as the German
Nibelungenlied. He seemed to think that Wagner's method was one
of "free expression." Yet thirty years earlier he had found the same
"free expression" in the music of the romantic composers of Italy and
had compared it to the method of *Leaves of Grass.* "Walt Whitman's
method in the construction of his songs is strictly the method of the
Italian Opera," he averred, which impresses the hearer "as if all the
sounds of the earth and hell were tumbled promiscuously together."[76]

Beginning with the first part of Whitman's sentence, Robert D.
Faner reaches the conclusion that grand opera not only influenced
Whitman but "it made a poet of him."[77] Faner also argues that the
Italian opera became the model for the construction of individual
poems, that the recitative and the aria provided his most distinctive
poetic style, and the musical phrase and measure were the models for
his poetic line and foot. Much as I agree with him in believing that
the opera was a shaping influence in the making of *Leaves of Grass,* I
am confident that he overstates the case. The dramatic stage, which
Faner ignores, was undoubtedly of equal, or nearly equal, importance. But great as it was, the entire theatrical experience was only
one of several. Obviously the reading of literature was a major experience, and perhaps even more important was Whitman's daily life in
Brooklyn and New York—in the streets, in newspaper offices, and in
the struggle for success in a competitive society. In *Specimen Days* he
seems to rate his early reading, his experience as a printer and jour-

[74] *WWC,* II, 116.

[75] *Prose Works 1892,* II, 481.

[76] For a fuller quotation and discussion of this passage, see the first chapter of
this book.

[77] Faner, pp. v, 82.

nalist, and even his passion for ferries and for omnibus "jaunts" on a par with plays and operas.[78] To these must be added his political activities and democratic ideals, his close association with nature as he knew it on Long Island and elsewhere, and his unorthodox but deeply religious intuitions. One looks in vain in his prefaces—those of 1855, 1872, and 1876, as well as in "A Backward Glance O'er Travel'd Roads"—for references to the Italian opera. Even the drama gets but little attention, although in the Preface of 1872 he compares the activities of modern nations to "some colossal drama" enacted under the open sun, in which the United States "are unquestionably designated for the leading parts."[79]

What he said of poetry in "A Backward Glance" is equally applicable to music. "Of the great poems receiv'd from abroad and from the ages, and to-day enveloping and penetrating America, is there one that is consistent with these United States, or essentially applicable to them as they are and are to be? Is there one whose underlying basis is not a denial and insult to democracy?"[80] He loved the romantic past, recreated in music by Donizetti and his contemporaries, in drama by Shakespeare, and in fiction by Walter Scott, and doubtless it became a part of him and entered into the making of *Leaves of Grass* in subtle ways; yet it was his intention to make his poem primarily the voice of democracy expressed through an individual personality in his own time and place. He recognized the truth that human nature changes little through the ages,[81] and that the moral qualities that made men great in the past can still make them great in a world that is outwardly quite different. Important as it is, then, the influence of opera and the drama, like the influence of Homer and other famous poets of the past, is far more apparent in the spirit of Whitman's poetry than in its form.

[78] *Prose Works 1892*, I, 13–21.
[79] *Ibid.*, II, 460.
[80] *Ibid.*, II, 720.
[81] He once compared the plot of Donizetti's "La Favorita" to Shakespeare's plays in a general way. "It is a type of the experience of the human kind, and, like Shakespeare's dramas, its moral is world-wide." (*UPP*, I, 258.)

VII. *Book Reviews and Related Reading*

D URING the months and years when he was chiefly responsible for editing a newspaper Whitman probably had little time to spend in libraries, but he received a considerable number of new books for the purpose of reviewing them. Some of these books were addressed to the popular taste and may be assumed to have left no lasting impression on the reviewer, but others were major works by great authors. A few of the latter were in the original editions, but most of them were reprints. Since there was no international copyright law then, English books could be reprinted quickly and cheaply in this country. In New York the most active reprint publishers between 1845 and 1850 were Wiley and Putnam and Harper and Brothers. There were no notices of new books, apparently, in the *Aurora* and but few in the Brooklyn *Evening Star*. One item in the *Star*, signed "W." and therefore presumably by Whitman, appeared on January 30, 1846, under the heading "A Great American Publishing House." Since, he says, "mind is molded nearly altogether from books," the Harpers' printing and publishing establishment is one of the "potential institutions of the world." They have published so many books that he thinks the character of the nation reflects their influence.[1]

In another item, the next day, headed "Books Worth Reading" and also signed "W.", the writer comments briefly on three books published by Wiley and Putnam: *Sketches*, by Lyman Blanchard, a book on capital punishment by Dr. Cheever, and "Carlyle's *Cromwell*." The Carlyle book was *Oliver Cromwell's Letters and Speeches: with Elucidations by Thomas Carlyle* (2 vols., London, 1845; reprinted the same year, also in 2 vols., by Wiley & Putnam of New York). Whitman —assuming the book review was his—calls it "a dashy rollicky, most readable book that sets at defiance all the old rules of English composition," and adds that it has the "distinguishing difference from nearly all European works relating to that era—the era of the great Cromwell—it tells the truth."[2] The first part of this comment refers

---

[1] *Walt Whitman Looks at the Schools*, ed. Florence Bernstein Freedman (New York, 1950), Appendix A, p. 216.

[2] *Ibid.*, pp. 216–17.

to Carlyle's hundred-page introduction and his running comment on the letters, but the last part suggests that the writer had read the letters also. For Whitman at that time, as for many others, Cromwell was a great hero, the champion of freedom against the tyranny of kings. Whether this book was Whitman's first introduction to Carlyle it is not possible to say; I am inclined to think it was.

Holloway found that Whitman had reviewed more than a hundred books while editing the Brooklyn *Daily Eagle*, and that he quoted from nearly a hundred more. Holloway printed extracts, most of them brief, from thirty-nine of the reviews in his *Uncollected Poetry and Prose of Walt Whitman* (1921).[3] A year earlier Cleveland Rodgers and John Black, in *The Gathering of the Forces* (2 vols., 1920), had published about fifteen of the same reviews in complete form as well as half a dozen or more from which Holloway had extracted nothing. Thus we have something like forty-five reviews, or notices, of books that he wrote for the *Eagle* and that have long been available. In addition Thomas L. Brasher has more recently quoted a few additional extracts in his study of Whitman's newspaper.[4] Holloway also lists authors and titles of about a hundred additional books that Whitman is said to have noticed briefly. Among the books listed but not excerpted by Holloway, several concerned Cromwell. The most important, perhaps, was John Forster's *The Statesmen of the Commonwealth of England*, in five volumes, the last two of which were devoted to a biography of Cromwell that Carlyle had praised. This work was edited by J. O. Choules and was reprinted by Harper in 1846. This reprint was undoubtedly the edition that Whitman reviewed.[5] Another work noticed, J. H. Merle D'Aubigné's *The Protector: A Vindication*, first published in New York in English in 1847, was also a defense of Protestantism and democracy. Still another was François Guizot's *History of the English Revolution of 1640*, translated by William Hazlitt, the younger (2 vols., New York, 1846), which Whitman noticed on March 5, 1846, calling it "one of the really valuable books of the age."[6]

[3] See *UPP*, I, 126–37. Thomas L. Brasher says Whitman reviewed 425 books in the *Eagle*, but he classifies only 203 of them: 100 as reviews of books of fiction, 22 of history, 14 of biography, 45 of religion, and 22 of poetry. He also mentions 30 reviews of periodicals. (See *Walt Whitman as Editor of the Brooklyn* Daily Eagle [Detroit, 1970], pp. 98, 100, 173, 191, 195, and 196.) Perhaps the difference between the figures of Holloway and Brasher is the consequence of different definitions of what constitutes a review.

[4] See *Walt Whitman as Editor of the Brooklyn* Daily Eagle, pp. 188–200.

[5] Brasher (p. 240) states that Whitman reviewed this book in the *Eagle* July 27, 1846, and again the following Sept. 7.

[6] *UPP*, I, 132. Whitman also noticed Merle D'Aubigné's *History of the Great*

Whitman made other references to Cromwell that express a lively interest in him at this period. Although Scott, like Shakespeare, was a favorite with Whitman early and late, he considered both to be anti-democratic and therefore bad for America. In the *Eagle* for April 26, 1847, he takes Scott to task for misrepresenting historical characters in his novels and in particular for portraying Charles II as better than he really was and Cromwell as worse.[7] Cromwell, he says, despite his faults, was "a heroic champion of his countrymen's rights—and the young Stuart was from top to toe a licentious, selfish, deceitful, and unprincipled man, giving his fastest friends to the axe and his subjects to plunder, when a spark of true manly nerve would have saved both. But the inference to be drawn from Scott's representation of these two men makes the villain a good-natured pleasant gentleman, and the honest ruler a blood-seeking hypocrite! Shame on such truckling! It is a stain black enough, added to his atrocious maligning of Napoleon, to render his brightest excellence murky!"[8] Fifteen years later, in *Brooklyniana*, he described Lion Gardiner, the first settler on the island that bears his name, as "one of those massive old characters of the English commonwealth—belonging to the republican party of the early portion of the 17th century, with Hampden, Cromwell, and other hearts of oak."[9]

His defence of Napoleon might have been influenced by his reading of William Hazlitt's *Life of Napoleon Bonaparte*, which he reviewed at some length on March 15, 1847, and again briefly on April 2.[10] The first review is in part an editorial on the state of Europe in

---

Reformation of the Sixteenth Century, which was frequently reprinted after 1842; and on March 27, 1847, he also noticed Henry Hallam's *Constitutional History of England*, reprinted in 1847 by Harper in one large volume from the 5th London edition in 2 vols. dated 1846. That he did not forget Forster is indicated by a brief note preserved and published in *Notes and Fragments* (*Complete Writings*, X, 30): "'Every accession of originality of thought,' says the author of *Statesmen of the Commonwealth of England*, 'brings with it necessarily an accession of a certain originality of style.'"

[7] I have noted earlier (Chapter III, p. 42) that Whitman cited Jefferson as opposed to the Waverley novels because they glamorized lords and ladies but treated poor people with contempt.

[8] *UPP*, I, 163–64. The characterization of Charles II and Cromwell in *Woodstock* might have evoked Whitman's protest. The "maligning of Napoleon" may be a reference to Scott's nine-volume biography of Bonaparte, published in 1827, though I doubt that Whitman had read much of it, if any.

[9] *UPP*, II, 314. Gardiner's Island is near the east end of Long Island.

[10] The first review was reprinted in *GF*, II, 284–87 and the second in *UPP*, I, 133. This book was published in three volumes in 1847 by Wiley and Putnam as part of their Library of Choice Reading. The text is the same as the original London edition in four volumes, the first two published in 1828 without Hazlitt's

1847, where, Whitman says, the people in some states are still unfree. "We too dread the horrors of the sword and of violence—of bloodshed, and a maddened people," he avers. "But we would rather at this moment over every kingdom on the continent of Europe, that *the people* should rise and enact the same prodigious destructions as those of the French Revolution, could they thus root out the kingcraft and priestcraft which are annually dwindling down humanity there to a lower and lower average—an appalling prospect ahead, for any one who *thinks* ahead!" Although Hazlitt does not mention Scott's life of Napoleon, Whitman seems to have sensed Hazlitt's purpose of making his own biography a kind of defense of Napoleon, and of democracy, against Scott's Tory condemnation of both. In his preface Hazlitt had said that Napoleon was "*a thorn in the side of kings* and kept them at bay," and so "kept off that last indignity and wrong offered to a whole people (and through them to the rest of the world) of being handed over like a herd of cattle, to a particular family, and chained to the foot of a legitimate throne." [11] In a letter dated December 7, 1827, Hazlitt wrote the publishers of the first two volumes, who had refused to include his preface as it was written: "It would be an impertinence in me to write a *Life of Buonaparte* after Sir W. without some such object as that expressed in the preface." [12] That purpose was not only to defend Napoleon against his calumniators, but to show that he was "the child and champion of the Revolution." Both Guizot and Hazlitt compared the English Revolution of 1640–88 to the French Revolution of 1789–1815, and both writers believed that Napoleon, like Cromwell, was the active agent of forces that for centuries had been at work moving English and continental governments from autocracy toward democracy. Yet both Cromwell and Napoleon were criticized for assuming the autocratic powers which it was their historical function to mitigate. They stood between feudalism and democracy, or rather they were like mighty bridges, attached to both sides, over which men might pass from one to the other.

For Whitman, Carlyle, too, was such a bridge. Although the pro-

---

preface, the second two with that preface incorporated into the text at the beginning of Vol. III. Since Hazlitt died before the third volume appeared, his son wrote a preface explaining his father's reason for writing the biography. This preface appears in the first volume of the American edition. There is also a three-volume edition, doubtless from the same stereotype plates used by Wiley and Putnam, published without date in Boston.

11 This quotation is from the first paragraph of Chapter XXXI and part of the preface originally intended for the first volume.

12 This letter was printed by Augustine Birrell in his biography of Hazlitt (1902) in the English Men of Letters series. It has since been several times printed elsewhere.

fessed enemy of democracy, especially in its equalitarian aspect, his human sympathies and his religious sense of mission made him a bridge spanning the gulf between the feudal past and the democratic future. Whitman's first mention of Carlyle in the *Eagle*, so far as I can learn, was made on July 8, 1846, when he quoted the last paragraph of a letter written by Carlyle to an unnamed young man who had asked his advice about reading. Dated March 13, 1843, this letter of about eight hundred words was printed, with a brief introduction, under the heading "Advice to Young Men," in *Chambers's Edinburgh Journal*, a weekly, for April 13, 1844. Whitman evidently saw this journal, probably in a library, and copied the last paragraph on the spot, later handing his notes, under the heading "How to Be a Man," to the *Eagle* printer, who in two places misread Whitman's handwriting. I quote Whitman's paragraph in full, indicating the correct words and punctuation in square brackets:

In conclusion, I will remind you that it is not books alone, or by books chiefly, that a man becomes in all points a man. Study to do faithfully whatsoever thing in your actual situation, then [there] and now, you find either expressly or tacitly laid to your charge; that is your post, [;] stand in it like a true soldier. Silently devour the many chagrines [chagrins] of it; [,] as all human situations have many; and see you aim not to quit it without doing all that it, [it,] at least, required of you. A man perfects himself by work much more than by reading. There [They] are a growing kind of men that can wisely combine the two things—wisely, valiantly, can do what is laid to their hand in their present sphere, and prepare themselves withal for doing other wider things, if such lie before them.[13]

The variations in the *Eagle* from the Chambers text are understandable. The changes in punctuation were either the result of careless copying by Whitman or were made by the printer. Whitman's hurriedly written "there" might easily have been mistaken by the printer for "then" and his "They" for "There." The paragraph is of interest

---

[13] Whitman's item was reprinted in *Walt Whitman Looks at the Schools*, p. 123, with no reference to its source. A note in *Chambers' Edinburgh Journal* (William and Robert Chambers, proprietors), states that the letter was originally published in a small country paper called *Cupar and St. Andrews Monthly Advertiser*. It has been reprinted in several places, including a small volume with the title *On the Choice of Books*, published by J. C. Hotten, 2nd ed., 1871, pp. 60–68, where the text is identical with that of *Chambers' Edinburgh Journal*. It is also in *Some Personal Reminiscences of Carlyle*, by A. J. Symington (1886), pp. 77–82, where the text varies slightly, both verbally and in punctuation and paragraphing, from that of Hotten and Chambers. In an introductory note Symington says the letter "had, somehow, got into print, and Carlyle used, on fitting occasions, to send copies of it to correspondents."

not only because it seems to indicate that Whitman was reading in libraries, but also because it suggests that, in copying only the last paragraph, his interest was primarily in Carlyle's statement that a man perfects himself more by work than by reading, but will, if wise, combine both. There is no indication that Whitman cared, at this time, for Carlyle's writing.

The first of Carlyle's books that Whitman reviewed in the *Eagle* was *Heroes and Hero-Worship*; this review appeared on October 17, 1846. In spite of Carlyle's distrust of democracy, Whitman calls him "a Democrat in that enlarged sense in which we would fain see more men Democrats," and notes approvingly that he was "quick to champion the downtrodden, and earnest in his wrath at tyranny." He does not approve, however, of his "rapt, weird" style, saying that it hides rather than reveals his thought. "No writer," he goes on, "achieves any thing worthy of him, by inventing merely a new *style*. Style in writing, is much as dress in society, sensible people will conform to the prevalent mode. . . ." The review of *Sartor Resartus* seems to have appeared in the same issue of the *Eagle*, but it consists of only a single sentence commenting on the book's "fiery-breath and profundity of meaning—when you delve them out." [14] His review on November 23, 1846, of *The French Revolution, a History* mentions Carlyle's notation on the verso of the title page authorizing Wiley and Putnam to be the sole publisher of this book in America and comments briefly on the need of an international copyright law, but it offers no criticism of the book, explaining that its subject is too broad "and provokes too many inferences, to be properly treated in one of these short notices." [15] By the time Whitman reviewed *Past and Present* and *Chartism*, on April 14, 1847, he had changed his mind somewhat about Carlyle. "One likes Mr. Carlyle," he wrote, "the more he communes with him; there is a sort of fascination about the man. His weird, wild way—his phrases welded together as it were, with strange twistings of the terminatives of words—his startling suggestions—his taking up, fish-hook like, certain matters of abuse—make an *original* kind of composition, that gets, after a little usage, to be strangely agreeable!" [16]

A few years later, Whitman himself, in notebooks that have been preserved, began to experiment with an original kind of composition, and he may have found encouragement in Carlyle's example. Even Carlyle's increasingly antidemocratic opinions were less offensive to

[14] *GF*, II, 290–91. The sentence review of *Sartor* is not dated in *GF*, but follows immediately after *Heroes and Hero-Worship*.

[15] *GF*, II, 292–93. *UPP*, I, 130, contains part of the review.

[16] *GF*, II, 293; *UPP*, I, 130.

Whitman than might be supposed. In *Macmillan's Magazine* for August 1867, Carlyle published an essay called "Shooting Niagara: and After?" in which he attacked the new British Reform Bill and had some uncomplimentary things to say about American democracy. In his own essay "Democracy," first published in the *Galaxy* for December 1867, Whitman allowed himself in a passage of four or five paragraphs to make an angry response to Carlyle's diatribe, declaring that "such a comic-painful hullabaloo and vituperative cat-squalling as this about 'the Niagara leap,' 'swarmery,' 'Orsonism,' etc." he had never encountered, "not even in extremest hour of midnight, in whooping Tennessee revival, or Bedlam let loose in crowded, colored Carolina bush-meeting." It was not surprising that Whitman was shocked by the change twenty years had made in Carlyle; but he too had matured, and on sober reflection he found he could take a more tolerant view of Carlyle's antidemocratic opinions. When he incorporated this essay in *Democratic Vistas* a few years later he deleted the angry paragraphs and inserted the following footnote instead:

I was at first roused to much anger and abuse by this essay from Mr. Carlyle, so insulting to the theory of America—but happening to think afterwards how I had more than once been in the like mood, during which his essay was evidently cast, and seen persons and things in the same light, (indeed some might say there are signs of the same feeling in these *Vistas*)—I have since read it again, not only as a study, expressing as it does certain judgments from the highest feudal point of view, but have read it with respect as coming from an earnest soul, and as contributing certain sharp-cutting metallic grains, which, if not gold or silver, may be good hard, honest iron.[17]

The first 367 and the last 730 lines of *Democratic Vistas*, constituting more than half of the whole, appear to have been written or rewritten after his anger had subsided. In the first part Whitman attacked the materialism, hypocrisy, and corruption in democratic America after the Civil War in terms almost as severe as those used by Carlyle; in the last part, he called for a democratic literature of high moral and religious purpose that, he believed, would be essential to the survival of a democratic society in America. It seems highly probable that both these parts of *Democratic Vistas* were in a large measure influenced by Carlyle's essay, including his call for an American literature of high seriousness that should be a kind of sacred history, like the Hebrew Bible and the Greek *Iliad*.

[17] See *Prose Works 1892*, II, 375–76; 749–50, where both the original and revised texts are recorded.

In the summer of 1846 Carlyle, with Emerson's assistance, had arranged for transferring to Wiley and Putnam all of the rights he controlled in the American publication of *Heroes and Hero-Worship*, *Sartor Resartus*, *The French Revolution*, *Past and Present*, and *Chartism*. He sent corrected copies of *Heroes* and *Sartor* to Wiley and Putnam on June 18, and of *The French Revolution* (with an index) on July 17. *Past and Present* and *Chartism* had been previously published by Little and Brown of Boston from copies sent by Carlyle for the purpose directly to Emerson. I find no bibliographical evidence that they were issued in a separate edition by Wiley and Putnam; more probably Little and Brown delivered to them all their remaining copies and also the plates for reprinting.[18] This would account for the delay in the reviewing of these books. Apparently Emerson did not complete the arrangement between Little and Brown and Wiley and Putnam until February 1847. The books just discussed are the only works by Carlyle which Whitman reviewed in the *Eagle*, but on November 2, 1858, he reviewed the "first installment" of *Frederick the Great* in the Brooklyn *Daily Times*, of which he was then editor.[19] Whitman's critical comment, the last paragraph of the review, is worth quoting: "Mr. Carlyle's style in the present volume—his manner of conducting his narrative—his startling outbursts of eloquence couched in language as startling—his wonderful sketches of character—are all Carlyleish and characteristic. We do not perceive that the hand that penned the 'History of the French Revolution' has, as yet, lost anything of its cunning."[20]

[18] The most authoritative information on these transactions will be found in *The Correspondence of Emerson and Carlyle*, ed. Joseph Slater (New York, 1964), pp. 400–415, 419–22, and 516–17. See also *A Bibliography of Thomas Carlyle's Writings and Ana*, by Isaac Watson Dyer (Portland, 1928), pp. 51–52, 64, 88, 105, 201–2, 223–25. Most if not all of these books were included in Wiley and Putnam's *Library of Choice Reading* and were popularly priced.

[19] This review was reprinted by Emory Holloway and Vernolian Schwarz in *I Sit and Look Out* (New York, 1932), p. 68. Whitman speaks of "the present volume," and yet Chapman and Hall, of London, published the first and second volumes both in Sept. 1858. There were eventually six volumes, the last issued in 1865. Harper and Brothers published concurrently a six-volume edition which the bibliographer dates 1858–66 without further particulars. It seems probable that Whitman had the first volume only of the Harper edition. A manuscript note (*Complete Writings*, IX, 230) left by Whitman reads: "Dec. '57, Carlyle's *Frederick the Great* is announced to be now in press." Apparently he planned ahead of time to review the book, or at least to read it.

[20] Nevertheless, Whitman told Traubel in 1888 that he did not like either Carlyle's *Frederick* or his *Cromwell*. "I am very impatient of stories which imply the concentration of all historical meanings in single eminent persons." (*WWC*, I, 157.)

If Whitman wrote anything on Carlyle for the Brooklyn *Freeman* or the New Orleans *Crescent* it has not survived.[21] There are many evidences, however, that his interest in Carlyle continued throughout his life. He was attracted early and late by what he called the "feudalism" of Carlyle, as well as of Shakespeare, Scott, and Tennyson,[22] and we have presumptive evidence that he subscribed to Carlyle's "Gospel of Work." He preserved a clipping which he found in Charles Knight's *Half-Hours with the Best Authors*, reprinted from *Past and Present*, in which this "Gospel" is developed.[23] He would have been struck by such a sentence as, "The latest Gospel in this world is, know thy work and do it," because by the time he read this excerpt he must have decided that his proper work was in the field of literature. Although he did not review Carlyle's *Critical and Miscellaneous Essays*, originally published in 1838, in Boston, through Emerson's enterprise, he certainly read them during the 1850's or earlier, for he made numerous notes based on them which he preserved and which were later published by Bucke in *Notes and Fragments*. I have identified notes quoting from or based on the following essays by Carlyle: "The Nibelungen Lied," "Goethe," "Goethe's Helena," "Goethe's Works," "Schiller," "Jean Paul Richter," "Jean Paul Richter Again," and "Diderot."[24] I have identified no specific borrowing from the essay "Characteristics," which in some respects was Carlyle's preview, or abstract, of *Sartor Resartus*, but many passages in *Leaves of Grass* are so closely parallel to portions of this essay that I can readily believe

[21] For Whitman and the *Freeman*, see *UPP*, I, lii–liii; for his contributions to the *Crescent* see W. K. Dart, "Walt Whitman in New Orleans," *Publications of the Louisiana Historical Society*, VII (1915), 97–112, and Emory Holloway, "Walt Whitman in New Orleans," *Yale Review*, n.s., V (Oct. 1915), 166–83.

[22] This is apparent in too many places to require documentation here. Its appeal was chiefly to his imagination, but he had more sympathy for the "natural aristocracy" that Emerson and Carlyle called for than one might think.

[23] This clipping is No. 341 of Bucke's list of clippings in *Notes and Fragments* and was annotated. It was taken from the first volume of the three-volume edition of *Half-Hours* published by Wiley in New York, 1848–49, and consists of all of Chapter XI, titled "Labour," and the first four paragraphs of Chapter XII. This clipping is not in the Trent Collection at Duke University, and I have not seen it. It will be recalled, also, that the Carlyle letter reprinted in part in the *Eagle* rates work above reading as a means of self-improvement. Emerson's "American Scholar" stresses the same idea.

[24] See my "Notes on Whitman's Reading," *American Literature*, XXVI (Nov. 1954), 344, 347–49, 357–58. Whitman's notes appear in *Complete Writings*, IX, 83, 110–14, 121–23, 226, 228. Holloway suggested that Whitman's article in *Life Illustrated*, May 10, 1856, owed something to Carlyle's essay on Voltaire. (*New York Dissected*, ed. Emory Holloway and Ralph Adimari [New York, 1936], p. 70.) For more on *The Nibelungenlied*, see Chapter X.

Whitman was influenced by it. I do not doubt that at one time or another he owned all of Carlyle's books that were published before 1860; and although he did not read them carefully before writing his newspaper reviews, there is every reason to believe that he returned to them and gave some of them at least close attention. We know that he still had the *Cromwell* in 1857, more than eleven years after he noticed it in the *Eagle*, for he offered it to James Parton in partial payment for the debt he owed.[25] I have been particular about these reviews because it is believed by some scholars that Carlyle had a strong influence on Whitman that is reflected in *Leaves of Grass*.[26] That Carlyle had a considerable influence on Whitman is beyond question, particularly during the latter's formative years, the late 1840's, for he was then widely recognized as a spokesman for German transcendental idealism; but the later Carlyle retained Whitman's respect more for what he had been than for what he was then, although he was also valued as the voice of dissidence, as a modern Jeremiah prophesying in agony the doom of a misguided world.[27]

Coleridge was another British author whose books were reviewed in the *Eagle* and who undoubtedly influenced Whitman's literary career, though not as much as Carlyle. *Aids to Reflection* is listed by Holloway as among the books reviewed, but he does not reprint the review. Whitman might have read any one of several editions published in America, but there is no way to determine which one. He reviewed *Letters, Conversations and Recollections of Samuel Taylor Coleridge* on February 20, 1847, and *Biographia Literaria* on December 4, 1847, both briefly. The *Letters, Conversations and Recollections* were first published in two volumes in London in 1836. It was immediately reprinted by Harper in New York in one volume. Whether there was a later American reprint I do not know, since the bibliographies do not list all of the American reprints, but I suspect

[25] See *WWC*, III, 239.

[26] Three articles deserve particular mention: (1) "The Literary Relations of Whitman and Carlyle with Especial Reference to their Contrasting Views on Democracy," by Gregory Paine, *Studies in Philology*, XXXVI (July 1939), 550–63; (2) "Whitman's Poet-Prophet and Carlyle's Hero," by Fred Manning Smith, *PMLA*, LV (Dec. 1940), 1146–64; and (3) "Whitman's Debt to Carlyle's *Sartor Resartus*," also by Smith, *Modern Language Quarterly*, III (March 1942), 51–65. By citing numerous parallels between *Sartor Resartus* and *Leaves of Grass*, as well as Whitman's prose works, both early and late, Smith undertakes to show that Carlyle's influence on Whitman was even greater than Emerson's.

[27] See Whitman's two articles, written after Carlyle's death, and published in *Specimen Days* (*Prose Works 1892*, I, 248–62). The numerous comments on Carlyle recorded in *With Walt Whitman in Camden* reflect Traubel's interest perhaps more than Whitman's.

there was in 1846 or 1847. *Biographia Literaria*, second edition, was published in London in 1847, announced as two volumes, but actually three since the first volume was issued in two parts. It was reprinted as two volumes in one by G. P. Putnam, New York, under the date 1848. It is probable that Whitman used this edition, which would have been possible if the book was actually released in early December 1847 and postdated, as sometimes happened. Whitman's review stated that it was published in two volumes, by which, of course, he could have meant two volumes in one or in three; there is no way of telling. In the review of *Letters, Conversations and Recollections* he calls Coleridge "that legitimate child of imagery, and true poet," and in the review of *Biographia Literaria* he calls him "that child of songs," and adds: "In some respects we think this man stands above all poets: he was passionate without being morbid—he was like Adam in Paradise, and almost as free from artificiality."[28] His comments on both books suggest that he had not read them very carefully and that he knew Coleridge, at that time, chiefly as a poet. "To a person of literary taste," he comments, "the first pleasure of reading any thing written by Coleridge will be, that it is written in such choice and unaffected style—next that the author evidently lays open his whole heart with the artlessness of a child—and next that there is no commonplace or cant. These are exceedingly rare merits, at the present day." He could hardly have found the "artlessness of a child" in *Biographia Literaria*; more likely he had in mind such poems as "Lewti," "The Ancient Mariner," "This Lime-Tree Bower My Prison," "Frost at Midnight," and perhaps "Christabel."[29]

I find only one additional reference to Coleridge in the portions of the *Eagle* that have been reprinted. In an article on "Brooklyn Schools," dated July 9, 1847, he wrote: " 'The boy,' says Coleridge, 'is father to the man.' The moral worth and usefulness of the latter depend upon the education of the former."[30] The quotation, probably, is not from Coleridge but from Wordsworth's "My Heart Leaps Up," and should read, "The Child is father of the man." The mistake may mean that Coleridge was much in Whitman's mind in 1847, or it may mean nothing. His interest in Coleridge's poetry, though never intense, continued into old age, for in *Specimen Days* he quotes the first six lines of "Work Without Hope" as an appropriate appendage to

---

[28] Both of these reviews were reprinted in *UPP*, I, 131, and the review of *Biographia Literaria* was also reprinted in *GF*, II, 298–99.

[29] The poems were easily accessible. Whitman may have seen *The Works of Samuel Taylor Coleridge, Prose and Verse, Complete in One Volume*, published by Crissy & Markley in Philadelphia, 1847, reprinted from an earlier edition.

[30] *Walt Whitman Looks at the Schools*, p. 200.

one of his nature notes on the frolics of the kingfishers.[31] He referred
to Coleridge a little later perhaps in a letter to Harry Stafford, February 17, 1881. He sent Harry two extracts, one from George D. Prentice and one from Coleridge and enjoined him to "read the piece
yourself," apparently at some public gathering. He requested that
both extracts be returned to him.[32] It is understandable that after he
had established his pose in *Leaves of Grass* as a poet without art or
learning Whitman should express little interest in Coleridge, who
was accomplished in both, as Whitman would have known then.
Moreover, as he grew older, Whitman tended to move away from
transcendental idealism in keeping with the general tendency of the
time toward realism. In the summer of 1888, Horace Traubel brought
him a copy of Carlyle's *Life of John Sterling*, which he had not read
earlier. He read it at intervals for several days. On August 8 he told
Traubel: "Today I struck upon the chapter on Coleridge—was intensely interested. It mainly hits the nail on the head—is just as true
as it is enjoyable."[33] Carlyle tells how the young Sterling "assiduously
attended" Coleridge during his last years, and took down many things
he said, though most of these notes were lost. Carlyle remarks that for
young men interested in German transcendentalism Coleridge was
an oracle. Carlyle himself was not wholly sympathetic toward Coleridge. "To the man himself," he concluded, "Nature had given, in
high measure, the seeds of a noble endowment; and to unfold it had
been forbidden him. A subtle lynx-eyed intellect, tremulous pious
sensibility to all good and all beautiful; truly a ray of empyrean light;
—but embedded in such weak laxity of character, in such indolences
and esuriences as had made strange work with it. Once more, the
tragic story of a high endowment with an insufficient will."[34] Whitman's modifying term "mainly" suggests to me that he may have
thought better of Coleridge's poetry than did Carlyle, who cared little for poetry of any kind.

[31] *Prose Works 1892*, I, 263. The poet says, "All Nature seems at work . . . /
And I, the while, the sole unbusy thing, / Nor honey make, nor pair, nor build,
nor sing."

[32] These were presumably poems although the letter (*Correspondence*, III, 212)
does not make the fact clear. Prentice, who died in 1870, had been editor of the
Louisville Journal. His poems were published in 1876 and went through several
editions. Whitman did not have the book himself, for he says both pieces were
copied for him by "a lady friend." The pieces themselves cannot be identified.

[33] *WWC*, II, 106.

[34] The passage may be found on p. 48 of Vol. XXI of the Scribner edition of
Carlyle's works, published in 1871. Whitman may have been reading a different
edition, but the text is the same in all. It was first published in 1851.

One of the books that undoubtedly influenced Whitman was Margaret Fuller's *Papers on Literature and Art*, which he reviewed in the *Eagle* very briefly on November 9, 1846.[35] A link between this book and *Leaves of Grass* exists in a note which he preserved: " 'Still lives the song tho' Regnar dies.'—*John Sterling*. The word is become flesh." [36] Whitman undoubtedly copied the quotation from Margaret Fuller's essay "The Modern Drama," originally printed in *The Dial* (IV, 329) and reprinted in *Papers on Literature and Art* in 1846. Whitman's addition, "The word is become flesh," suggests Whitman's identification of himself with his poems. There is no way to determine when this note was made, but it seems to belong to some time after Whitman had begun *Leaves of Grass*, possibly after 1855. Whitman used the quotation in *November Boughs* in "A Backward Glance o'er Travel'd Roads," [37] but did not remember where he got it. On November 17, 1888, he told Traubel, "Today it turned up: the mystery is revealed. It is from Sterling—Carlyle's Sterling." [38]

The mystery was not quite revealed, for when Traubel asked if he ever had a volume of Sterling's poetry, he "supposed" he had seen a copy and perhaps "had" one, but if so it had made little impression on him and was now "almost certainly" wholly forgotten. I doubt that he had ever seen a copy. Sterling's poems were published in London in 1839, were not widely circulated, and were not reprinted except in an unauthorized edition by Griswold published in Philadelphia in 1842, which Emerson said was "so ill got up that it did not succeed.[39] Emerson wrote Sterling on May 29, acknowledging receipt of a copy of his poems: "I have read these poems, and those, still more recent, in Blackwood, with great pleasure. The ballad of Alfred, de-

35 *UPP*, I, 132.

36 First printed by Bucke in *Notes and Fragments* (reprinted in *Complete Writings*, X, 15). The quotation is from Sterling's poem "Alfred the Harper." I reported the source of this quotation in "Notes on Whitman's Reading," *American Literature*, XXVI (Nov. 1954), 361.

37 See *Prose Works 1892*, II, 712.

38 *WWC*, III, 118–19 Whitman means Carlyle's friend Sterling, not his *Life of John Sterling*, where there is no such quotation.

39 *A Correspondence between John Sterling and Ralph Waldo Emerson*, with a biographical sketch, by Edward Waldo Emerson (Boston, 1897), p. 66. Quoted from Emerson's letter to Sterling dated June 30, 1843. Edward Emerson says (p. 6), "Little of what he wrote remains. His fine Strafford, a Tragedy, is now hard to obtain, and few people even know Daedalus, the best of his poems." "Daedalus," together with another poem called "Aphrodite," was reprinted by Margaret Fuller in "The Modern Drama," which discussed "Strafford" at length, but she quoted only the one line of "Alfred the Harper."

lighted me when I first read it, but I read it so often to my friends that I discovered that the last verses were not equal to the rest. Shall I gossip on and tell you that the two lines,

> 'Still lives the song though Regnar dies!
> Fill high your cups again,'

rung for a long time in my ear, and had a kind of witchcraft for my fancy?" These lines occur near the middle of "Alfred the Harper," a ballad of about 300 lines. In speaking of the first of the two lines, which she quotes, Margaret Fuller wrote, "One line we have heard so repeated by a voice, that could give it its full meaning, that we should be very grateful to the poet for that alone." This voice, we may be sure, was Emerson's. If Whitman ever saw the poem it was most probably in Emerson's collection *Parnassus* (1874), where he reprints both "Daedalus" and "Alfred the Harper." Whitman would surely have liked the ballad of Alfred, which tells how the King appears in disguise as a minstrel at the camp of the Danish King Guthrum, only to return later with an English army to defeat his enemy. Whitman told Traubel on January 15, 1889: "I never met Margaret Fuller, but I knew much about her those years: her life: the tragedy of her death . . . I remember the impression it made on me at the time." He said he had read the *Memoirs of Margaret Fuller Ossoli* at the time they were published, in 1852.[40] He preserved a clipping of a review of the *Memoirs*, published in the *American Whig Review* for April 1852 and signed "O.W.W."[41]

There are several references to Margaret Fuller in *Specimen Days*. One evening in September 1881 Whitman sat with Emerson and his friends in Concord, where letters to and from Thoreau were read. One of the best, he says, was written by Margaret Fuller, but he does not describe it further.[42] In a brief essay on the "Death of Longfellow," dated April 3, 1882, originally printed in the *Critic*, April 8, he said (in the original text): "To the ungracious complaint-charge—(as by Margaret Fuller many years ago, and several times since)—of his want of racy nativity and special originality, I shall only say that America and the world may well be reverently thankful—can never be thankful enough—for any such singing-bird vouchsafed out of the

---

[40] This work, in two volumes, was the joint enterprise of Emerson, J. F. Clarke, and W. H. Channing.

[41] The initials are those of O. W. Wight. This clipping, No. 507 of Bucke's list, is not in the Trent collection, and I have not seen it. Apparently Whitman made no annotations on it.

[42] *Prose Works 1892*, I, 279.

centuries, without asking that the notes be different from those of other songsters."[43] In a paragraph on American literature in a section of *Collect* called *"Notes Left Over,"* he closes with this comment: "The sharp warning of Margaret Fuller, unquell'd for thirty years, yet sounds in the air; 'It does not follow that because the United States print and read more books, magazines, and newspapers than all the rest of the world, that they really have, therefore a literature."[44] In an essay on "American National Literature," which appeared in the *North American Review* for March 1891 and was reprinted in *Good-Bye My Fancy*, Whitman wrote: "Yet the high-pitch'd taunt of Margaret Fuller, forty years ago, still sounds in the air: 'It does not follow, because the United States print and read more books, magazines, and newspapers than all the rest of the world, that they really have therefore a literature.' "[45] Whitman preserved a clipping of Margaret Fuller's essay (Bucke's No. 427) but he does not appear to have had it before him when he made his inaccurate quotations from it.[46]

In a clipping (Bucke's No. 322 probably) of a paragraph from Margaret Fuller's letter to the *Tribune* dated September 30, 1846, but published in the issue of November 13 as "Things and Thoughts in Europe. No. V," there is a mention of Ossian. Whitman pasted this clipping to a sheet of paper on which he wrote a note of about a hundred words under the heading: "An Ossianic paragraph: Margaret Fuller benighted and alone on Ben Lomond." The clipping was doubtless made in 1846, but the note seems to be of later date. The paragraph clipped is short enough to be quoted in full:

[43] *Ibid.*, I, 286. The allusion, made doubtless without reference to the book and from memory, is probably to the comment on Longfellow in the essay "American Literature," which begins as follows: "Longfellow is artificial and imitative. He borrows incessantly, and mixes what he borrows, so that it does not appear to the best advantage."

[44] *Ibid.*, II, 539. Again Whitman probably quoted from memory. What Margaret Fuller wrote, in the first three sentences of her essay "American Literature" (originally published in 1846 in *Papers on Literature and Art*), was: "Some thinkers may object to this essay, that we are about to write of that which has, as yet, no existence.

"For it does not follow because many books are written by persons born in America that there exists an American literature. Books which imitate or represent the thoughts and life of Europe do not constitute an American literature."

This paragraph was printed from what appears to be an old manuscript note made by Whitman long before 1882.

[45] *Ibid.*, II, 666–67. In writing this quotation Whitman may have referred back to his note in *Collect* and corrected his grammar; if not, it must have been corrected by the editors of the *North American Review*.

[46] This clipping is not in the Trent Collection and I have not seen it.

For about two hours, I saw the stars, and very cheery and companionable they looked; but then the mist fell, and I saw nothing more, except such apparitions as visited Ossian, on the hill-side, when he went out by night and struck the bosky shield, and called to him the spirits of the heroes, and the white-armed maids, with their blue eyes of grief. To me, too, came those visionary shapes. Floating slowly and gracefully, their white robes would unfurl from the great body of mist in which they had been engaged, and come upon me with a kiss pervasively cold as that of death. Then the moon rose. I could not see her, but her silver light filled the mist. Now I knew it was two o'clock, and that, having weathered out so much of the night, I might the rest; and the hours hardly seemed long to me more. What they might have told me, who knows, if I had but resigned myself more passively to that cold, spirit-like breathing![47]

Whitman himself describes "An Ossianic Night" in *Specimen Days*. It was a night in November 1881. He crossed and recrossed the Delaware River between Camden and Philadelphia, as he often did, but this time the moonlight, the mist, and the wind created for him "a real Ossianic night," in which he tenderly remembered dead or absent friends. He then quoted two passages from the *Poems of Ossian*, which he had at some former time copied out, one from Book VI of "Fingal" and the other from "Dar-Thula," with slight variations from the text.[48] He told Traubel that he had always had a copy of James Macpherson's *Ossian*, and he had one as late as 1885.[49]

More than once in his published writings he classed the *"bona fide* Ossian"* with genuine primitive poetry and with great primitive poets —the poems of the *Cid*, the Scandinavian *Eddas*, the *Nibelungen* legend, Homer, the Bible, and even Dante, Chaucer, Spenser, and Shakespeare—and he was proud to place *Leaves of Grass* in the same class as a product, like each of them, of its own time and place.[50] In "A Backward Glance o'er Travel'd Roads" he tells how, at intervals,

[47] When this paragraph was reprinted in *The Memoirs of Margaret Fuller Ossoli*, ed. R. W. Emerson, W. H. Channing, and J. F. Clarke, 2 vols. (Boston, 1852), II, 180–81, the last sentence was omitted.

[48] *Prose Works 1892*, I, 282–83.

[49] *WWC*, II, 17; see also *UPP*, 60–61, and W. S. Kennedy, *Reminiscences* (Boston, 1896), p. 12. *The Poems of Ossian* were first published as a whole in London in 1765, and in a revised form in 1773, but there were numerous editions thereafter for nearly a century in English and many foreign languages. The edition most frequently reprinted in the United States was published in Edinburgh in 1830, containing a "Preliminary Discourse," "A Dissertation Concerning the Aera of Ossian," and Hugh Blair's "Dissertation Concerning the Poems of Ossian." An undated edition, but apparently 1846, published by Edward Kearny of New York, seems to be identical with the 1830 edition and was probably the one Whitman would have read at the time.

[50] See *Prose Works 1892*, II, 556–57, 656, 722.

he used to go off "down in the country, or to Long Island seashores," for a week at a time, where he "went over thoroughly the Old and New Testaments, and absorb'd . . . Shakspere, Ossian, the best translated versions I could get of Homer, Eschylus, Sophocles, the old German Nibelung, the ancient Hindu poems, and one or two other masterpieces, Dante's among them."[51] He was careful, however, when he came to compose the *Leaves*, not to succumb to the temptation to imitate any of these. In the note on Margaret Fuller's "Ossianic paragraph," mentioned previously, he says that Ossian must not be despised, for it is an expression of a "kind of thought and character growing among a rude, combative, illiterate people, heroic dreamy, poetical," but without "benevolence, conscientiousness, agreeableness, or constructiveness." He describes it as "misty," "windy," and "full of diffused, only half-meaning words," and warns himself: "Don't fall into the Ossianic, *by any chance*." Yet in the same note he asks, "Is it not Isaiah, Job, the Psalms and so forth, transferred to the Scotch Highlands? (or to Ireland?)" This question may have been suggested by his reading of the poems themselves, but it would have been influenced by his reading of Hugh Blair's "Critical Dissertation on the Poems of Ossian," in which Blair points out that the language of Ossian "carries a remarkable resemblance to the style of the Old Testament." Blair also discusses at length the parallels between Homer's *Iliad* and Ossian's epic poem "Fingal," and concludes that the epic qualities of "Fingal" more nearly approach Aristotle's specifications than do those of the *Iliad*. He says also that "Homer and Ossian both wrote from nature," which would have interested Whitman.[52]

Four other clippings listed by Bucke, Nos. 22, 321, 323, and 324, are related to Ossian. Number 321, with the heading "Ossian's Hymn to

[51] He read Shakespeare early in connection with theatrical performances in 1833–35 if not earlier, and he doubtless also read the Bible as a boy. In both cases, however, his more serious reading probably came later. Ossian, as we have seen, he read in the middle 1840's. It is not likely that he read Homer, Eschylus, Sophocles, and the *Nibelungenlied* until much later. He may not have read any Hindu poetry before the middle 1850's. He himself says in *Notes and Fragments* (*Complete Writings*, IX, 91–93) that he read Dante's *Inferno* (John Carlyle's translation) for the first time in 1859, and that he had not then read the *Paradiso*. He was much in the country with his family, of course, between 1834 and 1845, but after that he is not likely to have spent as much as a week in the country or on the shores of Long Island except on visits to his sister Mary, who lived at Greenport, L.I. This was the terminus of the Long Island Railroad and was situated on a narrow channel connecting the waters of Peconic Bay with those of Gardiner's Bay.

[52] See the 1846 edition of *The Poems of Ossian*, pp. 104 and 108–11. Whitman's note on the clipping of Margaret Fuller's *Tribune* article is in *Notes and Fragments* (*Complete Writings*, IX, 94–95).

the Sun," is cut from an unidentified newspaper. Presumably this is the same passage from the poem "Carthon," usually called Ossian's "Address to the Sun," but I cannot be sure that it does not refer to some other passage where the sun is described or addressed. In the "Preliminary Discourse," which is unsigned but dated February 1, 1806, there is a literal translation of what is represented as Ossian's original "Address to the Sun," and it varies only in minor ways from Macpherson's translation of the same poem. Whitman preserved a clipping which Bucke called "Ossian's 'Address to the Sun,' " in a footnote to some Whitman notes which he printed in *Notes and Fragments*, but this is definitely Macpherson's version.[53] The clipping is pasted on a pink sheet of paper on which, above and below the clipping, Whitman made the following annotations in pencil: "Jas Macpherson 1737 1796 Ossian ossian very like a myth altogether bosky shield—wooden shield" Below the clipping, also in pencil, is this sentence: "The Irish swear that Ossian belongs to them—that he was born, lived, and wrote in Ireland." Between the words "Ossian" and "ossian" some original pencil writing has been obscured and the following inserted, probably at a later date: "The real Ossian, if ever there were one, is put down at 300 or 400 B.C." [54]

These notes have no bearing whatever on the poem, which might have been clipped from Robert Chambers's *Cyclopaedia of English Literature* (1844, p. 78), and they contain a remarkable number of errors. When the notes were made, reference books and encyclopedias usually gave Macpherson's birth year as 1738; later it was established as 1736. Ossian's time was believed by Macpherson and all authorities to have been late in the third or early in the fourth century after Christ—not before. There is, of course, no such word as "bosky" in the poems of Ossian as applied to a shield. However, in Margaret Fuller's essay, as printed in the *Tribune*, the term "bosky shield" does appear. This was obviously a misprint for "bossy shield," and it is not very creditable to Whitman that he did not perceive the printer's error. I presume he looked up the word "bosky" in a dictionary and carelessly interpreted the definition as "wooden." One is bound to conclude that a careful reader of *Ossian* like Margaret Fuller would not have made such an error, and also that Whitman at that time was not very familiar with the poems.

Bucke's clipping No. 22, presumably much later than No. 321, may be the source of Whitman's sentence about the Irish. It is thus de-

[53] These notes are reprinted in *Complete Writings*, IX, 94.

[54] The pink sheet on which the clipping is pasted contains several other miscellaneous notes, on Pythagoras, Zoroaster, and Jasmin. The clipping and notes are in the Trent Collection.

scribed by Bucke: "A newspaper report of a speech by Mr. Burke made on St. Patrick's, at foot W. writes—'Brooklyn *Eagle*, 18 March, '57!" The clipping reveals that the speech was in fact before the St. Patrick's Society; Burke not only claims Ossian as Irish, but says there was a succession of poets in Ireland before the eighth century.[55] Number 323 may be one of the clippings he cut from his copy of Thoreau's *A Week on the Concord and Merrimack Rivers.*[56] Thoreau's excellent opinion of the "genuine remains of Ossian, or those ancient poems which bear his name," and his acceptance of them as worthy to be classed with such primitive poetry as that of Homer and the Old Testament, must have reassured Whitman in his own respect for them.[57] I have not identified clipping No. 321, which Bucke says is like No. 323, from a book, but not from the same book. It may have been from this clipping that Whitman got his erroneous dates, for he did not get them from Chambers's *Cyclopaedia.*

There is no way of knowing when all these clippings were made, though it is probable that the Margaret Fuller clipping was made soon after her *Tribune* article was printed, and we can be sure that the clipping from *A Week* was made after November 1856. We can assume that there was a continuing interest in Ossian from 1846 to 1856 and later. Some of the notes on the pink sheet to which the "Address to the Sun" was pasted bear dates as late as 1856 and 1857. One of Whitman's notes in *Notes and Fragments* begins, "Reading Ossian awhile this morning"; its language suggests that he might have intended it for inclusion in a preface to *Leaves of Grass.* He says there is "so much race (to use an old Scotch word) of the prehistoric, primitively Irish and Caledonian thought and personality in these poems—notwithstanding their general mistiness and gossamer character"—that he has had "more or less good from what they give out."[58] This

---

[55] See also "Notes on Whitman's Reading," *American Literature*, XXVI (Nov. 1954), 345.

[56] When Thoreau visited Whitman in Brooklyn in 1856 he gave him a copy of this book, published in 1849. This copy is in the Charles Feinberg Collection, now in the Library of Congress, and shows the places where Whitman made cuttings, some of which are in the Trent Collection at Duke University. Clipping No. 323 can be identified in *Notes and Fragments* only by the words "Ossian-Thoreau" in a page of miscellaneous notes (*Complete Writings*, IX, 227). Although these words are followed in Whitman's notes by the words "Macpherson 1737–1796," he did not get this misinformation from Thoreau, who says nothing of Macpherson or his dates.

[57] Thoreau's comments on Ossian, including several selections, not from Macpherson's translation, may be found early in the section "Friday," the Riverside edition, I, 453–59.

[58] *Complete Writings*, IX, 187–88.

must have been written later than 1855, perhaps much later, since I do not find the word "race" as here used in any of Whitman's early writing. The note is, in effect, an admission that he had been influenced by the Ossianic poems of Macpherson, dating possibly from the inception of *Leaves of Grass.*

Many of the books reviewed in the *Eagle* obviously had no significant influence on the shaping of *Leaves of Grass* and need not be discussed. A few that may not have influenced Whitman's poems might, nevertheless, have made some impression on his mind and character. He was by temperament romantic and sentimental, a fact that becomes evident in his review of Fredrika Bremer's novels. He read them—he mentions six by title—in translations made by Mary Howitt for the Harper edition of her works. He praises them as studies of the soul, and adds, "We know nothing more likely to melt and refine the human character—particularly the young character." He recommends them to every family as household treasures.[59] In this review, as in his stories and early poems, one may detect the moralistic piety of the nineteenth-century schoolmaster. If she has any fault, "it is that in one or two of her novels there is a little infusion of transcendentalism"; but he thinks that can do "no great harm," and can be pardoned. It is evident that Whitman's taste in poetry was also romantic and sentimental. He was not able yet to appreciate Keats. On March 5, 1846, he printed a notice of Keats's *Poetical Works.* The best he could say of him was that he was "one of the pleasantest of modern poets," though he thought that if he had lived he might have become a distinguished poet.[60] Whitman later became interested in Keats and clipped a review of R. M. Milnes's *Life of Keats* from the *North British Review* for November 1848, on which he made numerous annotations. One of these, written in the margin beside a quoted letter in which Keats speaks of identifying himself with other people when he is in a room with them, reads as follows: "The great poet absorbs the identity of others and the experience of others and they are definite in him or from him; but he presses them all through the powerful press of himself . . . loads his own masterly identity." He also clipped an article on "The Hyperion of John Keats," by J. D. Whelpley, from the *American Whig Review* for October 1851. It was probably the

59 *GF,* II, 266–68; *UPP,* I, 128. Holloway reprints only extracts. This review is dated Aug. 18, 1846.

60 *GF,* II, 303–4; *UPP,* I, 133. In Holloway's excerpt this is said to be an edition in 2 vols. I can find no such edition in the catalogs of the Library of Congress or the British Museum, though a new edition in one volume was published by Moxon in London in 1846. Presumably Whitman had a cheap reprint in two volumes which would have sold probably for 25 cents a volume.

reading of these two reviews, and perhaps some reading from the poems themselves, that induced Whitman to make the comment which Bucke reprinted in *Notes and Fragments* describing Keats's poetry as "ornamental, elaborated, rich in wrought imagery," but having no more of life in the nineteenth century than the statues have. "It does not come home at all to the direct wants of the bodies and souls of the century."[61] In *Good-Bye My Fancy*, perhaps influenced by world opinion, Whitman placed Keats among the thirteen British poets of "unassail'd renown."

Longfellow pleased him much more than Keats. On October 12, 1846, he reviewed Longfellow's poems in the "handsome fifty cent edition" published by Harper, declared this edition contained "many of the finest poems in the English language," and gave Longfellow a rank equal to that of Bryant and Wordsworth. On November 20, 1847, he published a notice of "Evangeline," which he said ends "like a solemn psalm, the essence of whose deep religious music still lives on in your soul, and becomes a part of you." He regrets that there is not more of it, but then, remembering Keats, he adds, "But a thing of beauty is a joy forever."[62] Whitman was acquainted with Longfellow's *Poets and Poetry of Europe*. Bucke's clipping No. 13, a review of that book, was cut from the *American Whig Review* for December 1846 and was carefully read and annotated. Ranking Longfellow with Bryant was the highest praise Whitman could bestow upon him. In a notice of Bryant published September 1, 1846, on the occasion of his return from Europe, Whitman says that Bryant is "a poet who, to our mind, stands among the first in the world."[63] Bryant and Whitman were personally acquainted at this time, though never intimate. As fellow-editors and Democrats, they had much in common. Bryant was kind to the younger editor, and they sometimes took long walks together. But Bryant disapproved of *Leaves of Grass*, and after its publication, if not before, his association with Whitman was discontinued. But Whitman continued to rank him first among American poets, along with Longfellow, Whittier, and Emerson, and very high among all poets writing in English.[64] Some of Whitman's early mor-

[61] These are Bucke's clippings Nos. 33 and 54. Whitman's notes are reprinted in *Complete Writings*, IX, 120. See "Notes on Whitman's Reading," p. 348.

[62] *UPP*, I, 133–34. See also *GF*, II, 297–98. One other evidence that Longfellow's poetry pleased him at this time is the fact that he quoted from his works in the *Eagle*, according to Holloway, more frequently than from any other author. Holloway counted 22 quotations as compared with only 7 from Bryant, 6 from Whittier, 2 from Lowell, and none from Emerson. (See *UPP*, I, 130.)

[63] *GF*, II, 260–61. See also *UPP*, I, 128–29.

[64] See *Prose Works 1892*, I, 165–67 ("Death of William Cullen Bryant"), 266–67 ("My Tribute to Four Poets"), II, 658–62 ("Old Poets"), and *passim*.

alistic verses may have been influenced by Bryant, but it is not likely
that he had read Longfellow and Whittier at the time he wrote them.

The same moralism is evident in his review of *The Wigwam and
the Cabin*, Second Series, by William Gilmore Simms in the *Eagle* for
March 9, 1846. "Simms," he writes, "is unquestionably one of the
most attractive writers of the age; and yet some of his characters—to
our mind at least—are in exceedingly bad taste. It *may* be all well
enough to introduce a 'foul rabble of lewd spirits,' in order to show
that 'Virtue can triumph even in the worst estates,' but it is our impression that ladies and gentlemen of refinement—to say nothing of
heads of families—would rather take the maxim upon trust than have
it exemplified to them or their children through the medium of a
picture so very coarse and indelicate in its details, as that drawn by
Mr. Simms in his 'Caloya.' "[65] How much of Simms's fiction Whitman
read then and later I do not know; probably not a great deal. More
than ten years later he copied a paragraph from a review of the works
of Simms published in Emerson's *United States Magazine* for June
1857. What chiefly interested Whitman in this paragraph was the
writer's statement that the "man of great and commanding genius"
takes a point of view outside the current world and so "represents
posterity more than his compeers." Whitman then makes a comment
of his own about Simms, including the criticism that he was too wordy
and too self-conscious, though his descriptions are good and his characters well drawn. This comment, however, was obviously summarized from the review and not based on Whitman's own reading of
Simms.[66] He was perhaps more interested in Simms the critic than in
Simms the novelist, and he seems to have owned a copy of *Views and
Reviews*, Second Series (1846), for he cut out and saved two sections
of the book dealing with the writings of Cornelius Mathews, one on
the subject of humor, which he endorsed "Very fine," and the other
counseling "all honest writers" to pursue "some one single object,"
which he endorsed "Very good."[67]

So far as I can tell, Whitman was not interested in Cornelius Mathews or his writings. This is rather odd, since they were almost exact
contemporaries (Mathews was two years the older), and both Democrats and literary nationalists. Mathews was closely associated with
E. A. Duyckinck in founding and editing the magazine *Arcturus* in
the early 1840's. He was, like Whitman and Simms, a contributor to
the *Democratic Review*, but Whitman never recalled his name in con-

[65] *UPP*, I, 136.

[66] From *Notes and Fragments* (*Complete Writings*, IX, 166).

[67] Bucke seems to take these clippings as only one, which he numbers 431. They
are now in the Trent Collection.

versations with Traubel, although he does remember Duyckinck and his brother, associating them, however, with the "great bogums" of New York. "I met these brothers," he told Traubel; "they were both 'gentlemanly men'—and by the way I don't know any description that it would have pleased them better to hear: both very clerical looking —thin—wanting in body; men of truly proper style, God help 'em!' "[68] He was probably remembering them from the 1850's, and his peevish tone may have been due to the fact that they left him out of their *Cyclopaedia of American Literature*, published in 1856 but reprinted as late as 1875.

Whitman was always, in his mature years, a reader of history, both ancient and modern. This interest might have developed from his early reading of Scott's novels and his seeing the historical plays of Shakespeare presented on the stage. During the 1840's he was especially interested in the history of revolutionary movements in England and France. He was a child, or rather a grandchild, of the American Revolution, and shared his father's enthusiasm for its heroes, as well as for the radical writings of Thomas Paine and Frances Wright. As I have already noted, he admired Cromwell and Napoleon, seeing them as promoters of human freedom and the advancement of the common man. Besides Hazlitt's biography of Napoleon and Carlyle's *French Revolution*, he reviewed Jules Michelet's *History of France* and called it the fullest and clearest of the author's works, intimating that he had read others. This review was dated April 22, 1847. It is probable that he had read also Michelet's *The People*, translated, like the *History*, by G. H. Smith, which was published in New York in 1846.[69] He also noticed Lamartine's *History of the Girondists*, August 10, 1847, and called it "the most dramatic work" he had ever read. His interest in such books was stimulated by the contemporary revolutionary movements in Europe, which also inspired the poem "Resurgemus," first published in the New York *Tribune* June 21, 1850,[70] the only early poem that he reprinted, with revisions, in *Leaves of Grass*. In Bucke's list of Whitman's clippings, No. 6 is a newspaper review of De Tocqueville's *The Old Regime and the Revolution*, translated by John Bonner (Harper, 1856). Whitman dated the clip-

[68] *WWC*, I, 139.

[69] Gay Wilson Allen is confident that *Leaves of Grass* was influenced by *The People*. See *Walt Whitman Handbook* (Chicago, 1946), pp. 469–72; also Allen's article "Walt Whitman and Jules Michelet," *Études Anglaises*, I (May 1937), 230–37. See also Adeline Knapp, "Walt Whitman and Jules Michelet, Identical Passages," *Critic*, XLIV (1907), 467–68.

[70] Reprinted in *UPP*, I, 27–30. Brasher says (p. 99) that Lamartine's *History of the Girondists* got the longest review Whitman wrote for the *Eagle*.

ping October 1856 and wrote at the head of it, "Deserves Re-reading." In passages quoted by the reviewer, De Tocqueville emphasizes the danger of despotism in nations that most love freedom. Something of Whitman's revolutionary fervor survived in the 1850's and even later. It can be seen in the essay "The Eighteenth Presidency!" that he never published (1856), in *Democratic Vistas*, in "Origins of Attempted Secession," in *Two Rivulets* (1876), and in a discussion of Millet's pictures first published in the *Critic* in 1881.[71] It finds expression throughout *Leaves of Grass* in passages here and there too numerous to mention. Of his deliberate study of history, more will be said later.

The period between the English Revolution and the French and American Revolutions produced few books that aroused Whitman's interest, although he embraced many of the scientific and political ideas that originated in the late seventeenth and the eighteenth centuries. The period following the restoration of the Stuart family to the English throne offended his moral as well as his political sensibilities, and he completely rejected the patterns of formal correctness in neoclassical literature and manners. He noticed in the *Eagle* very few books by eighteenth-century authors, and he may be said to have reviewed only two, James Thomson's *Seasons* and James Boswell's *Life of Johnson*. I doubt if he read much in Thomson's poem, for most of the one long paragraph of his review is devoted to the pictorial "embellishments" that "fit in at the sides, tops, and corners of the pages, in a novel and most appropriate manner, while the text runs on side by side with them."[72]

He seems to have read Boswell with interest, for he wrote a relatively long review, about 700 words, and commented intelligently on a number of the people discussed—the "fiery-breathed Burke," the "heedless" but "good-hearted" Goldsmith, the "massive abstracted Gibbon,—clear as the ice of the topmost Alps—and as cold." Although he found Boswell's narrative compelling, he heartily disliked the chief character, Johnson, "a sour, malicious, egotistical man" who "insulted his equals" and "tyrannized over his inferiors." Whitman cared little more for Johnson's works, even his dictionary, though it is not clear whether he had read them.[73] He gives Boswell high praise

[71] See *Prose Works 1892*, I, 267–69; II, 426–33.

[72] Reviewed Nov. 24, 1847 (reprinted in full in *GF*, II, 300–301, and in part in *UPP*, I, 136). The first edition of this illustrated text was published in London in 1842 and a second edition followed in 1847; both were reprinted by Harper. Whitman used the Harper edition of 1847. The engraved illustrations were by E. Bookhout, from designs by various artists.

[73] The edition Whitman reviewed was the John Wilson Croker edition, first pub-

for presenting his characters "not as in waxwork, but the flesh and blood of breathing life."

Despite this evidence of a somewhat better than casual reading of Boswell's *Johnson* in 1846, Whitman borrowed the book from Thomas Harned in 1888, saying, "I have never so far read it." During the next several days he talked to Traubel from time to time about the book as he continued reading persistently to the end, but he confessed that he read it, "not because it interested me much but because I ought to know what the old man did with himself in the world." Johnson belongs, he asserted, "to the self-conscious literary class, who live in a house of rules and never get into the open air." Though he admitted in the end that the book "seems to have elements of life," the concession was more flattering to Boswell than to Johnson. Whether or not he had really forgot having reviewed this book in 1846, his opinion of Johnson after more than forty years remained the same.[74]

Some change can be observed, on the other hand, in Whitman's early and late opinions of Milton. In an essay published in the *American Whig Review* for November 1845, he quoted the third line of the first book of *Paradise Lost*, but that, of course, does not mean necessarily that he had read much of the poem.[75] I find nothing more than a casual mention of Milton until his review in the *Eagle*, January 10, 1848, of *The Poetical Works of John Milton*, edited with a Memoir by James Montgomery and illustrated with 120 engravings by William Harvey.[76] Whitman begins with a sentiment borrowed from the concluding paragraph of Montgomery's Memoir: "It has been said of Milton that he does not persuade but *commands* admiration." He also praises the beauty of the books, the morocco bindings, the paper, the type, and the illustrations, which he says explain as well as adorn the text. "With all his grandeur," he continues, "this poet certainly wants some endearing and softening accompaniments," such as this edition provides. "As a writer," he continues, "Milton is stern, lofty,

---

lished by J. Murray, London, 1831, 5 vols., but reprinted in 2 vols. by George Dearborn, New York, in 1834, 1835, and 1837, by A. V. Blake of New York, 2 vols., in 1843, and by Harper, also 2 vols., in 1846. The Harper edition was undoubtedly the one Whitman reviewed, the review dated Dec. 7, 1846. (See *GF*, II, 280–83 for the full review; *UPP*, I, 127–28 reprints a short extract.)

74 See *WWC*, I, 38, 45–47, 146.

75 "Tear Down and Build Over Again," reprinted in *UPP*, I, 97.

76 This edition, in 2 vols., was reprinted by Harper in 1847 from the original edition of 1843. The review is reprinted in *GF*, II, 287–89; see also *UPP*, I, 134. An earlier mention of Milton was in the essay in the *Eagle*, Feb. 10, 1847, "Independent American Literature" (*GF*, II, 237–41), where he is named along with Shakespeare, Spenser, Bunyan, and Defoe.

and grand; his themes are heavenly high, and profoundly deep." He concludes that a reader must have something of Milton's own "vast abruptness" to appreciate his poetry. It seems apparent that Whitman had not yet attained such abruptness.

It is possible that he did not attempt to read the shorter poems at this time. He must have kept the volumes, however, and perhaps taken them with him to New Orleans, for in a sketch written there and published in the New Orleans *Daily Crescent* May 2, 1848, he introduces a quotation and a paraphrase from *Comus* that suggests at least some familiarity with that poem.[77] During the next several years he continued to be interested in Milton, though he could hardly be said to have studied his works. In his notes on Shakespeare preserved in *Notes and Fragments* he records from his reading: "Milton admired and loved Shakespeare, writes praises of him,—But yet he charges harshly against Charles I. that the monarch had a copy of Shakespeare in his cabinet for his constant use."[78] The first sentence might have been based on Whitman's recollection of Milton's poem "On Shakespeare" read either in his edition of Milton's poems or as reprinted in J. Payne Collier's biography of Shakespeare, which was the source of most of this group of notes.[79] The second sentence might have come from any one of several sources, including Griswold's edition of Milton's *Prose Works*, but probably came from Isaac D'Israeli's *Amenities of Literature*, either directly or as quoted by L. Herrig in *British Classical Authors*.[80] Bucke's clipping No. 345, "Adam's

[77] This sketch, "Samuel Sensitive," which Holloway attributes on good evidence to Whitman, is reprinted in *UPP*, I, 216–18.

[78] *Complete Writings*, IX, 74. This is part of an original manuscript now in the Trent Collection. The first sentence is in ink, as are most of the notes; the second is in pencil and was perhaps added later.

[79] See my article "Whitman's Knowledge of Shakespeare," *Studies in Philology*, XLIX (Oct. 1952), 663.

[80] *The Prose Works of John Milton*, ed. R. W. Griswold, were published in 2 vols. in 1845 and reprinted in 1850 with the same text and pagination but bound in 1 vol. The passage about Shakespeare is on p. 450 of Vol. I, in the *Iconoclastes*. It is unlikely that Whitman was interested in that work. He reviewed, or discussed, in an article in the *Eagle*, D'Israeli's *Amenities of Literature* (Harper's reprint), on March 9, 1847, and had evidently read considerable parts of it. (See *GF*, II, 257–59.) He also owned a copy of *British Classical Authors*, for he clipped a number of items from it, including the text of Shakespeare's *Richard II* in its entirety. From evidence in several of these clippings, I would judge that Whitman's edition of *British Classical Authors* was either the first, 1851, or some other before 1855. It was reprinted annually at least until 1858. After quoting the passage about Shakespeare as the "closet companion" of Charles the First, D'Israeli explains that Milton "knew that he was casting the deepest odium on the royal character" in the eyes of the Puritans at that time. (See *Amenities*, I, 214, and *British Classical Authors*, p. 633.)

Morning Hymn," is probably clipped from *British Classical Authors*, pp. 121–22, where a section of *Paradise Lost* (Book V, lines 153–208) is printed with the title "Morning Hymn."

Within a few years after the date of Whitman's review of Milton's *Poetical Works*, Whitman had arrived at some rather positive and less favorable opinions of *Paradise Lost*. Among the clippings he annotated and preserved there is one consisting of two sheets (four pages) cut from the article "Christopher Under Canvass" (*Dies Boreales*, No. 1), by Christopher North (John Wilson), in *Blackwood's Magazine* for June, 1849. All of Whitman's notes are in pencil and were made at one sitting, possibly during the summer of 1849, but probably later.[81] His first note is at the top of page 763: "Some ideas on Hexameters Poetry & Prose, and on Milton."[82] On pp. 758–62 of the magazine, which Whitman did not clip, North had praised the hexameter of Homer's verse, but he praised equally the accented iambic pentameter of English verse, including *Paradise Lost*. He also discussed the contents of Milton's poem and declared that Milton is bolder than Homer, and more of a creator. Near the beginning of page 763 North says he finds in the *Iliad* "dim foreshadowings, which Milton, I doubt not, discerned and cherished. The Iliad was the natural and spiritual father of the Paradise Lost." This provoked Whitman to write in the margins of this and the following page:

The Paradise Lost is (to us), nonsense any how, because it takes themes entirely out of human cognisance and treats them as Homer treats his siege and opposing armies and their disputes.—The Iliad stands perfectly well and very beautiful for what it is, an appropriate blooming of the poet and what he had received, and what he believed, and what to him was so, and what *was so* in a certain sense.—The Paradise Lost is offensive to modern science and intelligence—it is a poetical fanaticism, with a few great strong features, but not a great poem. Another point of difference is, the Iliad *was wanted* to give body and shape to the nebulous float of traditions. . . . and it gives them the beautiful, swift, rolling, continuing shape.—The Paradise Lost was *not* wanted for any such purpose. What is in the Bible had better not be

---

[81] LXV, 763–66, near the end of the article. This is Bucke's No. 352, which he erroneously states is torn from a book. Another clipping, Bucke's No. 510, from *Blackwood's*, Aug. 1849, has but little about Milton and is not annotated. There are two newspaper clippings I have not seen: No. 291, a report of a lecture on "Dante and Milton"; and No. 346, "Daily Life of Milton." Bucke printed the annotations on clipping No. 352, with minor changes of his own, in *Notes and Fragments* (reprinted in *Complete Writings*, IX, 97–98). My quotations are made directly from the annotations on the clipping, which is in the Trent Collection.

[82] Bucke's clipping No. 403, which I have not seen, is called "Homer in English Hexameters." This may have no connection with North's discussion.

paraphrased. The Bible is indescribably perfect—putting it in rhyme, would that improve it or not?

North remarks that Book VII of *Paradise Lost* "is replete and alive with motion—with progress—with action, yes, with action—of an order unusual indeed in the Epos, but unexcelled in dignity—the Creative Action of Deity!" Above this passage Whitman comments: "Think of a writer going into the creative action of deity!" Among passages underlined by Whitman is the following: "A discourse in prose resembles a chain. The sentences are the successive links—all holding *to* one another—and holding one another. *All* is bound." But he not only underlines the following passage but brackets it and writes beside it "good": "A discourse in verse resembles a billowy sea. The verses are the waves that rise and fall—to our apprehension—each by impulse, life, will of its own. *All is free.*" After a digression on Wordsworth in which North says "His poems are, of necessity an Autobiography," on which Whitman comments, "Wordsworth lacks sympathy with men and women—that does not pervade him enough by a long shot," the text returns to Milton. In North's last comment on Milton at the end of page 766 he says that in *Paradise Lost* Milton argues the question of the origin of wrong and pain, and why they are permitted by God; and he concludes: "The Poem is, therefore, Theological, Argumentative, Didactic, in Epic Form" but "the intention is hidden in the Form. The Verse has transformed the matter." In the margin beside this Whitman wrote: "Yes, but the point is wrong at the start. If a poet take what is largely doubtful even he shall surely fail." At the top of this page is the note: "The difference between perfect originality and second hand originality is the difference between the Bible and Paradise Lost." In the left margin near the top of this page Whitman wrote: "Whoever believes in the Calvinistic theology, to him the thread of Paradise Lost may seem strong—to all others it will be weak." Lower in the same margin he set down his general opinion of Milton at that time. "Milton's mind seems to have had the grandest sort of muscle—and much of the other stuff that poetry wants.— His descriptions are large and definite. He has nothing little or nice about him—but he was *in* too much with sectarian theology and churchmen.—For instance what nations in Asia or Africa not Christian, would see any great point in his poem, if read to them?" Some, at least, of these notes on Milton seem to have been made after Whitman began to formulate the theory of poetry exemplified in *Leaves of Grass.*

Although Whitman came to understand *Paradise Lost* somewhat better in his later years he never grew to like what he called, not very accurately, its "Calvinistic theology." In the Preface to his 1855 edition of *Leaves of Grass,* and in the poems themselves, he made plain his faith in the rightness of natural law as the manifestation of God's will and in the power of the human spirit to respond to it wisely. He may have had *Paradise Lost* in mind when he declared in the Preface to the 1855 *Leaves* that "whatever would put God in a poem or system of philosophy as contending against some being or influence" is "of no account."[83] In "Song of Myself" he declared, "I find letters from God dropped in the street, and every one is signed by God's name."[84] For the preservation and promotion of American democracy he repeatedly called for a new literature tallying the spirit of nature and obeying its standards.[85] *Paradise Lost* seemed to him in 1888 pretty much what it had seemed in the 1850's, not only unnatural but "turgid, heavy, over-stately," as he told Traubel, "a copy of a copy—not only Homer but the Aeneid."[86] As he reviewed his career he conceived his commitment as the poet of democracy to have been no less than Milton's as the poet of Christian theology. In "A Backward Glance o'er Travel'd Roads" he wrote: "Ever since what might be call'd thought, or the budding of thought, fairly began in my youthful mind, I had had a desire to attempt some worthy record of that entire faith and acceptance ('to justify the ways of God to man' is Milton's well-known and ambitious phrase) which is the foundation of moral America."[87] It may be assumed, I think, that though Whitman never liked *Paradise Lost* he learned much from it that served his own purpose.

Another book that Whitman reviewed in the *Eagle,* and one of a very different kind, may have influenced him in the conception if not in the composition of *Leaves of Grass.* This was Parke Godwin's translation and edition of *The Autobiography of Goethe. Truth and Poetry: From My Life,* published by Wiley and Putnam in their Library of Choice Reading. It came out in four volumes, the first two in 1846, reviewed on November 19, 1846, and the last two in 1847, reviewed on June 28, 1847.[88] The first review contains about 450 words. It also contains, Holloway says, "four lengthy extracts, which, unfortunately,

[83] *Prose Works 1892,* II, 448. The language is the same in the 1855 text.

[84] Line 1286 in the *Comprehensive Reader's Edition* (New York, 1965).

[85] *Democratic Vistas (Prose Works 1892,* II, 416 and *passim;* see also *Prose Works 1892,* II, pp. 486, 657, 666, 719 ff).

[86] *WWC,* III, 185.

[87] *Prose Works 1892,* II, 729.

[88] Both reprinted in *UPP,* I, the first on pp. 139–41 under the title "Incidents in the Life of a World-Famed Man," and the second on p. 132. *GF,* II, 294–95, reprints part of the first review, but does not mention the second.

he does not reprint. The editors of *The Gathering of the Forces* make the following comment: "Whitman was so impressed with Goethe's autobiography that he published three columns of extracts from it, which he liberally interlaced with enthusiastic and appreciative comments."[89] The second review is only a short paragraph. There is evidence, especially in the first review, that Whitman read the volumes more carefully than usual and with genuine interest.

What a gain it would be [he comments], if we could forego some of the heavy tomes, the fruit of an age of toil and scientific study, for the simple easy truthful narrative of the existence and experience of a man of genius,—how his mind unfolded in his earliest years—the impressions things made upon him—how and where and when the religious sentiment dawned in him—what he thought of God before he was inoculated with books' ideas—the development of his soul—when he first loved—the way circumstance imbued his nature, and did him good, or worked him ill—with the long train of occurrences, adventures, mental processes, exercises within, and trials without, which go to make up the man—for *character* is the man, after all.

This is an outline of the first two volumes of the *Autobiography*.

Holloway suggests that Goethe's autobiography might have influenced Whitman's thinking about his own ideals as a poet, and he quotes, in a footnote, the following remark made by Whitman to Traubel on November 23, 1888: "Goethe impresses me as above all to stand for essential literature, art, life—to argue the importance of centering life in self—in perfect persons—perfect you, me: to force the real into the abstract ideal: to make himself, Goethe, the supremest example of personal identity: everything making for it: in us, in Goethe: every man repeating the same experience."[90] About two months before this date Bucke wrote Whitman a letter that became the theme of much discussion for weeks, though the significant sentence in the letter is not revealed until Whitman's conversation with Traubel on December 27. Traubel's father was German and a great lover of German poetry. Whitman said to Traubel on May 27, 1888: "Your father is a great man. He was here the other day—sat over where you are sitting now—spouted German poetry to me—Goethe, Schiller, Heine, Lessing. . . ." On June 10 he said: "Goethe's constraint was Roman (Stoic) not Greek: the Greek let go: in sorrow, in joy, let go." On July 15, he said: "Bucke sees a great deal more in Goethe than I do—sees Goethe as if come fresh from the soil. . . ." The

89 *GF*, II, 295. Unfortunately they too omit the extracts and the means of identifying them.
90 *WWC*, III, 159.

next day he continued, saying that Goethe, "in loving beauty, art, literature, for their own inherent significance, is not as close to nature as I conceive he should be." On September 25, he quoted Bucke as saying in his letter, "There are just two great modern books—Faust and Leaves of Grass." On December 21, he told Traubel that he had an idea of having Bucke's letter printed for a few friends. On December 27, he quoted Bucke's letter as saying of *Leaves of Grass*: "It is a gigantic massive autobiography, the first of its kind (though the trick had been tried before by Goethe, Rousseau and others; but even Goethe could not do it)." But we must go back to the evening of December 21 to learn Whitman's reaction to this sentence in Bucke's letter. He said,

The idea of the autobiographicality of the book—that is what hits me. . . . Can it be that the Doctor's theory is true? that the book is autobiography pure and simple—in its elemental form? . . . That the work all centres upon one point—that its origins, beginnings, inspirations have emanated, vitalized, all, centrally from one source: that comes more and more to me. The last two weeks especially have I questioned the whole case, turned it over, seen it on every side—and I have come to recognize a more marked centrality than I had ever observed before—a centrality actual, while not designed: but whether as autobiography—even in the high, the uncommon sense (the sense in which Doctor means it)—it excels the great, I may almost say, literatures of the past—that puts a severe and serious if not impossible strain upon our faith. Think of Rousseau, of Goethe—then consider what Doctor has undertaken to determine and declare.[91]

To the casual reader it might appear from Whitman's statement of December 21, 1888, that he had not thought of *Leaves of Grass* as autobiography until Bucke called it so. However, read carefully, the statement will be seen to affirm only that during the last two weeks he had come to recognize a "more marked centrality" than he had observed before. He also makes the point that this centrality, though actual, was not designed. This is "the high, the uncommon sense," he thinks, in which Bucke used the term. He questions whether it excels the great literatures of the past. These would include Shakespeare, among others, but especially those writers who might be classified as "subjective," not "objective." Every reader of *Leaves of Grass* is familiar with the proud boast in "So Long!" (1860): "This is no book, / Who touches this touches a man"; but the line preceding is less familiar: "From behind the screen where I hid, I advance personally."

[91] *WWC*, I, 217, 357; II, 2, 5, 378; III, 159, 354–56, 397–98. In mentioning the names of Rousseau and Goethe, he obviously refers to the specific works, Rousseau's *Confessions* and Goethe's *Autobiography*.

The screen, of course, is the mask presented by the early poems, before 1860. Because of it, Whitman's book is not quite the "simple easy truthful narrative" he described in his review of Goethe's *Auto-biography*; yet its "autobiographicality"—to use Whitman's awkward word—is apparent throughout, from "Song of Myself" to "Good-Bye My Fancy!"[92] Both the *persona* which was the mask, or screen, in the early poems and the "I" who advanced from behind it in 1860 were designed, despite his disclaimer, but the "I" of the later poems is closer to the real Whitman than the "I" which had been the mask.

Whitman's interest in Goethe was almost continuous from 1846 to the end of his life. He may have learned something of Goethe through Carlyle even before 1846. Carlyle's *Critical and Miscellaneous Essays*, originally published through Emerson's efforts in 1838–39 in four volumes, were reprinted, with Carlyle's approval, by Carey & Hart of Philadelphia in 1845 in one large volume. Among these essays were about twenty on German literature, including six on Goethe and his work. When Whitman first read these essays it is not possible to say, nor can one be sure that he ever owned a copy; what we do know is that he read them carefully and made notes on several of them at various times, in 1856 and probably earlier. But it is obvious from his notes that he read them for information only, not as the basis for his own opinions. He agreed with Carlyle, in 1856, that Goethe was a great literary artist, even a great man, but he did not accept Carlyle's almost idolatrous praise of him as a good man, a genuine man, morally and spiritually great, and destined to be the teacher of future generations.[93] It is not necessary to assume that he had read much of Goethe's work except the *Autobiography*, for Carlyle's essays had given him a knowledge of the general nature of it sufficient to enable him to form the opinion expressed in 1856. As he began to set down this opinion, he warned himself: "Had I not better read more of Goethe before giving an opinion?" but he went ahead and gave the opinion. He called Goethe "the most profound reviewer of life known" and "the first great critic," the "fountain of modern criticism"; but he added that he would never be beloved by his fellows,

---

[92] In a review of the 1860 edition of *Leaves of Grass* by "January Searle" (George S. Phillips) in the New York *Illustrated News*, May 26, 1860, reprinted (doubtless at Whitman's request) in the *Saturday Press*, June 30, 1860, *Leaves of Grass* is called "as genuine a piece of autobiography as that of Augustine, or Gibbon, or the Confessions of Rousseau." (See *A Child's Reminiscence*, by Thomas O. Mabbott and Rollo Silver [Seattle, 1930], p. 35.)

[93] See especially two essays written in 1832, "Death of Goethe," and "Goethe's Works," reprinted in *Critical and Miscellaneous Essays* (1858 ed.), pp. 341–45 and 345–65.

perhaps "because he knows too much," and fancied that he is not "well beloved of Nature for the same reason."

About a month after these notes were made, he continued with further criticism. "There is one point of the Goethean philosophy, which, without appeal and forever incapacitates it from suiting America and the forthcoming years. It is the cardinal Goethean doctrine too, that the artist or poet is to live in art or poetry alone apart from affairs, politics, facts, vulgar life, persons and things—seeking his 'high ideal.' " [94] A week or so later he added this: "The assumption that Goethe passed through the first stage of darkness and complaint to the second stage of consideration and knowledge and thence to the third stage of triumph and faith—this assumption cannot pass, cannot stand amid the judgments of the soul. Goethe's was the faith of a physical well being, a good digestion and appetite, it was not the faith of the masters, poets, prophets, divine persons. Such faith he perhaps came near and saw the artistical beauty of—perhaps fancied he had it—but he never had it." The ten paragraphs in *Notes and Fragments* from which these comments are drawn were written in pencil on both sides of two sheets of pink paper and bear the heading, "*Goethe's* Complete works, last complete edition of his own revision," apparently suggested by Carlyle's review (1832) of Goethe's complete works. These pink sheets seem to have been cut from unused pink wrappers collected by Whitman to be used as covers for certain unbound copies of *Leaves of Grass*. These wrappers, or some of them at least, bear the printed title "Leaves of Grass." They were extensively used for first drafts of poems in 1856 and perhaps later.[95]

Immediately following the ten paragraphs on pink paper, as printed in *Notes and Fragments*, are two paragraphs, also in pencil, written on one side only of two sheets of yellow paper under the heading, "Goethe—from about 1750 to 1832." This heading, however, is omitted in *Notes and Fragments*. These yellow sheets may also have been cut from wrappers made for *Leaves of Grass*; more likely they were cut from end papers of the second issue, which were yellow; in either case the notes must have been made after July 1855.[96] If the

[94] This seems to have been suggested by a passage in Carlyle's essay "Goethe," written in 1828 (*ibid.*, p. 83).

[95] These notes, from manuscripts now in the Trent Collection, are printed in *Complete Writings*, IX, 110–13. For a description of other manuscripts on pink wrappers now in the Barrett Library of the University of Virginia, see Fredson Bowers, *Whitman Manuscripts* (Chicago, 1955), pp. xli f.

[96] Ralph Adimari, in "Leaves of Grass—First Edition," *American Book Collector*, V (May–June 1934), 150–52, speaks of unbound copies in paper wrappers as the third issue, after Sept. 26, 1855. Frank Shay, however, in *The Bibliography of*

yellow sheets were not cut from wrappers or end papers, the notes, which are not dated, might have been made before 1855. The fact that the first date of the title is slightly inaccurate suggests that the notes were made from memory and at a time different, probably earlier, than the notes on the pink sheets, which accurately record the dates of Goethe's birth and death.

In the first of the two paragraphs on yellow paper Whitman raises the following questions about Goethe, which suggest his opinion of the great poet's deficiencies as well as the fact that he is measuring him by his own conception of the great poet: "Is he really an original creator or only the noblest of imitators and compositors? Would or could he have written anything without the studies of the antiques? Is a man or woman invigorated, made cleaner, grander, sweeter, by his poems? Or more friendly and less suspicious? Has he raised any strong voice for freedom and against tyrants? Has he satisfied his reader of immortality?" In the second paragraph he concludes his remarks with the following decisive opinion: "To the genius of America he is neither dear nor the reverse of dear. He passes with the general crowd upon whom the American glance descends with indifference. Our road is our own."

Obviously Whitman could have read Goethe's works as well as reviews and critical evaluations of them and of the man himself in the interval between 1846 and 1856. He had probably seen Longfellow's monumental *Poets and Poetry of Europe*, first published in 1845 and several times reprinted, which contained long passages on Goethe drawn from Börne, Menzel, Heine, Carlyle, and others, as well as selections from his poems. These were probably supplied by C. C. Felton, who had in 1840 published in three volumes his translation of Wolfgang Menzel's *German Literature*, which, of course, Whitman could have consulted directly. At any rate, he preserved a review of Longfellow's book, which he read carefully, marked, and annotated.[97] He bracketed and underlined the following lines in the review: "The cardinal doctrine of the Goethean philosophy, that an

---

Walt Whitman (1920), describes a copy in pink wrappers and calls it "unquestionably the first issue." In *A Concise Bibliography of the Works of Walt Whitman* (Boston, 1922), by Carolyn Wells and Afred F. Goldsmith, it is said that the earliest issue is probably the one bound in green cloth with gold stamped lettering and ornaments and marbled end papers. The second issue is described as the one in green cloth with less elaborate decoration and yellow end papers. Not many of the unbound copies in paper wrappers have survived, and I have heard of none with yellow wrappers.

97 This is Bucke's No. 13, now in the Trent Collection. This review was published in the *American Whig Review*, Dec. 1846.

artist may live in art alone, may hold himself aloof from the world of action, neglect the momentous questions that agitate society, refuse to take part by word or deed in the great events that are going on round him, is a doctrine which could not well be entertained by any but a cold and selfish spirit." Pasted on the verso of the first of the yellow sheets described above is a newspaper clipping with the title "The True Character of Goethe." It consists almost entirely of a quotation said to be from "one of his countrymen," who describes him as cold and evil, a polished worldling who thrived on sin and seduced females without remorse, in contrast with Byron, whose sins were the result of passion and who felt remorse for them. Neither the author nor the newspaper is identified, and Goethe's countryman is not named, though he might well have been Menzel, from whose *German Literature* Longfellow quotes a passage in which Goethe is said to be the image of his age—"an age of national degeneracy." Menzel goes on to say: "When we pierce through the many-colored cloud of the Goethean form, we perceive egotism to be the inmost essence of his poetry, as of his whole life; not, however, the egotism of the hero and the heaven-storming Titan, but only that of the Sybarite and the actor, the egotism of the passion for pleasure and the vanity of art." Whitman's clipping contains this passage, which he bracketed.[98]

With all this in mind, we are prepared for Whitman's final judgments. As the last paragraph of "A Backward Glance o'er Travel'd Roads" he wrote: "Concluding with two items for the imaginative genius of the West, when it worthily rises—First, What Herder taught to the young Goethe, that really great poetry is always (like the Homeric or Biblical canticles) the result of a national spirit, and not the

---

[98] Among other possible sources of Whitman's knowledge of Goethe and his work is Joseph Gostwick's *German Literature* (Philadelphia, 1854), which he himself cited in some notes on Barthold Niebuhr (*Complete Writings*, IX, 116). However, he was indebted to Gostwick chiefly for some of his ideas about German philosophy, about the *Nibelungenlied*, and about a few German writers other than Goethe. (See "Notes on Whitman's Reading," pp. 348, 351, 354, 361, and especially the sources listed in the footnote on p. 353.) He had also seen F. H. Hedge's *Prose Writers of Germany* (1847; 2nd ed. 1852), but he did not derive his estimate of Goethe from Hedge, whose criticism is restrained. In later years Whitman read with pleasure G. H. Lewes's *Life and Works of Goethe* (2 vols., 1856; 2nd ed. 1863. 3rd ed. 1875). Whether he read this book before 1873 is doubtful, since he told Traubel in 1888 (*WWC*, II, 394) that he once had an abridged edition and liked it so well he was not satisfied until he got the full book. The abridged edition was published in 1873 as *The Story of Goethe's Life*. Yet Whitman preserved two newspaper clippings which he pasted on a sheet containing notes on Schiller and others, both cut apparently from a review of Lewes's biography in its first edition. The first describes Goethe as a young man; the second describes him as an old man.

privilege of a polish'd and select few; Second, that the strongest and sweetest songs yet remain to be sung." And in a very late essay, "American National Literature," first published in the *North American Review*, March 1891, he wrote: "The Goethean theory and lesson (if I may briefly state it so) of the exclusive sufficiency of artistic, scientific, literary equipment to the character, irrespective of any strong claims of the political ties of nation, state, or city, could have answer'd under the conventionality and pettiness of Weimar, or the Germany, or even Europe, of those times; but it will not do for America to-day at all. We have not only to exploit our own theory above any that has preceded us, but we have entirely different, and deeper-rooted, and infinitely broader themes." [99]

Whitman made a clear distinction between Goethe's importance as a landmark of literary history, a man of his own time and place, and his worth to the future, particularly in America. It is the same distinction that he drew with respect to Walter Scott and even Shakespeare and Homer, the three writers he most loved and read with the greatest enthusiasm as representatives of their separate worlds. In an original note preserved in *Notes and Fragments* he said: "Shakespeare and Walter Scott are indeed the limners and recorders—as Homer was one before, and the greatest, perhaps, of any recorder. All belong to the class who depict characters and events and they are masters of the kind." But he continued: "I will be also a master after my own kind, making the poems of emotions, as they pass or stay, the poems of freedom, and the exposé of personality—singing in high tones Democracy and the New World of it through These States." [100]

Whitman might have derived from Goethe's *Autobiography* the idea that *Leaves of Grass* should be a record of his own interior life, but the record itself surely owed nothing, unless by contrast, either to the *Autobiography* or to any other of Goethe's works. He some-

[99] *Prose Works 1892*, II, 731–32 and 664–65. Whitman's version of what Herder said to the young Goethe might possibly have been derived from the *Autobiography* (II, 192), which contains its substance, but it is more likely to have come from Lewes's *Life of Goethe*. Lewes (I, 117) wrote that Herder taught Goethe "to look at the Bible, as a magnificent illustration of the truth that Poetry is the product of a national spirit, not the privilege of a cultivated few."

[100] Manuscript in the Trent Collection (*Complete Writings*, IX, 84). Bucke speculates in a footnote: "Probably written before 1850." This date is certainly too early, for the notes were written on a sheet of blue paper about 8 by 4 inches that was cut from one of the Williamsburg tax forms that Whitman acquired in quantity after Williamsburg was merged with Brooklyn by legislative act in April 1854, to become effective Jan. 1, 1855. It is possible that these remainders were acquired in the summer of 1854, when he could have been in need of scrap paper for early drafts of *Leaves of Grass*, but it is unlikely that he had them earlier.

times mentioned Goethe in connection with Homer and Shakespeare as a great literary figure, but he did not respond warmly to his books. He thought Goethe insincere, a mere artificer projecting an unreal world out of his own ego, whereas Homer and Shakespeare and Walter Scott recreated the realities of great men and events in human history. He could relate his American democratic world to their ancient or feudal worlds, however different, but the world of Goethe's art seemed to him an irrelevant abstraction.

His lack of sympathy with the exponents of formal art amounted almost to antipathy. This was partly a matter of temperament. He shared the romantic tendency to idealize primitive art, especially poetry, because he assumed that it was unselfconscious and natural. Even before he began to develop his own poetic style he was caught up in the movement toward literary nationalism, and in the Brooklyn *Eagle* he vigorously maintained the thesis that since America is a new world it should have a new literature, free of the aristocratic tone of European literature, democratic, grown out of native soil.[101] He borrowed the eighteenth-century concept of the "natural" man and conferred his supposed virtues on the American workingman of his own time as a kind of primitive. His own background contributed to this idealization of the self-reliant American workingman. It also provided fertile soil for the growth of his suspicion of any manifestation of literary formalism that could be attributed to European influence. His limited education and early practice of journalistic writing left him inadequately equipped to compete in polite letters with men like Longfellow and Lowell. Even in New York, where journalism was more closely associated with literature than in New England, most of the successful writers of near his own age, including even Cornelius Mathews, were college bred. If he had been a little more sophisticated he might have found congenial fellowship in the group gathered about E. A. Duyckinck known as Young America. He made some minor contributions to the *Democratic Review* during the early forties, and as editor of the *Eagle* he supported their nationalistic credo, but his credentials, social perhaps as well as literary, were evidently unacceptable. In the late forties and early fifties, through wide reading and attendance at the theater and opera, he broadened the horizon of his mind and acquired considerable sophistication, but by that time he had already made up his mind to be the poet of nature and the natural man, the spokesman of American democracy.

The image he presented to a somewhat inattentive world in the

---

101 See especially *GF*, II, 237–66. Whitman continued throughout his life to overpraise certain favorite American poets, Bryant in particular.

1855 edition of *Leaves of Grass* was that of a natural man, a native American, uncontaminated by European culture, who proposed to express himself in his poems without any inhibitions and without the assistance of conventional literary forms. Looking back from our advantage in the twentieth century, we can see that this image did resemble the actual Walt Whitman but that it was in fact a mask, or a pose. Having assumed the pose, however, he had no comfortable way of discarding it. In the poems written from 1859 on he did, in part at least, discard it, but in actual life he maintained it so successfully that, in the end, it ceased to be a pose; he had come to believe in it himself. Perhaps at first he did not recognize it as a pose either so much as an attempt to translate an ideal into reality. But this was likely to be confusing, for only the artist can recreate the real into the ideal. Inconsistently, he began to formulate rules for writing artlessly. Many of his surviving manuscript notes contain directions for writing naturally. One paragraph, headed "Rules for Composition," begins: "A perfectly transparent, plate-glassy style, artless, with no ornaments, or attempts at ornaments, for their own sake." [102] In the Preface to his first edition he wrote: "What I experience or portray shall go from my composition without a shred of my composition." [103] He continued to express this idea throughout his life, though he rarely, if ever, succeeded in fulfilling the injunction. In talking with Traubel in 1888 he said: "When you talk to me of 'style' it is as though you had brought me artificial flowers." Rightly understood, he added, "the style is to have no style." [104] He confessed to an antipathy for Matthew Arnold, apparently because he was a stylist, a writer of polished prose, and a critic. "Arnold is porcelain, chinaware, hangings," he told Traubel on another occasion.[105] He liked Arnold's poetry better than his prose. "It is fine—wonderful fine—like some delicate precious bit of porcelain, of china, but it is fragile, it lacks substance." [106] The subtleties of Henry James's novels pleased him even less perhaps than Arnold's criticism. "James is only feathers to me," he told Traubel.[107] Although he liked some of Poe's poems, he objected to what he called their "metrical niceties." [108]

---

[102] *Complete Writings*, IX, 34–35.

[103] Whitman kept this sentence unrevised in all texts. (See *Prose Works 1892*, II, 444–45.)

[104] *WWC*, I, 104–5.

[105] *WWC*, II, 391. The only example of Arnold's criticism for which he had high praise was his essay on Heine, a writer whom Whitman also admired.

[106] *WWC*, I, 47.

[107] *WWC*, I, 78.

[108] *WWC*, II, 518.

Yet Whitman's taste was broader than his theory, and when he was not consciously defending that theory he often confessed to a genuine pleasure in elaborate and sophisticated forms of art as well as in the simpler forms. His essay "Art-Singing and Heart-Singing" professes a love of simple music that he never lost.[109] But he was equally appreciative, as we have seen, of the formal music of the oratorio and the Italian opera, and he delighted in the virtuoso performances of Ole Bull and the Italian violinist Savori. He criticized American playwrights and some theaters for slavish imitation of the British and called for a truly American drama, yet he would not approve of poor plays and actors any more than poor books simply because they were American. He rather liked the "loud mouthed ranting style" of Edwin Forrest, but he deplored the imitation of his style by "vapid imitators." He readily admitted the superiority, in general, of the style of English actors, and had special praise for what he called the "mental style" of Macready, "which touched the heart, the soul, the feelings, the inner blood and nerves of his audience."[110] Heroic action and rhetoric deeply stirred him, especially as he knew them in Shakespeare's historical plays, and his favorite real historical characters were Cromwell and Napoleon. But he was equally moved by church hymns, the preaching of Father Taylor and Elias Hicks, the sentimental story of "Evangeline," and the verbal melody of Tennyson's poems. All of these characteristics can be detected in his own poetry, though they are not all provided for in his theory.

[109] *UPP*, I, 104–6. With minor changes, Whitman reprinted this essay in the *Eagle*, Dec. 4, 1846.
[110] See *GF*, II, 309–44, especially pp. 322–26 and 331–32.

VIII. *Self-Directed Reading: Whitman's Use of Clippings*

B Y 1846 Whitman's literary taste and ambition had developed to the point that he had grown weary of editing ephemeral newspapers and writing trivial poems and tales which he, as well as the editors who occasionally published them, recognized as mediocre at best and without promise of improvement. He could hardly have failed to compare himself unfavorably with William Cullen Bryant, who was friendly, and whom he admired both as an editor and as a poet, and very likely he had dreamed of emulating him in combining literary activity with editing a first-class newspaper. He knew well, of course, Bryant's *Evening Post*, as well as Greeley's *Tribune* and one or two other great New York papers, and when the opportunity came in 1846 to edit his hometown Democratic paper, the Brooklyn *Daily Eagle*, he seized it and was happy in his work there for a year at least. Although the *Eagle* was a local paper with relatively few readers interested in books, Whitman followed the example of the larger metropolitan newspapers in devoting some space to book reviews and literary matters in general. He wrote the reviews himself, but he was too busy with other duties to read the books carefully, and he must have discovered very soon that his literary education was insufficient to enable him to compete in this department with the *Tribune*, for example, where Margaret Fuller was contributing excellent critical reviews. Moreover, before many months had passed, he found himself at odds with the Tammany type of Democratic principles to which his employer subscribed and increasingly in sympathy with the Free-Soil party.

Although he had literary ambitions, he was probably not at this time wholly committed to a literary career. In discussing with Traubel in 1888 a newspaper report that Carlyle wanted to be a man of affairs rather than a writer, Whitman said that the same was true, in some measure, of himself, and cited as evidence his "addiction to the trades" and his work in the hospitals.[1] The "trades" he referred to were presumably those of the printer and carpenter, or builder. As a boy he had been apprenticed to a printer, and from there moved naturally into newspaper work. His father was a carpenter and

[1] *WWC*, II, 241.

builder, and he himself, by 1850, had turned to carpentry and house-building for part, at least, of his livelihood. Just what Whitman meant by "a man of affairs" I do not know, but he was certainly not a man of business, otherwise he would have stayed with the builder's trade during the middle 1850's. We have the testimony of his brother George that he might have made a good deal of money building houses, but that he willfully neglected his opportunity.[2]

He may have thought at one time of preparing himself for the legal profession, for he clipped and preserved an article from the *Democratic Review* for January 1846 with the title, "Prospects of the Legal Profession in America."[3] But he must have realized that his academic preparation was inadequate for the law, and indeed for literature or even journalism except on a low level of achievement. If he hoped for distinction in any career he must educate himself, for at his age and in his circumstances college was out of the question. In any case, few young men except the wealthy and those preparing for medicine, the law, or the ministry found a college education essential to success. He was encouraged by the example of others who had overcome the handicap of little formal education by self-directed study. On December 17, 1846, he wrote, in "A Few Words to the Young Men of Brooklyn": "Some of the wisest and most celebrated men, whose names adorn the pages of history, educated themselves after they had lost the season of youth."[4] He must have seen some of the many books and articles of the period on the subject of self-education. One of the most famous and influential essays on this theme was "Self-Culture," by the Rev. W. E. Channing, first delivered as a lecture in Boston in 1838, soon afterward printed in a pamphlet, and often reprinted. The first collected edition of his essays was published in 1841, and was reviewed in the *Democratic Review* for September 1841. The reviewer asserts that Channing is not only a democrat in the highest sense of the term, but feels "authorized by the testimony of his own writings to assert—he is a 'locofoco.' " Whitman was a "locofoco" at that time, but whether locofoco or Free-Soil Democrat, he would have approved of many of Channing's ideas. When he first read "Self-Culture" I do

[2] Horace Traubel, "Notes from Conversations with George Whitman, 1893," *In Re*, pp. 32–33. There was, as George pointed out, a great boom in housebuilding in the 1850's to provide for the city's rapidly expanding population.

[3] No. 467 in Bucke's list of clippings. It is a review of Samuel Warren's book *A Popular and Practical Introduction to Law Studies*, which the reviewer calls a "celebrated work," one calculated to awaken the enthusiasm of the law student" and inspire him "with a taste for the legal profession." Whitman also clipped from an unidentified magazine an article (Bucke's No. 535) with the title "The Legal Profession, Ancient and Modern," September 1846.

[4] Reprinted from the *Eagle* in *UPP*, I, 148, and in *GF*, I, 133.

not know, but he almost certainly read, or more probably reread, the essay as published in the collected edition of Channing's essays in six volumes that appeared in 1847. In the *Eagle* of June 28, he wrote of this essay: "We have always considered it an unsurpassed piece, either as to its matter or manner."[5] Whitman's "always" suggests that he had been acquainted with the essay for years, perhaps since he was a country school teacher on Long Island. He evidently had read other essays, for in the *Eagle*, July 26, 1847, he quotes a passage of several lines from the discourse on "War," originally delivered January 25, 1835.[6] Another evidence of Whitman's interest in Channing is that he preserved a clipping of the biographical sketch printed as the head note to several excerpts from Channing's essay "The Present" in *Half-Hours with the Best Authors.*[7] This interest persisted into old age. He told Traubel in 1889, "I have been dipping into the Stedman books again—reading Channing—William Henry Channing." When Traubel reminded him that it was William Ellery, not William Henry, he commented, "Is it that? I mean the great Channing, anyhow."[8]

Whitman did not have time to read carefully all the books he no-

---

[5] *UPP*, I, 130.

[6] *UPP*, I, 168. Holloway said he could not find this quotation in Channing's works. Probably he never expected to find it in the essay on "War." It is to be found in the 1847 edition, IV, 255. "Self-Culture" in this edition is in II, 347–411. Another quotation from Channing in the *Eagle*, April 6, 1846, is cited by Thomas L. Brasher in *Walt Whitman as Editor of the Brooklyn* Daily Eagle (Detroit, 1970), p. 176.

[7] This clipping is not listed by Bucke, but it is in the Trent Collection.

[8] In March 1889 E. C. Stedman sent Whitman the first seven volumes—all that had been published at the time—of his *Library of American Literature*, later completed in eleven volumes. (See *WWC*, IV, 446). Stedman's selections from Whitman's *Leaves of Grass* are in Vol. VII; the selections from Channing are in V, 3–19. It is easy to see how Whitman might have confused the first names of W. H. Channing with those of the "great" Channing, William Ellery the elder, who died in 1842. He probably knew W. H. Channing, nephew and biographer of the "great" Channing, since he lived in Washington during the war years 1861–65 and visited, as did Whitman, the battlefields in Virginia and the hospitals in Washington. He was also pastor of the Unitarian Church there and in 1863–64 was chaplain of the House of Representatives. Whitman may also have known W. H. Channing while he lived in Brooklyn and New York, 1842–45, for he preached often in both places, for a while in Stuyvesant Institute, where ten years later Whitman visited the Egyptian Museum. It is even possible that the poem "Present Good," signed "W," which appeared in Channing's short-lived magazine *The Present* in April 1844, was written by Whitman. The magazine was published on Fulton Street, near the ferry, on the New York side. He was more intimately acquainted during the 1860's with Dr. William F. Channing, son of William Ellery, whose wife was the sister of Mrs. W. D. O'Connor. He visited in the home of Dr.

ticed in the Brooklyn *Eagle*, but he saved some of the better ones for more careful study when he should have time for it. George Whitman said Walt "spent a good many hours in the libraries of New York."[9] No doubt he read, or read parts of, many more books than we have any record of, especially after 1849. Magazines and newspapers he read, of course. He must have been a fairly regular reader of the *Democratic Review* from 1841 to 1847, perhaps later, and during most of those years he was an occasional contributor. Moreover, as editor of Democratic newspapers he would naturally turn to that magazine more than to some others. Yet when in January 1845 Wiley and Putnam established *The American Review: A Whig Journal*, he not only read it but, in spite of politics, became a contributor. The many clippings he made from these two American magazines were most likely cut from his own files. He also made numerous clippings from the American editions of the leading British magazines and quarterlies, mostly from issues dated 1848 and later. He may have bought some of the copies he clipped soon after publication; others he acquired later, perhaps from leftover stock, but which ones cannot be determined. He read some of the articles first in a library, and if he found one that he wanted to study further, he bought the magazine containing it then or later, cut out what he wanted, and threw the rest away. Bucke said, on Whitman's authority, speaking of an uncertain period of time but probably the late 1840's and early 1850's: "These years he used to watch the English quarterlies and Blackwood, and when he found an article that suited him he would buy the number, perhaps second-hand, for a few cents, tear it out, and take it with him on his next sea beach excursion to digest."[10] He followed the same practice with some books, especially anthologies. Apparently he did not have the collector's respect for books as such, but only for that part of them which especially interested him. Something can be learned of the progress of his self-education from these clippings.

The largest significant collection of Whitman's clippings is that which Bucke listed in *Notes and Fragments* and later reprinted in *Complete Writings*, Vol. X, which consists of 554 items. Of these, approximately 350 are from newspapers, 120 are from magazines and reviews (45 British and 75 American), 50 or more are from books, and

---

Channing for several days in 1868 while he lived in Providence. All three Channings were liberal in their thinking and closely associated with Emerson and his circle.

9 *In Re*, p. 39.
10 *Walt Whitman* (Philadelphia, 1883), p. 21.

the rest are pamphlets, scrapbooks with maps and related material, and a few miscellaneous items. About 175 of these clippings, most of them marked in some way by Whitman and some extensively annotated, are now in the Trent Collection at Duke University. These include about two-thirds of all clippings from books and magazines and perhaps sixty from newspapers. The collection contains a few clippings not listed by Bucke. I have read most of the magazine articles listed by Bucke that are not in the Trent Collection, but usually without the advantage of Whitman's annotations. I have seen other collections, but much of what I shall have to say about Whitman's self-education in this chapter, and later chapters too, is based on a study of these clippings.[11] Most of the newspaper clippings were cut from papers published after 1855 and have little to do with *Leaves of Grass*, although some of them relate to other writers and their work. The clippings from magazines and reviews are the most important and contain the major portion of Whitman's annotations.

Nearly half of the book clippings are from *Half-Hours with the Best Authors*, edited by Charles Knight.[12] These are usually more biographical than critical and appear to have been made to assist Whitman in the study of literary history, perhaps with a view to lecturing on the subject. Several, perhaps a dozen, were clipped from *British Classical Authors*, edited by Ludwig Herrig in Germany for the use of German students of English, and consisting of selections, in English, from British literature from Chaucer to the middle of the nineteenth century.[13] Whitman clipped the selections he was especially interested in, perhaps to carry in his pocket. Among them were a number of pages of early Scottish poetry, English popular ballads, and the entire text of Shakespeare's *Richard II*. He removed the pages of the play and bound them separately as a pamphlet, which

---

[11] I spent several weeks studying and making notes on the clippings in the Trent Collection soon after they were received at the Duke University Library in 1942. Other collections I have seen are less important. The Library of Congress contains many hundreds of newspaper clippings. Some of these are obviously from papers received in exchange while Whitman was an editor. About 375 were cut by friends at or shortly after his death.

[12] Originally published in London, in 4 vols., 1847–48; frequently reprinted: in Philadelphia, in 6 vols., 1848, and in New York, by J. Wiley, 6 vols. in 3, 1849. Whitman's clippings are from the New York edition, the paging of which is different from that of the Philadelphia edition.

[13] The book was first published in Brunswick, Germany, in 1850, and reprinted annually for years. A revised edition, with a new Preface, came out in 1855, and it continued to be revised from time to time and used in German schools for half a century. Whitman seems to have owned a copy of the second edition, published in 1851.

he kept until 1888, when he showed it to Traubel, saying that he had often "spouted these first pages" from Broadway stagecoaches. Evidently he confused, for the moment, *Richard II* with *Richard III*, which he had often in his youth seen on the stage. The first pages of *Richard II* are not suited for "spouting," since they present a rather formal discussion between the King and his Counsellors intended to introduce the action, but the introductory lines of *Richard III* consist of a monologue by the Duke of Gloucester that is eminently suited for the purpose.[14] Whitman could not have seen *Richard II* played in New York, for it was not presented there as a stage play until 1865. Fanny Kemble read it to a public audience there in 1858, but only once.[15] Whitman also clipped a number of items from other books, including *A Week on the Concord and Merrimack Rivers*, which Thoreau gave him in 1856.

As might be expected, Whitman's first significant magazine clippings were made from the *Democratic Review* and the *American Review: A Whig Journal*, usually referred to as the *Whig Review*, and date from 1845.[16] He might have been expected to find something in the *Democratic Review* worth clipping during the years 1841–42, when he was contributing to it frequently, but I know of none either for those years or for 1843–44.[17] He clipped nothing from the *Columbian Magazine*, to which he contributed in 1844, nor from the *Aristidean*, to which he contributed in 1845.[18]

[14] *WWC*, II, 245–46. Traubel says that Whitman fitted the pages of the play back in their proper place in the volume, but he obviously did not keep them there, for they have long been in the Library of Congress, but the book itself is part of the Feinberg collection and only recently became part of the Whitman materials in the Library. For a more detailed discussion of this clipping, see my article, "Whitman's Knowledge of Shakespeare," in *Studies in Philology*, XLIX (Oct. 1952), 649–52. See also *Walt Whitman's Workshop*, ed. Clifton Joseph Furness (Cambridge, Mass., 1928), pp. 26, 35, 196, 209.

[15] *Annals*, VII, 96.

[16] There were only two earlier clippings listed by Bucke. One is an article on "The Dying Gladiator," published in the *Penny Magazine* (London, edited by Charles Knight, 1832–46), Jan. 12, 1833. Two stanzas describing the fallen gladiator are quoted from Canto IV of Byron's *Childe Harold*. The only thing remarkable about this clipping is the fact that Whitman preserved it. The other clipping, "America and the Early English Poets," is from the *Democratic Review*, 1839. Whitman was, at that time, probably less interested in these poets (Spenser, Drayton, Herbert, and Marvell) than in what they had to say of early America.

[17] He contributed prose tales and sketches to the issues of August, November, and December 1841; January, March, May, July, and September 1842; and the combined issue of July–August 1845. He also contributed "A Dialogue," an article opposing capital punishment, to the issue of November 1845.

[18] See *The Early Poems and the Fiction*, ed. Thomas L. Brasher (New York, 1963), Appendix A, pp. 335–39.

Bucke lists three clippings from the *Democratic Review* in 1845, one in 1846, and ten in 1847, but none thereafter. Of these fourteen, four are concerned directly and two indirectly with literature; four relate to history, two to geography and geology, one to philosophy and one to law. From the *Whig Review*, Bucke lists eight items in 1845, four in 1846, two in 1847, but none in 1848, 1849, or 1850; he lists nine in 1851, however, and six in 1852, the last year of its publication. Of the 28 items clipped from the *Whig Review*, nineteen were on literature (five in 1845, two in 1846, one in 1847, nine in 1851, and two in 1852). The only other important clippings from American magazines were one in *Graham's* in 1845 ("Egotism," chiefly about poets), and four in *Sartain's*, all by Charles G. Leland in 1849, and all on literature and art.

From British periodicals he clipped only one item before 1848; that was a review of two histories of Rome from the *Westminster Review* for April 1846. In 1848, however, he clipped ten items, and in 1849 twenty-one, but thereafter no more until 1857. Of the thirty-one items clipped in 1848–49, eleven were from the *North British Review*, seven from the *Edinburgh Review*, six from *Blackwood's Magazine*, six from the *Westminster Review*, and one from the *Quarterly Review*. Seventeen are on literature, six on history, four on geography and geology, two on botany, and two on art. In turning from American to British periodicals in 1848, Whitman may have been influenced by the general opinion, expressed by Caroline Kirkland a few years earlier, that American magazines were devoted to the entertainment, not the edification, of their readers, whereas the British quarterlies "embody a fund of information on almost every subject worth understanding." [19]

It is not possible to see from these clippings a definite pattern in Whitman's reading habits. It is apparent that his primary interest was in literature, and that his second greatest interest was in history and geography. But his interests changed somewhat between 1845 and 1852, as did his habits of work. In 1845 he was largely engaged in writing fiction for the magazines when not occupied with his editorial work. Presumably he was not then much interested in either writing or reading about poetry. Several, in fact most, of his clippings that year would have been useful to a writer of fiction or to a journalist trying to enrich his mind and improve his style. These include the articles "Words," "On Style," "Thoughts on Reading," "The Laws of Menu," "The French Moralists," "Lyell's Geological Tour,"

[19] "Periodical Reading," by Caroline Kirkland, in the *Democratic Review*, XVI (Jan. 1845), 59–61.

"Arnold's Lectures on Modern History," and "The Scotch School of Philosophy and Criticism." The only clippings that relate directly to poets or poetry are the "Hymn of Callimachus" and a review of Elizabeth Barrett's *A Drama of Exile and Other Poems*, which consist almost altogether of quotations and have no marks or annotations by Whitman. He clipped two articles published in 1846 that relate to poets and poetry, or more properly to literary history: a review of Longfellow's *Poets and Poetry of Europe* and an article on "Translators of Homer." In 1847 he clipped a review of P. J. Bailey's poem *Festus*, but he was obviously more interested in the poet's treatment of the theory of evil than in the poetry for itself.[20] Another clipping, "Nationality in Literature," dealt with a subject about which he had written a good deal in the Brooklyn *Eagle*. Even the clipping on "Characteristics of Shelley" seemed to interest Whitman chiefly for what it said of Shelley's personality and of the insubstantiality of his poetry.[21]

I cannot determine from the information available why he clipped eight items from the *Whig Review* in 1845 and only three from the *Democratic Review*, the organ of his party, in which he was still interested, or why he clipped ten from the *Democratic Review* in 1847, when he had begun to lose interest in the party, and only two from the *Whig Review*. So far as I can judge, the interest and literary quality of the articles were about the same in both periodicals. In both, however, the articles published in 1848, 1849, and 1850 seem to me to be inferior to those published in the years immediately preceding. After he became better acquainted with the British periodicals in 1848 he may have read American magazines more critically. The clippings from the magazines and quarterlies of 1848 and later reflect his growing interest in literary criticism and in poetry as an art. In these two areas, especially, the British quarterlies were superior to the American. They were not only more authoritative and more detailed; they were also more acute in critical analysis. For some reason which I shall not try to discover, the articles from 1851–52 issues of the *Whig*

[20] Whitman did not mark this clipping, but the following note appears in *Notes and Fragments* (*Complete Writings*, IX, 154): "Theories of Evil—*Festus, Faust, Manfred, Paradise Lost, Book of Job.*" This note may have been suggested to Whitman by another article he clipped (Bucke's No. 412), "Theories of Evil," from the *Whig Review*, Dec. 1851.

[21] In a biographical note on Shelley in *Notes and Fragments* (*Complete Writings*, IX, 84), Whitman expressed his opinion that Shelley "must have been quite such another as T. L. Harris." The reference is to Thomas Lake Harris (1823–1906), an American poet influenced by Andrew Jackson Davis, with whom he was associated in New York in 1848–50. About 1850 he began to compose long poems while in a state of trance and in communication, allegedly, with the spirit world.

Review in these areas were better than they had been in the years immediately preceding, and this improvement may account for the greater number of clippings Whitman preserved from the issues of those years. Among the better articles that he clipped were J. D. Whelpley's "Lessing's Laocoön" in January 1851 and the same writer's "The Hyperion of John Keats" in the October issue of the same year.

Until 1848, it seems, Whitman had been reading to improve his education without much consideration of the end to which it might be put. In any case, he was committed until then to political journalism in the interest of the Democratic Party. But during the year 1847 he began to lose his enthusiasm for that commitment, and the next February took his first step away from it by going to New Orleans with his brother Jeff. To be sure, he went there as a journalist, but was apparently not obligated to any political faction, and his known writing for the New Orleans *Crescent* proves that he was more interested in the life of the streets than in political affairs. He did not intend to remain in New Orleans longer than would be necessary to save enough money to build a house on his lot on Myrtle Street, or, possibly, to buy a place in the country.[22]

The brothers returned to New York in May, and during the winter of 1848–49, Whitman says he built a large house on Myrtle Street in which the family lived until September 1852. Part of this time Whitman operated a printing shop and also a bookstore in the same building. It is possible that he acquired some copies of the British quarterlies for sale in his bookstore, but finding in certain issues articles that especially interested him, retained these issues for himself and then or later clipped from them. This would explain perhaps why he clipped often from the British quarterlies of 1848–49 but not from earlier issues.[23] I am inclined to think that the years 1848–52 were for Whit-

---

[22] See *Correspondence*, I, pp. 33–34. See also p. 43.

[23] Gay W. Allen has suggested in *The Solitary Singer* (New York, 1955, p. 130) that Whitman might have received the British periodicals for review in the Brooklyn *Freeman*, which he edited from September 1848 until September 1849; yet that does not seem probable since he did not review British periodicals during the two years he edited the Brooklyn *Eagle* although he did review some American periodicals. In 1847 he praised Littell's *Living Age*, according to Thomas L. Brasher. (See *Walt Whitman as Editor of the Brooklyn* Daily Eagle, p. 198.) This periodical reprinted articles chiefly from the British quarterlies, and it may be that his reading the reprinted articles there led him to turn eventually to the periodicals themselves. No clippings from British quarterlies were made by Whitman after he became editor of the Brooklyn *Daily Times* in 1857, although during the two years of his editorship he printed a number of reviews of them: seven of the *London Quarterly Review*, and four each of the *Edinburgh Review*, the *North*

man a period of indecision as to what would be his permanent career. After he gave up editing the *Freeman*, he was largely engaged for two or three years in the building trade, with writing only a secondary occupation; yet his education continued, and it is unlikely that he ever seriously considered building houses as a permanent trade despite the fact that he was making money at it.

Whitman clipped very few magazine articles after 1852, possibly because he had by that time committed himself to the career of a poet. The evidence of such a commitment is not conclusive from an examination of the clippings, but is very nearly so in his preserved manuscripts, especially his notebooks. It has generally been thought that Whitman's earliest notebooks containing verse that he later worked over and included in the 1855 and 1856 editions of *Leaves of Grass* date from 1847–49.[24] It is my own opinion however, after a careful study of microfilm copies of the notebook Holloway thought the earliest, as well as other early notebooks, that they are of later date, and that the experimental verse Whitman wrote into them belongs to the years 1853–55, and most of it to 1854–55. My opinion is based on internal evidence chiefly, evidence that Holloway and others who have concerned themselves with the subject have neglected to some extent. Yet there are marks and dates in one of the books that seem to support Holloway's conjecture and to be inconsistent with my conclusion. I think the apparent inconsistency can be satisfactorily accounted for, but the problem is a thorny one.[25]

The magazine articles which most interested Whitman he read and reread several times over a period of years though perhaps not after he became editor of the Brooklyn *Daily Times* in 1857. The evidence of these readings can be seen in the kinds and number of marks Whitman made on the clippings. The most common mark is the marginal bracket, which may enclose single lines or groups of lines, sometimes whole paragraphs. The next most common mark is the underlining of words, phrases, lines, and occasionally groups of lines. Many lines have been bracketed and underlined more than once, with different

---

British Review, and the *Westminster Review*. Of *Blackwood's Magazine* he printed about twenty. Among American magazines he printed twelve reviews of the *Atlantic Monthly* and eleven of *Harper's Magazine*. (See William White, "Walt Whitman's Journalism: a Bibliography," *Walt Whitman Review*, Sept. 1968.)

24 Emory Holloway was the first to suggest these dates, as he was the first to examine the notebooks carefully and reprint portions of them in *Uncollected Poetry and Prose of Walt Whitman*.

25 See my article on "Dating Whitman's Early Notebooks," *Studies in Bibliography*, XXIV (1971), 197–204. See also Edward F. Grier, "Walt Whitman's Earliest Notebook," *PMLA*, LXXXIII (Oct. 1968), 1453–56.

types of pencil or with ink, showing the different readings. Frequently
a hand is drawn in the margin, side, top, or bottom, with index finger
pointing to the word or passage to which Whitman wished to call
special attention. Many of the clippings are annotated by Whitman;
these annotations may vary from a single word to many lines or even
paragraphs of comments, some of which were printed by Bucke in
Notes and Fragments and reprinted in Vols. IX and X of *Complete
Writings.*

The statistics on newspaper clippings are quite different. Out of
approximately 350 clippings listed by Bucke, only about 65 are dated,
either from a printed dateline on the clipping or from a notation by
Whitman. The earliest of those dated is given as 1849. There are none
from 1850–52, 3 from 1853, 7 from 1854, 2 from 1855, 10 from 1856,
20 from 1857, 12 from 1858, 4 from 1859, and 2 from 1860. The large
number from 1857 and 1858 as compared to other years is presumably
accounted for by the fact that he received during these years many
papers in exchange while editing the Brooklyn *Daily Times.* There
are perhaps 75 newspaper clippings related in some way to literature,
50 to science, 60 to geography and history, and 70 to travel and descriptions of places. A great many contain miscellaneous information
not easily classified. Only about half a dozen are marked or annotated
by Whitman except for identification and dating. Many of the clippings from newspapers, with a few from magazines, on science, geography, history, and travel, found their way into a huge scrapbook
which Whitman made by taking apart four geographies and atlases
and recombining them so that he might insert clippings next to the
maps to which they are related.[26]

It is obvious that the materials of *Leaves of Grass* derive chiefly
from Whitman's personal experience and observation in the streets,
theaters, and newspaper offices of New York and in the neighboring
countryside of Long Island. To a considerable extent they derive also
from current events as reported in the daily and weekly newspapers.
Books of history, geography, and science, or the reviews of such books,
also contributed much factual information. As a rule, clippings containing factual information used in *Leaves of Grass* are not marked

[26] The following books were used for this purpose: R. C. Smith's *Atlas of Modern and Ancient Geography* (1855); *Geography and History, Ancient and Modern*
(J. H. Colton & Co., 1855); *Pelham's Pictorial Voyage* (1854), describing scenes along
the border between the United States and Canada; a chart called *Pictures of Nations, or Perspective Sketch of the Course of Empire*, to accompany *Willard's Universal History in Perspective* (date of publication uncertain). I examined and
made notes on all of these and the inserted clippings many years ago when the
scrapbook was in the collection of W. D. Bayley, of Springfield, Ohio.

by Whitman. The fact that they were clipped at all proves that he was more than usually interested in their contents, and many of the notes preserved in *Notes and Fragments* are based on reading that was not annotated. Yet in clippings that are marked, the degree of his interest may be indicated, more or less accurately, by the kind of marks he made on them. Brackets were used to set apart passages of more interest than unmarked portions of the article. Underlining of words and lines is evidence, I believe, of a still greater interest. Double and triple brackets and heavy underlinings, or underlinings in both pencil and ink, indicate matter of the greatest interest. The hand drawn in the margin with index finger pointing to a passage or place on the page clearly shows that Whitman wished to call very special attention to what was written or printed there. As a rule, markings in ink appear to be of later date than markings in pencil on the same clipping, but clippings of late date may be marked with pencil equally with clippings of an early date. I suspect all the ink markings were made at a second, third, or later reading.

Magazine articles were clipped more often for the ideas they contained or suggested than for factual information, especially if those ideas related to poetic art or the function of the poet. I suspect that many articles clipped primarily for information were later marked for ideas. Articles on science, history, and philosophy have fewer marks and annotations than articles on literature, or even on literary history. Many of the marks and annotations on literary history, especially, were in all probability made in 1855 or 1856 in connection with his preparations for lecturing. It is often impossible to determine whether marks and annotations on clippings of magazines, especially those published before 1852, were made early, in connection with his self-education, in 1855–56 while he was preparing to give lectures, or some time between while he was developing the techniques and principles that went into the making of the first *Leaves*. Doubtless some passages were marked because they contained opinions that confirmed his own ideas previously formed. The lack of marks on a clipped article is not necessarily evidence that Whitman did not read it carefully.

IX. *Science, Phrenology, and Geography*

W HITMAN preserved only five clippings on subjects of a strictly
scientific nature. One of these, on "Botany," was cut from the
Westminster Review in 1849, two were on Lyell's *Geological Tours
in America*, 1845 and 1849, one from the *Quarterly Review* and one
from the *Democratic Review*; two were on "Herschel—Southern
Heavens," from the *Edinburgh Review*, also in 1848. A few newspaper
clippings deal with strictly scientific subjects, but most of these are
only journalistic reports of scientific lectures or conventions. None
of these clippings are marked. So far as I have found he clipped none
of the numerous reviews and discussions of Robert Chambers' *Vestiges of Creation*, first published in 1843.

Nevertheless, he must have read summaries or excerpts from authoritative works on all the sciences, for *Leaves of Grass* is full of the
evidences of his knowledge, as a number of scholarly studies have
shown.[1] Many of the notes Bucke published in *Notes and Fragments*
relate to his scientific studies, and some of them mention poems he
hoped to write on specific topics involving a knowledge of science.
Some of these notes were certainly written before or while he prepared the first edition of *Leaves of Grass*; others were written later.
In one he suggests: "A poem in which is minutely described the whole
particulars and ensemble of a *first-rate healthy* Human Body—it,
looked into and through, as if it were transparent and of pure glass—
and now reported in a poem."[2] This was surely written before or
early in the year 1855, and though he wrote no poem exactly like the
one projected, parts of "Song of Myself" and "I Sing the Body Electric" come close to it. Another note, I suspect, was written after the
publication of the 1855 edition but before he completed the 1856 edition. In it he tells himself: "Read the latest and best anatomical

---

[1] See especially Alice Lovelace Cooke's excellent article, "Whitman's Indebtedness to the Scientific Thought of His Day," University of Texas *Studies in English*,
No. 14 (1934), 89–115; Clarence Dugdale's "Whitman's Knowledge of Astronomy,"
ibid., No. 16 (1936), 125–37; and Joseph Beaver's *Walt Whitman—Poet of Science*
(New York, 1951). The first chapter of Beaver's book contains a useful review of
what had been written before 1951 on Whitman's knowledge and use of science.

[2] *Complete Writings*, IX, 106.

works. Talk with Physicians. Study the anatomical plates—also casts and figures in the collections of design." [3] He must have read and talked as directed before setting down the long list of anatomical terms without comment a few pages farther on in *Notes and Fragments*,[4] which he transferred with but little modification to the 1856 text of "I Sing the Body Electric," in what is in late editions Section 9. In a long list of terms and their definitions he mentions Cuvier's division of reptiles into four orders, and he notes that the term "biology" was "introduced by Treviranus of Bremen instead of physiology." [5] These notes seem to have been taken from a dictionary. In a note on phenomena most closely identified with the air, such as the orbs, space, light, and heat, he cites Silliman as calling them "cosmical not terrestrial." [6] Among the numerous suggestions in *Notes and Fragments* for poems, one note calls for "Poems identifying the different branches of the Sciences," and another calls for a "Poem of Insects. Get from Mr. Arkhurst the names of all insects—interweave a train of thought suitable—also trains of words." [7] These notes on the sciences were obviously written by a person who had made no serious study of them, but had picked up his information from newspapers, magazines, dictionaries, and perhaps a few popular textbooks. He might have been genuinely interested in science for its own sake, but these notes prove only that he wished to include the sciences in his comprehensive plan for *Leaves of Grass*. He knew something of geology and biology, including some evolutionary theory that he could easily have found in *Vestiges of Creation*, or perhaps in reviews, but there is no evidence in the poems of the 1855 edition that anything more than the romance of science had interested him seriously. Readers of *Leaves of Grass* should be thankful that he never wrote most of these poems that are projected in *Notes and Fragments*.

For Whitman the romance of science did not inhere in scientific facts themselves, but in what they led to, what they symbolized. As he wrote in the 1855 "Song of Myself," "The facts are useful and real . . . they are not my dwelling . . . . I enter by them to an area of the

---

[3] *Ibid.*, X, 10.

[4] *Ibid.*, X, 22–23.

[5] *Ibid.*, IX, 208, 209. The reference is to Gottfried Reinhold Treviranus, whose *Biologie; oder die Philosophie der lebenden Natur* (1802–5) is said to have introduced the term.

[6] *Complete Writings*, IX, 47. The reference, presumably, is to Benjamin Silliman, Jr., who published widely used textbooks of both chemistry and physics. I think it unlikely that Whitman based this note on either of these books.

[7] *Ibid.*, X, 20–21 and 25. So far as I know, none of these poems was written. I cannot identify "Mr. Arkhurst."

dwelling." [8] This area of his dwelling is a sense of the immensity and unity of the universe, spiritual as well as material, and of his identity with it. The concept of progressive evolution governed by law, with man at the apex of the organic scale, excited his imagination. "I am an acme of things accomplished, and I an encloser of things to be. . . . Rise after rise bow the phantoms behind me. . . ." [9] He may have derived his ideas of evolution directly or indirectly from *Vestiges of Creation.* The book, originally published in 1843, was discussed in magazines and newspapers for many years, being both defended and condemned, so that Whitman could hardly have failed to become acquainted with its main ideas.

Another book that he may have read was the first volume of William Fishbough's *The Macrocosm and Microcosm; or, The Universe Without and the Universe Within.* [10] The scientific journals did not review the book, and yet it did not go unnoticed or unappreciated. In the *American Phrenological Journal* for July 1854, I find the following notice: "A remarkable work. The book noticed below is equal if not superior to the 'Vestiges of Creation.' We copy the article from the *Philadelphia Sunday Ledger*, and commend it as the most appreciative yet critical notice of that work which has yet appeared." The review in the *Ledger* (about five or six hundred words) states, in part: "For accuracy of analysis, solidity of thought, discriminating sagacity; extent of knowledge, and cogency of reasoning, that portion which treats of the physical or material creation will favorably compare with the writings of Lord Bacon, Sir Isaac Newton, Dr. Franklin, Arago, Humboldt and Espy; whilst the spiritual portion, in *mysticism*, resembles the writings of Baron Swedenborg and the German transcendentalists." [11] The reviewer did not care for "mysticism," but notes that Horace Greeley had noticed the book favorably in the *Tribune* and quoted two columns from it. Fishbough was almost certainly influenced by Andrew Jackson Davis, who, when a youth of 19 and 20 delivered, while in a state of trance, a series of 157 lectures, which, as his amanuensis, William Fishbough copied down verbatim. These were published in 1847 as *Principles of Nature. Her Divine Revelations, and a Voice to Mankind.* After that Davis dispensed with

[8] P. 28. As later revised (lines 491–94): "Your facts are useful, and yet they are not my dwelling, / I but enter by them to an area of my dwelling."

[9] P. 50. Lines 1148 and 1152 of the revised poem.

[10] The book was to be in two volumes; the first was on the world without, but was published in New York in 1852 under the full title. Fishbough was still working on the second volume, which was to be devoted to the world within, in 1854, but there is no record of its ever having been published.

[11] *The American Phrenological Journal, and Repository of Science, Literature, and General Intelligence*, XX, 12.

dictation, and in 1850–52 published *The Great Harmonia; Being a Philosophical Revelation of the Natural, Spiritual, and Celestial Universe.*" I have seen only Volume II, "The Teacher," and Volume III, "The Seer," which seem most likely to have been of interest to Whitman. In the former he said, "The God of the human mind is the magnified perception of itself—and sometimes it is a prophecy of its *future* self!" [12] In another place he said, "Mind and Matter, or God and his Body, are universal and eternal! There never was a time when nothing existed; nor can there ever be a period when nothing shall exist." [13] These are two of numerous passages that contain ideas essentially identical with some of the key ideas in "Song of Myself." Davis also says, "If there exists an Evil principle, would not that principle be an integral element in the constitution of the Divine Mind?" [14] This, of course, is one basic idea of "Chanting the Square Deific." The third volume of *The Great Harmonia*, which develops the author's theory of the "Seven Mental States," is primarily concerned with Spiritualism. The publication of this volume may have been the main reason why Fishbough never published his second volume of *The Macrocosm and Microcosm*, which also was to deal with the life of the spirit and to utilize the magic numbers three and seven and the Swedenborgian doctrine of correspondence.

Another Swedenborgian idea that may have influenced Whitman through Fishbough was his doctrine of spheres. This doctrine was involved in Fishbough's "law of the seven-fold correspondential series," or "harmonial scale of creation," and is discussed at some length in Chapter VIII of the *Macrocosm*, where he describes the experiments of the German scientist, Karl, Baron von Reichenbach, as proof.[15] Fishbough returned to the idea in a short article entitled "Spheres" in the *American Phrenological Journal* for January 1853, where he wrote: "The idea, I believe, was first distinctly set forth by Swedenborg, that all forms and existences, whether inorganic or organic, or whether in the natural or spiritual world, respectively send forth their own peculiar emanations, by which is formed around each an enveloping sphere or atmosphere." He says further, "The

12 *The Great Harmonia*, II, 261. The text cited is the 1856 edition of Vol. II; the first edition was copyrighted in 1851. Vol. I was subtitled "The Physician," Vol. IV "The Reformer," and Vol. V "The Thinker."

13 *Ibid.*, II, 278. Cf. "Song of Myself," sections 3, 20, 38, 41, 45, 48, and *passim.*

14 *Ibid.*, II, 289.

15 These experiments are described in the Baron's book, which has the imposing title of *Physico-Physiological Researches on the Dynamics of Magnetism, Electricity, Heat, Light, Crystallization, and Chemism, in Their Relation to Vital Force.* The first American edition of this work, in translation, was published in New York in 1851.

sphere of each body, therefore, is the exact aromal counterpart of the
body, and may be said to be its identical self spiritualized."[16] Whitman's images representing the identity of body and soul and the "ef-
flux" of the soul may have come from Fishbough, or from Swedenborg through him.[17] In Section 2 of "Song of Myself," where he says
that houses and rooms are "full of perfumes," he must refer to the
"aroma" that belonged to the persons living in the houses and writing the books on the shelves. The sphere may also be the "fluid and
attaching character" of individuals described in the same poem. It
is the "necessary film" which envelops the individual soul, as stated
in Section 9 of "Crossing Brooklyn Ferry." Many other parallels might
be cited.

In the *Phrenological Journal* for April 1854, Fishbough tells how
Dr. J. R. Orton, of Brooklyn, when deeply abstracted and mentally
excited while writing on a metaphysical subject, "suddenly found
himself separated, as it were, from his own body, and standing several
feet from it, and looking upon it as it sat by the table with the pen in
its hand. . . . This is one among the thousands of phenomena which
might be related as proving that while the soul is normally connected
with the body, and is in a great degree dependent upon it, it still may
exist as a *separate entity*, entirely independent of the physical orga-
nism." Whether Whitman accepted this story as a scientific fact or
not, it may have suggested the lines in "Song of Myself" where the
soul is represented as a separate entity yet properly one with the body,
notably lines 75–79 and 82–90. The "Calamus" poem "That Shadow
My Likeness" also involves the idea of double-consciousness.

Although few if any of the contributors to the *Phrenological Journal* were scientists of any note, some of them were well acquainted
with the literature of science and became intermediaries between the
learned and the unlearned. For example, during the year 1853 a series
of nine articles on *The Natural History of Man*, by William C. Rog-
ers, was published. The author says he will "endeavor to bring the

[16] *American Phrenological Journal*, XVII, 8–10. Fishbough continues with examples of how the union of two or more spheres produces clairvoyance.

[17] Whitman was interested in Swedenborg. He preserved a long newspaper
clipping on him with the title "The New Jerusalem" (Bucke's No. 278); and in
Notes and Fragments, in a brief note on him, he says, "He is a precursor, in some
sort, of great differences between past thousands of years and future thousands."
(*Complete Writings*, IX, 79–80.) He seems to have formed this judgment from his
own reading of Swedenborg; at least he did not get it from the clipping. He also
mentions him in *Democratic Vistas* and in notes on Elias Hicks in *November
Boughs*. Helen Price wrote Bucke that Whitman and John Arnold, a Swedenborgian who lived in the same house with her and her mother, discussed Swedenborg a great deal in her presence in the late 1850's. (*Walt Whitman*, pp. 26–27.)

researches of the most profound Anatomists, Physiologists, and Naturalists, within the reach and comprehension of all, divesting the subject of the formalities of a strictly scientific investigation, and yet adhering closely to all the facts and arguments which such an investigation sets forth." In the course of his work he quotes extensively from J. C. Prichard's *Natural History of Man* (1843), W. B. Carpenter's *Principles of Human Physiology* (1843), and others.

Whitman was almost certainly a regular reader of the *American Phrenological Journal* during the years 1850–56. While editor of the *Eagle* he had reviewed several books on phrenology and spoken well of them. There is a strong probability that he read them either before writing the reviews or later. He became a frequent visitor at the phrenological cabinet, or museum, maintained by the firm of Fowler and Wells (before O. S. Fowler withdrew from the firm in 1854, Fowlers and Wells), consisting originally of O. S. and L. N. Fowler and S. R. Wells. In July 1849 he had a phrenological reading signed and dated by L. N. Fowler in a manuscript now in the Trent Collection.[18] He preserved several clippings from the *Phrenological Journal*, one dated as late as May 1857. He labeled one clipping "Cosmos Clock," though the printed title is "Universal Time." It has a chart consisting of a large central clock face showing time in New York surrounded by numerous smaller clock faces showing corresponding times in several American and foreign cities. It is from the issue for March 1854. In addition to the *Phrenological Journal*, Fowler and Wells published the *Water Cure Journal and Herald of Reforms*; the two periodicals had a combined circulation of 100,000 copies each month. They also published the *Illustrated Hydropathic Quarterly Review*, a professional magazine devoted to medical reform. In October 1854 they began to issue a weekly, *Life Illustrated*, devoted to literature, science, and the arts. Whitman contributed a number of articles to this weekly between November 1855 and August 1856 and may, for a time, have filled an editorial post on it.[19]

It is reasonable to assume that when Whitman had his phrenological reading in 1849 he had some degree of confidence in the scientific accuracy of the report given him by L. N. Fowler. The fact that he preserved the manuscript throughout his life and incorporated some

18 Whitman's interest in phrenology has been discussed by many scholars. The first thorough study of the subject was made by Edward Hungerford and published as "Walt Whitman and His Chart of Bumps," in *American Literature*, II (Jan. 1931), 350–84. For Whitman's dealings with Fowler and Wells, see Madeleine B. Stern, *Heads and Headlines* (Norman, Okla., 1971), pp. 99–123 and *passim*.

19 Articles by Whitman and attributed to him are printed with annotations in *New York Dissected*, ed. Emory Holloway and Ralph Adimari (New York, 1936).

of its terms in *Leaves of Grass* suggests that he never wholly lost his belief in its value. When he reviewed his 1855 edition for the Brooklyn *Times* in September 1855, he boasted of his "rugged phrenology," and printed with obvious pride the statistics of Fowler's report. I doubt, however, that he continued to be an uncritical believer in phrenology as a legitimate science, or even in his phrenological reading except as it offered presumptive support for his own egotistic appraisal of himself. Although in his twenties he had been an enthusiastic supporter of temperance and other reform movements, in his thirties he became worldly-wise and a bit skeptical of all reform movements. Yet he sympathized with the general aims of the reformers. Commenting in the Brooklyn *Times* of June 29, 1858, on "The Radicals in Council," as he termed a meeting of reformers in Rutland, Vermont, he wrote with mixed amusement, tolerance, and sympathy: "This gathering, like other gatherings of the kind, we look upon as significant of a grand upheaval of ideas and reconstruction of many things on new bases—not in the manner indicated by these excrescences who have just finished their pow-wow at Rutland, but on an infinitely larger, grander and nobler scale—all in God's good time. Nevertheless, these, too, have their uses." [20]

That Whitman maintained a fairly close relationship to some of the editors of the *Phrenological Journal* during the middle 1850's is beyond question. In an editorial comment on the paintings of Jesse Talbot in the issue of February 1853, I find the following paragraph: " 'Christian and the Cross' is another warm and glowing work by Talbot, in the possession of Walter Whitman, of Brooklyn. It has some exquisite touches of color and delicate outlines. The large picture, of which it is a reproduction, in smaller size, equally delighted the critics and the public, on its first appearance some years ago." [21] In 1855 and 1856 he was glad to have Fowler and Wells sponsor the first and second editions of *Leaves of Grass* until he could find a publisher who could do more for the book. It is fairly certain that the poems in "Children of Adam" were written to illustrate the phrenological characteristic of "Amativeness" and that the poems in "Calamus" were designed to exemplify "Adhesiveness." Critics who interpret "Calamus" as homosexual poems would do well to take their phrenological significance into consideration.

Whether or not Whitman ever believed in phrenology as a genu-

[20] Reprinted in *I Sit and Look Out*, p. 46.

[21] XVII, 45. This was a picture that in 1857, Whitman included with other merchandise as part payment of a debt he owed James Parton. Whitman wrote O'Connor in 1869 that the painting was worth four or five hundred dollars but that he thought he put it in for one hundred. See *WWC*, III, 236–39.

ine science, it may have supported his natural inclination to value science for its humanistic potential rather than for its strictly intellectual appeal. In any case, he moved easily from science to a wider reading in geography, history, and philosophy. Into his huge atlas-scrapbook went articles from newspapers and magazines on travel, geography, history, archeology, and philosophy indiscriminately so long as they had human interest, although articles on travel, geography, and history predominate. There are newspaper reports of lectures on subjects ranging from geology to art, travel letters by Bayard Taylor and others, and reviews of books. Several lectures on geology by "Dr. Boynton" are there; of the sixth lecture the reporter writes: "The lecture was particularly successful in exposing the errors of the Lamarckian theory that each order of animals formed links in one chain of animated being, connecting the superior with the inferior, and making man the off-shoot of the monkey."[22] There are articles on China, India, and Japan, on the travels of Dr. Livingstone and Henry Barth in Africa, and other similar works. Whitman must have pored many hours over these until he had built a solid foundation of fact upon which his imagination could erect the vast structures of time and space that we find in "Song of Myself," "Starting from Paumanok," "Salut au Monde!" and other poems. Some of the geographical statistics preserved in *Notes and Fragments* derive largely from these atlases and the clippings related to them.[23] One of the books of which the atlas is made, Colton's *Geography and History, American and Modern*, contains a brief history of Texas, including an account of the massacre of Colonel Fannin's men at Goliad in violation of the terms of their surrender to General Santa Anna. Whitman used this account in writing Section 34 of "Song of Myself." The language of the poem is quite similar to that of the book. Most of the clippings are from New York newspapers and weeklies, but there are several long reviews from British quarterlies, including the review of Herschel's observations of the southern heavens published in the *Edinburgh Review*, February 1848. Other major reviews in the scrapbook include one of *The Physical Atlas*, by Alexander Keith Johnston in the *Edinburgh Review* for April 1849, and one of *Nineveh and Its Remains*, by Austin Henry Layard, in the *North American* for May

22 I have not definitely identified this Dr. Boynton. I suspect he was Charles Brandon Boynton (1806–83), clergyman and man of affairs. He was awarded the degree of Doctor of Divinity by Marietta College in recognition of his acquirements as a biblical scholar, and from 1865 to 1869 he was Chaplain of the House of Representatives in Washington, succeeding W. H. Channing in that office. The dates of these lectures are not available.

23 See especially *Complete Writings*, IX, 47–62 and 207–20.

1849.[24] There is also in the scrapbook a review of Prescott's *Conquest of Peru* from the *Democratic Review* for August 1847 and an article on "China and the Chinese," from the *Westminster Review* for April 1857. Numerous other articles on China and India are listed by Bucke. It is obvious that Whitman's geographical interests were wide and enduring.

[24] Whitman also clipped a review of Johnston's *Physical Atlas* from the *North British Review*, Aug. 1848, and a review of Mrs. Mary Somerville's *Physical Geography* from the *North British Review*, May 1848. These are not in the scrapbook; I read them in the Trent Collection. There are no annotations.

X. *Ancient and Medieval History and Literature*

A CAREFUL examination of the poems in the 1855 edition of *Leaves of Grass* reveals the fact that when Whitman wrote these poems he was primarily interested in the people and geography of the United States, and to a lesser extent in those of Canada and Latin America. Most of the gods mentioned in Section 41 of "Song of Myself" were well known. One of them, "Adonai," was apparently an erratic spelling of Adonis, perhaps vaguely associated with Shelley's "Adonais." In the 1856 edition he dropped it and substituted "Buddha."[1] "Mexitli" is another name for Huitzilopochtli, the Aztec war god. I think "Mexitli" was more commonly used in 1855 than it is now, but I have not found it in Prescott's *Conquest of Mexico*, which Whitman most probably had read. "Teokallis" in Section 43, usually spelled with a "c" instead of a "k," is the plural of Teocalli, an Aztec temple. I do not know where he got "circle of obis" in Section 43 unless he had picked it up from some description of Negro fetish worship.

In the poems first published in 1856 there is evidence that since writing the poems of the first edition he had read much about the customs of antiquity as well as about modern geography. This is notable in "Salut au Monde!" and "Song of the Broad-Axe," where we find not just a list of names or places; but descriptive phrases, showing considerable detailed knowledge. Just when he first became interested in ancient Egypt and neighboring countries of Asia Minor is not clear. In an article on "Indian Life and Customs" in the *Eagle* November 7, 1846, he says "it is singular to see that 'the public' will rush in crowds to hear Dr. Giddon's lectures on the ancient Egyptians, while a baker's dozen only could be got together by the most graphic and authentic narrative of aboriginal matters."[2] Whitman may have

[1] If he checked on the meaning of the word after the 1855 *Leaves* was published he discovered that "Adonai" is a Hebrew word for God or Lord. Since he had mentioned Jehovah in a preceding line, he would not have used "Adonai" as one of the heathen gods if in 1855 he had known its true meaning.

[2] Reprinted in *GF*, II, 136–40. "Giddon" is obviously a typographical error for "Gliddon." George R. Gliddon, born in England in 1809, went with his father at an early age to Cairo and remained there twenty-three years, part of the time as vice-consul for the United States. He wrote many books on archeological subjects,

heard some of these lectures, but I conclude from the context of his
statement on Egypt that he was then more interested in aboriginal
American Indians than in Egyptian antiquities. In 1854 and 1855,
however, and perhaps in 1853, he made frequent visits to the Egyptian museum of Dr. Henry Abbott, and his deep interest in Egyptian
antiquities probably dates from that time. Bucke says that Whitman
visited this Museum "for over two years off and on . . . became friends
with the proprietor, Dr. Abbott, a learned Egyptologist, and gleaned
largely from his personal narrations."[3] In *Good-Bye My Fancy* Whitman himself says, "The great 'Egyptian Collection' was well up in
Broadway, and I got quite acquainted with Dr. Abbott, the proprietor—paid many visits there, and had long talks with him, in connection with my readings of many books and reports on Egypt—its antiquities, history, and how things and the scenes really look, and
what the old relics stand for, as near as we can now get."[4] This would
have been, most probably, between the middle of 1853 and the latter
part of 1855. Abbott brought his collection to New York in 1853
hoping to sell it to the city. During that year he issued his first American catalogue (a previous one had been published in London), and
in 1854 he issued a larger one. In 1855 he returned to Cairo.[5]

In a manuscript notebook in the Library of Congress dating from
1854, the first four pages contain notes on Egypt, including the following sentence: "Dr. Abbott tells me that Lepsius told him of finding monuments in Ethiopia with inscriptions and astronomical signs
upon them."[6] Karl Richard Lepsius was a distinguished German
scholar and Egyptologist. He wrote many books, some of which Whitman may have read, though I cannot be sure of that. He was a friend
of Christian C. J. Bunsen, another German scholar of many interests,
some of whose many books on Egypt Whitman surely had read, or at

the best known of which was *Ancient Egypt*, originally published in 1843 as a special number of the *New World*, where Whitman's *Franklin Evans* had been published the preceding year. It was several times reprinted. Gliddon lectured on
Egypt in New York at various times during the 1840's, and in New Orleans in
March 1848, as reported in the *Daily Crescent*, perhaps by Whitman. He died in
1857.

  3 *Walt Whitman* (Philadelphia, 1883), p. 21.

  4 *Prose Works 1892*, II, 696.

  5 I have examined the 1854 catalogue. Abbott was unsuccessful in selling his
collection, but he left it in New York when he returned to Cairo. Later it was
acquired by the New York Historical Society. Abbott died in 1859.

  6 This notebook is item No. 84 in the catalogue of the Walt Whitman Collection
in the Library of Congress. For the bases on which I date this notebook see my
article "Dating Whitman's Early Notebooks" in the University of Virginia *Studies
in Bibliography*, XXIV (1971), 197–204.

least consulted. An article on "The Egyptian Museum" published in *Life Illustrated* for December 8, 1855, was almost certainly written by Whitman.[7] This article shows that Whitman had absorbed a good deal of information about ancient Egypt, some of it from Abbott, no doubt, some of it from lectures by Gliddon and others, but probably a good deal more from his reading of the many books, reviews, and magazine and newspaper articles on Egypt published during the 1840's and 1850's. He mentions the account of Egypt by Herodotus and cites such nineteenth-century Egyptologists as Champollion, Ippolito Rosellini, Sir John Gardner Wilkinson, and Lepsius. Of Rosellini he says he "has issued a complete civil, military, religious, and monumental account of the Egyptians, with magnificent plates. This work is of such cost that only wealthy libraries can possess it. There is a copy in the Astor Library in New York." Since it had not been translated, Whitman could not have read this book, but in all likelihood he had looked at the plates with intelligent interest. He does not mention Bunsen, which may mean that he had not read any of his books at the time of writing his essay.

There is a passage in the essay, part of which is repeated in *Notes and Fragments*,[8] on "Remesis Second, supposed to be the same as Sesostris, 1355 years before Christ," who was "six feet ten inches high," and who "conquered all Asia and part of Europe in nine years," and where the people resisted him bravely he erected monuments with phallic symbols, but where they gave easy tribute he inscribed feminine symbols. "In the programme of Egyptian greatness he is the first after Osiris. His reign was long continued, being over sixty-two years. He partitioned the land among the peasants, and compounded with them to pay him a fixed tax." All of this is almost word for word from Wilkinson, even to the spelling of the king's name, usually "Rameses."[9] In 1854 Wilkinson published in New York *A Popular Account of the Ancient Egyptians*, but if Whitman read this he made no notes from it that I can identify. A considerable portion of the facts about Sesostris and Rameses cited in Wilkinson could have been derived from Bunsen's *Egypt's Place in Universal History* (Vol. II, pp. 292–304), but Wilkinson's language is much

---

[7] It is reprinted, with notes establishing the authorship, by Emory Holloway and Ralph Adimari in *New York Dissected* (New York, 1936), pp. 27–40 and pp. 204–7.

[8] See *Complete Writings*, IX, 102, 215.

[9] Most of this appears in the chronological table on p. 29 of Vol. I of Wilkinson's *Manners and Customs of the Ancient Egyptians* (London, 1837), and the rest on pp. 64–65. The substitution of an "i" for the second "e" in "Remeses" was probably a typographical error in Wilkinson's book.

closer to Whitman's than is Bunsen's. Much of what Wilkinson and
Bunsen say is drawn from Herodotus, and Whitman might have gone
directly to that source, which was frequently published in English;
one translation, by Henry Cary, was reprinted in New York by Harper in 1855.[10] However, modern historians had access to several other
early sources of information about Egypt, including Diodorus and
Manetho. The prose passage in Whitman's *Notes and Fragments*
which seems to have been used in the poem "Unnamed Lands," first
published in 1860, may have been suggested by Bunsen's Prefaces to
Vol. I and Vol. II.[11] In the section on "Religions—Gods" Whitman
credits Bunsen with dating Zoroaster as far back as 3000 B.C.[12] He
must have got this from Vol. III, p. 583 of *Egypt's Place,* where it is
alleged that the foundation of Zoroastrian doctrine dates back to
between 4000 and 3000 B.C.[13] Another work of Bunsen's that Whitman certainly knew was *Outlines of the Philosophy of Universal History, Applied to Language and Religion,* published in English in two
volumes in 1854. Several notes from that work have survived in manuscripts now in the Trent Collection and printed with some omissions
in *Notes and Fragments.* These notes are in black ink on pink paper
like one type of the wrappers used on the 1855 edition of *Leaves of
Grass,* and were therefore probably made after June 1855. The sheet
containing these notes bears the superscription "resume (from Bunsen)," and beside the paragraph on the inscriptions at Sinai (the last
paragraph of the item) is the reference "Bunsen, p. 231)." Both of
these references are omitted in *Notes and Fragments.* I think it likely
that he had read widely in Vol. 1 at least.[14] I can cite no specific references from Vol. II, in which Bunsen discusses the origin of language,
the great language systems, and evidence in language of the unity of

[10] See pp. 134–35 of that edition. (*Euterpe,* II, 102–10.)
[11] This is the passage in *Complete Writings,* IX, 49–50, beginning "The most
immense part of ancient history is altogether unknown."
[12] *Ibid.,* p. 211.
[13] There is a newspaper clipping (Bucke's No. 104) on "Bunsen's Chronology" in
the Trent Collection that contains some statistics evidently borrowed from Bunsen's *Egypt's Place,* Vols. I and II, which deal at great length with Egyptian chronology and in such detail that I doubt if Whitman would have had the patience
to read very much of it. He may not have read any of Vols. IV and V. Vol. I was
published in 1848, II in 1854, III in 1859, IV in 1860, and V in 1867, after Bunsen's
death.
[14] See *Complete Writings,* IX, 51–52, and Bunsen's *Outlines,* Vol. I, pp. 190, 193–
94, 201–2, 211, and 231. Another manuscript which has "Bunsen" written at the
top of the sheet (*Complete Writings,* IX, 214) containing the sentence "Abrahamic
movement 28th or 29th century before Christ" may derive either from Bunsen's
Outlines, I, 227, or *Egypt's Place,* III, 351. The note on Buddhism is from *Outlines,*
I, 341.

the human race, but Whitman's ideas on language and religion might well have been influenced by Bunsen's theories developed in this volume.

The beginning of Whitman's interest in India is of uncertain date. From the first issue of the *Whig Review*, May 1845, he clipped an article by J. D. Whelpley called "The Laws of Menu," which was in fact a review of Sir William Jones's translation of the *Institutes of Menu*. Some of the notes on India in the section of *Notes and Fragments* on religions and gods might have derived from this article, but it is more likely that they were taken from a dictionary or encyclopedia. Another note, printed in *Notes and Fragments*, "Menu son or grandson of Brahma and first of created beings," was undoubtedly drawn from Thoreau's *A Week on the Concord and Merrimack Rivers*, and therefore dates from 1856.[15] Whelpley states that he was thought to be the grandson of Brahma. Another clipping, "Indian Epic Poetry," from the *Westminster Review* for October 1848, was the source of Whitman's notes on the *Ramayána* and the *Mahabhárata*.[16] I have not seen this clipping. I suppose it was cut in 1848, but whether the notes were made then or later I cannot say; I suspect it was later. I find no positive evidence that Whitman had read much on Hindu literature before 1855. In "Song of Myself" I find the phrase "to Shastas and Vedas admirant," but these two words could have come from a dictionary or from casual reading.[17] Whitman's interest in reading about Indian literature, as was the case with Egypt, was primarily in the development of language. There is a clipping from an unidentified newspaper on the "Sanscrit Professorship at Cambridge" dated April 1849 which Bucke says is annotated, but I have not seen it. Whitman told Thoreau, who visited him in October 1856, that he had not read anything of Oriental literature, though he surely had read some reviews and extracts of poetry. It was then that Thoreau gave him a copy of his *A Week*, from which he made a number of clippings, including some on Indian literature. The earliest poem of *Leaves of Grass* that reflects any specific knowledge of Indian literature is "Salut au Monde!" (first published in 1856). Line 92 of that

[15] *Complete Writings*, IX, 212 and X, 8.

[16] *Ibid.*, IX, 229. Several review articles on Sanscrit poetry appeared in the British quarterlies around 1830–32, but I think it unlikely that Whitman read them.

[17] Section 43, line 9. The usual spelling was "Shastras," though some writers on India used Whitman's spelling. The spelling "Shaster" can also be found. In *Notes and Fragments* the section on religions and gods (*Complete Writings*, IX, 212) contains the word "Shastras," listed along with Pouranas and Vedas as Indian sacred books. Whelpley's article says that in Sanscrit the word "shastra" means "any inspired work."

poem reads: "I see the falling of the Ganges over the high rim of Sankara." The most likely source of this line is a translation of some lines from the Ramayána in "Indian Epic Poetry": "Falling from heaven upon peaks of Sancara, and thence falling upon the earth." Most of the newspaper clippings on India relate to the mutiny of native troops against the British army in 1857. He published an editorial on "British Rule in India" in the Brooklyn *Times*, August 8, 1857. He saved a newspaper clipping of Emerson's poem "Brahma," reprinted from the *Atlantic Monthly* for October 1857, and in the *Times* of November 16, 1857, he wrote in explanation of the poem: "The name of the poem is a facile key to it; Brahma, the Indian Deity, is the absolute and omnipresent god, besides [beside?] whom all is illusion and fancy, and to whom everything apparent reverts in the end." [18] Whitman owned a copy of William Rounseville Alger's book *The Poetry of the East*, which the author gave him in Boston, presumably in 1860, and he said he had read the Introduction "over and over again." This would have given him considerable knowledge of Hindu literature and also something of Persian and other poetry of the East.[19] Alger mentions the 1848 *Westminster Review* article on "Indian Epic Poetry" that Whitman clipped and calls it "very valuable." Alger then quotes from the article two long selections of verse, one from the *Ramayána* and the other from the *Mahabhârata*. In *Notes and Fragments* Whitman has notes on this article, which evidently he had read with some care. From the article he derived the following sentence: "The style of a great poem must flow on 'unhasting and unresting.' "[20] In conversations with Edward Carpenter in 1877, Whitman "told the story of Yudisthura," an episode of the *Ramayána*, which is related in the clipping and also in Alger's book.[21] Another brief passage from the *Ramayána* concludes Alger's quotation. It tells how a Brahmin enters the arena of a tournament

> . . . wearing his white raiment, and the white sacrificial cord,
> With his snow-white hair and his silvery beard, and the white
>   garland round his head,
> Into the midst of the arena slowly walked the Brahmin with his son,
> Like the sun with the planet Mars in a cloudless sky.

[18] Reprinted in *I Sit and Look Out*, p. 64.

[19] See Horace L. Traubel's article "Notes on the Text of *Leaves of Grass* in the *Conservator*, IX (March 1898), 9–11. Whitman's note on the flyleaf states that it was given to him "in Boston it must have been in 1861—or '2." Evidently this note was made long after he received the book.

[20] *Complete Writings*, IX, 229.

[21] See *Days with Walt Whitman* (New York, 1906), p. 23. See also *The Poetry of the East*, Introduction, pp. 38–45.

Whitman must have had this incident from the *Ramayána* in mind when on the night of October 28, 1876, seeing Jupiter in a cloudless sky with "a little star for companion," he wrote, quoting imperfectly from memory or consciously revising to suit his own experience:

> Clothed in his white garments,
> Into the round and clear arena slowly entered the brahmin,
> Holding a little child by the hand,
> Like the moon with the planet Jupiter in a cloudless night-sky.[22]

Another quotation occurs in "The Bible as Poetry" as follows:

> One terrible to see—blood-red his garb,
> His body huge and dark, bloodshot his eyes,
> Which flamed like suns beneath his turban cloth,
> Arm'd was he with a noose.[23]

This portion of the *Mahabhárata* is not translated in "Indian Epic Poetry." It may be Whitman's verses are a variation of the version of the lines as given by Sir Edwin Austin, describing Yama, the god of Death:

> Red his garments were,
> His body vast and dark; like fiery suns
> The eyes which burned beneath his forehead-cloth;
> Armed was he with a noose, awful of mien.[24]

In the same conversation with Carpenter Whitman "spoke of 'Sakuntala,' its 'modernness'—the comic scenes especially being as of the times of Shakespeare." This might have been derived from "The Hindu Drama," a review of several books, including Monier Williams's translation of the *Sakoontala; or the Lost Ring,* an episode from the *Mahabhárata* by the Indian dramatist Kalidasa. The review discusses the comic characters of the play and compares them to some Shakespearean characters. The reviewer refers to Kalidasa as the "Hindu Shakespeare."[25] Only scattered lines from the play are quoted in the review and I doubt that Whitman had read more than these quotations. Carpenter does not say that he had read the play.

[22] *Specimen Days (Prose Works 1892,* I, 134). The manuscript, in pencil, originally had "Mars" instead of Jupiter, and "brahmin" is inserted in ink.

[23] *November Boughs (Prose Works 1892,* II, 547).

[24] *Indian Idylls, from the Sanscrit of the Mahabhárata* (Boston, 1883), p. 34. I first pointed out this parallel in my notes to Whitman's verses in *Prose Works 1892,* cited in note 22.

[25] *Westminster Review,* LXVII (April 1857), 200 and 208 especially.

Alger discusses the *Sakuntala* briefly and calls it "the 'As You Like It' of the Eastern Shakespeare." The two different spellings of the title tell us nothing as to Whitman's reading, since he never mentioned it in his published writing or in *Notes and Fragments*. In "A Backward Glance o'er Travel'd Roads" he names "the ancient Hindoo poems" along with Homer and Dante among the works he had read in "the best translated versions" he could get, but it is incredible that he should have read all of the almost interminable epic poems.[26] He had undoubtedly read some short poems and a few extracts from the epics, but this reading could hardly have been sufficient to contribute substantially to the philosophy of *Leaves of Grass*. It is possible that Whitman's verse form in *Leaves of Grass* owed something to the long lines, some rhymed and some unrhymed, of the translations printed in "Indian Epic Poetry," but insofar as he was influenced by Hindu ideas, the influence came chiefly through Emerson and Thoreau and their contemporaries and reached him at second or third hand.[27]

Whitman's reading about ancient Persia was not extensive and seems to have been ancillary to his interest in Egypt and Greece.[28] He mentions Zoroaster two or three times in *Notes and Fragments*, but only to give his date in relation to Menu, Moses, and other ancient notables. In his notes on English history he observes that some writers identify the Celts with the Persians and the Irish language with a Persian dialect.[29] The Persian poets and poetry of the Middle Ages interested him somewhat more, but he never admired them as Emerson and Thoreau had done. In *Notes and Fragments* he comments briefly on Ferdousi, Hafiz, and Sadi, giving Sadi the date

[26] *Prose Works 1892*, II, 722.

[27] Caleb Wright, who had traveled extensively in India and had lectured widely on Indian customs, wrote a book on *India and Its Inhabitants* which was published in 1852 and often reprinted. It contains many of his lectures, and also a long "Description of the Shasters," by J. J. Weitbrecht, long a resident of India, with specimen pages from the Vedas, the Upanishads, and other sacred writings of the Hindus. "Shasters" here is evidently a variant spelling of "Shastras."

[28] In his article on "The Egyptian Museum" in *Life Illustrated* he said that Egypt was conquered by the Persians under Cambyses in 525 B.C., and long remained a Persian satrapy; both countries being conquered by Alexander the great about 332. He may have got this information from Lepsius, *Letters from Egypt, Ethiopia* (1843), pp. 251–52. This book is listed in the catalogue of the Brooklyn Library published in 1878.

[29] *Complete Writings*, X, 40–41. The notes were taken from *The Pictorial History of England*, by George L. Craik and others, I (New York, 1846), 13. The Brooklyn Library had this work, and he may have read it there.

"about 1000 A.D."[30] The *Whig Review* for January 1849 contained an article on "Ferdousi the Persian Poet" that Whitman probably saw. It is based on James Atkinson's translation (abridged) of Ferdousi's *The Shah Námeh* and critical comments, which was published in 1832. Whether Whitman had read this book I cannot say, but I think it unlikely. He had read some or all of the selections from Persian poets in W. R. Alger's *Poetry of the East*, but this reading was probably too late to have influenced the early *Leaves*.

Although Whitman preserved a number of newspaper and magazine clippings on China, he was less interested in ancient Chinese culture than in that of Egypt or India. It was the emergence of China and Japan as modern nations that interested him. He does mention Confucius twice in *Notes and Fragments*,[31] but only to fix his date in relation to Socrates and others. He preserved a clipping of the article "The Central Nation" in the *American Whig Review* for April 1852 (No. 229 on Bucke's list), which was a review of several books on China. The reviewer makes the statement that "this eastern extremity of civilization in the old world will one day freely answer back to the western; and the unity of the human race, which has been so slow in its dawn upon the human condition, will be seen and felt in China, to the overthrow of its powerfully cemented exclusiveness." This would have interested Whitman and supported views later expressed in *Leaves of Grass*.

Whitman's interest in the history of ancient Greece and Rome may have begun before his reading about Egypt and India, and it was more lasting. He preserved a clipping (Bucke's No. 113, "Early Roman History") from the *Western Review*, of Columbus, Ohio, for April 1846 (the only issue published), of a review of the first two volumes of B. G. Niebuhr's *History of Rome* and the first two volumes of Thomas Arnold's *History of Rome*. The clipping is annotated by Whitman in pencil and in ink. A note in pencil on a strip of paper pasted to the first page of the clipping reads: *"See to Roman History. I discover that I need a thorough posting up in what Rome and the Romans were."*[32] Whitman brackets a passage stating that Roman history has been perverted and made "the armory from which the priests and advocates and soldiers of oppression have drawn their

[30] *Complete Writings,* X, 8 and 14. These references are drawn from Thoreau and Carlyle. See my article "Notes on Whitman's Reading," *American Literature,* XXVI (Nov. 1954), 359–61.

[31] *Complete Writings,* IX, 99 and X, 9.

[32] This is printed by Bucke in *Notes and Fragments (Complete Writings,* X, 35), but he does not there mention the review.

craftiest maxims, their foulest pleas, and their sharpest weapons, to be used in the service of their god." In the margin Whitman comments, sarcastically no doubt: "good American doctrine." The reviewer blames the teaching of Roman history "for conventionalisms, and disregard of abstract right, upon which are based the crying sins of our age." He attributes Rome's sway to "the great practical energy of the Roman people, and the absence of many of the higher qualities of pure intellect." In the margin beside this passage Whitman wrote in pencil: "America *now* of all lands has the greatest practical energy. —(But has it not also the highest infusion of pure intellect?)" Under this pencil note a line is drawn in ink and in ink these words are written: "Well, if it has, does it not want something *besides* intellect? What are you after in people? merely their intellect?" The annotation in ink is undoubtedly of later date than the one in pencil. Whitman also brackets and draws a hand pointing to these words in the review: ". . . a people never swerving from their purpose, and more resolute in the hour of defeat than in that of triumph." An extra wavy line is drawn under that part of the phrase beginning with the words "more resolute," and at the top of the page he wrote in pencil: "A man 'more resolute in the hour of defeat than in that of triumph,'" evidently applying the quotation to himself. This annotation I believe was also later than most of the penciled annotations, and may have been as late as 1856, when he was somewhat discouraged over the reception of *Leaves of Grass*. Beside a passage stating that "the old annalists glossed over the degradation of their country, after the true Roman fashion, which never hesitated at a falsehood, no matter how egregious likely to minister to their ambition, their vanity, or their avarice," Whitman wrote sarcastically: "important hint for American historians." Below a passage describing the usefulness of Etruscan public works and monuments, Whitman wrote: "Is not our putting up of 'monuments,' statues to Washington, &c., a poor relic of the old Asiatic, Greek, or Roman spirit?" At the top of a page praising Frederick Schlegel's *History of Literature*, Whitman wrote in pencil: "Get 'History of Literature,' by Fr. Schlegel."[33]

The author of the *Western Review* article calls Niebuhr the greatest of the historians of Rome in a passage that Whitman marked, and he evidently continued his interest in Niebuhr because he clipped a

[33] Whitman's annotations, with some exceptions, are printed by Bucke in *Notes and Fragments (Complete Writings*, IX, 215–16). Bucke omits some marginal annotations that merely summarize passages in the review, but he also omits the two sarcastic comments and the reminder to himself to get Schlegel's *History of Literature*. Whitman's reference to "monuments" might help to date his comment, since the cornerstone of the Washington monument was laid in 1848.

review-essay on Niebuhr and his various works on Roman history from the American edition of the *North British Review*, issue of February 1849. Whitman made only a few marks on this clipping, including a penciled note on the first page calling Niebuhr the "founder of a new theory of history." Another evidence of his continued interest in Niebuhr is a paragraph that Bucke printed in *Notes and Fragments* giving a few biographical facts and adding that he "became the great reformer of Roman History (and ancient History generally)." These notes were based on page 249 of Joseph Gostwick's 1854 edition of *German Literature*.[34] Whitman may have read these reviews in the late 1840's or early 1850's, but there is no mention of Rome or the Romans in his prose or poetry before the 1856 edition of *Leaves of Grass*.

Many scholars have supposed that Whitman read Homer as a boy or a young man in the late 1840's. The basis of this belief is probably Whitman's own statement about shouting Homer and Shakespeare on the beach at Coney Island or from the tops of omnibuses in New York City;[35] yet I find no evidence in his earlier writing that he had read either the *Iliad* or the *Odyssey* before 1855. Buckley's prose translation of the *Iliad*, which he read "first thoroughly on the peninsula of Orient, northeast end of Long Island," was first published in London in 1851, but Whitman read it in the Bohn edition, London, 1857, or, most likely, in the Harper Classical library edition also published in 1857.[36] The *Odyssey* as translated by Buckley was published in London by Bohn in 1855 and reprinted several times. It was reprinted by Harper in 1859. He might, of course, have read selections from Pope's translations, but he disliked them so heartily that it is unlikely that he read much of them.

He preserved a clipping of C. A. Bristed's article on "Translators of Homer" from the *Whig Review* for October 1846 (Bucke's No. 404), and made some annotations on it. When he first read this article there is no way of knowing, but his annotations were probably made in 1856 and 1857. The article is a review of William Munford's translation of the *Iliad*, published in 1846. After a few introductory pages it is devoted to a comparison of passages from Munson's translation with translations of the same passages by Chapman, Pope, Cowper,

---

34 *Complete Writings*, IX, 116. Whitman gives credit to this book and cites pp. 249–51, but all his notes are from p. 249. At one time he probably owned a copy, since it is not listed in the catalogues of the Brooklyn Library.

35 *Specimen Days (Prose Works 1892*, I, 12 and 18).

36 "A Backward Glance," *Prose Works 1892*, II, 722. The place indicated by Whitman was probably in the general area of Greenport, where his sister Mary lived.

and Sotheby. Two passages in the introductory part are annotated by Whitman. In the first, Bristed writes: "Great poets are usually great translators. There is Pope, and Byron, and Shelley, and Coleridge, &c." In the margin next to this sentence Whitman writes: "The greatest poets can never be translators of the poetry of others—that is in any other way than Shakespeare translated—which was by taking the poor or tolerable stuff of others and making it incomparable." Later in the article, after naming nine complete English translations of Homer, Bristed adds: "Of partial translations from one book to ten the number is very considerable. A friend recently enumerated to us eleven, to which we were able to add five, and there is little doubt that the list might be still further extended." At the bottom of the page on which these statements occur, Whitman notes: "16 English translations of Homer, and more, besides." Here he seems to have been confused as between complete and partial translations.

Bucke prints these annotations in *Notes and Fragments* as the last two items in Section 18 of Part III.[37] Preceding these in the same section are two other items that Bucke derived from other Whitman notes. He put them with the notes in the Bristed article because he perceived that they related, directly or indirectly, to the translations of Homer. The first of these notes reads as follows: "Leigh Hunt—born 1784— is he now living? aged 72. Yes (July, '57) he lives, old and in fair condition, in London, aged 73. Died, Aug., '59, aged 75." I cannot be sure where Whitman got these facts about Hunt, whose *Autobiography* was published in 1850, and was reviewed January, 1851, in the *Whig Review*. One other indication of the date of these notes is the fact that a clipping of a page of translations of Pindar from Thoreau's *A Week on the Concord and Merrimack Rivers*, which Thoreau gave Whitman in 1856, is fastened to the Bristed clipping. Another clipping on translations of the *Iliad* is also attached to it. This may, in part, be the source of the second item in Bucke's *Notes and Fragments*, which reads: "Hexameter translation of Homer—Prof. Newman's translation. Get Buckley's prose trans. of Iliad —republished here by Harper." Newman's translation, published in London in 1856, is in unrhymed verse, but not hexameters. There is in Bristed's review a brief passage, apparently his own translation, in hexameters. There is also a brief article on "The Hexameter and the Pentameter," by Carl Benson, in the *Whig Review* for November 1846, which Whitman must have seen. Benson wrote that "at present two hexametrical translations of the Iliad are in course of publication in England." *Blackwood's Magazine* for March 1846 published a translation of the twenty-fourth book of the *Iliad* in English hexameters, and in the May number, at the Editor's request, a similar translation of the first book, both signed "N. N. T." The issues for July, September, and October 1846 contain "Letters on English Hexameters," in which these translations are discussed. C. C. Felton mentions these *Blackwood* translations, which he says were done "with fair success."[38] These notes have been dwelt on at length because they strongly indicate that Whitman had little if any direct knowledge of Homer's works before 1855.[39] The notes on the *Iliad*, the Bible, the Aeschylean tragedies, and Shakespeare's tragedies, published in *Notes and Fragments,* are written in ink on small blue sheets cut from blank forms of the Williamsburg Tax Assessor's office, and therefore date from 1855 or later.[40]

Whitman probably first read the *Odyssey* in Buckley's prose translation, published by Bohn. A copy of this edition, or a reprint of it, was in Whitman's library at the time of his death.[41] He also had the edition of Pope's translation of the *Odyssey* with notes by the Rev. T. A. Buckley and Flaxman's designs, published in London by F. Warne & Co., in the Chandos Classics series. The British Museum catalogue lists this edition as first published in London, 1875.[42] A letter of Whitman's to an unnamed person whom he salutes as "My

[38] *Greece, Ancient and Modern* (Boston, 1866), I, 103–5. Whitman may have seen these *Blackwood* translations.

[39] Whitman brackets the sentence in Bristed's article stating that Chapman was the first translator of Homer, 1600, but makes no note on it. However, in the notes on Shakespeare in Section 27 of Part II of *Notes and Fragments (Complete Writings,* IX, 71) Bucke records this pencilled note, obviously out of place, "Chapman's translation of Homer printed 1600," which might have derived from the Bristed review.

[40] *Complete Writings,* IX, 100. Whitman acquired a large supply of these unused forms, presumably in 1855, or late in 1854, after Williamsburg was legally united with Brooklyn, and for an indeterminate time, perhaps two or three years, used them as note paper.

[41] See the *Catalog of an Exhibition of the Works of Walt Whitman* (Detroit, 1955), p. 123. It bears this inscription in Whitman's autograph: "Walt Whitman, posses'd by me from 1868 to 1888 and read by me during those times—some times in Washington & sometimes in Camden—small or larger readings—often in Camp or Army Hospitals. Walt Whitman." The catalogue gives the date of publication as 1863, but the description corresponds exactly to the Library of Congress description of the 1855 edition. I have not found an 1863 edition listed. The edition of the Harper Classical Library is dated 1861. Whitman must have inadvertently written "1868" for "1858," since he read it in Army camps.

[42] The *Exhibition* catalogue gives no date, but the description fits the British Museum catalogue description of the 1875 edition in the Chandos Classics.

dear friend," dated June 9, 1865, begins with the sentence, "The Homer has come & is now lying before me. I thank you deeply."[43] The editor assumes that the "dear friend" is John Swinton, and in a footnote suggests that the "*Homer*" is Buckley's translation of the *Odyssey* which was in his library when he died, but Whitman told Traubel in 1888 that "John Swinton sent me Derby's translation of Homer."[44] When Whitman refers to a work of Homer as "Homer," without naming a title, he usually means the *Iliad*, as here. The Earl of Derby made no translation of the *Odyssey* so far as I have found. Whitman's article "Walt Whitman in Camden," published in the *Critic*, February 28, 1885, under the pseudonym "George Selwyn," describing Whitman's room and books, mentions "a nook devoted to translations of Homer and AEschylus and the other Greek poets and tragedians."[45] Horace Traubel concluded from his talks with Whitman that he was "very familiar with the formal classics in a general way."[46] In addition to the works of Homer mentioned above, his library contained an edition of the *Tragedies of Euripides*, translated by Buckley (London, Bell & Daldy, 2 vols., 1866), and Volume II of Buckley's translation as published by Harper in 1857. The latter, he notes on a flyleaf, he had in Washington and Camden "altogether all of 20 years."[47] Whitman also had at his death a copy of *The Odes of Anacreon*, translated by Thomas Moore, which was given him in 1877, and a copy of *The Odes of Pindar*, literally translated into English prose by Dawson W. Turner, originally published in 1852 (Bohn's Classical Library). At one time he owned a copy of the *Works of Hesiod, Callimachus, and Theognis*, literally translated into English prose by the Rev. J. Banks, published in the Bohn Classical Library in 1856. This volume is now in the Van Sinderen Collection at Yale University. He learned something of Epicurus early by reading Fanny Wright's *A Few Days in Athens*. He told Traubel that he had bought a secondhand copy of a book by Epictetus and had read it at the age of sixteen.[48] This is puzzling, because the earliest English translation of Epictetus that he is likely to have seen was that of George Long, published in Bohn's Classical Library in 1848, and re-

---

43 *Correspondence*, I, 263.

44 *WWC*, I, 126. This would have been the blank verse translation of the *Iliad* by Edward, Earl of Derby, originally published in 2 vols. in London in 1864, reprinted as 2 vols. in 1 in New York in 1866 and in Philadelphia in 1867.

45 Reprinted in *UPP*, II, 58–62.

46 *WWC*, II, 332.

47 *Catalog of an Exhibition*, p. 123. The two-volume edition must have been acquired late.

48 *WWC*, II, 71–72.

printed without date in Philadelphia, probably much later. T. W. H. Rolleston translated the *Encheiridion* of Epictetus in 1881 and sent Whitman a copy, which he read assiduously during the 1880's.[49] I have noted elsewhere that Whitman's notes on Plutarch and on Lycurgus in *Notes and Fragments* were taken from John and William Langhorne's edition of *Plutarch's Lives,* especially the editors' Preface and biography of Plutarch, but also apparently some of Plutarch's biographies.[50] Plutarch's biographies are mentioned a number of times in Whitman's later writings, but there is no specific evidence that he remembered or had read them.

Much of Whitman's knowledge of Greek history in his old age was derived from George Grote's *History of Greece,* which he probably read in one of the Harper reprints, of which there were several between 1851 and 1859. The first Harper edition contained only the first eight volumes, but that was all of the London edition that had been issued at that time. Harper added others as soon as they were published in London, Vols. 9 and 10 in 1853, 11 in 1855, and 12 in 1856. In 1857 Harper reprinted the entire 12 volumes. Whitman probably had only the first eight, for he told Traubel in 1888 that Grote's history contained not one volume only, "or even two or three, but eight or nine: I have read them all—carefully, fully, more than once—more deliberately than usual with me."[51] If he bought them as soon as published by Harper, it was probably in 1852, or 1853 at the latest. He might, of course, have picked them up secondhand later, obviously thinking he had a complete set. I doubt if he had read the volumes as carefully as he said, or else he read them after he had lost the habit of taking notes. I have been able to trace very few of his notes to Grote.[52] I think his interest in Grote was primarily in

49 See Whitman's letter to Rolleston dated Dec. 2 (*Correspondence,* III, 254); see also *WWC,* I, 207, 337, and later volumes, *passim.*

50 See my "Notes on Whitman's Reading," previously cited. The Langhorne edition was reprinted by Harper in 1844, but Whitman probably read the later reprint published in Cincinnati in 1854 and 1855. Whitman's notes are in *Complete Writings,* IX, 126.

51 *WWC,* I, 39–40.

52 Perhaps some of the notes in *Complete Writings,* IX, 98–99, were from Chapter LXVII, on the Drama, in Vol. 8. The reference to dating time by Greek olympiads (IX, 214) could have been derived from Grote's Preface, I, p. vii. One reference (X, 16) citing Grote, II, 383, in reference to Aeschylus, is incorrect. Almost certainly the reference should be to I, 383, which, together with some pages before and after, is concerned with Aeschylus. He probably was familiar with Grote's account of Greek myths, gods, and legends in Vol. I, and he certainly read his account of Homer and the Homeric poems in Vol. II. Vols. III–VII, which deal almost exclusively with history, may have been read very little or not at all. The Feinberg Collection contains two notebooks on his Homeric studies based chiefly

what he had to say of Greek literature, for in a later conversation
with Traubel he refers to these books as "Grote's History of Greek
Literature."[53]

In his later years Whitman owned a copy of C. C. Felton's *Greece,
Ancient and Modern*, lectures delivered before the Lowell Institute
between 1851 and 1860. Whitman probably learned more from Felton's lecture on Homer, which he told Traubel was the best, than he
did from Grote.[54] In *Notes and Fragments* he cites page references to
passages in Volume I on Aeschylus, Sophocles, Hesiod, and Tyr-
taeus.[55] We can be sure, therefore, that he read the first half of this
volume, incorporating the first course of lectures, on Greek language
and literature. However, since Felton's book was not published until
1867, it could have had no influence on the early poems. In any case,
he had already read, most likely, all of Homer's work that he would
ever read. At this time he was interested in Homer chiefly as a great
poet, representative of his time and culture, as he considered himself
representative of his time and culture. He may have read Friedrich
Schlegel's *Philosophy of History*, which he mentions in a biographical note on Schlegel,[56] but his notes there are drawn from Joseph
Gostwick's 1854 edition of *German Literature* (p. 279). He had read
parts, perhaps all, of Schlegel's *Lectures on the History of Literature*,
for the two paragraphs in *Notes and Fragments* beginning, "Plato
treated philosophy as an *art*—Aristotle as a *science*," were drawn almost literally from that work.[57]

There is a great deal in this book that Whitman would have found
intensely interesting, including medieval as well as Greek and Latin
literature. Indeed, he may have been led to read Lucretius by what
Schlegel said of him as a poet of nature and science.[58] It is unlikely
that Lucretius influenced Whitman in writing *Leaves of Grass*,

---

on Grote, Vols. II and III. (See the *Catalog of an Exhibition of the Works of Walt
Whitman*, p. 14. The cataloguer dates these 1872.)

[53] *WWC*, IV, 109.

[54] *WWC*, V, 306. "I am reminded of an expression of Felton's—C. C. Felton's—in
one of his lectures on Greek literature—the best lecture of the lot, that on Homer:
. . . 'The great poet is a rare bird.' "

[55] *Complete Writings*, X, 16.

[56] *Complete Writings*, IX, 120–21. These notes were written on the blue paper
cut from the tax forms of the city of Williamsburg.

[57] *Complete Writings*, X, 16. He might have quoted from the Langley edition,
New York, 1841 (pp. 99 f.) or, more probably, the Bohn Library edition, London,
1859 (pp. 82 f.).

[58] In *Democratic Vistas* (*Prose Works 1892*, II, 421) he wrote: "What the Roman
Lucretius sought most nobly, yet all too blindly, negatively to do for his age and
its successors, must be done positively by some great coming literatus, especially

though the two had much in common. Whitman, at one time, possessed a copy of *De Rerum Natura* in the translation of the Rev. J. S. Watson published in 1851, and made a brief outline of its six books and commented on its main ideas.[59] These notes were made on stationery from the Attorney General's office, where he began to work in 1865, and so could hardly have been made before that year, and might have been made three or four years later.[60] The Feinberg Collection contains a 12-page notebook on Plato. The notes are all apparently from Vol. I of the 1858 Bohn Library edition in 6 vols. Only Volume I was translated by Henry Cary.[61]

As we have seen, Whitman developed his literary taste on the novels of Scott, the historical plays of Shakespeare, and other novels and plays featuring the stirring life of medieval and feudal times in England, and his reading of the poems of Ossian in the 1840's stimulated his interest in primitive poetry. He read Shakespeare and Ossian more carefully in the 1850's with a deeper appreciation of the former and a clearer understanding of the genuine element of primitiveness in the latter.[62] Throughout his mature life he maintained an ambivalent attitude toward Shakespeare's plays and Scott's novels. He loved their heroic action, the pageantry of kings, the rhetorical flourishes, and the poetry of the plays, but he acknowledged that they were antagonistic and "poisonous" to American democracy.[63] In "Poetry To-day in America," he condemns Scott, along with Shakespeare and Tennyson, for exhaling "that principle of caste which we Americans have come

---

poet, who, while remaining fully poet, will absorb whatever science indicates, with spiritualism, and out of them, and out of his own genius, will compose the great poem of death."

[59] For more details, see Gay Wilson Allen, *The Solitary Singer* (New York, 1955), pp. 139–40. These manuscript notes are in the Library of Congress. (See the catalogue of the Walt Whitman Collection, item 107.)

[60] The portion of *Democratic Vistas* in which the statement about Lucretius appears was not in the two component essays published in the *Galaxy* in 1867 and 1868, but in the last section, which was probably written in 1868 or 1869.

[61] See the *Catalog of an Exhibition of the Works of Walt Whitman*, p. 7.

[62] Commenting in *Notes and Fragments* (*Complete Writings*, IX, 94–95) on an "Ossianic paragraph" in one of Margaret Fuller's letters to her mother, published in *Memoirs of Margaret Fuller Ossoli* (Boston, 1852), Whitman says: "Ossian must not be despised," and yet he adds that it is "misty," "windy," and "full of diffused, only half-meaning words," and warns himself not to "fall into the Ossianic, *by any chance.*" This was apparently written after he had begun to compose the poems first published in the 1855 edition, probably in 1854 or 1855.

[63] For examples see the *Eagle*, April 26, 1847 (*GF*, II, 264–65), the fragment on Voltaire in *Life Illustrated* for May 10, 1856 (*New York Dissected*, ed. Emory Holloway and Ralph Adimari [New York, 1936], p. 71), and many passages in *Democratic Vistas* and later prose.

on earth to destroy," yet in the very next paragraph calls him "the noblest, healthiest, cheeriest romancer that ever lived."[64] Shakespeare's plays and Scott's novels presented the feudal world only in retrospect, and Macpherson's *Ossian* was mostly spurious, but he came closer to it in reading Scott's *Minstrelsy of the Scottish Border.* In "A Backward Glance" he says, "Along in my sixteenth year I had become possessor of a stout, well-cramm'd one thousand page octavo volume (I have it yet,) containing Walter Scott's poetry entire—an inexhaustible mine and treasury of poetic forage (especially the endless forests and jungles of notes)—has been so to me for fifty years, and remains so to this day." In a footnote Whitman implies that this volume was Lockhart's edition of the *Poetical Works,* published in 1833–34. However, that edition, in twelve volumes, illustrated by J. M. W. Turner, was not reprinted in a single volume until 1841, and that contained 823 pages, and did not include any poems from *Minstrelsy of the Scottish Border* except the poems written by Scott in imitation of the authentic poems in his edition. Whitman's volume contained, he says, not only Scott's poems, but the whole of *Minstrelsy of the Scottish Border,* and in addition "all the dramas; various Introductions, endless interesting Notes, and Essays on Poetry, Romance, &c."[65] In an interview printed under the heading "Personal," in *Harper's Weekly* for April 23, 1887, Whitman said, "The only poetry that had nourished him was Sir Walter Scott's Border Minstrelsy, particularly Sir Walter's memoranda of interviews with old Scotsmen and Scotswomen respecting the folk-lore of their earlier days. The folk-lore of witchcraft was especially interesting to him." The only single volume of Scott's works that contains all that Whitman said he found in the one he owned is Volume I of the seven-volume edition of Scott's *Complete Works,* published in New York by Conner & Cooke in 1834.[66] If Whitman remembered the time correctly he came into possession of this volume in 1834 or 1835. Since he did not own the other volumes, I suspect he picked it up secondhand, possibly a little later.

Other works that Whitman mentions as part of literary "heredita-

[64] *Prose Works 1892,* II, pp. 476–77.

[65] *Ibid.,* II, 722–23.

[66] The date on the title page is 1833, but the prefixed "Advertisement," signed "Conner and Cooke," is dated July 1834. The text of Scott's poems is the same as that of Lockhart's edition of 1833, 34. Another "advertisement" preceding the first section, *Minstrelsy of the Scottish Border,* is signed "J.G.L." and dated London, March 12, 1833. There is no essay in the volume on poetry, so titled, but Whitman probably had in mind Scott's essay on the Drama, which is concerned chiefly, though not exclusively, with the poetic drama, classical and modern. The volume also contains Scott's ten letters to J. C. Lockhart that later constituted his essay

ments" of European feudalism and chivalry, and presumably known
to him, were "Percy's collection, Ellis's early English Metrical Romances, the European continental poems of Walter of Aquitania, and
the Nibelungen, of pagan stock, but monkish-feudal redaction; the
history of the Troubadours, by Fauriel; even the far-back cumbrous
old Hindu epics, as indicating the Asian eggs out of which European
chivalry was hatch'd; Ticknor's chapters on the Cid, and on the Spanish poems and poets of Calderon's time." [67] So far as I know Whitman
did not own a copy of Bishop Percy's *Reliques of Ancient English
Poetry*, but he undoubtedly knew it in some form, and in his essay
"Walt Whitman in Camden" he said he had "a collection of the works
of Fauriel and Ellis on medieval poetry." [68] Whitman said to Traubel,
speaking of Percy's *Reliques*: "It takes you in to the birth of man: it
is always a young book." [69] C. C. Fauriel's *Histoire de la Poesie Provençale* was published in Paris in 1846, in three volumes. In 1860
George J. Adler published a translation, in a single volume of 496
pages, of most of Volume I and part of Volume II, including Fauriel's
chapters on the *Nibelungenlied*, on Walther of Aquitaine, and on
Provençale lyric poetry, which apparently were the portions in which
Whitman was most interested. This was undoubtedly the edition
owned by Whitman.[70] Whitman clipped a review of the original edition of Fauriel's book, along with several others, entitled "Provençal
and Scandinavian Poetry," from the *Edinburgh Review* for July 1848.
This clipping (Bucke's No. 330) was the basis for most of Whitman's
notes from Fauriel.[71] He also clipped "Littérature du Moyen Age"
(Bucke's No. 311), a review of A. F. Villemain's book by the same title,
from the *Westminster Review* for July 1849, and made a few notes on
it.[72] There is no reason to suppose he had seen Villemain's book,
which had not been translated into English. Traubel says Whitman
handed him his copy of George Ellis's *Specimens of Early English*

"Demonology and Witchcraft," and two or three other short essays. There are 828
pages of the poems, the dramas, and the *Minstrelsy*. The other materials are separately paged, amounting to 247 pages, making a total of 1,075. This edition is not
listed in the catalogues of the Library of Congress and the British Museum.

[67] From *Democratic Vistas* (*Prose Works 1892*, II, 366).

[68] Published in the *Critic*, Feb. 28, 1885, under the pseudonym of "George Selwyn" (reprinted in *UPP*, II, 58–62). An 1855 edition of Percy's *Reliques* is listed
in the 1877 catalogue of the Brooklyn Library.

[69] *WWC*, I, 127.

[70] Adler's translation has become very rare, but it was reprinted recently by
Haskell House, New York. There was apparently no other English translation of
Fauriel's work.

[71] *Complete Writings*, IX, 228.

[72] *Ibid.*, IX, 90.

Metrical Romances, saying: "I think it better than Percy's Reliques: richer, deeper, larger." At another time Whitman said: "It is a text-book for me—a sort of work-tool. I have made use of it time and again."[73] Just how it was used as a "work-tool" is not clear, but it was certainly a textbook of medieval literature and the fashions of feu-dalism.

Whitman's inclusion of what he terms "the European continental poems of Walter of Aquitania" seems to imply that these, along with the collections of Fauriel and Ellis, were part of his own reading. He could not have read them, of course, because they had not been trans-lated into modern English in his time. There was really only one poem, as in the *Nibelungenlied,* but it existed fragmentarily in many dialects and versions. Of course they were not poems "of" Walter, but about him, for he was a legendary character. The Walther saga de-rived from a combination of myths and historic events in the province or kingdom of Aquitania about the fifth or sixth century and is closely related to the Nibelungen story. The most complete version exists as *Waltherius,* in Latin of the tenth century, but others exist in Gothic, Old Norse, and Polish, as well as fragments in still other lan-guages.[74] It is possible, but not likely, that Whitman confused Wal-ther of Aquitaine with Walther von der Vogelweide, one of the Minnesingers of the late twelfth and early thirteenth century, some of whose many lyrics were available to him in several collections, in-cluding Longfellow's *Poets and Poetry of Europe.* On the other hand, if he read his Fauriel before writing the passage quoted from *Demo-cratic Vistas* he should have known a great deal about the Walther poems, though not the poems themselves, since Chapters XI and XII, which were in Adler's translation, contain a summary and analysis of them and their relation to the Nibelungen poems.

Whitman might have read the whole of the *Nibelungenlied* in the English translation of W. N. Lettson (*The Fall of the Nibelungers,* 1850) which was in the Brooklyn Library, but he probably did not. He undoubtedly read Carlyle's essay on the poem in *Critical and Miscellaneous Essays,* probably in the 1848 edition, and he also read about it and saw translations of portions in Gostwick's *German Lit-erature* (1854). He even versified, in his own way, a brief passage that Gostwick had translated literally.[75]

[73] *WWC,* II, 23, 464.

[74] The fullest account published in Whitman's lifetime is "The Saga of Walther of Aquitaine," ed. M. D. Learned, *PMLA,* VII (1892), vi, 208. This, obviously, was too late to have influenced Whitman.

[75] For other details see my article "Notes on Whitman's Reading," *American Literature,* XXVI (Nov. 1954), 337–52. For Whitman's verses, see *Faint Clews &*

When Whitman acquired George Ticknor's three-volume scholarly *History of Spanish Literature* or how well he knew it, I cannot say. It was originally published in 1849 and was reprinted in 1854 and in 1863, as well as later. I suspect he had the 1854 edition, for he would have been too much engaged with other matters in Washington to have read it in the 1863 edition and he was not yet ready for it earlier than 1854. He made notes from Ticknor's account of *Amadis of Gaul* and the Palmerin Romances.[76] He summarized in his notes a considerable part of Ticknor's extended account of Cervantes, limiting himself almost entirely to biographical facts.[77] Although he mentions Calderon and the "poems and poets" of his time, I do not believe he cared much for any Spanish writer except, perhaps, Cervantes, and I doubt if he read much of *Don Quixote*. I think he read Ticknor merely for self-education. Certainly there is no evidence that his own poems were influenced by any Spanish writer.

Whether Whitman's interest in the early history of France extended beyond Provençal poetry and the legendary stories related to the break-up of the Roman empire, one cannot be sure. At one time he reviewed for the *Eagle*, and presumably read, portions of Jules Michelet's *History of France* in G. H. Smith's translation and made the following comment: "Of the many standard works from his pen, the history of France is on some accounts the best: he appears to have taken pride and pains in making it the fullest and clearest."[78] Gay W. Allen has pointed out several parallels between Whitman's idea of the relation of a poet to the people and Michelet's idea of the relation of a historian to the people.[79] These parallels could be accidental, but more probably they reflect Whitman's acquaintance, more or less, with Michelet's *The People*. Whitman also drew on Michelet's later book, *The Bird* (1869), for some lines of "To the Man-of-War Bird," first published in 1876. The *History of France* relates in considerable detail the events in Western Europe and Britain consequent to the decline of the Roman power there. *The People* and other books of

---

Indirections (1949), pp. 20–22. Most of Whitman's notes on the poem may be found in *Complete Writings*, IX, 83, 117, 187.

76 These notes are on twelve sheets of paper folded to form a small book. They have the label "Literature Romance of the 15th & 16th centuries." They are taken from Chapter XI of the first period of the history, *Complete Writings*, I, 218–40. They are not in *Notes and Fragments*.

77 These notes are based on Chapters X, XI, and XII of the second period, *Complete Writings*, II, 52–119. The notes on Cervantes were printed in *Notes and Fragments* (*Complete Writings*, IX, 64–69).

78 The Brooklyn *Eagle*, April 22, 1847 (reprinted in *UPP*, I, 134).

79 Allen, "Walt Whitman and Jules Michelet," *Etudes Anglaises*, I (May 1937), 230–37, and also the *Walt Whitman Handbook* (Chicago, 1946), pp. 469–72.

Michelet's are advertised in the final pages of the *History of France*. He noticed Guizot's *History of the English Revolution of 1640*, in William Hazlitt's translation, and called it "one of the really valuable books of the age."[80] He may also have known Guizot's *History of Civilization*, also in Hazlitt's translation (four volumes, New York, 1846), the first volume of which has a detailed account of the fall of the Roman Empire. At any rate, he clipped from *Half-Hours with the Best Authors* a selection of about ten pages taken by the editor from Guizot's introductory discussion of the various definitions of "civilization." He seems not to have read Froissart, though he clipped from *Half-Hours* a brief sketch of his life introducing a selection from his works, and in "New York Dissected," an article in *Life Illustrated*, July 12, 1856, he wrote: "As Froissart said of the English, 'We take our pleasure sadly.' "[81]

It is clear that Whitman approached European history chiefly through two main interests: popular literature, especially poetry, and revolutions leading toward a more democratic society.[82] The history of England was naturally a subject of considerable interest, from the point of view of a developing literature and a developing democracy out of which the literature and politics of his own time emerged. The "Notes on English History," published in *Notes and Fragments*, are the most extensive that Whitman preserved on a single topic. They were drawn, with minor exceptions, from the first 138 pages of Vol. I of the *Pictorial History of England* by George L. Craik, Charles MacFarlane, and other contributors, as reprinted by Harper and Brothers in 1846.[83] In a footnote in *Notes and Fragments* Bucke states that these notes "are written on the back of unused copies of the fly-title of the 1855 *Leaves of Grass* which was printed quite early in that year." The notes end abruptly with the year 633, shortly after King Edwin

[80] The Brooklyn *Eagle*, March 5, 1846 (reprinted in *UPP*, I, 132).

[81] Reprinted in *New York Dissected*, p. 84.

[82] In *Notes and Fragments* he makes this comment on D'Israeli's reported statement that a philosopher "would consent to lose any poet to regain an historian": "Then poets must arise to make future D'Israelis unable to say this. Why the best poetry is the *real* history." (*Complete Writings*, IX, 69.)

[83] As originally published this history extended only to the accession of George III in 1760. It was issued by Charles Knight in 44 monthly installments that later were gathered into four volumes. These installments were reprinted by Harpers, and the four large volumes were also reprinted, Vol. I in 1846, Vols. II and III in 1848, and Vol. IV in 1851. It can be established that this was the edition used by Whitman because in two places he mentioned pages on which certain facts were found, and these pages correspond only to the Harper edition. The standard edition of the completed work, which was extended to 1815, was published in 1849, in London, in 8 vols. This was in the Brooklyn Library.

became a Christian and his people after him. I have not seen the manuscripts and do not know whether they are still extant. The notes were probably made in 1855 or earlier; if earlier, they must have been made in a library and later transferred to the unused fly-title leaves. Bucke notes one sentence in the notes that Whitman used in "Salut au Monde!" first published in 1856: "I see where druids walked the groves of Mona, I see the mistletoe and vervain." It appears in the notes as: "I see where Druids walked the groves of Anglesey—I see in their hands the mistletoe and Vervain." In a footnote Bucke says this line in the notes, before revision, read: "I see the Druids in the groves of Anglesey—I see the sprigs of mistletoe and vervain." The revision must have been made before he finished "Salut au Monde!" but the original might have been considerably earlier. I do not know what induced Whitman to make these notes, but I suspect one stimulus was the opera *Norma*, which he heard early in 1854 sung by the incomparable Marietta Alboni. Norma was the high priestess of the Druids, and the setting was at Mona, or Anglesey, during the Roman occupation of Britain. In their barbaric way, the Druids, like the Hebrew prophets, suggested to Whitman the function he would assign to the poets of democracy.[84]

[84] As he intimates in "Poetry To-day in America," *Prose Works 1892*, II, 485–86.

XI. *Primitivism and German Romantic Philosophy*

Whitman's interest in the theory of poetry was greatest during the 1850's, when he was developing his own theory and writing the poems that first appeared in the 1855, 1856, and 1860 editions of *Leaves of Grass*. His theory was derived, in large part, from the study of ancient Biblical poetry and from the German romantic critics and philosophers, sometimes directly and sometimes through English romantic critics and the American Emerson. In primitive times, as he states in *Notes and Fragments*, "bards were the only historians," and through them the struggles and aspirations of the people of those times have been transmitted to our times. Egypt, he declares, "represents that phase of development, advanced childhood, full of belief, rich and divine enough, standing amazed and awed before the mystery of life—nothing more wonderful than life, even in a hawk—a bull or a cat—the masses of the people reverent of priestly and kingly authority." In Indian passiveness he saw the beginning of European feudality; the Greeks illustrated the aesthetic and intellectual development of the race, the Romans the physical and legal, and the Hebrews expressed "the spiritual element, the indefinite, the immortal, sublimity, the realm to which the material tends. . . ." He saw his chances for greatness and estimated them in the light of the past. "Sustenance for the great geniuses of the world is always plenty and the main ingredients of it are perhaps always the same. Yet nothing ever happened to former heroes, sages and poets so inspiring to them, so fit to shine resplendent, light upon them and make them original creators of works newer, nobler, grander, as the events of the last eighty years. I mean the advent of America."[1]

As a boy in Sunday School and under the usual influences of a Protestant Christian home, he had absorbed much of the Old and New Testaments, but so far as I can discover, he never thought of the Hebrew Bible as poetry until 1850 or later. At any rate, by the time he began to set down and preserve his thoughts in the scraps later gathered into *Notes and Fragments*, he had arrived at the interpretation

[1] *Complete Writings*, IX, 101–6. The last two sentences certainly, and probably the entire statement, was written in 1856, eighty years after the Declaration of Independence.

of the Bible as a great poem like the *Iliad* and the Indian epics, but not a complete and infallible guide to religious worship. In this judgment he excluded the New Testament so far as the poetical character of the Bible was concerned. The Bible, like nature, is incomplete and without obvious unity; and he wonders how it has held together, or, he adds, "is this diversity the very reason it has held together?"[2] All primitive poetry is alike in exemplifying, like nature, the principle of unity in diversity. He would apply the same principle to history, it seems: "The History of the World,—viz.: An immense digested collection of lists of dates, names of representative persons and events, maps and census returns."[3] There is no question but that in the 1855 edition, and perhaps also the 1856 edition, of *Leaves of Grass*, Whitman allowed himself to be guided by this principle, not trying for unity but trusting that it would come naturally out of the diverse materials of his poems. As late as June 1857 he thought of himself as constructing a New Bible, which would round itself into a unity in 1859 as the year rounds itself in fulfilling its three hundred and sixty-five days.[4]

The Old Testament may also, as some critics have thought, have influenced Whitman in determining the verse form of his poems. Gay W. Allen has pointed out the similarity of Whitman's use of various types of parallelism and other verse patterns to those used in the Hebrew poetry of the Bible, but he did not address himself to the question whether Whitman discovered these patterns in his own reading of the English Bible or learned of them from books and articles on Hebrew poetry.[5] While no such thorough analysis of the rhythmic patterns of Biblical poetry was available to Whitman as R. G. Moulton's *Literary Study of the Bible* (1895), he might have found all he required in a number of places. The earliest extended discussion of the subject was Robert Lowth's *Lectures on the Sacred Poetry of the Hebrews,* originally published in 1753. These lectures were written in Latin and delivered in the early 1740's while Lowth was Professor of Poetry at Oxford.[6] They were translated into English in 1787 by G. Gregory, but earlier (1758–1761) they had been translated into German by the distinguished philologist of Goettengin, J. D. Michaelis, with extensive notes. A new edition, edited by C. E. Stowe,

---

2 *Ibid.,* p. 101.

3 *Ibid.,* p. 49.

4 *Ibid.,* p. 6.

5 See his "Biblical Analogies for Walt Whitman's Prosody" in the *Revue Anglo-Américaine,* X (Aug. 1933), 490–507 and also his chapter on Whitman in *American Prosody* (New York, 1935), pp. 217–43.

6 Lowth was born in 1710 and died in 1787. He became Bishop of London in 1777.

with additional notes, was published in Boston in 1829, and the original English edition was reprinted in London in 1816 and in 1847.[7] The nature of the sentences of Hebrew poetry, Lowth noted, is "that a complete sense is almost equally infused in every component part, and that every member constitutes an entire verse." The poetic style is parabolic and includes three modes of speech: the sententious, which is most evident in the prophetic books, the figurative, and the sublime. The sententious style "prevents a prosaic mode of expression, and always reduces a composition to a kind of metrical form." In the figurative style, the metaphor is the most common figure of speech, and the images are borrowed from common life and familiar objects.[8] Lowth's discussion of parallelism became the basis of all later interpretations. He names three principal types: (1) synonymous, "when the same sentiment is repeated in different but equivalent terms"; (2) antithetic, "when a thing is illustrated by its contrary being opposed to it"; and (3) synthetic, "in which the sentences answer to each other, not by the iteration of the same image or sentiment, or the opposition of their contraries, but merely by the form of construction."[9]

The next important study of Hebrew poetry was J. G. Herder's *The Spirit of Hebrew Poetry*, originally published in German in 1782, and translated into English by James Marsh and published in Burlington, Vermont, in 1833.[10] Herder says that Hebrew poetry "exhibits actions and events as present, whether they be past, or passing, or future," for "among the Hebrews, history itself is properly poetry, that is the transmission of narratives, which are related in the present tense." Parallelism is a characteristic form, appealing to the feelings, for "so soon as the heart gives way to its emotions, wave follows upon wave, and that is parallelism." Parallelism also appeals to the understanding in this way: "It changes the figure and exhibits the thought in another light. It varies the precept, and explains it, or impresses it upon the heart." Hebrew poetry "should be read under the open sky, and if possible in the dawn of morning." The natural parallelism of Heaven and Earth, the spirit and the body helps the poet to perceive that "sublimity requires the boundless and immense," and that beauty and truth require definite limits, which is the condition of earth. Every age must make its poetry consistent with its ideas of the great system of being, or if not, must at least be assured

---

[7] The Brooklyn Library had a copy of Gregory's translation, 2nd ed., 1816.

[8] These ideas are drawn from the 1829 edition, chiefly from pp. 38–58.

[9] *Ibid.*, 1829 ed., p. 157.

[10] This translation is not listed in the Brooklyn Library nor in the Astor, but was no doubt accessible.

of producing a greater effect by its poetical fictions than systematic truth could secure to it." [11]

There were several other important German works on the poetry of the Bible but they were not translated in Whitman's time and he could have known them, if at all, only in reviews. The only significant American studies of the subject were those of George R. Noyes, Professor of Hebrew at Harvard, who published *An Amended Version of the Book of Job* in 1827 and *A New Translation of the Book of Psalms* in 1831, which was reprinted in 1846. The same year he published in Boston *A New Translation of the Proverbs, Ecclesiastes and the Canticles*, with introduction and explanatory notes.[12] In these volumes he explains and illustrates the three main types of parallelism in the poetry of the Bible, following in general the pattern set by Lowth. His translations arrange the poetry in verse form, each line beginning with a capital letter and usually constituting a complete statement, the whole illustrating the principles of parallelism and repetition. If Whitman saw the translation of Noyes he might have derived from it some suggestions later used in *Leaves of Grass*. A review of each of Noyes's books was published in the *North American Review*. The review of the 1846 volume briefly explains the several types of parallelism illustrated by Noyes.[13]

In 1851 George Gilfillan published *Bards of the Bible*, later published also with the title *Poets and Poetry of the Bible*, a book Whitman is very likely to have seen.[14] Gilfillan names the four principal characteristics of Biblical poetry as (1) figurative language, especially in the use of the metaphor; (2) simplicity approaching artlessness; (3) what the author calls "unconsciousness," by which he means that "men of genius are conscious, not of what is peculiar in the individual, but what is universal in the race; of what characterizes not a man but Man"; and (4) a high moral tone and constant religious reference. The equal of these Hebrew poets, he affirms, we shall not see "till poets are the organs, not only of their personal belief, but of the general sentiment around them, and have become the high-priests in a vast sanctuary, where all shall be worshipers because all is felt to be divine." [15] Whitman would not have liked Gilfillan's sentimentality

11 *The Spirit of Hebrew Poetry*, trans. James Marsh, I, 37, 41, 45, 60, 94.

12 All these were in the Brooklyn Library.

13 *North American Review*, LXIII (July 1846), 201–10.

14 Published by Harper, which published many books read by Whitman. In the final leaves of this book other Harper books known to Whitman are advertised, among them Leigh Hunt's *Autobiography*, Ticknor's *History of Spanish Literature*, and Craik's *Pictorial History of England*.

15 *Bards of the Bible*, pp. 42–57.

and inflated style, perhaps, but there is no denying that his characterization of the Hebrew poets of the Bible resembles Whitman's ideal
of the future poets of America. There is nothing in the book about
the rhythmical structure of Biblical poetry, but a review of it in the
North American Review for July 1851 supplies the deficiency by calling parallelism the "great and fundamental law of Hebrew poetry"
and naming its three forms as (1) *synonymous* parallelism, in which
two clauses or sentences are placed side by side, the second expressing
the same sentiment as the first but with a variation of phraseology;
(2) *antithetic* parallelism, in which the second clause is the antithesis
of the first; and (3) *synthetic*, in which the second clause is a continu-
ance of the thought of the first, or coordinate, or correspondent in
respect to length or measure.[16]

There can be no doubt that Whitman read with pleasure Macpherson's *Poems of Ossian* and was influenced by them in the same way
that he was influenced by all primitive poetry. In so far as they were
authentic, or even as imitations of authentic primitive poems, they
were examples of how natural poetry reflects the spirit of the age in
which it is written—examples that helped Whitman to understand
the spirit of his own time and place, though very different, and to
reflect it in his poems.[17] Other imitations of primitive poetry that
might have influenced Whitman were Martin F. Tupper's *Proverbial
Philosophy* (1849) and Samuel Warren's *The Lily and the Bee* (1851).
Bliss Perry pointed out some similarities long ago.[18] *Proverbial Philosophy* is written in long end-stopped lines like *Leaves of Grass*, but
it may be termed poetry only by a kind of license. The long lines may
have interested Whitman, and occasionally Tupper's diction and use
of parallelism in the lines resemble Biblical poetry. Whitman probably had seen this book, for on February 20, 1847, he reviewed one of
Tupper's prose works, *Probabilities; an Aid to Faith*, in the *Eagle*.
His notice is brief, but he says "justice to it would require many
pages."[19] The one of Tupper's "probabilities" most likely to have
interested Whitman, then or later, is that evil is not a principle existing of itself, but only relative, a limitation of the good.

Whether Whitman read *The Lily and the Bee* I do not know, but
if he did he surely found it interesting at the time he was cogitating

16 LXXIII, 238–67.

17 For a detailed account of Whitman's interest in Ossian, see Chapter VII.

18 *Walt Whitman* (Boston, 1906), pp. 91–95. An American edition of *Proverbial
Philosophy* was published by Wiley and Putnam, New York, in 1847; *The Lily and
the Bee* was reprinted by Harper in 1851, soon after it appeared in England. *The
Works of Samuel Warren* were published in five volumes in 1854–55.

19 Reprinted in *UPP*, I, 136.

the form and meaning of his own projected poems. In the author's introductory "Exposition" of his poem he says its subject is "Man, in his threefold relations to the Earth, to his fellow-man, and to God. . . . These threefold relations are all pervaded by the idea of a Unity: on which the eye settles most steadily, at the moment when otherwise it would be wandering, dazzled and bewildered by the endlessly varying splendours attracting it: and as soon as the beholder has caught a glimpse of this Unity, and not till then, he sees the true and deep significance of the spectacle, speaking to the mind of Statesman, Philosopher, and Divine, in sublime accents; and he exclaims, 'O! rare unity in multiplicity! uniformity in endless variety.' " The Lily and the Bee symbolize nature and art as well as man's spiritual and material relations. The first part of the poem describes the Crystal Palace during the day; the second part represents the poet alone in the Palace at night, when especially its spiritual connotations are revealed to him. The idea of universality is conveyed through a description of the many people, from all parts of the world, who visit the Palace. As for the form of the poem, the author says, "Poetry depends essentially upon Thought; which should be trusted for the selection of such forms of expression as it may deem suitable, in order to reach an attuned imagination. . . . Apparent orderliness of method was designedly discarded. Guided by the impression which so stupendous a spectacle was calculated to produce on the susceptible imagination, the author sought to excite in that of the reader, a sense of lustrous confusion, slowly subsiding into distinctness, and then developing grand proportion, harmony, and system." In *Notes and Fragments*, we may remember, Whitman said: "My poems when complete should be a *unity*, in the same sense that the earth is . . ."[20] As to the form of the verse, Warren describes it as "rhythmical prose," and yet he calls it a "Lyrical Soliloquy." It employs parallelism and repetition and occasionally the declamatory style of much of Whitman's verse, but its language is far more prosaic than Whitman's. A few lines from the beginning of the second part will have to do for illustration, although there is such variety of form that no single passage can be called representative. It is night in the Crystal Palace.

> The seventy thousand gone! All gone
> And I, Alone!
> —How dread this silence!
> The seventy thousand, with bright sunshine, gone,
> And I alone,
> And moonlight all irradiates, solemnly.

[20] *Complete Writings*, IX, 3.

All gone! The living stream, with its mysterious hum:
My brethren! and my sisters! gone!
From every clime, of every hue, and every tongue!
But a few hours ago, all here: gleeful, eager, curious, all,
Admiring, all: instructed, thousands:
Some, stirred with deep thoughts, and fixed on musings strange:
But now, thus far on in night, all, all, asleep,
Past, Present, Future, melted into One!

Whitman was not averse to the use of these and other undistinguished poets if they might serve his purpose, but he could have found plenty of precedents for the use of repetition and parallelism among English and American poets of the highest rank.[21]

The apparent kinship of the style of *Leaves of Grass* to the rhetoric of orators, great and less great, that he heard in New York, has often been remarked,[22] and Whitman himself expressed ideas of oratory that suggest some of his statements about *Leaves of Grass*. In "Father Taylor (and Oratory)," first published in the *Century Magazine*, February 1887, he wrote: "Talking of oratory, why is it that the unsophisticated practices often strike deeper than the train'd ones? . . . In my time I have heard Webster, Clay, Edward Everett, Phillips, and such *célèbres*; yet I recall the minor but life-eloquence of men like John P. Hale, Cassius Clay, and one or two of the old abolition 'fanatics' ahead of all those stereotyped fames."[23] Earlier, however, he thought better of elocutionary art. He admired what he called the "mental style" of Macready as well as, perhaps more than, the more boisterous style of Forrest. In his notes on oratory and directions to himself for public speaking he tells himself: "Restrain and curb gesture. Not too much gesture. Animation and life may be shown in a speech by great feeling in voice and look. Interior gesture, which is perhaps better than exterior gesture." Yet he also tells himself in these notes that the "fullest type of live oratory" involves "animation of limbs, hands, arms, neck, shoulders, waist, open breast, &c."[24] Ac-

---

[21] In the early English ballads, in the works of Shakespeare, and in those of Poe and Tennyson and other poets of Whitman's own time.

[22] See T. B. Harned, "Walt Whitman and Oratory," *Complete Writings*, VIII, 244 ff. See also Clifton Joseph Furness, *Walt Whitman's Workshop* (Cambridge, Mass., 1928), pp. 27–84 and Notes, *passim*.

[23] *Prose Works 1892*, II, 551. In "Memoranda" (*ibid.*, II, 697), he speaks of attending meetings of the "windy and cyclonic" reformatory societies and the "tumultuous Anti-Slavery" meetings in the large "Tabernacle" on Broadway before the Civil War, and says he "was sure to be on hand when J. P. Hale or Cash Clay made speeches."

[24] Quoted by Furness in *Walt Whitman's Workshop*, pp. 37–38.

tually Whitman's taste embraced both art and nature, and this is evident in his poems as well as in his preferences in opera, dramatics, and oratory. In dramatics, therefore, he was best pleased with Booth and Charlotte Cushman, who had, in great measure, both the power of Forrest and the art of Macready.

Similar ambivalences of temperament overlying a basic unity of character find expression throughout *Leaves of Grass*. It would be a mistake, therefore, to stress Whitman's love of the primitive in poetry without giving due consideration to his genuine appreciation of the more deliberate art of his modern antecedents and contemporaries. He says he has constructed his poem on the principles of nature; yet nature works unconsciously, whereas he admits he has sweated "in the fog with the linguists and learned men." He loved the "florid, rich, first phases of poetry, as in the oriental poems, in the Bible," but in his early directions to himself on composition he requires "a perfectly transparent, plate-glassy style." He says there is in the soul "an instinctive test of the sense and actuality of anything," and yet he advises the opera singer that to sing well his part is not enough; he should "be master of the composers of all operas—and of all tenors—and of all violins and first violins." For the poet, the implication is that he must master all the great poets and poetry of the past.[25] He sounds like Wordsworth when he says that "originality must be of the spirit and show itself in new combinations and new meanings and discovering greatness and harmony where there was before thought no greatness"; but in the same note he sounds a bit like a classicist in saying the style must be "carefully purged of anything striking or dazzling or ornamental."[26] Yet Whitman was to no appreciable extent a classicist. Insofar as there was conflict between two literary methods it was between the method of the philosophical romanticist and the graphic realist. These two methods are well illustrated in the *Calamus* group and the *Children of Adam* group respectively. Philosophically the same kind of duality prevails. "My two theses—animal and spiritual," he says in *Notes and Fragments*, "become gradually fused in *Leaves of Grass*,—runs through all the poems and gives color to the whole."[27] The *Children of Adam* poems are "full of animal fire," whereas the *Calamus* poems express a love which is not animal but spiritual—he calls it "ethereal," yet "athletic."[28] These contrasting groups illustrate the phrenological qualities of "amativeness" and

[25] *Notes and Fragments* (*Complete Writings*, IX, pp. 34, 42, 43, and *passim*).

[26] *Ibid.* (p. 37). This note was suggested by a review of Keats's "Hyperion" in the *American Whig Review*, Oct. 1851.

[27] *Complete Writings*, I, 15.

[28] See *ibid.*, IX, 150, and the *Calamus* poem "Fast Anchor'd Eternal O Love!"

"adhesiveness"—woman-love and manly love, or friendship. It is true, as he says, that these two issues become "gradually fused" in *Leaves of Grass*, yet they both appear prominently in "Song of Myself" and to some extent are fused there, while in the later poems the spiritual thesis is predominant.

In developing his literary method and his two theses he was undoubtedly influenced by his early journalistic background, his work as a mechanic—printer and carpenter—his attendance at the theater, and his reading of the great romantic writers of his time—Wordsworth, Coleridge, Carlyle, and Emerson; yet the threads of the web, as we have seen, extend, however tenuously, into areas more remote and sometimes inaccessible. I have tried to suggest the extent of his interest in ancient cultures and the workings of the primitive mind. He was no less concerned with the cultures of his own time and the periods in between the present and the remote past, especially during the years just before and just after the completion of the first edition of *Leaves of Grass*. He was never a student of philosophy, strictly speaking, but he picked up the basic ideas of the philosophies current in his day, sometimes from sources of doubtful authority.

Bucke's list of clippings contains only three articles purporting to deal with philosophy. The earliest of these, on the "Scotch School of Philosophy and Criticism" (No. 14), is from the *American Whig Review* for October 1845. Its anonymous author says little about philosophy, being concerned with what he calls the "leading characteristic" of writers of this school, their addiction to the "exclusive employment of the analytic process," whereas, in his opinion, "the best part of art is that which no analysis can seize, no method can subjugate." The best of our aesthetical critics, whom he designates as Hazlitt, Coleridge, and Carlyle, he thinks are the least methodical. In a brief annotation, Whitman compared the negative criticism of the Scotch school to that of Voltaire. He adds that many "present writers" are followers of Voltaire without knowing it. The tone of this brief note suggests that it was written somewhat earlier than Whitman's article on Voltaire in *Life Illustrated* (1856), which was on the whole favorable.

The next earliest of the three clippings (No. 520) is titled "System of Positive Philosophy" and was cut from the *Democratic Review* for March 1847. It was the second of a series of four articles published between February and May. Bucke says it was "scored," but it is not in the Trent collection, and I have not seen it. I doubt if Whitman was much interested in Auguste Comte's "Positive Philosophy," for it is the May installment, which he did not clip, that contains the summary of this philosophy. The March number has the subtitle "Of Social Science, or the Science of History." It contains a brief summary of human development from ancient times to the present, including some comments on Kant, Fichte, Schelling, and Hegel, and on the "eclectic school" of Victor Cousin in France.[29]

The third clipping (Bucke's No. 554), was titled "Philosophy, Psychology and Metaphysics," and was cut from the *Eclectic Magazine* for April 1871, where it was reprinted from the *North British Review*. It is likely that by the time he read this essay Whitman's philosophical attitudes were already fully formed, but he might have been interested in reviewing the German Romantic philosophy while preparing his proposed "Sunday evening lectures."[30] Among these notes is a reference to his "*Vistas*." This must have been written after the publication of *Democratic Vistas* in 1871, since the word "*Vistas*" does not occur in the two contributory essays published in the *Galaxy* in 1867 and 1868. The article cut from the *Eclectic Magazine* may have contributed little, if anything, to these notes, but if it contributed nothing it corroborated a great deal. Several of the passages Whitman bracketed on the clipping express philosophical views closely paralleling his own. Metaphysics is defined in the article as "the endeavor to demonstrate and bring clearly to light the spiritual unity of the world, not as contradictory of the material unity, but as underlying it, and being the source from which it proceeds" (p. 395). This sounds somewhat like the passage in Whitman's notes where he submits what he calls a "better description" of metaphysics than Kant's: "that which considers the whole concrete show of things, the world, man himself, either individually or aggregated in History, as resting on a spiritual, invisible basis, continually shifting, yet the real substance, and the only immutable one." "This," he adds, "was the doctrine of Hegel."[31] This article was written by J. R. Morell, who in 1852 had edited and revised Arthur Johnson's translation of W. G. Tennemann's *A Manual of the History of Philosophy*, originally published in 1832. J. R. Morell was a cousin of J. D. Morell, whose *Historical and Critical View of the Speculative Philosophy of Europe in the Nineteenth Century* was originally published in London in two volumes in 1846 and reprinted in 1847. It was reprinted in New York in one large volume in 1848 and again in later years. Whitman could have read the 1853 edition in the Brooklyn Library. This was the

29 These essays were originally published in *Le National*, translated from the French of Emile Littré by J. H. Young.

30 See *Complete Writings*, IX, 166–86.

31 *Ibid.*, IX, 168.

most authoritative and influential work on the philosophy of Germany and France at that time. Morell's personal views were very close to those of Victor Cousin. If Whitman had been a serious student of philosophy in the 1850's he would certainly have known J. D. Morell's book and probably also J. R. Morell's edition of Tennemann's volume. He may have clipped a review of J. D. Morell's book from the *American Whig Review* for May 1851, but if so it was probably not preserved and is not on Bucke's list. The review begins on page 458, immediately following a review of Wordsworth's *Prelude* that begins on page 448. On page 447, which is the reverse side of 448, Whitman has written the titles of both reviews: "Wordsworth's Prelude" and "Speculative Philosophy in the Nineteenth Century," as if he clipped both. Actually the clipping in the Trent Collection contains only the title page, 448, and pages 455–57 of the review of the *Prelude*, with, of course, page 458, which is the first page of the review of Morell's book. Whether or not he clipped this review, he must surely have read it. The reviewer praises Morell's book and says with it as his guide he has no difficulty understanding German transcendentalism. He calls Morell an idealist and says he is "partial to the views of Cousin and the German philosophers."

There were many opportunities in the 1840's and 1850's for Whitman to secure at least an elementary knowledge of German philosophy. One need only read René Wellek's survey-article, "The Minor Transcendentalists and German Philosophy" to realize that fact.[32] Among other books that he might easily have seen was Johann Bernhard Stallo's *General Principles of the Philosophy of Nature*, also in the Brooklyn Library, which provided a somewhat detailed outline of the philosophies of Schelling, Hegel, and others. Stallo lectured at St. John's College (now Fordham) from 1844 to 1847, while preparing his book, and it is of course possible that Whitman heard some of his lectures, though he does not mention him so far as I have discovered.[33] Emerson owned a copy of Stallo's book and quoted from it several times in his journal. Stallo was a Jeffersonian Democrat until about 1850, when, like Whitman, he became first a Free-Soiler and then a Republican. He was an elector for Fremont in 1856. Asa Mahan's *A System of Intellectual Philosophy*, based on classroom lectures at Oberlin Institute and Cleveland University, draws heavily on Coleridge, Cousin, and Kant, and would have provided an excellent introduction to philosophy in general. It was first published in

---

[32] *New England Quarterly*, XV (Dec. 1942), pp. 652–80.
[33] See Herbert W. Schneider, *A History of American Philosophy* (New York, 1946), p. 332.

1847, then revised and reprinted in 1854. A notice of the first edition appeared in the *Democratic Review* for March 1847 (XX, 287).

More important as a source of Whitman's knowledge of the German philosophers was Frederic H. Hedge's *Prose Writers of Germany*, originally published in 1847; reprinted in 1849 and 1852; revised in 1870. It contains selections from many writers, including Kant, Lessing, Moses Mendelssohn, Lavater, Jacobi, Herder, Goethe, Schiller, Fichte, the Schlegels, Hegel, and Schelling, and introductory biographical notes. Whitman owned a copy of this book as late as 1891, according to Horace Traubel, and probably at the time of his death.[34] Sister Mary Eleanor pointed out passages in Whitman's *Notes and Fragments* that are identical with some of Hedge's comments on Hegel, Fichte, Schelling, Kant, and Herder, and similarities in the selections from these and other writers to passages in *Leaves of Grass*.[35] In making my own comparison, I have found a number of passages Sister Mary Eleanor might have cited but did not. Also, the selections themselves contain material from which Whitman borrowed, though sparingly, including the section from Hegel entitled "History as the Manifestation of Spirit," Fichte's "The Destination of Man," and Herder's "Love and Self." I think it may be reasonably assumed that Whitman read all or most of this volume at one time or another. I have not seen Whitman's copy and do not know which edition he owned. I suspect his notes were taken from the edition of 1852.

Another book that Whitman read carefully and cited in *Notes and Fragments* was Joseph Gostwick's *German Literature*, originally published in Edinburgh in 1849 as one of the 26 volumes of W. and R. Chambers's *Instructive and Entertaining Library*. The title page of this edition gave the author's name as "Gostick." According to the catalogue of the British Museum all of Gostwick's early volumes on German literature bore that name on the title page. Later books by the same author spelled his name "Gostwick." The edition Whitman used, not listed in the British Museum catalogue, was published in Philadelphia in 1854, and was undoubtedly a reprint of the Edinburgh 1849 edition since the letters "W & R C," standing for William and Robert Chambers, are printed in gold on the covers, front and back. In 1873 a volume with the title *Outlines of German Literature*, by Joseph Gostwick and Robert Harrison, was published in London

---

[34] See Traubel's article, "Walt Whitman at Date," *New England Magazine*, May 1891 (reprinted in *In Re*, pp. 109–47 [see p. 137]).

[35] "Hedge's *Prose Writers of Germany* as a Source of Whitman's Knowledge of German Philosophy," *Modern Language Notes*, LXI (June 1946), 381–88.

and New York. It was "respectfully inscribed" to Thomas Carlyle. It is not simply a revised edition of Gostick's *German Literature,* but a new work, although some of the materials of the earlier version are used. Gostwick's *German Literature* is not mentioned in the Preface or anywhere in the 1873 volume. There is no evidence at all that Whitman drew any of his notes from Gostwick and Harrison's 1873 volume. That he did make notes from the 1854 *German Literature* is proved by a page reference in *Notes and Fragments* and by identical or nearly identical comments in these notes and in *German Literature.*[36] If the use of this volume were not otherwise proved, it is proved by Whitman's free verse paraphrase, in nine lines, of Gostwick's literal unrhymed English translation of 12 lines of the *Nibelungenlied* which he quotes in the original and in a modern German translation. Whitman also made a free-verse paraphrase in 29 lines of the last 32 lines of the *Nibelungenlied* in Gostwick's rhymed English translation. The 12 lines come from near the middle of the *Nibelungenlied* whereas the 32 lines paraphrased by Whitman are the last of the poem, but Whitman juxtaposes them neatly in his version to make it appear they are consecutive. *German Literature* contains about 350 lines of the *Nibelungenlied,* whereas the 1873 *Outlines of German Literature* contains none.[37]

Whitman also made considerable use of encyclopedias, especially the *Encyclopaedia Britannica,* eighth edition, published from 1853 to 1860, and the *New American Cyclopaedia,* edited by George Ripley and Charles A. Dana, both personally known to Whitman, published from 1858 to 1862. His notes on Kant and Fichte were drawn almost entirely from the eighth edition of the *Britannica,* and his briefer notes on Schelling were from the *New American Cyclopae-*

[36] At the end of Whitman's notes on Barthold Niebuhr he writes, "See pages 249–50–51 *German Literature"* (*Notes and Fragments* in *Complete Writings,* IX, 116). The pages are correct for the 1854 volume. Most of the paragraph "summing up" Kant (*ibid.,* IX, 176) is almost word for word from this volume, pp. 266–69. Other parallels might be cited.

[37] Clarence Gohdes and Rollo G. Silver, who printed Whitman's free verse translation in *Faint Clews & Indirections* (Durham, N.C., 1949), state in their headnote that "it bears little resemblance to the discussion of and translation from the poem in Joseph Gostwick's *German Literature."* It seems obvious to me that they are mistaken. I have compared Whitman's translation with the texts of the translations by Carl Lachmann (1848) and W. N. Lettson (1850), which were the only complete English translations available to him, and I feel sure he used neither. The passage is not quoted by Carlyle in his review of Karl Simrock's modern German translation (1831). Wm. A. Little also recognized the source of Whitman's translation as Gostwick. ("Walt Whitman and the *Nibelungenlied," PMLA,* LXXX [Dec. 1965], 562–70.)

dia.[38] Whitman could not have formed his favorable opinion of Hegel from the *Britannica* article, which was strongly anti-Hegelian, but he would have found the *New American Cyclopaedia* article somewhat more agreeable. It is my opinion, however, admittedly based on inconclusive evidence, that he got his first taste of Hegel's philosophy in Gostwick's *German Literature* or in Hedge's *Prose Writers of Germany* about 1854 and later developed his own ideas of it from more extensive reading, perhaps including some of Hegel's own writing. He is most likely to have read the *Philosophy of History* among Hegel's major works, but he probably read excerpts from other works. He probably also read Victor Cousin's *History of Modern Philosophy*, where many ideas were drawn from Hegel, though he nowhere mentions Cousin's name. Whether he made his notes from Gostwick before or after writing the poems of the first edition of *Leaves of Grass* I cannot be sure, but there seem to be more ideas akin to German philosophy in the 1856 edition than in the 1855 edition. Some of the notes preserved in *Notes and Fragments* contributed to Whitman's comments on Hegel in his essay on "Carlyle from American Points of View," where he says he is "much indebted to J. Gostick's abstract," but they suggest much wider reading. Since he was familiar with G. H. Lewes's life of Goethe, he might also have consulted the same author's *Biographical History of Philosophy*, published in 1845 in four small volumes, reprinted several times during the next ten years, and made the basis of the much enlarged and more valuable work, *The History of Philosophy from Thales to Comte*, published in two volumes in 1871 and reprinted in one large volume in 1875. He would have learned a good deal about Herder, including his general ideas on a national literature, from reading Goethe's *Autobiography*, and he may well have read Herder's *Outlines of a Philosophy of the History of Man* (translated by T. Churchill, 2 vols., 2nd edition, 1803), a book which he could have found in the Brooklyn Library.

[38] See Newton Arvin's *Whitman* (New York, 1938), pp. 191–95, 308–9, and my "Notes on Whitman's Reading," *American Literature*, XXVI (Nov. 1954), 337–62, especially p. 353. See also Pochmann, *German Culture in America*, pp. 471–72 and 787. Arvin found a manuscript note in the Library of Congress in which Whitman refers to the seventh edition of the *Encyclopaedia Britannica* as containing an article on Fichte in Vol. IX and an article on Kant in Vol. XII, but since Kant does not appear in the seventh edition, Whitman must have cited it by mistake. The Library of Congress catalogue does not list either the seventh or the eighth edition. Whitman could have seen the eighth edition earlier in the Brooklyn Library, but not the seventh, which, however, was available after 1852 in the Astor Library of New York. The *Brooklyn Daily Times* printed two notices of the publication of the *New American Cyclopaedia* while Whitman was editor of the paper, on Aug. 9, 1858, and on Dec. 20, 1858. (See the *Walt Whitman Review*, Sept. 1968.)

The ideas of God and Nature in *Leaves of Grass* resemble Herder's, but there is no other evidence that he read the book, and he could have got his ideas from other and later sources. However, since he did read some of the works of Bunsen, most probably in the Brooklyn Library, the extent of his reading in such erudite literature may have been greater than any one has supposed.[39]

How much Whitman read of German philosophy in the periodicals of his time it is idle to speculate, but I suspect he read a good deal. I have earlier discussed the clippings he made from British periodicals in 1848 and 1849 and later. Many articles were reprinted from these periodicals in American magazines, especially the *Eclectic* and the *Living Age*.[40] The *Eclectic Magazine* for June, 1851, contains an article, "Victor Cousin," which is a review of several editions of the works of Cousin, reprinted from the *Edinburgh Review*, from which Whitman might have learned much and been stimulated to read more, both about Cousin and about German philosophers, especially Schelling and Hegel, on whom Cousin drew for elements of his own philosophy. The following passage on Cousin's "Natural Theology," quoted from one of his lectures, has much in common with Whitman's conception of the relations of man, nature, and God in *Leaves of Grass*: "Man is not in consciousness without Nature, nor Nature without Man; but both meet there, at once in their opposition and their reciprocity; just like relative causes and substances, whose nature is always to develop themselves, and always by means of each other. The God of Consciousness is not an abstract Deity—a solitary monarch retained on the other side of creation, upon the desert throne of a silent eternity and an absolute existence; he is a God at once real and true; one and many; eternity and time; space and number; essence and life; indivisibility and totality, principle, end, and

[39] Gene Bluestein, in "The Advantages of Barbarism: Herder and Whitman's Nationalism" (*Journal of the History of Ideas*, XXIV [Jan.–March 1963], 115–26) says that "Whitman's program for the establishing of a national literature followed closely the conceptions" of Herder, and implies that he was acquainted with Herder's edition of German "Volkslieder." I find no evidence that he knew Herder's ideas on folk literature, which had apparently not appeard in English. He could hardly have derived them from *The Spirit of Hebrew Poetry* or the *Outlines*.

[40] He may have been led to read the poems of Alexander Smith by seeing first a review of his poems in the *Eclectic*, July 1853, reprinted from the *Westminster Review*. The review quotes some of the same lines about a "mighty Poet" who will soon arise that Whitman quoted in his article "An English and an American Poet," published anonymously in the *Phrenological Journal*, Oct. 1855. The reviewer, like Whitman in a note on Smith's poems in *Notes and Fragments*, mentions the images drawn from Shakespeare, but does not mention a likeness to Tennyson, as Whitman does.

middle; at the summit and at the base of existence; infinite and finite at once; in brief, a trinity which comprehends at once God, Nature, and Humanity."[41] This passage may be found in various places in Cousin's works with minor verbal variations. Whitman could have seen it in Cousin's Preface to *Philosophical Fragments*, which was re-printed as "Exposition of Eclecticism," in George Ripley's translation, in Vol. IX of *The Students' Cabinet Library of Useful Tracts* (Edinburgh, 1843). The passage is also quoted by J. D. Morell in his *Speculative Philosophy of Europe*, p. 655. It could have been read in O. W. Wight's translation of Cousin's *Course of the History of Philosophy* on pp. 112–113 of the first volume.

There is an article on Fichte in the *Living Age* for August 2, 1851, and a review of *Herder's Remains* in the same periodical for July 4, 1857. On June 21, 1858, Whitman's newspaper, the Brooklyn *Times*, contained a notice of the June issue of the *Atlantic Monthly* which contained an article by Hedge on "Gottfried Wilhelm von Leibnitz," that Whitman probably saw. It did not provide him with his first knowledge of Leibnitz, but it would have proved useful since it summarizes the main events of the life of Leibnitz and the main points in his philosophy, including his theory of monads. Hedge later published a translation of the *Monadology* of Leibnitz in the *Journal of Speculative Philosophy*.[42] Whitman's poem "Eidólons" (1876) may have been suggested by Leibnitz's theory of monads.[43] In "Sail Out for Good, Eidólon Yacht" (1891) he refers to his spiritual and permanent self as the "Eidólon Yacht of Me." He does not use the term in connection with *Leaves of Grass*, so far as I know, but I am sure he considered his book, in its various forms, as a succession of "eidólons" of himself. It is possible, if not probable, that before setting down his notes for "Sunday evening lectures," which must have been about 1870 or a little before, he had read a good deal about German philosophy in the *Journal of Speculative Philosophy*, edited by W. T. Harris in St. Louis, which was chiefly devoted to German philosophy from Leibnitz to Hegel, with the emphasis on Hegel. He told Traubel in 1888, handing him a copy of the *Journal*, that there was nothing in it to interest him, but this does not necessarily mean that no other issue interested him. He met Harris in Concord in 1881 and was pleased to

[41] *Eclectic Magazine*, XXIII, 195. The reviewer says this shows the influence of Schelling's pantheism and that Cousin's philosophical treatment of history shows "a close affinity with the Hegelian view of human consciousness, as a process of thought in which the divine idea perpetually realizes and unfolds itself."

[42] I (1867), 129–37.

[43] See also the Preface to the Centennial edition of *Leaves of Grass* and *Two Rivulets (Prose Works 1892*, II, 472–73).

think he approved of *Leaves of Grass,* but he might well have become familiar with the *Journal* long before he met its editor. The three volumes (1867, 1868, and 1869) which Whitman might have seen before writing his notes for lectures on philosophy were especially rich in more or less authoritative essays on the works of Leibnitz, Kant, Schelling, and Hegel, and would have enlarged his knowledge of these philosophers considerably.

Whitman could, of course, have been introduced to German literature and philosophy through Coleridge and Carlyle, particularly the latter. I doubt that he had read the *Biographia Literaria,* or any other prose of Coleridge, with understanding or care prior to 1855, and he always seemed to think of him as a poet rather than as a critic or philosopher. But, as I have pointed out earlier,[44] Whitman was much indebted to the writings of Thomas Carlyle, and may have derived his first impressions of German transcendental philosophy from Carlyle's *Critical and Miscellaneous Essays.* All of these essays were written and published between 1826 and 1840 and were undoubtedly in Whitman's mind when he wrote the following, printed in *Notes and Fragments*: "Carlyle certainly introduced the German style, writers, sentimentalism, transcendentalism, etc. etc. etc. from 1826 to 1840—through the great reviews and magazines—and through his own works and example."[45] I cannot tell precisely when he read these essays for the first time, but I believe it could not have been earlier than 1847 and was probably two years or more later. The latest of his Carlyle reviews in the *Eagle,* dated April 14, 1847, suggests that he was then well on the way to become an admirer of Carlyle, but I see no evidence in it that he had yet read the *Critical and Miscellaneous Essays.* His article dated April 26, 1847, on "The Anti-Democratic Bearing of Scott's Novels" is like Carlyle's review-essay, the "Memoirs of the Life of Scott," in finding fault with the Author of *Waverly,* but it is not the same fault. I doubt if Whitman had read Carlyle's essay before writing his own opinion. Much has been said of the influence of *Sartor Resartus* on *Leaves of Grass,* and apparently it was considerable. However, the essay "Characteristics," which was written about the same time as *Sartor* and has many of the same ideas but without the story element and the stylistic peculiarities, was probably a more immediate influence.

The *Critical and Miscellaneous Essays* were first published in book form in Boston in four volumes in 1838. Emerson was directly responsible for their publication. Only 1000 copies were printed. This edi-

---

44 See Chapter VII; for Carlyle, pp. 101–10; for Coleridge, pp. 110–12.
45 *Complete Writings,* IX, 123.

tion was reprinted in London without change in 1839. In 1840 a new edition, called the second, was published in London in five volumes and reprinted without change in 1842. In 1847 a third edition was published in London in four volumes, but apparently it was not a reprint of the first Boston edition. In June 1845 Emerson wrote to Carey and Hart, of Philadelphia, stating Carlyle's "concurrence in this new edition of his Essays." So far as I have discovered, Carey and Hart's large one-volume edition of the essays was first published in 1849.[46] This edition was reissued in 1852 and again in 1855, the latter in Boston and New York. It is my belief that at one time Whitman owned one of these one-volume editions that were issued between 1849 and 1855, since the English editions in four or five volumes would have been very expensive, but I have not been able to determine which one. After his reviews in 1846 and 1847 of the cheap Wiley and Putnam editions, also authorized by Carlyle through Emerson, it is not likely that he waited longer than necessary to acquire the essays. He did not review this volume because after 1848 he had ready access to no newspaper that has survived. If he had the book between 1850 and 1853 the essays would surely have been an influence on the first poems of *Leaves of Grass*, and his reading of them might have preceded his serious reading of Emerson's essays.

There was one grand idea prominent in *Leaves of Grass*, especially in the poems written between 1860 and 1875, that Whitman could not have derived from either Carlyle or Coleridge, but which is suggested in Hegel's *Philosophy of History* and more specifically developed in Cousin's *History of Modern Philosophy*. This is the idea that history is "the manifestation of God's supervision of Humanity," and that it consists of three epochs and three only, representing the three elements of thought: the infinite, the finite, and the relation of these two. The epoch representing the infinite has for its geographical theater Asia, the epoch of the finite, Europe, and the epoch of their relation, or fusion, America. On Asia's broad plateaus man's consciousness dwells chiefly with the infinite, and the results are vast states controlled by systems of government that allow little freedom of the individual and little progress in society. In Europe, on the other hand, where rivers, inland seas, and small mountain ranges divide the area at the same time that they encourage communication between the different nations, the human intellect is developed and progress is made toward individual freedom and democracy. The process of re-

46 This edition is not mentioned in I. W. Dyer's *Bibliography* (Portland, 1928), though he mentions "a new edition complete in one volume" published by A. Hart in 1850. Dyer also omits a Boston reprint of this edition in 1858.

lating or fusing the finite and the infinite is to be completed in America, which has some of the geographical characteristics of both Asia and Europe, but no one in excess, so that it is destined to become the theater of man's highest development and greatest achievements in the realms of the intellect and the spirit. Its culture is not original, but transmitted in a highly developed state from Europe.[47] In one way or another this conception of America as the destined theater of man's highest development through the union of the characteristic features of Asiatic and European culture appears in perhaps a dozen poems, notably "With Antecedents" (1860), "A Broadway Pageant" (1860), "Passage to India" (1869), "Thou Mother with Thy Equal Brook" (1872), and "Song of the Redwood Tree" (1874). The final greatness of humanity will come when, after his long separation, man is reunited with Nature and God. In *Democratic Vistas* (1871) Whitman calls for great poet-prophets in America by whose means this reunion and the culmination of democratic culture may be brought about.

Cousin describes in some detail the history of man through the epochs of the infinite and the finite, which he makes clear relate to Asia and Europe respectively, and he intimates that the third epoch is to have America for its theater. Whether Whitman had read Cousin's *History of Modern Philosophy* I cannot be sure, but it was readily available in an English translation.[48] Another book deals at great length with what appears to be Cousin's third epoch, and could have had great influence on *Leaves of Grass*. This was Arnold Guyot's lecture series, *The Earth and Man*, originally published in 1849 and reprinted in a second and revised edition in 1850.[49] Besides the book's general import, the influence of man's environment on his mental

[47] Hegel's *Lectures on the Philosophy of History*, translated by J. Sibree, was published by Bohn in London in 1857. The ideas here summarized, more or less closely, are to be found in Hegel's "Introduction" (pp. 1–107), the latter part of it especially. The 1861 edition of this translation was in the Brooklyn Library. The Astor Library had no English translation.

[48] An edition in two volumes, translated by O. W. Wight, was published by Appleton in New York in 1852, and reprinted in 1853, 1854, and later. These ideas are to be found in I, 152–71, and suggestions of them elsewhere in the book, which was available in the Brooklyn Library.

[49] This book was also in the Brooklyn Library. Guyot, a native of Switzerland, delivered these lectures in French, without a manuscript, in 1849, in Boston. After each lecture he wrote out a manuscript the next day, which was immediately translated into English by C. C. Felton and published in a Boston newspaper. Soon after the series was completed the lectures were gathered and published in book form. Extensive and important revisions were made by the author in consultation with the translator before the second edition was published. This edition was reprinted several times, the fourth time in 1851. Guyot remained in America, at-

and moral culture, there are a great many passages that would certainly have interested Whitman in the 1850's if he had seen them, as
I suspect he did. I must be content with quoting two or three. He
accepts the nebular hypothesis and compares the evolution of the
physical universe to the organic development of the egg. At first there
is "liquid animal matter, without precise form. . . . Soon, in the interior of the egg, the elements separate, diverging tendencies are
established; the matter accumulates and concentrates itself upon
certain points; these accumulations assume more distinct forms and
more specific characters; we see organs traced, a head, an eye, a heart,
an alimentary canal. But this diversification does not go on indefinitely. Under the influence of a special force, all these diverse tendencies are drawn together towards a single end; these distinct organs
are united and coordinated in one whole, and perform their functions
in the interest and for the service of the individual commanding
them." The mode of progress is diversity, the establishment of difference; the end is a new and harmonious organic unit. He perceives a
striking analogy between this organic development and the development of the physical universe from an original chaos of gaseous matter spread uniformly throughout space; then the principle of gravita-
tion "counterbalances the unlimited expansion of the gaseous matter,
brings the molecules nearer together, and groups them in a spheroidal
mass. This approximation allows the molecules, different in nature,
to act upon each other according to their chemical affinities; the process of life commences, and its earliest manifestation is light and
heat." The same principle controls the development of human societies: "that which excites life, that which is the condition of life, is
difference. The progress of development is diversity; the end is the
harmonious unity allowing all differences, all individualities to exist,
but coordinating and subjecting them to a superior aim." So, he concludes: "All is order, all is harmony in the universe, because the whole
universe is a thought of God; and it appears as a combination of or-
ganisms, each of which is only an integral part of one still more sublime. God alone contains them all, without making a part of any." [50]

tained distinction as a geographer, and in 1854 became professor of physical
geography and geology at Princeton, where Guyot Hall was named in his honor.
He had been influenced as a student in Germany by Carl Ritter, who in turn had
been influenced by Humboldt. Ritter developed the theory that, as a man's physical body is largely determinative of his life, so the structure of each country is an
important element in the progress of its culture. He thought the relation of the
physical globe to mankind is analogous to the relation of the individual man's
body to his soul. (See W. L. Gage, *The Life of Carl Ritter* [New York, 1867], p. 213
and *passim*.)

[50] *The Earth and Man*, pp. 96–102.

This idea of individuality preserved in a unified society is central to Whitman's "One's-Self I Sing," and indeed to the whole of *Leaves of Grass*. Another passage suggests Whitman's attitude toward the past and is especially relevant to "Passage to India": "Asia, Europe, and North America, are the three grand stages of humanity in its march through the ages. Asia is the cradle where man passed his infancy, under the authority of law, and where he learned his dependence upon a sovereign master. Europe is the school where his youth was trained, where he waxed in strength and knowledge, grew to manhood, and learned at once his liberty and his moral responsibility. America is the theatre of his activity during the period of manhood; the land where he applies and practices all he has learned, brings into action all the forces he has acquired, and where he is still to learn the entire development of his being and his own happiness are possible only by a willing obedience to the laws of his maker." [51] If Whitman read this book, his attention might have been directed to it by an anonymous review in the *American Whig Review* for September 1851. In addition to full summaries of the main arguments of the book, the review contains some sidelights on contemporary America that are outside the limits of the work reviewed. For example, this passage: "The world has never seen so strange a spectacle as is today witnessed in California; a kingdom built up in an hour by the free hands and bold hearts and thoughtful brains of *un*organized, not disorganized, men." Asia was colonized by fire and sword, but "this Minerva-kingdom by the Pacific created itself."

[51] *Ibid.*, p. 327.

XII. *French Literary Influences*

THE romantic philosophy of the Germans from Herder to Hegel, of Victor Cousin and the French eclectics, of the British Wordsworth, Coleridge, and Carlyle, and of the American Emerson and his circle, was all-embracing within the cultural limits of Europe in the late eighteenth and early nineteenth centuries, including religion, history, and the arts within its scope, and to some extent politics and science. To a considerable degree it constituted the intellectual and spiritual foreground of *Leaves of Grass*. Its political philosophy was not perfectly suited to Whitman's ideal democracy, and its science was somewhat outmoded, but he was able eventually to reconcile them with Darwinism and the equalitarian aspects of American democracy. At the time he was occupied with *Democratic Vistas* he could write in *Notes and Fragments* that, in his opinion, Hegel "most fully and definitely illustrates Democracy by carrying it into the highest regions.[1] Elsewhere in *Notes and Fragments*, in a note probably written in the middle 1850's, he says his poems when complete should be a unity as the earth is, or the human body (including the soul), and that their two great constituent elements will be materialism and spirituality.[2] In *Leaves of Grass* and elsewhere he often described his poems as essentially religious. In "Song of Myself" he concentrated on materialism and the physical body, but he made it clear that the soul, in its finite aspect, is inseparable from the body and in its infinite aspect is the real body, retaining after death the spiritual properties that have accrued to it through experience. In "Starting from Paumanok" he says he will make no poem nor any part of one that does not have reference to the soul. In the same poem he says, "I too, following many and follow'd by many, inaugurate a religion." *Leaves of Grass* is the Bible of that religion. In *Notes and Fragments* he wrote in June 1857: "The Great Construction of the New Bible. . . . It ought to be ready in 1859."[3] He came to conceive democracy in America as developing in three stages: the first stage was completed with the carrying out of the principles of the Declaration of Independence and

[1] *Complete Writings*, IX, 184.
[2] *Ibid.*, IX, 3.
[3] *Ibid.*, IX, 6.

the Constitution; the second stage was the building of material prosperity in the nineteenth century; the third stage, which he announces
at length in *Democratic Vistas*, "rising out of the previous ones to
make them and all illustrious," was to be "a sublime and serious Religious Democracy sternly taking command" and democratising society.[4] The priests of this democratic religion were to be artists, and
especially poets, and he calls for a special class of dedicated American
poet-prophets—"poets not only possess'd of the religious fire and
abandon of Isaiah, luxuriant in the epic talent of Homer, or for
proud characters as in Shakspere, but consistent with the Hegelian
formulas, and consistent with modern science."[5] Thus "illumin'd and
illuming," he hoped to see America "become a full-form'd world, and
divine Mother not only of material but spiritual worlds, in ceaseless
succession through time—the main thing being the average, the bod-
ily, the concrete, the democratic, the popular, on which all the super-
structures of the future are to permanently rest."[6]

This conception of the poet-prophet and a special class of artists
would seem to be inconsistent with his description of himself as "one
of the roughs," without art or literary sophistication, writing in a
simple "plate-glassy" style for carpenters, firemen, and stagedrivers.[7]
The apparent inconsistency is resolved in the identity of body and
soul in the finite individual and in the soul's access, through intui-
tion, to the universal, which can lead to the recognition of the truth
that the hand of God is the promise of his own.[8] In "Out of the Cradle
Endlessly Rocking" (1859) the boy's soul recognizes the song of the
bird as the voice of his demon, which will awaken in him his potential poetic genius. Thus without losing his status as one of the democratic mass, he is dedicated and, so to speak, set aside to become a
teacher to his fellows. In *Democratic Vistas* Whitman develops a
theory of personalism, already provided for in the early poems, to
account for superiority in some individuals. The strong individuals
rise out of the democratic mass somewhat as, in the nebular theory,
individual suns and systems are formed, to become the "Chandeliers
of the universe."[9]

---

[4] *Prose Works 1892,* II, 410.

[5] *Ibid.,* II, 421.

[6] *Ibid.,* II, 426.

[7] See "Song of Myself," Section 24. "One of the roughs" appears in the 1855
text but was dropped in 1867. (See also *Notes and Fragments* in *Complete Writings,*
IX, 34–36.) These notes are undated but they must have been written about 1855
or before.

[8] "Song of Myself," Section 5. In the 1855 edition the text reads "elderhand"
instead of "promise."

[9] See *Prose Works 1892,* II, 404. In "Song of Prudence" (1856) he had written:

Whitman's faith in the individual was undoubtedly to a great extent indigenous; even so, it was a characteristic of the romantic philosophy. These words of Herder, written in the eighteenth century, or their equivalent, might be Whitman's:

The power which thinks and acts in me, is, from its nature, as eternal as that, which holds together the stars: its organs may wear out, and the sphere of its action may change, as earths wear away, and stars change their places, but the laws, through which it is where it is, and will again come in other forms, never alter. Its nature is as eternal as the mind of God; and the foundations of my being (not of my corporeal frame) are as fixed as the pillars of the universe. For all being is alike an indivisible idea; in the greatest, as well as in the least, founded on the same laws. Thus the universe confirms the eternity of the core of my being, of my intrinsic life. Wherever or whatever I may be, I shall be, as I now am, a power in the universal system of powers, a being in the inconceivable harmony of some world of God.[10]

As a matter of fact, Whitman's philosophy united transcendentalism not only with Darwinism and Hegelianism but with Jacksonian equalitarianism as well and even found the naturalism of Rousseau acceptable. It is true that, like Emerson, he became a bit more conservative as he grew older, but he was not even in his youth wholly antagonistic to conservative movements. He contributed to Whig periodicals, and read them, as readily as Democratic ones. He read Voltaire as well as Rousseau, accepted such of their ideas as agreed with his own, but rejected their personalities with equal distaste.

In 1856 he published a fragment of an essay on Voltaire in the phrenological publication *Life Illustrated,* in which he passed the verdict that though the "mighty infidel" helped on a great work—the preparation of men's minds for the French and American Revolutions—he was neither a humanitarian nor a democrat, but "the friend and advocate of kings and empresses." [11] Yet in old age he called Voltaire a great man, "whose ridicule did more for justice than the battles of armies." [12] This good opinion of Voltaire might have been influ-

---

"Charity and personal force are the only investments worth any thing." And in the 1856 version of "By Blue Ontario's Shore" he wrote: "Produce great Persons, the rest follows" (Sec. 3). In *Notes and Fragments (Complete Writings,* IX, 95) he wrote: "Produce great persons and the producers of great persons . . . all the rest surely follows."

10 *Outlines of a Philosophy of the History of Man* (T. Churchill's translation, 2nd ed., 1803), I, 5.

11 This fragment is reprinted in *New York Dissected,* ed. Emory Holloway and Ralph Adimari (New York, 1936), pp. 70–73.

12 *WWC,* II, 16. In conversation with Traubel July 18, 1888.

enced by his reading of James Parton's biography (1881) and John Morley's (1886). Parton reprints excerpts from Victor Hugo's eulogy of Voltaire on the one hundredth anniversary of his death, May 30, 1878. Whitman had read this eulogy either in Parton's biography[13] or in a periodical with the title *Man*, a liberal journal of progress and reform published between 1878 and 1884, copies of which are now very rare. W. D. O'Connor wrote to Whitman on March 15, 1883: "I got the Man this afternoon with Parton's version of Hugo's magnificent oration on Voltaire. Also the Tribune catalogue which I have not yet had time to look into. Thanks."[14] O'Connor was a great admirer of Hugo. Where Whitman got a copy of *Man* I do not know. Whitman's comment on what Voltaire did for justice may have been suggested by a passage in the first chapter of Morley's book: "Wrong-doing and injustice were not simply words on his lips; they went as knives to the heart; he suffered with the victim, and consumed with an active rage against the oppressor."[15] John Morley, then editor of the London *Fortnightly Review*, visited Whitman in 1868, and in December, Whitman sent him a manuscript with the title "Thou Vast Rondure Swimming in Space," which afterward became "Passage to India," which Morley agreed to publish in the issue of April 1869; however, it was not published there or elsewhere with that title.[16] In a letter to Bucke, October 28–29, 1889, Whitman said he had been reading a book about Voltaire, adding: "I wonder if some of his causticity han't got in me."[17] It seems probable that it was Morley's book to which he referred here.

However, he did not have to depend on secondary sources for his knowledge of Voltaire's "causticity," for he owned and doubtless read at various times Voltaire's *Philosophical Dictionary*, and wrote his name in heavy black ink on the title page. It is now in the Van Sinderin Collection in the Yale University Library. The book is described as "the first American stereotype edition" and was published in Boston in 1836. It is a reprint, containing two volumes in one, of the 1824 English edition published in six volumes, edited with some additions and notes by Abner Kneeland. On the blank page before the title of the book is pasted a scrap of paper with the following in ink:

13 II, 634–36, which concludes the book.

14 *WWC*, IV, 360. The word "Man" is followed by *sic* in brackets. This was inserted not by Traubel, presumably, but by the editor of Vol. IV, Sculley Bradley, who may not have known that *Man* was the title of a periodical. There is a marked copy of *Man* for April 1882 in the Whitman Collection in the Library of Congress.

15 *Voltaire*, p. 13.

16 See *WWC*, I, 216–17; II, 237; III, 322, 426–27; and *Correspondence*, II, 77.

17 *Correspondence*, IV, 391.

"*Directions to Binder.* bind in plain, strong, light-colored leather, with the words, *Voltaire's Dictionary* on the back." This is in Whitman's handwriting, but there is no date given and it is impossible to tell if the book really was rebound for Whitman, and, if so, when. A newspaper clipping from the *London Daily News*, dated in pencil, "Dec. 20, 1891," is pasted under the directions to the binder. The clipping is headed "Ferney's Statue of Voltaire" and is about the unveiling of the statue. The name plate of William F. Gable, who owned the book before Van Sinderin purchased it in 1924, is in the present binding, which is green and apparently not the one Whitman specified. A plate at the end of the volume dates Gable's Whitman collection at 1910, and he may have acquired the volume at that time. I have found nothing to indicate who the owner was before that.[18]

When Whitman acquired the book I do not know, but I suspect it was purchased secondhand just before or after he published the article in *Life Illustrated* in 1856. If it had been a new copy he probably would not have wanted it rebound. There are no marks in the volume except three that Whitman himself made. Among the scraps preserved now in the Trent Collection are the following: "Two samples of Voltaire's writings.—Translated from his *Philosophical Dictionary.* See what is marked on pages 173 and 174." This note is written on the verso of the paper containing geographical notes on Europe, which seem to have been made in the late 1850's.[19] Along the margin of Voltaire's article "Character," beginning on page 173 and ending on page 174, a pencil line is drawn, and in the margin to the right of this heading, in pencil, apparently in Whitman's handwriting, "side / head / and / set close." The same type of marks and notation are made on pages 403–4 beside Voltaire's article "Great—Greatness." Page 403 is folded down as if to direct the printer's attention to it. It looks as if Whitman wanted to reprint these two excerpts in his article for *Life Illustrated*, assuming he had Voltaire's book then; though they might have been intended for his own newspaper, the Brooklyn *Daily Times*, which he edited from about May 1857 to about June 1859. As I have noted, the *Life Illustrated* article on Voltaire is called a fragment. As submitted by Whitman it may have been complete and much longer, including the two quotations from the

---

[18] I am much indebted to Nolan E. Smith, who provided much of the information about the volume given above. I examined the book myself many years ago and made some notes, but overlooked a few particulars. W. F. Gable contributed a brief article to the *Conservator*, "On Whitman's Lincolnism," in 1919, XXX, 42.

[19] The population statistics appear to be based on census figures made after 1850 and before 1860. Presumably the note on Voltaire was written about the same time.

Philosophical Dictionary as samples of Voltaire's style, editorial cutting having reduced it to its fragmentary form. If the marked passages were printed in the *Daily Times*, there is no mention of the fact in the materials reprinted or the editorial matter in *I Sit and Look Out*. The only other mark in the book is the underlining in black ink, like that of Whitman's signature on the title page, of the word *amours* on p. xxxiv of the Preface to the London edition, which is reprinted. There doesn't seem to be any significance in this mark except possibly as an indication of Whitman's interest in French words at this time.

Voltaire is mentioned one other time in *Notes and Fragments*, this time in connection with the theater. "I fancy the classical tragedies of Corneille, Racine, Voltaire &c., must illustrate the vital differences between a native and normal growth (as the Greek tragedies themselves) and all that comes from the mere study of that growth." Immediately below this sentence, in the same note, is the following: "November, 1855, I saw Rachel in *Athalie* at the Academy of Music." Actually she appeared in only the second act November 16, and William Swinton may have been with Whitman when he saw her then.[20]

Whitman in the 1850's may have been more in sympathy with Rousseau than with Voltaire, or, if not with the man, at least with some of his ideas. Sadakichi Hartmann said Whitman told him that he had not read Rousseau,[21] but this was not true as Whitman must have been aware when he made the statement. When and how much he had read of the works of Rousseau is uncertain. In one way or another he may have known Rousseau's ideas of education in the late 1830's and early 1840's, when he was a country schoolteacher, though it is doubtful that he ever read *Émile*, Rousseau's so-called novel, which is subtitled *A Treatise on Education*.[22] In the *Eagle* for July

---

[20] *Complete Writings*, IX, 82. Whitman preserved a clipping of an article on Racine's *Rachel* in *Putnam's Magazine*, Sept. 1855 (Bucke's No. 421). Part of Whitman's note may have been drawn from an article on "The Drama in France—Classic and Romantic," possibly written by William Swinton, in the October number of *Putnam's*, or he might have got his information directly from William Swinton. (See my "Notes on Whitman's Reading," pp. 343–44. See also "Whitman and William Swinton," by C. Carroll Hollis, *American Literature*, XXX [Jan. 1959], 428, note 14. This article contains the fullest available account of the relations of Whitman and William Swinton.)

[21] *Conversations with Walt Whitman* (New York, 1895), p. 26.

[22] *Émile* is listed in an English translation in four volumes in the 1878 catalogue of the Brooklyn Library, with the title *Emilius and Sophia; or, A New System of Education* (London, 1767). The catalogue does not show when books were acquired. Some of Rousseau's ideas on education were doubtless available through secondary sources, such as the lectures of Horace Mann, whom Whitman may have heard in

11, 1846, he names Rousseau as one of the "great intellects of Europe" and speaks of his "fascinating melancholy," but of course he may have been echoing opinions then available from secondary sources.[23]

It is certain that he read parts or all of Rousseau's *Confessions* in the translation of his friend William Swinton, published in 1856. He called it a "frivolous, chattering, repulsive book that still has a great lesson in its pages, and whose revelations one keeps reading somehow to the end."[24] His biographical notes were probably drawn from Swinton's introduction and are probably correct so far as information was available at that time. He ends his note with the question, "Did he or did he not die of suicide?" In his article on Voltaire in *Life Illustrated* he quotes a paragraph on Voltaire's last days and death from Julia Kavanagh's *Woman in France during the Eighteenth Century*, and immediately after it introduces another quotation from the same source on Rousseau's death with the following sentence: "There was another equally great character, from whom, in France, the first can hardly be separated, much as they contrast against each other."[25] The account of Rousseau's death is romantic fiction, and of course makes no mention of suicide. It quotes his dying request as "Let me behold once more the glorious setting sun," and says his last glance was toward the sun. In Whitman's talk to the Brooklyn Art Union on "Art and Artists" he quotes the same request of Rousseau and describes his death in a similar way, obviously drawing on Julia Kavanagh's book.[26] In his talk Whitman identifies Nature and Art, but it is obvious from the context that he conceives both nature and art in the terms of William Cullen Bryant, whose "Forest Hymn" he quotes in part, and not in those of *Leaves of Grass*. His conclusion is that despite Rousseau's "sarcasms upon art" he was an artist because he loved the beauty of nature represented by the "glorious setting sun." He could hardly, at this time, have read much of Rousseau or conceived the central philosophy of *Leaves of Grass*.

Among the manuscripts in the Trent Collection is a brief summary in Whitman's handwriting of the Preface and the nine short chapters of Book I of Rousseau's *Social Contract*.[27] Hollis suggests that Swin-

---

1842. (See *Walt Whitman Looks at the Schools*, ed. Florence Bernstein Freedman [New York, 1950], pp. 54–56.)

[23] In the article on " 'Home' Literature" (reprinted in *UPP*, I, 121–22, and *GF*, II, 242–43).

[24] See *Notes and Fragments* (*Complete Writings*, IX, 80–81).

[25] Reprinted in *New York Dissected*, pp. 72–73.

[26] *UPP*, I, 241–47; reprinted from the Brooklyn *Daily Advertiser*, April 3, 1851. Julia Kavanagh's book was published in 1850. The talk was made March 31, 1851.

[27] Published in *Faint Clews & Indirections*, ed. Clarence Gohdes and Rollo G.

ton may have been reading the French text of the *Contrat Social* and translating as he read, with Whitman sitting near and taking rapid notes. This may be true of some of the notes, but perhaps not all. Hollis does not attempt to identify the French text, but that can be done by comparing Whitman's translation with available texts in his time. What Whitman designates *"Preface,* to the First Edition" is really in that edition the "Avertissement," to which Whitman has added, as if they were part of the main text of the Preface, several statements drawn from the footnote to the "Avertissement." Whitman's paragraph beginning with "Montesquieu" is the first paragraph of the footnote and is in quotation marks in the French text; it is credited as "(Note de Brizard.)" The reference is to G. Brizard, one of the editors of the *Oeuvres completes de Jean Jacques Rousseau* (38 volumes, Paris, 1788–1793). Whitman's paragraph beginning "Rousseau" is part of the note, not in quotation in the French text, of the editor of this text of the *Contrat Social,* signed "G.P.," the identifying initials of Louis Germain Petitain. This is in *Oeuvres de J. J. Rousseau, avec des notes historiques,* 20 volumes, published in Paris in 1819–20. This edition was reprinted complete in 4 large volumes in Paris in 1837. *Du Contrat Social* is in Vol. I. This "Avertissement" and the notes by the editor, including the one quoted from Brizard, are to be found in no other edition. It is not likely that Swinton, then a youth of twenty-three, owned the 20-volume set, but not at all unlikely that he owned the 4-volume reprint and made his translation of the *Confessions* from that edition. This edition is not listed in the Brooklyn Library or the Astor Library catalogue; hence it was probably Swinton's, and could have been seen by Whitman. Yet Whitman's rendering of the name "Brizard" as "Brissard" suggests that he was depending on his ear, not his eye, for the spelling. But Whitman interpolated a number of comments of his own in his translated notes, which would have been difficult if he was translating from Swinton's reading. My conclusion is that Whitman originally made notes from Swinton's reading but later went over them, perhaps with the French text before him.

Whitman undoubtedly learned something of the French language from William Swinton to supplement what he had previously picked up in miscellaneous reading and during his brief residence in New Orleans in 1848. Swinton may also have stimulated his interest in words and contributed indirectly to the writing of the manuscript of

Silver (Durham, N.C., 1949), pp. 33–41. Book I is the shortest of the four books constituting the *Social Contract,* and includes but little more than one-eighth of the entire work.

his *American Primer*. Hollis believes that Whitman contributed substantially to the writing of Swinton's first book, *Rambles among
Words* (1859) and undertakes to identify a considerable number of
paragraphs written wholly by Whitman. I am inclined to disagree
with that judgment. In examining some of these paragraphs I have
found numerous words not listed in the Whitman Concordance and
apparently not used anywhere in *Leaves of Grass*, the Prefaces, or
Democratic Vistas.[28] In the Preface to his first edition of *Rambles
among Words*, dated April 23, 1859, Swinton states that "the whole
book was written half-a-dozen years ago," and he implies that this
was about the same time that he wrote the two articles for *Putnam's
Magazine* under the title "Rambles over the Realms of Verbs and
Substantives," published in the issues of November and December,
1854; and in the Preface to the edition of 1872 he says: "The material
of this little book originally appeared in the form of articles contributed to *Putnam's Magazine* . . . during the years 1853 and 1854.
Afterwards the papers were put together in book form, and published in 1858."

Actually Swinton's two articles were the only contributions on the
subject published by *Putnam's*, but it is quite possible that he contributed others in 1853 that were not published, and that these together with the published articles constituted the chief subject matter
of the later *Rambles among Words*. It is also possible that the brief
review of Maximilian Schele de Vere's *Outlines of Comparative
Philology*, published in *Putnam's* for December 1853, was written by
Swinton, and that in this way he came to possess the copy later owned
by Whitman which has inscribed on the flyleaf: "Wm. Swinton,
Greensboro, North Carolina." An anonymous biographical article
in the *Historical Magazine* for November 1869, when Swinton was
at the University of California, evidently written by Swinton himself or someone close to him, states that he left Amherst in 1853 to
assume the Chair of Ancient and Modern Languages at Edgeworth
Female Seminary, but that "his residence in the South was not agreeable, and in 1854, he removed to New York, and occupied a Chair in
the Mount Washington Collegiate Institute in that City."[29] Whether
he first "occupied" the Chair in 1854, or in 1855, as stated in the *Dictionary of American Biography*, is not certain. As suggested previously, he probably began to write for the New York *Times* in 1855
and, according to the writer in the *Historical Magazine*, became a

---

[28] Such words as "ejects," "effete," "humanitary," "opulences," "propulsive,"
"poetries," and "siderial," which I suspect Whitman would have avoided as
pretentious.

[29] XVI, 295–98.

member of the editorial staff in 1858. If Swinton was not known to Whitman until he began to write for the New York *Times* after the middle of the year 1855, as seems probable, he could not have influenced the writing of any of the poems of the first edition of *Leaves of Grass*, nor most of the new poems in the 1856 edition.[30] Whether Whitman wrote any appreciable portion of *Rambles among Words* also seems to me doubtful, though he probably read the manuscript before publication and made some suggestions. The only portion of the book that seems to me unmistakably in the style of Whitman is the last short chapter, six pages, with the subtitle "English in America."

The only other French writer likely to have influenced the writing of *Leaves of Grass* was George Sand.[31] On September 27, 1847, Whitman reviewed Francis George Shaw's translation of *Le Compagnon du Tour de France,* which was published in New York by W. H. Graham in 1847 under the title *The Journeyman Joiner; or, the Companion of the Tour of France.* Between the title page and the Preface a statement is reprinted from Joseph Mazzini's essay on George Sand, published in the *People's Journal,* of London, which I quote in part: "The evil that she has pictured is not *her* evil, it is *ours.* It does not come to us from her; it was and is yet around us, in the air we breathe, in the foundations of our corrupt society, in the hypocrisy, above all, which has spread its ample cloak over all the manifestations of our life . . . she has, with daring hand, torn away the veil; she has laid bare the festering wounds, and she has cried to us: *Behold your Society!*"[32] Since Whitman's review, as reprinted by Holloway, is brief, it may be quoted in full: "That Madame Sand's works are looked upon by a portion of the public, and of critics, with a feeling of great repugnance, there is no denying. But the talented French woman is nevertheless one of a class much needed in the world—needed lest the world stagnate in wrongs merely from precedent. We are fully of the belief that 'free discussion,' upon any subject of general and profound interest, is not only allowable, but in most cases desirable. And this is all we have to say to those who put Madame Sand's books down by

---

[30] According to his brother John, as reported by Robert Waters in *Career and Conversation of John Swinton* (Chicago, 1902), pp. 27–28, William Swinton began writing for the *Times* about September 1855. Professor Hollis suggests that Whitman's friendship with him began about November 1855.

[31] After 1870 Whitman had a good deal to say of Victor Hugo, but I find no evidence that he knew either Hugo's poetry or his fiction during the early years, although he did hear Verdi's opera based on Hugo's drama *Hernani.* He read Taine's *History of English Literature,* but that was not available in English until 1871.

[32] The entire article was reprinted in *The Harbinger,* May 29, 1847, where Whitman might easily have read it.

a mere flourish of prejudice. . . . The 'Journeyman Joiner' is a work of very great interest as a story. Indeed we know of few that are more so." [33]

The "prejudice" referred to by Whitman was widespread among English critics, especially those who wrote for the conservative journals. Her well-publicized liaisons with other men after she separated from her husband as well as the sexual irregularities of some of her heroines accounted for some of the prejudice. Also, probably, her social criticism and her association with Pierre Leroux, Lamennais, and other radical democrats, subjected her to suspicions of Tory journals like the *Quarterly Review* and some American critics aping their British fellows. Whitman could have found most of the sentiments of his review in the essay by Mazzini reprinted in the *Harbinger* mentioned earlier. For example, Whitman's statement that George Sand is one of a class much needed "lest the world stagnate in wrongs merely from precedent," is much like statements by Mazzini found in the *Harbinger*, including this sentence: "Human indolence and apathy are the greatest enemies that truth, and the genius which proclaims truth, can encounter upon earth." [34] William and Mary Howitt were among those in England who admired George Sand's works. In their *Howitt's Journal* they published several brief articles and reviews praising her work in 1847, but whether Whitman read that journal I cannot say. [35] He clipped and preserved an article (Bucke's No. 274) called "Shakespeare *versus* Sand" from the *American Whig*

[33] *UPP*, I, 135. I have not seen the text in the *Eagle* and cannot say whether the three dots in Holloway's text represent significant omissions.

[34] See the *Harbinger*, IV, 393. See also the essay on George Sand in VI, 39, where this and other portions of this essay are reprinted in *Life and Writings of Joseph Mazzini*, 6 vols., London, 1864–70. This volume might have been included in the box of books, including works by Mazzini, Carlyle, and others, sent by Thomas Dixon, of Sunderland, England, to Whitman in 1870 and acknowledged by Whitman in a letter dated June 30, 1870 (reprinted in *WWC*, II, 310). A volume of selected essays, edited by William Clarke and published by Walter Scott, London, 1887, was in Whitman's possession in March, 1889. This contained Mazzini's essay on Byron and Goethe, but not the essay on George Sand. (See *WWC*, IV, 349. See also *Correspondence*, II, 99–100, note 22.) He said, on a later occasion, "I knew these essays as many as forty—at least 30—years ago." (*Correspondence*, V, 395.) The only place he could have seen them as much even as twenty years before was in the sixth volume of the *Life and Works*, though, as indicated above, he could have seen the essay on George Sand in the *Harbinger* almost forty years before.

[35] *Howitt's Journal*, a weekly, in support of popular causes, was published from Jan. 2, 1847, until June 24, 1848, three volumes, when the Howitts went into bankruptcy under circumstances related to their connection with the *People's Journal*, which supported the same causes. There is a picture of George Sand as a young woman in the issue of March 3, 1847.

Review for May 1847. The author, who is not named in the *Review*, out-Toried the Tories in his prejudice against all French writers and especially against George Sand. He admits, or rather boasts, that he had read only one of her novels, and that was not *Consuelo*. He does not name the novel, though if one may judge by his comments on it, it was certainly one of her earlier ones, perhaps *Indiana*, or *Lelia*, or *Jacques*, but what he says sheds little light on what he had read. Most of the essay is concerned with praise of Shakespeare, and indeed all British writers, the worst of whom, he believes, are better than the best of the French.

Although Whitman notes that *The Journeyman Joiner* is "of great interest as a story," it is apparent that his chief interest was in the author's airing of the principles of the movement for the organization of workingmen. Whitman remembered *The Journeyman Joiner* and mentioned it to his friend Helen Price as one of his favorites.[36] Even as late as 1889 he remembered very well, he said, the subject matter of the story, although he was not certain he remembered the title correctly. He told Traubel, "Madame Dudevant's story was an extra fine one—I read it—ah! what was its name? Its subject matter is quite plain to me—the title is gone—'A Journey Through France' or something like that was the sub-title."[37] Esther Shephard, in *Walt Whitman's Pose*, suggests that Whitman had tried to read the French edition of this book, published in 1851, with the help of Shaw's translation,[38] but the main title of Shaw's translation, *The Journeyman Joiner*, is not in the French text nor in any translation other than Shaw's, and what Whitman takes for a subtitle is in fact a poor translation of the main and only title in the French text. Whitman also mentioned *Consuelo* to Helen Price, and a short novel with the title *The Devil's Pool*, a translation by F. G. Shaw of *La Mare au Diable*, published in New York in 1847. This is a simple story of the love of two young peasants and has been much admired and several times reprinted as a text for American students of French. The fact that Whitman liked it as well as *The Journeyman Joiner* proves that his interest in George Sand's writing was in no way limited to her social and philosophical ideas. A writer in the *London Spectator* said that "Truth, justice, and love are the ruling objects and powers of her ethics," and that several of her books, including *La Mare au Diable* were "directed to illustrate the power of goodness and kindness in

36 This would have been after 1856 and probably before 1860, the period of her closest association with Whitman. See Bucke's *Walt Whitman* (Philadelphia, 1883), pp. 29–30.

37 *WWC*, V, 350.

38 *Walt Whitman's Pose* (New York, 1936), p. 426.

elevating the soul and diffusing happiness."[39] It is likely that Whitman read this novel about the same time that he read and reviewed *The Journeyman Joiner*. How many other novels by George Sand he read I do not know. He sent Peter Doyle a copy of *A Rolling Stone* in early January 1874, which presumably he read before sending it, though he does not state that he has in his January 9 letter to Doyle asking if he had received the book.[40] It is the story of a handsome youth, son of a peasant, who traveled with a minor theatrical group for several years because he was in love with one of the pretty actresses; because she rejected him he returned to his native town where, thereafter, he sought the company of homely girls and avoided the pretty ones. It is an interesting narrative of adventure but has little literary worth, and was apparently sent to Peter Doyle as the kind of novel an uneducated man might enjoy reading.

The two novels of Madame Dudevant that Whitman most enjoyed and longest remembered were *Consuelo* and its sequel *The Countess of Rudolstadt*, in the translations of Francis G. Shaw, published in 1847. Consuelo, a talented Spanish Gypsy girl who never knew her father and whose mother was a wandering streetsinger, is the heroine of both stories. Whitman usually referred to the two novels as though he thought of them as really one. In the Shaw translation *Consuelo* was in three volumes, *The Countess of Rudolstadt* in two. He told Traubel that he thought he or his mother had acquired the books in 1841, unless Traubel misread his own notes and took a 7 for a 1. It would be strange if he said 1841 since he had the books on the table before him at the time bearing the date of publication. He had an exaggerated opinion of the novel's literary value, presumably formed at the time he first read it, although he must have reread it later. "The book is a masterpiece: truly a masterpiece," he told Traubel; "the noblest work left by George Sand—the noblest in many respects, on its own field, in all literature."[41]

In *Walt Whitman's Pose*, Esther Shephard undertakes to prove that Whitman's whole conception of the poet of *Leaves of Grass* was derived from his reading of the "Epilogue" to *The Countess of Rudolstadt*, or rather that part of it which George Sand entitled "Letter of Philo to Ignatius Joseph Martinowicz," which presents Consuelo, who had long before lost her singing voice, with her husband, the former Count of Rudolstadt, now dispossessed of his title and his wealth, and mentally deranged after many persecutions, wandering

[39] This article was reprinted in *The Harbinger*, IV (Feb. 13, 1847), 183–85.

[40] *Correspondence*, II, 265. This was a translation by Carroll Owen of *Pierre qui roule* (Paris, 1870), published in Boston in 1871.

[41] *WWC*, III, 422–23.

in the forests of Bohemia, where they are questioned by Philo and his friend Spartacus, whom George Sand identifies with Adam Weishaupt, the historical founder of the Order of Illuminati. "*Consuelo*," Mrs. Shephard maintains, "and *The Devil's Pool* had no influence on Whitman that would be traceable in *Leaves of Grass*; *The Journeyman Joiner* influence belongs mainly to the prose phase of the early years of the long foreground, carrying over probably a little to the comradeship preaching in *Leaves of Grass*."[42] This is rather surprising, since most if not all of the social and philosophical ideas stated by Albert in Philo's letter can be found expressed or implied in *Consuelo* and in the main story of *The Countess of Rudolstadt*.[43] *The Journeyman Joiner*, in fact, could have had little influence on what she calls "the prose phase" of Whitman's early writing, but it may have been one of many books that confirmed views already formed as to the corruption of European statecraft and priestcraft and the imminence of revolution and social change in Europe.[44]

The first English translation of *Consuelo* and *The Countess of Rudolstadt* was made by Francis G. Shaw and published serially in *The Harbinger*, an Associationist weekly sponsored by Brook Farm supporters and published simultaneously in Boston and New York. The first issue is dated June 14, 1845, and the last, apparently, in February 1849. It was edited at first by George Ripley and later by Parke Godwin, and among its regular contributors, besides the editors, were the Fourierist Albert Brisbane, Horace Greeley, Charles A. Dana, and Francis G. Shaw. Several of the contributors, notably Dana and Godwin, were well known personally to Whitman. The publication of Shaw's translation began with the very first issue and continued regularly at the rate of two or three chapters each week until June 27, 1846, when the last two chapters of *Consuelo* were printed. The first chapter of *The Countess of Rudolstadt* appeared in the issue of July 4, 1846, and the last section of the "Epilogue," concluding the story, in the issue of March 20, 1847. In the *Harbinger* text, as in all other texts that I have seen, *Consuelo* has 105 chapters and the unnumbered "Conclusion," and *The Countess of Rudolstadt* has 41 besides the unnumbered "Epilogue." Also, in *The Countess of Rudolstadt* the 41 chapters are divided into two volumes as in most other texts, but in *Consuelo* the 105 chapters are divided into seven vol-

42 *Walt Whitman's Pose*, p. 221.

43 For some examples see *Consuelo*, Chapters 24 and 25 and *The Countess of Rudolstadt*, Chapters 11 through 17.

44 For examples of Whitman's views on these matters before he read *The Journeyman Joiner*, see the articles he published in the *Eagle* in 1846 and early in 1847 (reprinted in *GF*, I, 1–50).

umes, as in no other text, English or French, that I have seen. Both novels were originally published in the *Revue Indépendante* of Paris, founded by Pierre Leroux with the support of George Sand herself. The first installment of *Consuelo* appeared in the issue of February 1, 1842, and on the following December 24 the publication of the first two volumes of the novel was announced. The remaining volumes, three and four, were announced on May 6, 1843. The first installment of *La Comtesse de Rudolstadt* came out in the issue of June 25, 1843, and the last volume of that novel was announced on June 8, 1844. On January 18, 1845, an edition of both *Consuelo* and *La Comtesse de Rudolstadt*, in six volumes, was announced by Charpentier.[45] I have not seen a file of the *Revue Indépendante*, but I suspect no volume divisions were indicated in that publication and that Shaw translated directly from the *Revue* text rather than from the first book publication. Since the book divisions of the *Countess of Rudolstadt* agree with other book publications, it is likely that it was translated from the Charpentier edition of January 1845.

There is no way to determine when Whitman first read these novels. The first book publication of Shaw's translation of *Consuelo* was announced in the *Harbinger* of June 20, 1846; it was in two volumes totaling 1,000 pages, by Ticknor & Co. of Boston. The second edition of Shaw's translation of *Consuelo*, in three volumes, was issued by Ticknor in 1847, probably early in that year, since a third edition came out the same year, together with Shaw's *The Countess of Rudolstadt*, in two volumes. This must have appeared after March 20, since the *Harbinger* presented the last installment of the "Epilogue" on that date. I doubt that Whitman, in 1845, would have had a sufficiently lasting interest in a French novel to enable him to follow Shaw's translation through the fifty or more issues of the *Harbinger*, but it is possible that he first noticed it there and found it sufficiently interesting to justify his purchasing the three-volume edition and its two-volume sequel in 1847. At that time he would not have been interested in the mystical philosophy briefly suggested in *Consuelo* and more fully developed in the "Epilogue" to the *Countess of Rudolstadt*, and in any case he would have found this only after reading several hundred pages at least. What would have interested him in 1847 and for several years thereafter was the fact that the heroine, Consuelo, was an opera singer, for during that period he was tremendously impressed by the Italian opera in New York, first as represented by the Havana Company, and later by such singers as Bettini

45 These dates are to be found in the chronologies printed in Vols. V and VI of *Correspondence de George Sand*, ed. Georges Lubin (Paris, 1969).

and Alboni, whom he heard in the early fifties.[46] A few years later he
talked often with Helen Price about his great love of music. "In talking to him once about music," she wrote, "I found he had read George
Sand's 'Consuelo,' and enjoyed it thoroughly. One passage he liked
best was where Consuelo sings in church at the very beginning of her
musical career. He said he had read it over many times." [47] The passage that Whitman liked so much may be found near the end of
Chapter X, very early in the first volume of *Consuelo*. Consuelo was
only eighteen then, and though not entirely untaught, was untried
by a public appearance, but as she rose to sing the psalm selected for
her, she was transformed by religious exaltation. "A divine fire rose
to her cheeks and a sacred flame flashed from her eyes as she filled the
building with that unequalled voice and that victorious accent, pure
and truly grandiose, which can spring only from a great intelligence
united to a great heart." [48] In other auditions, outside the church,
Consuelo proved her skill in nonreligious music to be equally great.
When she sang a dramatic love song she was able to identify her emotions with those of the character. "She was sublime in her pathos, her
simplicity, and her grandeur, and her face was even more beautiful
than it had been in church. . . . She was no longer a saint, but what
was still better, a woman utterly possessed and carried away by the
passion of love." [49] The characteristics of fine Italian singing illustrated by Consuelo were precisely those which appealed most to Whitman in the Italian opera of New York. He heard and admired the
"vocal dexterity" of Jenny Lind, but "there was a vacuum in the head
of the performance," and even her singing of the "grandest religious
airs" did not touch his heart. It was quite otherwise with the Italian
tenor, Bettini, whose voice affected him to tears. Others, the critics
said, were more perfectly artistical. "But the singing of this man has
breathing blood within it; the living soul, of which the lower stage
they call art, is but the shell and sham." [50] He was thrilled "by the
deep passion of Alboni's contralto" as by the voice of no other woman
singer.[51]

The only external evidence that Whitman was especially interested
in the "Epilogue" and the mystical philosophy of Albert Podiebrad
(the Count of Rudolstadt, or Tresmigistus, as he was sometimes

46 See Chapter VII, pp. 92–97.

47 Bucke, *Walt Whitman*, pp. 29–30.

48 I quote from Frank H. Potter's translation, I, 87, published in four volumes
by Dodd, Mead & Co., New York, 1889.

49 *Ibid.*, p. 105.

50 Reprinted from the New York *Evening Post*, Aug. 14, 1851, in *UPP*, I, 257.

51 "The Old Bowery," *Prose Works 1892*, II, 592.

called) in his later years of apparent madness and flight from the officers of the Austrian authorities is a passage which he copied, with some amendments, and which is printed in *Notes and Fragments*:

"The unknown refused to explain himself. 'What could I say to you that I have not said in another (my own) language? Is it my fault that you have not understood me? You think I wished to speak to your senses, and it was my soul spoke to you. What do I say! It was the soul of the whole of humanity that spoke to you through mine.' "[52] There is no way to determine whether Whitman made this note before or after 1855. He made a few slight alterations, as he usually did in quoting, and one more important one that needs some comment and explanation. This is the substitution of "another (my own) language" for "a more beautiful language." Mrs. Shephard argues that this change is "positive evidence" that Whitman "conceived of himself as an incarnation or impersonation of such a poet in America"— that is, such a poet as the "unknown" of the passage quoted.[53] She assumes that the words "my own" referred to Whitman's language, whereas obviously they refer to the language of music—the language of the music of the unknown's violin, which he had just been playing. Another gross misconception is Mrs. Shephard's argument that Whitman borrowed his image of the poet of *Leaves of Grass* from this unknown, who in reality is not a workman but the Count of Rudolstadt (Albert Podiebrad), who is disguised and has adopted a wandering life with his family for the sole purpose of escaping recognition. There is in fact little or no similarity between Whitman's person, or habits, or dress and those of George Sand's disguised violinist-poet aristocrat. Many other weaknesses in Mrs. Shephard's argument are apparent to any close reader of her book who is familiar with Whitman's life and poetry. The philosophical ideas which she assumes Whitman derived from Albert's mystic "poem" pronounced in a trance-like state, were accessible, as I have already demonstrated, in dozens of books by authentic philosophical writers of the eighteenth and nineteenth centuries in Europe and America. I do not maintain that George Sand's books were wholly without influence on Whitman, only that they were agreeable to his pre-existent taste. Most likely he liked them because they confirmed ideas already formed in his mind before he read them carefully.

[52] *Complete Writings*, IX, 19.
[53] *Walt Whitman's Pose*, pp. 178, 187.

XIII. *Heinrich Heine and Others*

I N HIS later years Whitman showed some interest in the works and
the personality of Heinrich Heine. He might have seen a few
poems in collections, such as Longfellow's *Poets and Poetry of Europe*
(1845), and fragments of prose in Hedge's *Prose Writers of Germany*,
but he could have acquired no considerable knowledge of Heine until
1856, when he read Charles G. Leland's *Pictures of Travel*, a translation of Heine's *Reisebilder*, and made the following note: "Heinrich
Heine (just dead 1856) Pictures of Travel (1856), portrait—leaning,
sleeping head. Poems (as translated) seem to be fanciful and viva-
cious, rather ironical and melancholy with a dash of the poetical
craziness." [1] Whitman apparently owned a copy of the book, for he
had it in 1888 and had been reading it on May 5, when Traubel came
to his room. Whitman said, "I have the book here; it is good to read
any time." When Traubel came on July 13, Whitman suggested he
read the book, saying of Heine: "He was the master of a pregnant
sarcasm: he brought down a hundred humbuggeries if he brought
down two. At times he plays with you with a deliberate, baffling
sportiveness." On July 27 he remarked that although most translations did not satisfy him, "Leland's translation of the *Reisebilder*
is . . . a joy and a delight." [2] I doubt that Whitman had read any other
translation, or that he was capable of making an informed judgment,
since he could not read the original. His statement probably means
no more than that he had a high opinion of Leland and his talents.

1 *Notes and Fragments* (*Complete Writings*, IX, 88). Leland's translation was
first published in several monthly installments beginning about May 1855. The
first edition in book form bears the publication date 1855, although some copies
I have seen contain, inserted before the title page, several "Notices of the Press,"
one of them from the *Knickerbocker Magazine*, Feb. 1856. Another issue, identical
with this but dated 1856 and designated "Second Edition," seems to have been the
one Whitman read, shortly after Heine's death Feb. 16, 1856. The first and second
editions were published by J. Weik of Philadelphia. The Library of Congress
catalogue lists what is designated a "2nd edition," dated 1858, but since the paging
and other particulars are identical with the second edition of 1856 I assume it is
really the same. The only copy of Leland's translation listed in the British Museum
catalogue is called the "Fifth revised edition," and was published in New York
in 1866.

2 *WWC*, I, 106, 461; II, 53.

Although he mentions Leland to Traubel only as the translator of Heine, he knew him quite well at that time. In Leland's journal for April 30, 1881, he notes that he had talked with Whitman, and later entries prove that the two met a number of times thereafter. When Leland's book on *The Gypsies* came out in 1882 he gave Whitman a copy and wrote in it a short complimentary poem.[3] It is possible, though not certain, that Whitman had met Leland in New York in the late 1850's, when for six months he was foreign editor of the New York *Times* and later connected with various publications of Frank Leslie and with the *Knickerbocker Magazine.* Leland was well acquainted with the Bohemian circle that foregathered at Pfaff's restaurant on Broadway, although he never became one of them, apparently because of his wife's distaste for bohemianism. For about ten months, from July 1860 to May 1861, he was editor of *Vanity Fair*, succeeding its founder, Frank Wood, one of the Pfaff circle of Bohemians, many of whom were contributors. It may be that Whitman himself contributed either before or after Leland became editor. The author of the sketch of Whitman in the *National Cyclopaedia of American Biography* (I, 255) makes the following statement about Whitman: "During the first years of the war he wrote for 'Vanity Fair' and other comic or satirical papers in New York, and was a recognized member of a group of young 'Bohemians,' as they were called, made up of musical, dramatic and literary critics attached to the daily and weekly press. At this time, he led the life of a free-lance."[4] Of his work with *Vanity Fair* Leland said, "I held myself very strictly aloof from the Bohemians, save in business affairs."[5]

One reason for supposing that Whitman was aware of Leland during the latter's New York years is that he had previously clipped and preserved four articles by him published in *Sartain's Union Magazine* in 1849. The first was "The Head of Christ, by Steinhauser," in the February number. Of this work Leland says, "We have in it, to borrow the expression and test of Schelling, 'the Infinite made Finite,' to a degree seldom witnessed in modern works of art." In "The Phi-

3 Elizabeth Robins Pennell, *Charles Godfrey Leland, a Biography*, 2 vols. (Boston, 1906), II, 111, 194.

4 In his article "Charles Leland and 'Vanity Fair' " in the *Pennsylvania Magazine of History and Biography* (LXII [July 1938], 309–23), Charles I. Glicksberg quotes this passage from the *National Cyclopaedia* and attributes it to John Burroughs, on what authority I do not know. The articles in the *National Cyclopaedia* are not signed, but John Burroughs is named in a list of contributors to Vol. I.

5 Charles Leland, *Memoirs* (New York, 1893), pp. 233–35. Of his earlier work with Frank Leslie, he wrote that "there was much rather shaky Bohemianism about the frequenters of our sanctum, and all things considered, it was a pity that I ever entered it."

losophy of Art—and Steinhauser's Psyche," in the March number, Leland says, "the character of a genuine work of art, can be determined by the predominance of one of three elements," which he specifies as the Spiritual, the Material, and the Romantic. He thinks the "Psyche" has all three elements, though the spiritual and material predominate; and "the joint action of one or both of these upon the mind of the observer, calling into play his imaginative, associative, and creative powers, beyond the pale of its intended unity" constitutes the statue's *Romance*. In "The Romantic in Literature and Art," in the November issue, Leland says; "Classic Art strove to limit the personal or individual peculiarities of the artist, which constituted his style. Romantic Art extends them. . . . Romantic Art dares to employ everything. . . . From this view of Romantic Art the critic will be disposed to admit the expediency of a progressive philosophy, which shall rather be disposed to examine carefully into, and find a place within its sphere for any new development, than to reject it as inapplicable. . . . A great Romantic Age in the fullest, highest sense, is undoubtedly dawning upon us." On this clipping Whitman noted: "This essay has many good suggestions—the principal fault is that 'Romantic' is not the right word to use, as used in it—(what should be the word?)." The fourth article, clipped from the December issue, is a brief and unimportant note on Victor Hugo.[6] All or most of Leland's ideas in these essays were derived from Schelling, the Schlegels, or other spokesmen of the German Romantic philosophy, and Whitman may already have been familiar with them at the time he made his comment on Leland's use of the term "Romantic." The first item in Part I of Bucke's *Notes and Fragments* might have been a by-product of Whitman's thought on this subject: "Great constituent elements of my poetry—Two, viz.: Materialism—Spirituality—The Intellect, the Esthetic is what is to be the medium of these and to beautify and make serviceable there."[7]

Charles Leland had a younger brother, Henry, whose connection with Whitman and with *Leaves of Grass* in the 1850's, though important, has never been fully reported. His name was apparently not mentioned in Whitman's conversations with Horace Traubel, and we must turn to Charles Leland's biographer and to his own published *Memoirs* for the story of this connection. In his journal, as quoted by his biographer, Leland wrote of Whitman: "Once he told me that—in the darkest years of his life, when he almost despaired, he

<hr>

[6] These clippings, Nos. 527, 528, and 533 of Bucke's list, and the fourth, not on Bucke's list, are in the Trent Collection.
[7] *Complete Writings*, IX, 3.

had been kept up to hope by two letters—one from my brother Henry, who, then in Italy, had seen some of his first scattered poems, and, not knowing him, had written to him very encouragingly, or well,—or however it was. Therefore, he is so much interested in me." [8] This statement is significant as indicating that Whitman's interest in Charles Leland was not so much because he was the translator of Heine, as Traubel's work leads one to believe, as because he was Henry's brother. It is further significant because it links the letter from Henry Leland with a second important letter, which I suspect was none other than the famous letter from Emerson. For more light on the story, we must turn to Charles Leland's *Memoirs*. Henry P. Leland was four years younger than Charles, and much less successful as a writer. He was also interested in painting and apparently went to Rome to study in 1855 or thereabouts.[9] Either before he left this country or soon after arriving in Rome, he read some of Whitman's poems. These could not have been, as Charles thought in the passage quoted above, "scattered poems," for none were then published. He must have seen a copy of the 1855 edition. This would seem to be confirmed by what Charles says in his *Memoirs*. Whitman told him, he says, twelve years after Henry's death, which occurred in 1868, "that there was one year of his life during which he had received no encouragement as a poet, and so much ridicule that he was in utter despondency. At that time he received from Henry, who was unknown to him, a cheering letter, full of admiration, which had a great effect on him, and inspired him to renewed effort. He sent my brother a copy of the first edition of his *Leaves of Grass*, with his autograph, which I still possess. I knew nothing of this till Whitman told me of it. The poet declared to me very explicitly that he had been much influenced by my brother's letter, which was like a single star in a dark night of despair, and I have no doubt that the world owes more to it than will ever be made known." [10]

I do not know whether Whitman ever met Henry Leland, or how much correspondence they had, now all apparently lost. An article praising Whitman and a poem related to him with the title "Enfants de Soixante-Seize" were written by Henry and published in the Philadelphia *City Item* and reprinted in the *Saturday Press* on June 16,

---

8 Pennell, II, 111.

9 Biographical information on Henry is scanty, and I am not sure of dates, but Charles was engaged to be married for five years before he was able, through his father's generosity, to marry in January 1856. I should guess that sending Henry to Rome was another instance of such generosity. (See *ibid.*, I, 243).

10 Charles Leland, *Memoirs* (1893), p. 256. The phrase "dark night of despair" suggests that Henry's letter came to Whitman several months later than Emerson's.

1860.[11] Henry Leland may have sent Whitman clippings of these articles, or he may have sent them directly to Clapp. In any case, Whitman had seen them when he wrote to Clapp on June 12, 1860, to make a "special request" that he reprint them in the next issue of the *Saturday Press*.[12]

Several contributors to the *Saturday Press* used pseudonyms. Clapp himself used the pseudonym "Figaro." Whitman always contributed under his own name, so far as I can tell. On December 24, 1859, he published a poem with the title "A Child's Reminiscence," later changed several times, finally to "Out of the Cradle Endlessly Rocking." Two weeks later, in the issue of January 14, he published, under the title "You and Me To-Day," the poem that later became "With Antecedents." In the next issue, January 21, appeared a clever parody with the title "Yourn and Mine, and Any-Day" attributed to "Saerasmid from Philadelphia." This parody was included in *Leaves of Grass Imprints*, published early in 1860. On January 28 appeared Whitman's poem beginning "Of him I love day and night," thirteen lines, under the title "Poemet." On February 4, also with the title "Poemet," appeared the five-line poem beginning "That Shadow my likeness," which in the 1860 edition was No. 40 in the Calamus group.[13] On February 11 appeared a parody, also signed "Saerasmid," of Whitman's "Poemet" in the issue of January 28. Also on February 11 appeared "Autopathaea. Dedicated to Walt Whitman." This was a general parody of Whitman by "Saerasmid" and applied to no specific poem. A few other parodies of Whitman's poems were published in 1860, including one of "Manahatta" on June 9. "Saerasmid" was a pseudonym of Charles Desmarais Gardette, and was an anagram of his middle name. It may also have been a satiric anagram of "Dims a Seer." Gardette was a newspaperman in Philadelphia at this time and was probably acquainted with Henry P. Leland.[14]

The frequent mention of Heine in Traubel's record of his conversations with Whitman in 1888 was the consequence, in part, of his association with Charles Leland, the translator. Horace Traubel, moreover, kept Whitman's interest alive in all things German, being himself of German origin and a great admirer of German literature.

[11] See Charles I. Glicksberg, "A Friend of Whitman," *American Book Collector*, VI (March 1935), 91–94.

[12] See Whitman's letter, *Correspondence*, I, 55, and note 23 on p. 54.

[13] At one time Whitman considered using the title "Poemet" for "With Antecedents." See manuscripts in the Barrett Collection at the University of Virginia; see also Arthur Golden's *Walt Whitman's Blue Book*, 2 vols. (New York, 1968) I, 174.

[14] See George P. Clark, " 'Saerasmid,' an Early Promoter of Walt Whitman," *American Literature*, XXVII (May 1955), 259–62.

But even in the intermediate years, while Whitman was resident in Washington, he did not lose touch with Heine. In a manuscript notebook in the Library of Congress he made a number of personal notations, some of them seeming to compare his own situation to that of Heine. The following note is of particular interest: "After an Extract from Heine's Diary Nov. 25, 1868—(night)—paraphrased & varied—to live a *more Serene Calm, Philosophic Life—reticent, far more reticent*—yet cheerful, with pleased spirit and pleased manner—far less of the gusty, the capricious—the puerile—

"No more attempts at smart sayings, or scornful criticisms, or actions, or private or public affairs."[15] Heine left no diary in the ordinary sense of the term, but there is much autobiographical material in his published writings.[16] It may be that Whitman had been rereading *Pictures of Travel* in 1868, at a time when he himself was a center of considerable controversy and when he was perhaps undergoing some emotional disturbances connected with Peter Doyle and other young men whom he had known and become attached to in the hospitals of Washington. The parallel of his situation and that of Heine at any time is certainly not very close, but another entry in the same notebook under the date June 17, presumably 1870, may also be related to Heine. "It is imperative," he writes, "that I obviate & remove myself (& my orbit) *at all hazards*, from this *incessant, enormous & abnormal perturbation*." The words are written in black ink, but the underlining, a drawn hand pointing, and some tracings are in wine-colored ink. The word "perturbation" is in large letters. The markings in wine-colored ink were probably made July 15 when he added this endorsement in red pencil: "Good!—July 15." On another sheet, dated July 15, 1870, are the well-known notes advising himself "To give up absolutely & for good, from this present hour, this feverish pursuit of 164." Most recent commentators have thought that 164 is a cipher for "P. D." (Peter Doyle), the sixteenth and fourth letters of the alphabet. Attached to one sheet is a newspaper clipping on Carlyle, dated March, 1870, describing him as unhappy and bitter and irritable of late, indulging in fierce sarcasms. Whitman has a drawn hand pointing to this and the words: "A warning to Literary men philosophers & poets." In this connection it may be noted again that Whitman was angered by Carlyle's essay "Shooting Niagara: and After," published in *Macmillan's Magazine* for August 1867, and

15 See *UPP*, II, 94–95.

16 In 1888, in Germany, Gustav Karpeles published what he called *Heinrich Heine's Autobiographie: Nach seinen Werken*. In 1893 Arthur Dexter's English translation of this book, with the title *Heinrich Heine's Life Told in His Own Words*, was published in New York.

made a rather abusive reply in his essay "Democracy," first published in the *Galaxy* the following December. But when he went to revise this essay for inclusion in *Democratic Vistas* in late 1868 or 1869, he eliminated the abusive language. All of these notes and warnings to himself were related in one way or another, perhaps, to his notes in paraphrase of Heine.

His renewed interest in Heine in the late 1860's might possibly have been aroused by his reading Matthew Arnold's essay on Heine, first published in the *Cornhill Magazine*, August 1863, and reprinted in *Essays in Criticism* in 1865, but there is little in this essay to suggest Whitman's notes. He did read the essay, however, perhaps then, certainly later, for he told Traubel in 1888 he thought it "the best thing Arnold ever wrote: it gives me a vein in which I can run companionably with Arnold." [17] To find any comments on Heine that might reasonably have suggested Whitman's notes we have to go back to 1856. Of the two or three essays published about that time, the most suggestive is the essay-review by George Ripley of Alfred Meissner's *Heinrich Heine* in *Putnam's Monthly* for November 1856. There he might have read, and probably did read, the following acute characterization of Heine:

He was one of the restless and yearning souls, which inclosed in a tender and almost weak organization, experience both rapture and the wretchedness of life, with the exaltation of enthusiasm. The perpetual literary wars in which he was engaged, in order to burn the castles of his enemies, but more frequently to protect his own realms from invasion, kept him in a state of injurious excitement. The slightest unfavorable criticism, though proceeding from an insignificant pen, was enough to cause a sleepless night to his laurelled brow. His fame was great, but his ambition was still greater, and sensitive as the vanity of the most susceptible woman. . . . Not material excitements, but the intensity of emotion, acted on his delicate organization, and destroyed him. He perished by the element in which he lived.[18]

If Whitman read, or remembered, this essay during the years 1868 through 1870, he might well have seen in Heine's emotional disturbances a parallel with his own about that time.

Emanuel Swedenborg may have had some influence on Whitman's

---

[17] *WWC*, III, 184 (Nov. 26, 1888). This essay, in fact, was about the only thing of Arnold's that he liked, so far as I can discover.

[18] *Putnam's Monthly*, VIII, 519. Whitman often spoke of Ripley to Traubel in 1888. "He was a noble scholar: I read him at one time with assiduity." Again he said Ripley was superlatively equipped for the office of critic. "I met him here and there but we were never on close terms. His great learning always impressed me." (*WWC*, I, 62, 246; II, 111.)

thinking, as he had also on Emerson's, though I doubt that Whitman had read any of his books. What he knew of Swedenborg was probably derived from newspaper and magazine articles and conversations with Swedenborgians. Swedenborgianism was much talked and written about in this country during the 1840's and 1850's. I have already indicated something of the nature of Whitman's sources for Swedenborgian ideas in an earlier part of this book, and need not go further into the matter here.[19] One other great European may have contributed to the development of Whitman's poetic or stylistic principles. That was Dante, though he did not know his work until 1859, and then read only the *Inferno*, in John A. Carlyle's translation.[20] Whitman's comments on the poem, preserved in *Notes and Fragments*,[21] were made in 1859, and emphasize its simplicity of style in contrast to the "tangled and florid Shakespeare." He says the poem is "a great study for diffuse moderns." Whether Whitman was influenced by the style of Dante in his own poems is doubtful. *Leaves of Grass*, unlike the *Inferno*, is not noted for its "economy of words." Whitman kept this book into old age, and had it with him during the Civil War years.[22] How he happened to read that particular translation I cannot say. It was possibly because John A. Carlyle was the younger brother of Thomas Carlyle, who may have first directed his attention to Dante. In *Notes and Fragments* appear the following phrases from Carlyle's *Miscellaneous Essays*: "The lurid fire of Dante" . . . "The auroral light of Tasso."[23] In the same note, Whitman wrote of Dante, quoting: " 'Master of heaven [hell], of purgatory and of paradise, owning them by right of genius—he could bestow situation upon friend or foe, in any of them.' " He then mentions Tasso, Petrarch, and Boccaccio. Then, again quoting: " 'Next to Dante Boccaccio was the greatest contributor to the formation of the Italian language. To the former it was indebted for nerve and dignity, to the latter for elegance, wit and ease.' " All of the passage beginning "Master of heaven" except the name of Tasso is from the article "Literature of the Middle Ages" in the *Westminster Review* for July 1849, slightly modi-

[19] See above, pp. 154–56.

[20] Published in 1849, with the literal prose translation on the upper part of the page and the Italian text below, together with the translator's notes.

[21] *Complete Writings*, IX, pp. 91–93.

[22] See *Whitman and the Civil War*, ed. Charles I. Glicksberg (Philadelphia, 1933), pp. 82–83, note 51. See also, for a general examination of Whitman's knowledge of Dante, Joseph Chesley Mathews, "Walt Whitman's Reading of Dante," University of Texas *Studies in English*, No. 19 (1933), pp. 172–79.

[23] *Complete Writings*, X, 14. See also my "Notes on Whitman's Reading," *American Literature*, XXVI (Nov. 1954), 360–61.

fied by Whitman.[24] In a manuscript in the Library of Congress, dated
1862, Whitman says: "Sept. '62—looked carefully over the quarto
Dore's illustrations of Dante—very, very fine—yet some of them too
melodramatic."[25] W. R. Thayer said Whitman told him in 1885 that
he had read Longfellow's translation of the *Divine Comedy*, but I
have found no reference to the fact in Whitman's writing.[26] There
are numerous brief references to Dante throughout Whitman's
works.[27] Although Whitman's interest in Dante was genuine and lasting, there is no evidence that he was a direct influence in the writing
of *Leaves of Grass*.

In his notes, as I have indicated, Whitman borrowed a phrase from
Thomas Carlyle contrasting the "lurid fire" of Dante with the "auroral light" of the sixteenth-century Italian poet Tasso, and in *Notes
and Fragments* there is a relatively detailed account of Tasso's life
and work.[28] This account is drawn almost word for word from J. H.
Wiffen's biography, *The Life of Torquato Tasso*, edited by O. W.
Wight and published in New York in 1859, the same year in which he
read John Carlyle's translation of Dante's *Inferno*.[29] I have no doubt
that Whitman's reading this book and making notes on it was the consequence of Carlyle's description linking Tasso with Dante. I have
found only one other mention of Tasso in Whitman's works, and
that, oddly enough, in one of his general essays published in the
Brooklyn *Eagle*, where Tasso is named along with Petrarch and
Shakespeare as one who wore "the ancient and manly beard."[30]
Doubtless he was merely remembering a picture he had seen, and at
that time knew nothing of Tasso or his work. Doubtless, also, he discovered in reading Wiffen's biography that Tasso and his work were
of little interest or value to him.

[24] The word "hell" in brackets was probably inserted by Bucke, or just possibly
by Whitman in the manuscript, which is not available for comparison. It does not
appear in the *Westminster Review* article.

[25] Quoted by Mathews in "Walt Whitman's Reading of Dante," cited in note 22.

[26] Thayer's statement is quoted by Mathews, *ibid.*

[27] See *Prose Works 1892*, I, 114, 188, 214; II, 406, 533, 557, 656, 772; and *Correspondence*, I, 82; V, 49, 63.

[28] *Complete Writings*, IX, 163–66.

[29] I first reported this in "Notes on Whitman's Reading," *American Literature*,
XXVII (Nov. 1954), 352.

[30] See the *Eagle*, Aug. 14, 1847 (reprinted in *GF*, II, 171).

XIV. *British Poets*

I N SURVEYING the wide-stretching foreground of *Leaves of Grass*, reaching in time down from the most remote civilizations to his own day, and in space from India and Egypt through Asia Minor to Greece and the medieval and modern cultures of Europe, I find the most surprising fact to be the relatively minor place occupied by Britain and British literature in the panorama. In the "General Notes" to *Democratic Vistas* (1871), Whitman wrote that

while England is among the greatest of lands in political freedom, or the idea of it, and in stalwart personal character, &c.—the spirit of English literature is not great, at least is not greatest—and its products are no models for us. With the exception of Shakspere, there is no first-class genius in that literature—which, with a truly vast amount of value, and of artificial beauty, (largely from the classics,) is almost always material, sensual, not spiritual—almost always congests, makes plethoric, not frees, expands, dilates—is cold, anti-democratic, loves to be sluggish and stately, and shows much of that characteristic of vulgar persons, the dread of saying or doing something not at all improper in itself, but unconventional, and that may be laugh'd at.[1]

The literature of ancient India, of the Bible, and even the medieval and modern literature of continental Europe, he thought, come closer to fulfilling the requirements of democratic America.

A fair notion of Whitman's estimate of British poets is to be obtained from his reply in the New York *Critic* of November 24, 1888, to a question propounded by that paper as to whether any American not then living deserved a place beside the thirteen British poets before Tennyson named as "greatest" by Edmund Gosse in an article published in the *Forum* for October. The poets named by Gosse were Chaucer, Spenser, Shakespeare, Milton, Dryden, Pope, Gray, Burns, Wordsworth, Coleridge, Byron, Shelley, and Keats. Whitman seemed to accept Gosse's judgment that these thirteen are the only British poets whose fame was already firmly and permanently established. He wrote: "Of the thirteen British immortals mention'd—after plac-

---

[1] Reprinted as "British Literature" in *Collect* (*Prose Works 1892*, II, 521–23).

ing Shakspere on a sort of pre-eminence of fame not to be invaded yet—the names of Bryant, Emerson, Whittier and Longfellow (with even added names, sometimes Southerners, sometimes Western or other writers of only one or two pieces,) deserve in my opinion an equally high niche of renown as belongs to any on the dozen of that glorious list."[2] Something must be allowed for the exaggeration due to national pride, but even with that allowance it is shocking that Whitman rated the poetry of Bryant, Emerson, Whittier, and Longfellow (not to mention the unnamed Southern and Western poets) as equal to that of Milton and Wordsworth, or even to that of Chaucer and Byron.

His feeling was ambivalent even toward Shakespeare and the two later British writers whom he most admired, Scott and Tennyson. All three illustrated the evils of feudalism that survived in the social structure of the British Isles. They "exhale that principle of caste which we Americans have come on earth to destroy."[3] His feeling was equally ambivalent, though for different reasons, toward Burns and Carlyle. Burns, though personally attractive and to be applauded for his democratic sympathies, has "little or no spirituality," and that is "his mortal flaw and defect."[4] Of Carlyle, whom, for the moment, I will include with the poets, he said there were two "conflicting agonistic elements" in him "pulling him different ways like wild horses." He made, says Whitman, "the most indignant comment or protest anent the fruits of feudalism to-day in Great Britain—the increasing poverty and degradation of the homeless, landless twenty millions, while a few thousands, or rather a few hundreds, possess the entire soil, the money, and the fat berths."[5] In another place, however, he said of Carlyle: "The great masses of humanity stand for nothing—at least nothing but nebulous raw material. . . . All that is comprehended under the terms republicanism and democracy were distasteful to him from the first, and as he grew older they became hateful and contemptible."[6] Whitman was somewhat like Carlyle in that he valued personal worth above social equality, and sometimes, as in *Democratic Vistas,* he succumbed, briefly, to something like Carlyle's

---

[2] *Prose Works 1892,* II, 675–76.

[3] "Poetry To-day in America—Shakspere—the Future," first published as "The Poetry of the Future," in the *North American Review,* Feb. 1881; revised and reprinted in *Specimen Days & Collect (Prose Works 1892,* II, 475–76).

[4] "Robert Burns as Poet and Person," first published as "Robert Burns" in the *Critic,* Dec. 16, 1882; reprinted with revisions in the *North American Review,* Nov. 1886. (See *Prose Works 1892,* II, 565.)

[5] "Death of Thomas Carlyle," *Prose Works 1892,* I, 251.

[6] "Carlyle from American Points of View," *ibid.,* I, 256.

pessimistic view of democracy. Carlyle appealed to his critical sense, whereas Shakespeare and Scott early captured his imagination and never relaxed their hold. Tennyson's poetry appealed to his natural love of the beautiful, often, it seems, consciously suppressed, and for the most part left uncultivated.

For other British poets, he cared surprisingly little. Some of them he read in the 1850's chiefly to prepare himself for proposed lectures on literature, but even in this preparation he cared more for historical and biographical facts than for essential literary values in the works he read. His notes on Chaucer, many of which were drawn from a review article in the *North British Review* for February 1849, were professedly made for a lecture on "The Poet."[7] The two books reviewed were *The Poetry of Chaucer*, with a memoir, by Sir Harris Nicolas (1845), and *Selections from the Poetical Works*, with a concise life of Chaucer, by Charles D. Deshler (1847). The latter, according to Holloway, was among the books "noticed or reviewed" by Whitman in the *Eagle*.[8] Some of Whitman's notes were unmistakably drawn directly from Deshler's book; in fact, all of the notes on Chaucer's influence on later poets, particularly Spenser and Dryden, and the sentence stating that Dryden preferred the story of Palamon and Arcite in the *Knight's Tale*, above all other poems by Chaucer, were taken directly from Deshler's biography. There can be no doubt that he had the volume with him when he made the notes, as well as the review. Among the poems reprinted by Deshler is a selection from the *Romaunt of the Rose* to which he gives the title, "Apparel and Demeanor of the Gallants in Chaucer's Time."[9] This selection must have suggested Whitman's article in the *Eagle* for December 8, 1847, called "A Foot and Boot Article." He quotes from Deshler's text the following six lines, introducing them with the sentence: "What says old Chaucer—that venerable father of English song?"

> Of shoon and boot'es new and faire,
> Look at least thou have a pair,
> And that they fit so fetously
> That these rude men may utterly
> Marvel, sith they sit so plain,
> How they come on and off again.[10]

[7] See *Notes and Fragments* (*Complete Works*, IX, 85–87 and 226–27). The reference to the lecture on "The Poet" is in the second passage cited, which contains notes Whitman made directly on the margins of the clipping of the review (Bucke's No. 327). The longer passage contains notes preserved separately.

[8] *UPP*, I, 127, note. In this note Deshler is mistakenly printed Desher.

[9] Deshler, pp. 239–42.

[10] *GF*, II, 157. Whitman made a number of changes in his quotation: dropping

The fact that Whitman chose to quote from so improbable a source as the *Romaunt of the Rose* does not prove that he read Deshler's book with attention; it was Deshler's title, not in the original, that struck his fancy. I doubt if Whitman was ever interested in Chaucer's poetry, but he would have had to include the "father of English song" in a lecture on "The Poet." He is not mentioned in Whitman's later prose except as a representative of early English "culture" and as one of the thirteen English poets generally recognized as the greatest.[11]

Whitman probably had even less interest in Spenser than in Chaucer, and it is inconceivable that he could have endured to read much of the *Faerie Queene.* In a clipping from *Half-Hours* of a portion of Macaulay's review of Southey's edition of Bunyan's *Pilgrim's Progress* (1831), published in the *Edinburgh Review* for December 1831, Macaulay has the following comment on Spenser: "One unpardonable fault, the fault of tediousness, pervades the whole of the Fairy Queen." Whitman's comment in the margin by this was: "Brava!" In the essay "Independent American Literature" in the *Eagle* for February 10, 1847, he praises Spenser along with Shakespeare, Milton, Bunyan, and DeFoe, as one of the "treasures" left by England to America,[12] and in the 1850's, presumably in preparation for a lecture, he had made notes on two books on Spenser: G. L. Craik's *Spenser and His Poetry* (1845), and Mrs. C. K. Kirkland's *Spenser and the Fairy Queen* (1847).[13] According to Holloway, Whitman reviewed Mrs. Kirkland's book in the *Eagle* but he does not summarize the review or give the date.[14] It is pretty certain that Whitman made these notes in the middle 1850's; hence he must have preserved his copy of Mrs. Kirkland's book until that time. His last paragraph is a brief summary of Book I of the *Faerie Queene,* but it is likely that Whitman got his facts from Mrs. Kirkland's summary, not from reading the poem himself. He clipped Spenser's "Heavenly Beauty" from *Half-Hours,* but did not mark it. He mentioned Spenser only twice in his prose writings, and these were the passages cited above in con-

the final "e" on some but not all words having it, writing "boot'es" for "bootes," and "marvel" for "marvaile," and introducing the word "men" after "rude." Deshler uses the text of Thomas Tyrwhitt (*Poetical Works,* 1843, p. 227) but writes "shoone" for "shone" and "again" for "againe."

[11] In "A Thought on Shakspere" (1886) and in the *Critic* in 1888 as mentioned earlier in this chapter. (See *Prose Works 1892,* II, 557, 676.)

[12] Reprinted in *GF,* II, 239–41.

[13] These notes are printed by Bucke in *Notes and Fragments,* where by his error or that of a printer Spenser's name is spelled "Spencer." The manuscript shows that the error was not Whitman's. (See *Complete Writings,* IX, 77–79; X, 15.)

[14] *UPP,* I, 128 note.

nection with Chaucer, from "A Thought on Shakspere" and the *Critic* article about thirteen British poets.

As I have noted earlier, Whitman's opinion of Milton became somewhat less favorable in his later years than it was in January 1848, when he reviewed James Montgomery's edition of *The Poetical Works of John Milton*, with 120 engravings.[15] Whitman seemed to be more interested in the "beautiful pictorial designs" and in "the superb outward embellishments" of Harper's two-volume edition than in the poems themselves. He is willing to accept the general opinion of Milton's "grandeur," but he thinks the poet certainly "wants some endearing and softening accompaniments." He annotated a clipping of the article "Egotism" in *Graham's Magazine* for March 1845 and starred the statement that "Milton's egotism touches the sublime." He underlined the next sentence: "The Satan of Paradise Lost is a representation of what John Milton would be, if he were placed 'high on the gorgeous seat' of Pandemonium, as the ruler of its powers; and consequently the devil has perhaps a little more than justice done to him." These notes on egotism were probably made after Whitman began to write, or plan, *Leaves of Grass*. In general, his mature judgments on Milton in his published works were more favorable than his private opinions recorded by Horace Traubel in *With Walt Whitman in Camden*.[16]

Whitman never cared for the neoclassical poetry of the late seventeenth and early eighteenth century in England. In *Specimen Days* he tells how, on his western tour in 1879, while "lying by one rainy day in Missouri," he tried to read "a big volume" of "Milton, Young, Gray, Beattie and Collins," but gave it up "for a bad job" and turned with pleasure to his old favorites, Scott's "Marmion" and the "Lay of the Last Minstrel."[17] Although in his *Critic* article he accepted Gray as one of the thirteen greatest British poets, he mentions Gray's name nowhere else either in his published work or in his conversations with Traubel.[18] In the Trent Collection at Duke University I found the following note in pencil on a sheet of pink paper, evidently cut from one of the wrappers used in the 1855 edition: "Dryden 1631 to 1701. Dryden seems to have been of vigorous make, sharp-tempered—used

---

[15] This review was reprinted in *GF*, II, 287–89, and more briefly summarized in *UPP*, I, 134.

[16] See Chapter VII, pp. 125–29, for more details on Whitman's opinion of Milton.

[17] *Prose Works 1892*, I, 222.

[18] On one occasion, however, he says he shares Traubel's statement that he has an "equal lack of affinity with Milton, Dryden, Pope, Gray." (*WWC*, III, 258.)

his poetical talent to make money, show up his enemies,—those of the opposite party, noblemen, politicians, &c.—He sings a good deal in the inflated, distressingly classical style of those times."[19] I have found no source for this; it may have been based in part on his own reading of the poems. Traubel records that he often heard Whitman quote the following couplet:

> Not heaven itself upon the past has power,
> But what has been has been—and I have had my hour.

Looking through Whitman's effects later, he found the couplet written out in Whitman's hand on an old slip of paper with the superscription: "Horace, translated (improved) by Dryden."[20] The couplet is lines 71–72 of the "Twenty-ninth Ode of the First Book of Horace. Paraphrased in Pindaric Verse" by Dryden, and inscribed by him to the Earl of Rochester. Whitman would not have said the lines were by Horace "improved" by Dryden, if he had at the time he made the note seen Christopher Smart's literal prose translation of Horace's works, which he afterward owned in the edition of 1864. Dryden's poem is really not a paraphrase at all, but an original poem. Its theme might be said to be vaguely related to Horace's ode, but the lines which Whitman quotes do not occur in the original, nor anything like them. Actually Smart's literal prose translation of this ode contains only thirteen lines, a short paragraph, whereas Dryden's poem contains well over a hundred. Whitman might have picked up the lines from some secondary source, or he could have been reading Dryden's poem in the 1851 one-volume reprint of the four-volume edition of 1811, with a biographical introduction by Samuel Johnson and notes by the Wartons and others.[21]

Whitman linked Dryden's work closely with that of Pope. In his notes on Chaucer we find the following sentence: "Driden founded the school under which Pope's style comes. Driden's forte was satire— his poems all have it more or less—visibly or invisibly."[22] In his clipping of Aubrey De Vere's review-essay, "Modern Poetry and Poets," in the *Edinburgh Review* for October 1849, Whitman underlines the

[19] This is printed in *Notes and Fragments* with one or two minor changes. (See *Complete Writings*, IX, 127–28.)

[20] *WWC*, II, 142.

[21] George Gilfillan's two-volume edition of 1855 does not contain the translations.

[22] *Complete Writings*, IX, p. 86. The source of these two sentences was C. D. Deshler's introduction to his *Selections* from Chaucer, pp. 54–56. The spelling "Driden" in *Notes and Fragments* is a misprint; Whitman's manuscripts have "Dryden."

statement that in the "silver age of English poetry" Dryden was the greatest in mental power and Pope left the most perfect works.[23] In his clipping of Thomas De Quincey's review of *The Works of Alexander Pope* (8 vols., 1847) in the *North British Review* for August 1848, Whitman's markings indicate that he was interested in Pope's alleged insincerity and in his didacticism, but that he probably saved the clipping because of what De Quincey had to say about poetry in general. Attached to this clipping is another, cut from Charles Knight's *Half-Hours With the Best Authors*, of Pope's "Imitation of Horace," which contains no markings. In his reminiscences in *Specimen Days*, apparently of the years 1845–50, Whitman wrote: "I went regularly every week in mild seasons down to Coney Island, at that time a long, bare unfrequented shore, which I had all to myself, and where I loved, after bathing, to race up and down the hard sand, and declaim Homer or Shakspere to the surf and sea-gulls by the hour."[24] In another place in *Specimen Days* he writes from notes made on July 25, 1881, how on a "jaunt" with friends to the beach at Far Rockaway, Long Island, he "had a leisurely bath and naked ramble as of old" while his companions were off in a boat in deeper water, and shouted to them "Jupiter's menaces against the gods, from Pope's Homer."[25] It is probable that Pope's was the only translation Whitman had read before T. A. Buckley's prose translation in 1857, and that he thought very well of it during the late 1840's and early 1850's. For purposes of declamation it, apparently, ranked with Shakespeare's *Richard III*. It was not until he began to read the English romantic critics of the period of Carlyle and Emerson, and not long before he read Buckley's work, that he lost his enthusiasm for Pope. In discussing, late in life, how literary judgments change with time, Whitman remarked, apropos of nothing so far as I can see, that "Byron thought Pope's verse incomparably ahead of Homer and Shakspere."[26] He had read Goldsmith's *Vicar of Wakefield* several times, he told Traubel, but had not read "The Deserted Village" or "The Traveler," or, presumably, any of the other poems.[27]

[23] This was a review of Tennyson's *The Princess*, Mrs. Shelley's *Poetical Works of Shelley*, and R. Monckton Milnes's *Life, Letters, and Literary Remains of John Keats* in two volumes.

[24] *Prose Works 1892*, I, 12. This, he says, was while he lived in Brooklyn, hence it was after 1845, and might have been as late as 1851–52.

[25] *Ibid.*, p. 273. The lines shouted must have been 7–34 of Book VIII.

[26] "Old Poets," originally published in the *North American Review*, 1890 (*Prose Works 1892*, II, 659).

[27] *WWC*, I, 64. In his review of Boswell's "Life of Samuel Johnson" in the *Eagle*, Dec. 7, 1846 (*GF*, II, 281) he wrote: "We read of the poverty-pressed Goldsmith, the heedless but good-hearted one."

Nineteenth-century British writers usually fared somewhat better in Whitman's judgments. He reviewed William Hazlitt's *Napoleon Bonaparte* with enthusiasm in the *Eagle* March 15, 1847, calling it "a noble, grand work! a democratic work!" and again on April 2, 1847, praising it as "a masterpiece of style, earnestness, clearness, and spirit"; but he never mentioned Hazlitt again, either in his published work or in *Notes and Fragments*, and not in *With Walt Whitman in Camden*, so far as I have found.[28] He knew something of Coleridge's work, both prose and poetry, but how much I cannot be sure. He reviewed *Letters, Conversations, and Recollections* in the *Eagle* on February 20, 1847, and *Biographia Literaria* on December 4, but there are no notes on Coleridge or his work in *Notes and Fragments*, and he had little to say of him in later years; nevertheless he must have known more of his work than appears evident.[29]

Whitman did not review in the *Eagle* any of Wordsworth's poems, perhaps because no important new poem or collection of poems was published while he was editor, but in a review of Longfellow's poems on October 12, 1846, he says Longfellow is "deserving to stand on the same platform with Bryant and Wordsworth."[30] To place Wordsworth in the same class with Bryant was high praise, for in an earlier issue of the *Eagle*, September 1, 1846, he rated Bryant as "one of the best poets in the world."[31]

Whitman clipped four magazine articles on Wordsworth (Bucke's list Nos. 28, 37, 42, and 43). The first is a review in the *Whig Review* for May 1851 of Wordsworth's *Prelude*, first published in 1850. Actually only three leaves are clipped, including pages 447–48 and pages 455–58. The review really begins on page 448 and ends on page 457. On page 447, the reverse of 448, Whitman has written the title of the review clipped, "Wordsworth's Prelude." On page 458, the first of a review of J. D. Morell's *Historical and Critical View of the Speculative Philosophy of Europe in the Nineteenth Century*, Whitman wrote this title, "Speculative Philosophy in the Nineteenth Century," and also on page 447, as if he intended to clip that review also, but if he did the clipping was lost either by Whitman or by Bucke. The review of the *Prelude* is signed "O.W.W.," probably O. W. Wight, the translator of Victor Cousin's *History of Modern Philosophy*, discussed earlier. Apparently Whitman was not interested in the *Prelude*, but only in the biographical data of the review, which are all on the pages he clipped. In the margin beside the paragraph on page

28 The first review is reprinted in *GF*, II, 284–87 and the second in *UPP*, I, 133.
29 For a more detailed account, see Chapter VII, pp. 110–12.
30 *GF*, II, 297.
31 *GF*, II, 261.

457 telling of Wordsworth's appointment as Distributor of Stamps, his legacy from a friend, his pension in 1842, and his appointment as Poet Laureate in 1843, Whitman wrote in pencil: "So it seems Wordsworth made 'a good thing,' from the start, out of his poetry: legacies! a fat office! pensions from the crown!" He was also, apparently, interested in Wordsworth's self-criticism, which he had surely seen in his prefaces, and in self-criticism by poets in general. On the upper half of page 447, under the titles Whitman wrote at the top and above an English translation of a poem by Uhland under the title "Crossing the Ferry" and signed "S. N. N.," Whitman pasted a clipped paragraph from a review of Leigh Hunt's *Autobiography* in the *American Whig Review* for January 1851. On this clipping he wrote the following notations: in ink, "Leigh Hunt criticising his own poems—Also the same sort of self-criticism by other poets," and in pencil, "Spenser criticised himself."[32] I do not know when Whitman clipped these reviews, but the annotations were probably made after the publication of the first edition of *Leaves of Grass*. These self-criticisms may have influenced his publishing anonymous reviews of the book.

The second of the Wordsworth clippings, Bucke's No. 37, is an article with the title "Recollections of Poets Laureate: Wordsworth and Tennyson," from the *American Whig Review*, June 1852 (XV, 516–23). There are no marks on the first four pages, which are about Wordsworth, except the bracketing and underlining of a statement quoted from Leigh Hunt's autobiography saying that on meeting Wordsworth after nearly thirty years Wordsworth said little and made

---

[32] Underneath the six-stanza poem by Uhland, Whitman has written a different version of the last stanza, as follows:

> Take O boatman thrice thy fee
> Take—I give it willingly
> For unwittingly to thee,
> Spirits twain have crossed with me.

Whitman is quoting, probably from memory and therefore inaccurately, the last stanza of the translation of Uhland's poem, under the title "The Passage," that Longfellow included in *Poets and Poetry of Europe*, and that was reprinted in the review of that volume in the *American Whig Review*. This review is in two installments, in the issues of November and December 1846. Whitman clipped the second installment only. The clipping is in the Trent Collection. The translation is not by Longfellow, who credits it to the *Edinburgh Review*. It appeared in that periodical October 1832 (LVI, 45), unsigned. In the bibliography of W. T. Hewitt's edition of *Poems of Uhland* (1896, p. 340), the translation is attributed to George Moir. Whitman's version differs considerably from Moir's in punctuation, and differs verbally by substituting "unwittingly" for "invisible" in the third line. Whitman's version is published in *Notes and Fragments* as item 141 of Part I, where commas are placed after the first and second lines, possibly by Bucke. Part I was not reprinted in the *Complete Writings*.

no criticisms. "He had found out that he could at least afford to be silent."[33] On page 516, preceding the reference to Hunt, is the following: "The writer of this sketch had the pleasure of bringing Leigh Hunt and Wordsworth into friendly intercourse after an estrangement of above twenty-eight years." He describes Wordsworth as "Tall, bony, and broadly formed. . . . His face was oval, nose slightly aquiline and large. . . ."[34] Inserted between pages 516 and 517 is a brief clipping about Landor's letter to Emerson in which he says Hazlitt told him Wordsworth looked like a horse.[35] Whitman made no marks on this inserted clipping, but it may have influenced some of the comments he made on other clippings. Whitman's notes on the *Whig Review* clipping were presumably made in 1856, for on page 523, in reference to Tennyson, he notes: "Age now, (1856) 48 years." On the same page is the note: "Sept. 1855—Tennyson published *Maud,* & other Poems."

The third clipping, Bucke's No. 42, which he describes simply as a magazine article on "Wordsworth," is a review by O. W. Wight of Christopher Wordsworth's *Memoirs of William Wordsworth* (1851) and of *The Poetical Works* (1851), cut from the *American Whig Review* for July 1851, pp. 68–80. This is, in a sense, a continuation of the review by Wight of the *Prelude* in the May issue (Bucke's No. 28). It is not in the Trent Collection, and I have not seen it, but Bucke says it was "carefully read and annotated." These annotations, or some of them at least, are printed in *Notes and Fragments* and read as follows: "A good article [*added later*] yes it is. Yet with all this glorification of Wordsworth read the personal traits of him, with sayings, looks, foibles, etc., as given by those who knew him. Died 1850—aged 80."[36]

---

[33] See II, 20–21 of Roger Ingpen's edition of the *Autobiography* (1903).

[34] The writer of this article is not named in the *American Whig Review* and I have been unable to identify him.

[35] This letter was really a pamphlet published in Bath in 1856 and was a kind of review of Emerson's *English Traits,* which had just been published. Landor's pamphlet was reprinted by the Rowfant Club (Cleveland, 1895), together with Emerson's paper on Landor reprinted from the *Dial,* edited by S. A. Jones. On p. 52 of the Rowfant edition Landor says that when Hazlitt asked if he had seen Wordsworth and Landor replied that he had not, Hazlitt said, "Sir, have you ever seen a horse?" Landor said "Assuredly." "Then, Sir," said Hazlitt, "you have seen Wordsworth." Two years earlier Landor had written to John Forster a slightly different version. When Hazlitt visited Landor in 1825 and asked him if he had seen Wordsworth, Landor replied that he had not; then Hazlitt said: "Well, sir, if you have seen a horse, sir, I mean his head, sir, you have seen Wordsworth." Landor's letter was dated Oct. 23, 1854. (See R. H. Super, *Walter Savage Landor: A Biography* [New York, 1954], p. 177 and p. 544 note.)

[36] *Complete Writings,* IX, 125. In a footnote Bucke says the date of the notes

The fourth clipping, Bucke's No. 43, is from an unidentified source, perhaps a newspaper, and is listed by him under the title "The First Mild Day of March." The correct title of the poem, of course, is "To My Sister." I have not seen it. It is not in the Trent Collection, but Whitman's comment on it is printed in *Notes and Fragments*: "Wordsworth, it seems, is the originator of this kind of poem—followed here by Bryant and others."[37]

Whitman was interested in Hunt during the 1850's as one who criticized his own poems, and he was also interested in what he had to say of poetry. I find no real evidence that he had seen Hunt's little book "Imagination and Fancy" (1845), which contained an essay answering the question "What is Poetry?" We know only that he clipped the last pages of this essay from the anthology *Half-Hours with the Best Authors*. This is item No. 402 of Bucke's list, and he says it is "much scored and annotated." This clipping is not in the Trent Collection and I have not seen it. I suspect the initial date in the following note in *Notes and Fragments* was derived from the biographical headnote prefixed to the selection in *Half-Hours*: "Leigh Hunt—born 1784—is he now living? aged 72. Yes (July '57) he lives, old and in fair condition, in London, aged 73. [*Added afterwards:*] died, Aug., '59, aged 75."[38] Obviously this note was begun in 1856, and his adding to it in 1857 and 1859 shows an interest in Hunt spanning several years, but there is no reference to him in Whitman's published work or in his conversations with Traubel.[39] Hunt's work was not much read after his death.

Byron, Shelley, and Keats were very nearly of Hunt's generation, and the first two were closely associated with him. Of the three, only Byron achieved fame before his death. How much Whitman knew as a young man of Byron's poems I do not know, but it is evident that he knew of Byron's irregular love adventures, real and imaginatively represented in his poems, and that, being a moralistic youth, he did not like them. In one of the "Sun-Down Papers," written in 1841, he condemned "the puerile, moping love, painted by such trashy writers

---

was about 1856. The original note, "A good article," was presumably made earlier, perhaps at the time Whitman clipped the review and as early as 1851. Bucke apparently based his opinion of the date on the note on Tennyson mentioned in the preceding paragraph.

37 *Ibid.*, IX, 125. In a footnote Bucke gives the title, still incorrectly, as "It is the first mild day of March," which is the first line.

38 *Ibid.*, IX, 222.

39 Holloway mentions the fact that he printed three quotations from Hunt in the *Eagle*. He probably picked them up from secondary sources, though Hunt was still a literary force of some consequence in the 1840's.

as Byron and Bulwer."[40] By 1846 he had come to know and appreciate "the fiery breath of Byron," which may reflect an interest in his revolutionary sympathies, and by 1848, as a contributor to the New Orleans *Crescent,* he knew enough of the poems to quote casually from *Childe Harold* and *Don Juan.*[41] In the *Eagle* for August 28, 1846 appeared the following item under the heading "Yankee Impertinence," "Does the audacious *Boston Post* mean to insinuate that *we* have any of Bryon's *weak* spots?"[42] In a manuscript originally containing a distinction between "the poet" and "the singers," Whitman has named Horace and Byron, apparently, among the singers. The note probably dates from 1855 or 1856.[43] By June 1858 he was evidently familiar enough with Byron's *Childe Harold* to quote phrases from several stanzas of Canto III.[44] The dates of Byron's birth and death are noted in *Notes and Fragments,*[45] but if one may judge by the lack of clipped articles and the absence of preserved notes on Byron during the 1850's, he was at that time not much interested in him or his poetry. After all, at the time he was planning *Leaves of Grass* his interest in poets was almost exclusively in the "makers of poetry," as he called them in "Song of the Answerer," and hardly at all in the "singers." In later years, specifically after 1865, Whitman thought much better of Byron. This change, I suspect, was due to the influence of his friend William Douglas O'Connor, who was an admirer of Byron. In a letter to O'Connor dated August 23, 1869, Whitman wrote: "William, do you see how Mrs. Stowe & the Atlanticites are getting cuffed & smitten front & rear, anent of the Byron resurrectionism? The papers are all having articles about it—& all condemn the Atlantic article."[46] The

[40] Reprinted in *UPP,* I, 48.

[41] See *ibid.,* I, 121, 197, 203, 207, and 212.

[42] Reprinted in *GF,* II, 277.

[43] *Faint Clews & Indirections,* ed. Clarence Gohdes and Rollo G. Silver (Durham, N.C., 1949), p. 31. See also catalogue of the Trent Collection, p. 28. The editors suggest, correctly I think, that this manuscript dates from about 1855 while Whitman was writing his Preface. The naming here of Horace and Byron together may have been suggested by an undated newspaper clipping (Bucke's No. 347) on "Horace and Byron," which I have not seen.

[44] *I Sit and Look Out,* pp. 104–5. I suspect he owned a copy of the poem, though he might have quoted from memory.

[45] *Complete Writings,* IX, 230. This note follows immediately a note dated December 1857, announcing that Carlyle's *Frederick the Great* is "now in press," but Bucke's placing it there does not prove that the two notes were made at the same time.

[46] *Correspondence,* II, 86. In 1871 a relation of Byron's, Roden Noel, wrote a favorable article on Whitman and sent the poet an inscribed copy, in return for which Whitman sent him a copy of the 1876 edition of *Leaves of Grass.* (See *Correspondence,* II, 162, note 55.)

Atlantic article referred to was Harriet Beecher Stowe's "The True Story of Lady Byron's Life" (September 1869). The following year Mrs. Stowe published her book *Lady Byron Vindicated* (Boston), in the introduction to which she said, "The interval since my publication of 'The True Story of Lady Byron's Life' has been one of stormy discussion and of much invective." Whitman undoubtedly had Mrs. Stowe in mind, among others, when he wrote in the "General Notes" to *Democratic Vistas* (1871): "Observe that the most impudent slanders, low insults, &c., on the great revolutionary authors, leaders, poets, &c., of Europe, have their origin and main circulation in certain circles here. The treatment of Victor Hugo living, and Byron dead, are samples. Both deserving so well of America, and both persistently attempted to be soil'd here by unclean birds, male and female."[47] In his essay "Edgar Poe's Significance" dated January 1, 1880, he puts Byron with a group including Burns, Schiller, and George Sand, in whom "the perfect character, the good, the heroic, although never attain'd, is never lost sight of, but through failures, sorrows, temporary downfalls, is return'd to again and again, and while often violated, is passionately adhered to as long as mind, muscles, voice, obey the power we call volition"; whereas Poe's verses are "almost without the first sign of moral principle . . . and, by final judgment, probably belong among the electric lights of imaginative literature, brilliant and dazzling, but with no heat."[48] O'Connor's writing *The Good Gray Poet* in 1865 (published January 1866) in defense of Whitman put him, so to speak, in the same position as others O'Connor had defended, including Byron. In his preface to O'Connor's posthumous volume of essays and tales (1891), Whitman says he "defended every attack'd literary person," and "always applauded the freedom of the masters, whence and whoever."[49] In this as in many other matters, including the theory that Bacon wrote the plays attributed to Shakespeare, Whitman was drawn, irresistibly it seems, to agree with the opinions of O'Connor.

Whitman's opinions of literary men and the grounds for them are always hard to establish, and this is particularly true of his opinion of Shelley. He did not mention him in the Brooklyn *Eagle*, so far as reprints from that paper reveal, although he acquired while he was editor or later a copy of Mrs. Shelley's edition of *The Works of Percy Bysshe Shelley*, published in one volume in 1847 by Moxon in Lon-

[47] Reprinted in *Two Rivulets* (1876) and in *Specimen Days and Collect*. (See *Prose Works 1892*, II, 526.)

[48] This essay was published in the *Critic*, June 3, 1882. (See *Prose Works 1892*, I, 231.)

[49] *Prose Works 1892*, II, 691.

don and reissued in 1850.[50] A reprint in one volume of the 1839 edition of the *Poetical Works* was published in Philadelphia by Crissy and Markley in 1847 and reissued in 1851, but so far as I have learned no edition of the poems or the prose was published in New York during the 1840's. A copy of the 1847 edition by Moxon was in Whitman's possession at the time of his death and in the division of his literary remains went to Thomas Harned, one of the literary executors. It is now in the library of Bryn Mawr College, where it has been examined by at least two persons, Roland A. Duerksen and Mary K. Sanders.[51] Duerksen suggests that Whitman received his copy from the London publisher for the purpose of review in the *Eagle*, but this is very unlikely. The *Eagle* was too obscure a paper for Moxon to have desired a review in it, and if Whitman had bought the book himself while he was editor he would almost certainly have noticed it in his paper. Duerksen wisely refrains from trying to date Whitman's marks on the book, but does note that none appear on the poems, and that most of them are on those portions of the prose where Shelley discusses the nature of poetry and the function of the poet. It is probable, therefore, that the notes were made by Whitman after he had begun to write the poems published in the 1855 edition of *Leaves of Grass*, about 1854, and perhaps later than that. Mary K. Sanders, accepting 1847 as the date of what Holloway called Whitman's first notebook, assumes that the notes were made at that time and argues that they reflect Whitman's reading of Shelley. As I have tried to show elsewhere, the entries in this notebook were probably made in 1854,[52] and certainly not in 1847. Whether they were influenced by Shelley is an arguable point; very likely there were many sources, perhaps including Shelley.

On September 19, 1888, Traubel reports this conversation between Whitman and Thomas Harned: " 'No indeed Tom: I am not a reader of Shelley—I don't come so near him, or he to me, as some others.' Harned alluded to a handsome Shelley once possessed by W. 'Yes, I had that: you mean the one in red canvas? I sold it—a friend of mine came here one day and wanted it badly, offered to buy it: so I let him take it away.' "[53] Mary Sanders thinks this is the book that went to

---

[50] This edition was in two parts, one based on Mrs. Shelley's edition in four volumes of the *Poetical Works* in 1839, and the other on her edition in two volumes of the *Essays, Letters from Abroad, Translations and Fragments* in 1840.

[51] See "Markings by Whitman in His Copy of Shelley's *Works*," by Roland A. Duerksen, and "Shelley's Promethean Shadow on *Leaves of Grass*," by Mary K. Sanders, both published in the *Walt Whitman Review*, Dec. 1968.

[52] "Dating Whitman's Early Notebooks," *Studies in Bibliography*, XXIV (1971), 197–204.

[53] *WWC*, II, 345.

Harned after Whitman's death. She says that the Bryn Mawr book is canvas, "and taking into consideration the discoloration of age upon the reddish brown cover—appears to be the same volume Whitman disclaimed any interest in when Harned wanted to discuss Shelley connections." But if, as Whitman says, he sold this book to a friend prior to the date of his conversation with Harned, it could not have been in his possession at the time of his death unless, somehow, he had recovered it during the interval. I do not know who bought the book from Whitman, but my guess would be his wealthy jeweler friend in New York, John H. Johnston, who, on a visit to Whitman January 20, 1888, had bought for $9.00 and taken away his four-volume edition of Pepy's diary and his two-volume edition, by H. Buxton Forman, of Shelley's poems dated 1882.[54] Whoever was the purchaser of the book bound in red canvas I can imagine no reason for his returning it. It was probably the one-volume reprint, issued by Moxon in 1840, of the four-volume edition of the *Poetical Works* edited by Mrs. Shelley that he published in 1839. Both the 1839 edition of the *Poems* and the 1840 edition of the *Essays, Letters from Abroad,* etc., in two-volumes, were bound in red canvas. Whether the one-volume reprint of the *Poems* was also bound in red canvas I do not know since I have not seen it, but I suspect it was. If this was the volume Whitman sold, its early date and rarity would explain Harned's opinion that it was worth four dollars, though Whitman said he did not get that for it. He would naturally have parted with it more readily than with a volume of Shelley's essays and prefaces, especially the 1847 edition of the *Works* that he had marked.

As a matter of fact, Whitman cared little for English poetry, or poetry of any kind, either before or after 1855, though he was much interested in the biography of poets. He quotes, evidently with satisfaction, O'Connor's contrast of Rabelais—"of the earth earthy"—with Shelley—"a wind, a perfume: pure, ethereal." He also said, "Shelley is interesting to me as Burns is, chiefly as a person," and it is obvious that Burns as a person, with all his faults, pleased him more than Shelley did. Yet he could not entirely deny a poet that some of his most admired friends called great. He admitted that "there must have been a heap in Shelley that I never reached to: see the people who believed in him—Mrs. Gilchrist, Forman, Symonds."[55] He repeats to Traubel "a story that Mrs. Shelley tells" that makes him think of

---

[54] See Whitman's letter to Johnston, acknowledging payment of $9.00 "for the books" and the editor's footnote. (*Correspondence*, IV, 165–66.) David McKay, Whitman's Philadelphia publisher, gave him the Pepys diary, and Forman, presumably, had given him the Shelley books.

[55] *WWC*, III, 97.

himself: "We always know when the bad are about to happen: when we are perfectly well, when all is at peace, then we know that the clouds are gathering—that a blow is preparing."[56] If this is an accurate quotation I do not know its source; I suspect it is rather Whitman's paraphrase of Mrs. Shelley's words, which he might have derived from her letter to Mrs. Gisborne on August 15, after Shelley's death. While they lived at Lerici, just before the fatal boat trip, Mary wrote that Shelley "never was in better health or spirits," but she herself was ill. "My nerves," she said, "were wound up to the utmost irritation, and the sense of misfortune hung over my spirits."[57] Whitman may have had in mind Mrs. Shelley's "Note on the Poems of 1822," first printed in her edition of the poems in 1839 and reprinted in later editions, including that of 1847. In this note Mrs. Shelley wrote: "During the whole of our stay at Lerici, an intense presentiment of coming evil brooded over my mind, and covered this beautiful place, and genial summer, with the shadow of coming misery."[58]

I find it hard to believe that Whitman's *Leaves of Grass,* even the first edition, was influenced in any specific detail by any of Shelley's poems, though it is possible, as Duerksen believes, that "The Sleepers," or rather the idea in "The Sleepers," owed something to "The Witch of Atlas." Other poems of Shelley, as well as his prose, have ideas that appealed to Whitman, but whether he derived these ideas from Shelley or from one or more of the dozens of other possible sources, some of which have been suggested earlier in these pages, it would be nearly if not quite impossible to determine. Shelley's diatribes against priests and kings have their counterpart in Whitman's early writing, but it would be absurd to argue that these came from Shelley rather than Thomas Paine and other American revolutionaries, or Rousseau, or Voltaire, or from political conversations in newspaper offices in the 1830's and 1840's. Mary Sanders's theory that Whitman's statements about style in the early notebooks—"Be simple and clear," etc.—were a reaction to his reading of Shelley's poems, which are not simple nor always clear, is largely speculation. However, Whitman might have been influenced by some of the magazine

56 *WWC,* IV, 452.

57 This letter is printed in Dowden's *Life of Percy Bysshe Shelley* (2 vols. [London, 1886], II, 510). Perhaps Whitman had read it in Dowden's *Life,* but I find no real evidence that he owned a copy of this biography or had read it. Of course he could have seen this letter elsewhere; it was reprinted by Richard Garnett in *Selected Letters of Percy Bysshe Shelley* (London, 1884), pp. 223–40.

58 See the 1847 edition, p. 351. See also II, 222 of the two-volume reprint of the four-volume edition of the poems published in Boston, 1855, as Vols. XLVIII and XLIX (1880) of *British Poets.*

criticism of Shelley that he read. He clipped Shelley's "To a Skylark" from *Half-Hours with the Best Authors* but did not annotate it or mark it in any way. He marked with underlinings and brackets several passages in the article "Characteristics of Shelley," which he clipped from the *American Whig Review* for May 1847 (V, 533–36). He underlined and triple-bracketed sentences that seemed especially to interest him: "His intellect seems to have held in solution all beautiful things in the universe; but wanted the cold addition of experience, which alone could precipitate his visions, in bright and regular forms. . . . But the sphere of the true poet is among the common elements of humanity. . . . Shelley never lost his favorite defects. He never unlearned his nice, elaborate system of embellishment. With him this was all in all." This sentence is bracketed and underlined: "Perhaps no one can perfectly enjoy this poet, who has not some portion of his sickly delicateness." I think this must have suggested a comment by Whitman in *Notes and Fragments* (*Complete Writings*, IX, 31): "No one will perfectly enjoy me who has not some of my own rudeness, sensuality and hauteur." The date of these markings is uncertain, but he certainly handled the clipping as late as 1855, for pasted to it is a strip of blue paper cut from a leftover form of the Williamsburg tax assessor's office which Whitman acquired in late 1854 or early 1855. On this strip he has written in ink in large capital letters "Egotism," and below this, in pencil, "or rather Vanity." The notes on Shelley in *Notes and Fragments* are based on a review of several works on Shelley in the *North British Review* for November 1847, but apparently Whitman did not clip the review; it is not, in any case, on Bucke's list. The notes are written in pencil on a piece of paper about 4 by 5 inches cut from a proof sheet, apparently of a grammar. Almost certainly Whitman made the notes directly from the journal, probably in a library. The source of the paper is probably of no consequence. Only one of the works reviewed, which included Mrs. Shelley's edition of the *Poetical Works* (3 vols., London, 1847), interested Whitman enough to induce him to make notes on it; that was T. J. Hogg's *Shelley at Oxford*, where Hogg was intimately associated with Shelley. Hogg's description and account of Shelley are exaggerated and sensational, but they are what captured Whitman's attention, and accounted for his comment that Shelley "must have been quite such another as T. L. Harris." Whitman may have heard Thomas Lake Harris preach between 1847 and 1850 in the independent Christian Church he founded in New York, of which Horace Greeley was a member. At that time Harris was much under the influence of Andrew Jackson Davis, the mystic, and had, like

Davis, adopted many Swedenborgian ideas. It is by no means incredible that Whitman was influenced by one or both of these men.[59] Harris seems to have left New York about 1850; therefore Whitman's note on Shelley may, as Bucke suggests in a footnote, have been "written before 1850."[60]

One of Whitman's more important clippings was the review with the title "Modern Poetry and Poets," by Aubrey De Vere, in the *Edinburgh Review* for October 1849.[61] The article purports to be a review of Tennyson's *The Princess* (edition of 1848), Mrs. Shelley's 1847 edition of the *Poetical Works of Shelley*, and Richard Moncton Milnes's *Life, Letters, and Literary Remains of John Keats* (1848), but the reviewer surveys a wide range of poets and poetry from Chaucer and Dante to Tennyson. He does not discuss Shelley until page 221, where Whitman brackets and places a large exclamation point opposite these lines: "He gazed in admiration at all things, whether the triumphs of the human mind or the commonest achievements of mechanic skill; yet in all his poetry we find no trace of his having possessed the kindred, but nobler habit—that of veneration." He triple-brackets a passage saying Shelley's impetuous temper deprived his poetry of "that perfect sanity which we find in the great masters." Whitman's exclamation point is a bit ambiguous; it might indicate surprise that Shelley lacked veneration or disagreement with De Vere's judgment that he lacked it. In the words I quote about "perfect sanity" I am sure that Whitman agreed, but it is not certain whether the idea was new to him or only one agreeing with an opinion he had already formed.

De Vere's discussion of Keats is much more extensive and suggests that his Catholic sympathies were less offended by Keats's Greek paganism than by Shelley's opposition to Christian orthodoxy. Whitman bracketed much of the section on Keats, but he also underlined and seemed especially interested in the following sentences: "His mind had itself much of that 'negative capability' which he remarked on as a large part of Shakespeare's greatness, and which he described as a power 'of being in uncertainties, mysteries, doubts, without any irritable reaching after fact and reason.' " This, the reviewer adds, is

[59] For more on Davis and his associates, see pp. 154–56. My principal source of information on T. L. Harris is *The Life and World-Work of Thomas Lake Harris* (Glasgow, 1908), which the author says was "written from Personal Knowledge" by "an almost Life-Long Associate."

[60] *Complete Writings*, IX, 84.

[61] Whitman clipped the review from the American edition, XC, 203–27 (388–433 in the regular edition). The review begins on p. 204, but at the top of p. 203, the reverse side, he wrote "Tennyson, Shelley, Keats."

the doubt of one "who prefers the broken fragments of truth to the imposing completeness of delusion. Such is that uncertainty of a large mind, which a small mind cannot understand." Whitman placed an exclamation point beside the last lines here quoted. I suspect he disagreed with the reviewer's last sentence, although not with Keats's idea of "negative capability."

Whitman clipped two other articles on Keats. One was a review of Milnes's *Life, Letters, and Literary Remains of John Keats* in the *North British Review* for November 1848.[62] Whitman underlined and bracketed a number of passages in this review but made only two annotations. At the top of page 39 he wrote, "Poets *now in all lands.*" This apparently refers to a passage in the first paragraph praising Keats's "powers of merely sensual perception and expression," and adding that he "may claim the honour of having assisted more than any other writer, except Mr. Wordsworth, in the origination of the remarkable school of poetry which is yet in its vigorous youth, and exhibits indications of capabilities of unlimited expansion." The reviewer quotes from a letter in which Keats argues that a poet is not poetical because he has no identity, no self. "When I am in a room with people," Keats declares, "if I am free from speculating on creations of my own brain, then, not myself goes home to myself; but the identity of every one in the room begins to press upon me, so that I am in a very little time annihilated; not only among men, but in a nursery of children it would be the same." Whitman draws an ink line along this entire letter up to the top, where he writes: "The great poet absorbs the Iden[ti]ty and the exp[erience] of others, and they are definite in him or from him; but he p[resses] them all through the powerful press of himself . . . his own masterly identity."[63] The sense here, in spite of imperfections, is clear enough. Whitman obviously does not agree with Keats's opinion that a poet may lose his identity in the presence of other people. Around the fourth paragraph of the review, in which the reviewer develops the idea that poetical genius is not infrequently the result of some deep-seated disease, Whitman places two rows of question marks, altogether more than a score, obviously to express strong disagreement and shock. He makes no further annotations, but he double-brackets the following quotation from a Keats letter: "That which is creative must create itself. In 'Endymion' I leaped headlong into the sea, and

62 Whitman's clipping is from the American edition, X, 38–51. It is No. 33 on Bucke's list of clippings.

63 *Notes and Fragments* (*Complete Writings*, IX, 120). Bucke interprets the imperfect manuscript as I do except that he writes "loads" for what to me is an undecipherable word just before "his own." The ellipses are Whitman's.

thereby have become better acquainted with the soundings, the quick-sands, and the rocks, than if I had strayed upon the green shore, and piped a silly pipe, and took tea and comfortable advice. I was never afraid of failure, for I would rather fail than not be among the great-est." If Whitman saw this before writing the first of his poems of *Leaves of Grass* it would have encouraged him to make his own head-long leap; if he read it afterwards it would have confirmed his judg-ment in making the leap. Early in his review the reviewer says Keats's poems are certainly not simple, nor even sensuous and passionate in Milton's sense of these terms. On the contrary, "His verses constitute a region of eye-wearying splendour, from which all who can duly appreciate them, must feel glad to escape, after the astonishment and rapture caused by a short sojourn among them." Whitman brackets and underlines these statements, which may have contributed to his general opinion of Keats and his poetry. In *Notes and Fragments* he makes this summation: "Keats' poetry is ornamental, elaborated, rich in wrought imagery, it is imbued with the sentiment, at second-hand, of the gods and goddesses of twenty-five hundred years ago. Its feeling is the feeling of a gentlemanly person lately at college, accept-ing what was commanded him there, who moves and would only move in society, reading classical books in libraries. Of life in the nineteenth century it has none any more than the statues have. It does not come home at all to the direct wants of the bodies and souls of the century." [64] If Whitman had read a biography of Keats, or even the biographical portions of the review with care, he could not have had so false a notion of Keats's life. He certainly would not have char-acterized him as "a gentlemanly person lately at college." He might have read some of the poems, however, and evidently had read "Hyperion."

He clipped J. D. Whelpley's article "The Hyperion of John Keats" from the *American Whig Review* for October 1851; or, rather, he clipped the last six pages, which survive, while the first six are miss-ing. Nevertheless, he read the entire review, since at least three notes in *Notes and Fragments* are drawn from or based on the pages not now in the clipping. In one of these Whitman wrote: "See how these fellows always take a *handsome man* for their God." [65] As Bucke sug-gests, Whitman had in mind, very likely, two lines (371–72) of the poem in a passage describing Hyperion's entrance to the great hall where the defeated Titans sat in dejection: "Golden his hair, of short Numidian curl; / Regal his shape majestic . . ." On the same page

[64] *Complete Writings*, IX, 120.
[65] *Ibid.*, IX, 128.

of *Notes and Fragments* Bucke has printed the following note: "Every great artist, poet, etc., will be found to have some precursors or first beginners of his greatness. Doubtless Homer had though we know them not." This is undoubtedly based on a portion of Whelpley's discussion of originality and imitation (pp. 314–15), and especially the sentence: "Every artistic age refines upon former ages, holding to a certain taste, and improving the 'school.' " A third passage, which Bucke prints in the section on "Meaning and Intention of 'Leaves of Grass,' " as if it were a comment on his own poems, reads: "The originality must be of the spirit and show itself in new combinations and new meanings and discovering greatness and harmony where there was before thought no greatness. The style of expression must be carefully purged of anything striking or dazzling or ornamental—and with great severity precluded from all that is eccentric." In a footnote Bucke says this was written as a note to the following sentence in the magazine: "It is perhaps safe to affirm that originality cannot be attained by seeking for it, but only eccentricity—oddity and eccentricity, which the great artist avoids as he values his immortality." [66] Presumably Bucke meant that the note was written on the page of the magazine (p. 315); if so, he must have had pages of the clipping not now surviving in the Trent Collection. On page 316 of the portion not in the clipping as it now exists, Whelpley wrote: "To be original, therefore, it is necessary to live the life, not of a recluse, given up to meditation, nor of a scholar buried in books, but to unite with a certain degree of scholarship and speculative thought a large experience of men, and a knowledge of things and their uses." This sounds a good deal like Whitman's summary statement about Keats quoted earlier and may have been one of the bases of it. In concluding my comments on Whitman and Keats, I am inclined to believe that Keats had some influence on the early *Leaves*, perhaps more as an example of what the American poet should avoid than of what he should follow, but it seems fairly obvious that he made no impression on the later Whitman.

[66] *Ibid.*, IX, 37.

XV. *Contemporary British Poets: Tennyson*

O F THE British poets who were his contemporaries, or near contemporaries, only Tennyson made a lasting impression on
Whitman. He reviewed the *Ballads* of Mary Howitt on February 2,
1847, commenting, "Among the Brooklyn *Eagle's* most favored favorites stands the sweet authoress of these poems!"[1] It is incredible that
Whitman was beginning to write, or even plan, *Leaves of Grass* at
the time he expressed this opinion. Whether he had read any of her
poems before 1847 I do not know, but he knew and admired her as a
translator of one of his favorite writers, Fredrika Bremer, whom he
first mentions in the *Eagle* on April 9, 1846. He says she "tells us a
beautiful and sublime thought which she learned from flowers," and
he urges his readers to place flowers where they can be seen every day,
since "we may learn many a fine moral from the flowers!" In the *Eagle*
on August 18, 1846, he reviewed several of her novels in the Harper's
edition of her works, translated by Mary Howitt, and called them
probably "the best books the whole range of romance-writing can
furnish."[2] Mary Howitt often collaborated in literary ventures with
her husband, William Howitt, and he wrote a number of books up-
holding the rights of the common people and condemning "kingcraft
and priestcraft" that Whitman would have approved, yet I do not
know whether he read any of them or not. Holloway says he quoted
five times in the *Eagle* from Mary Howitt and once from William
Howitt. In 1846 William Howitt became associated with John Saunders, founder of *The People's Journal,* but quarreled with him before
the end of the year and left it to found, with the help of his wife,
Howitt's Journal of Literature and Popular Progress, also a weekly
supporting radical reform movements, beginning January 2, 1847.
Howitt's Journal had a wide circulation, for a while at least, and
must have been well known in the United States to persons interested

---

[1] Reprinted in *UPP,* I, 133. Whitman must have had a copy of the London edition (1847), since no American edition, so far as I can find, was published before
Putnam's in 1848.

[2] Reprinted in *GF,* II, 266–70, and in part in *UPP,* I, 128. Many of Fredrika
Bremer's books described the family life in the home, and many of Mary Howitt's
poems also were on home life.

in popular causes. It published a number of articles against capital punishment. It ceased to exist as a separate publication on June 24, 1848, and soon after was merged with *The People's Journal.*[3] It is not at all unlikely that Whitman saw copies of *Howitt's* or *The People's Journal* between 1847 and 1849, when he was very much interested in the reform and revolutionary movements of the time in Europe. A number of articles on the Howitts were published in American periodicals, and they were well known to many American literary liberals, including Margaret Fuller and Emerson, who visited them at their home in 1847 when he went to England on a lecture tour. More than fifty of Mary Howitt's poems were published in American literary annuals.[4] The public libraries of New York and Brooklyn contained most of their books, but not, so far as I have found, files of *Howitt's Journal* or *The People's Journal.* I should like to think that Whitman sent them a copy of the 1855 *Leaves of Grass,* for William Howitt wrote a favorable review of the book published in the London *Dispatch* that Whitman reprinted in the 1856 edition and again in *Leaves of Grass Imprints* in 1860.[5]

Whitman's interest in wood engravings may have dated from the early 1830's and possibly also his interest in Thomas Bewick. *The Penny Magazine,* published from 1832 to 1846 for the Society for the Diffusion of Useful Knowledge, used wood engravings extensively. William Howitt, in *Rural Life of England,* said that the direct consequence of Bewick's revival of the art of wood engraving was that "we have now tens of thousands of volumes embellished with woodcuts, and upwards of two hundred engravers in this department. *The Penny Magazine* alone is said to pay for its wood-cutting 2000£ per annum."[6] Undoubtedly Whitman knew something of the *Penny Magazine,* for he clipped from the issue of January 12, 1833, an article on "The Dying Gladiator," in which the stanzas from Byron's *Childe Harold* were quoted.[7] In the same volume from which he made the clipping there is an article tracing the history of woodcut-

---

[3] For articles on George Sand in *Howitt's Journal* and *People's Journal* see pp. 214–15.

[4] See Bradford A. Booth's article, "Taste in the Annuals," *American Literature,* XIV (Nov. 1942), 299–302.

[5] It was also reprinted by Holloway and Ralph Adimari in *New York Dissected* (New York, 1936), pp. 166–67. It is probable, however, that the *Dispatch* received one of the copies Fowler and Wells sent to Horsell and Company for sale in England. But see Gay Wilson Allen, *The Solitary Singer* (New York, 1955), p. 177. Harold Blodgett, in *Walt Whitman in England* (Ithaca, New York, 1934), pp. 4, 14, states that this review was written by William J. Fox, apparently an error.

[6] See p. 341 of the 1840 edition.

[7] This clipping is mentioned in Chapter VIII, note 16.

ting as an art from the fifteenth century to the end of the seventeenth,
when it gradually disappeared in English publishing until it was revived by Thomas Bewick late in the eighteenth century.[8] William
Howitt used numerous wood engravings in the second edition (1840)
of *Rural Life of England*, including some of Bewick's given to him
by the artist's daughters when the Howitts visited his birthplace in
1836.[9] Chapter II of Part IV of *Rural Life of England* is devoted almost entirely to the life and work of Bewick, and in Chapter III
Howitt discusses the work of his successors, which he thought inferior
to Bewick's. Howitt also published a biographical sketch of Bewick,
with his picture on the first page, in *Howitt's Journal* for September
18, 1847.[10] Wood engravings were a prominent feature of *Howitt's
Journal* and of other British periodicals, such as *Punch, Illustrated
News*, and *Pictorial Times*. They were also extensively used in the
United States throughout the 1840's and 1850's, especially in the illustrated weeklies, such as *Gleason's* (later *Ballou's*) *Pictorial*, the
Illustrated News that Charles Leland edited for a time, *Leslie's Weekly*, and *Harper's Weekly*, all of which Whitman seems to have read
regularly.

We know from various sources that Whitman was interested in art
and artists as early as 1846, when he wrote familiarly of art exhibi-
tions in Brooklyn, that he had a number of artist friends, acquired
some original paintings of his own, and in 1851 felt sufficiently sure
of himself to address students of art on the subject of their own profession.[11] He never lost his interest in artists. On October 17, 1888,
Traubel found him reading the "Memoirs of Bewick," as Traubel
calls the book, and when he asked if Whitman was particularly interested in artists, Whitman replied, "I suppose I am. . . ."[12] Whitman
described this work as "autobiographical, simple, interesting," and
added: "The book just accidentally turned up—I have had it for
years: so I tackle it again." He implies that it had been "a long long
time mislaid."[13] It is pretty evident that he had acquired his copy
soon after its first publication. It is also more than probable that it

8 *Penny Magazine*, II (Oct. 26, 1933), 417–24. It was probably from this article
that Howitt learned that the *Penny Magazine* spent £2,000 a year for its woodcuts.

9 Carl Ray Woodring, *Victorian Samplers: William and Mary Howitt* (Lawrence, Kansas, 1952), p. 67.

10 *Howitt's Journal*, II, 178–80.

11 See, for examples, *UPP*, I, 142–43 and 236–47.

12 The book is described in the catalogue of the Library of Congress as "A
Memoir of Thomas Bewick, written by himself, embellished with numerous engravings designed and engraved by the author for a work on British fishes and
never before published." It was published for the first time in 1862, and reprinted.

13 *WWC*, II, 492.

did not turn up "accidentally." His interest in Bewick might have
been revived by his reading of Austin Dobson's two articles in the
Century Magazine: "Thomas Bewick" in September 1882 and "The
Pupils of Thomas Bewick" in October 1883. He may also have seen
Dobson's book based on these articles, *Thomas Bewick and His Pu-
pils*, published in London and Boston in 1884.

Another minor contemporary of Tennyson whose work interested
Whitman for a time was Martin Farquhar Tupper, whose prose work,
Probabilities: an Aid to Faith, was reviewed briefly in the *Eagle* of
February 20, 1847. Whitman must have had the original edition, published in London in 1847, for it was not reprinted in America, apparently, until it appeared in Tupper's *Complete Prose Works*, published at Hartford, Connecticut, in 1850 and reprinted in 1851 and
1853.[14] Whitman says the book "has a lofty, an august scope of intention! It treats of the great mysteries of the future, of God and his
attributes, of the fall of man, of heaven and hell! The author, Mr.
Tupper, is one of the rare men of the time. He turns up thoughts as
with a plow, on the sward of monotonous usage. We would like well
to go into this book, in a fuller article; but justice to it would require
many pages."[15] Unless these comments were ironical, which is unlikely
in view of Whitman's temperament, he meant to praise the book. It is
short, but whether Whitman read it all one cannot be sure. The subjects mentioned in the second sentence are subheads in the book, but
the opinion expressed in the fourth sentence must have been based
on some knowledge of the contents. The sentence calling Tupper
"one of the rare men of the time" suggests that Whitman knew more
of his work than the book under review; if he did not then, he almost
surely made a point of looking him up later.

Tupper was well known, even famous, at the time as the author of
a volume of poems with the title *Proverbial Philosophy: A Book of
Thoughts and Arguments, Originally Treated*, the first "series" of
which was published in 1838 and the second in 1842. A third series
was added in 1867 and a fourth in 1876, but the first two are the only
parts worth noticing here. The first two series were incredibly popular, reaching to the eighteenth edition by 1854 and the fiftieth edition in 1880. Wiley and Putnam reprinted the book in 1846, and in
1847 made it one of the books in their Library of Choice Reading.
Whitman reviewed a number of books published by Wiley and Putnam, and he must have known of their edition of *Proverbial Philoso-*

---

[14] The catalogue of the British Museum does not list an edition of the *Complete
Prose Works*; presumably it was published only in the United States.

[15] Reprinted in *UPP*, I, 136; not reprinted in *GF*.

phy. The only reason I can think of why he did not review it in the *Eagle* is that it was already too well known to make a review worth while. The poem, if such it is, consists of thoughts and arguments on themes of universal interest, such as truth, wisdom, friendship, ambition, fame, life, death, and immortality, arranged in long lines of ten to twenty syllables, usually, each beginning with a capital letter and containing various poetic features somewhat in the manner of the Bible, with alliteration and several types of parallelism. The poetic qualities are somewhat more apparent in the second series than in the first, but in neither is there much music or imagination. Tupper had some skill in verse, though there is little evidence of it in *Proverbial Philosophy,* for in the same year, 1838, that he published the first part of that poem he published "Geraldine," a continuation of the theme of Coleridge's "Christabel" in irregular lines like those of that poem. He continued to write verse in the orthodox manner until his death in 1889. None of it is particularly good, and yet it hardly deserved the ridicule some critics heaped upon his work as a whole, provoked in the first place, no doubt, by *Proverbial Philosophy.*

More than one competent reader of *Leaves of Grass* has compared Whitman's long unrhymed lines with those of *Proverbial Philosophy,* usually, but not always, in ridicule. One of the reviewers of the 1855 edition wrote in the London *Leader*: "The poem is written in wild, irregular, unrhymed, almost unmetrical 'lengths,' like the measured prose of Mr. Martin Farquhar Tupper's Proverbial Philosophy, or some of the Oriental writings."[16] The reviewer in the London *Examiner,* less kind, used a comparison with Tupper to ridicule Whitman's poem: "Suppose that Mr. Tupper had been brought up to the business of an auctioneer, then banished to the backwoods, compelled to live for a long time as a backwoodsman, and thus contracting a passion for the reading of Emerson and Carlyle? Suppose him maddened by this course of reading and fancying himself not only an Emerson but a Carlyle and an American Shakespeare to boot when the fits came on, and putting forth his notion of that combination in his own self-satisfied way, and in his own wonderful cadences? In that state he would write a book exactly like Walt Whitman's *Leaves of Grass.*"[17]

Swinburne, who in the 1860's had written in admiration of *Leaves*

[16] Whitman reprinted this review in his 1856 edition and in 1860 in *Leaves of Grass Imprints.* It was also reprinted in *Life Illustrated,* probably at Whitman's request, on July 19, 1856. I quote from this source as reprinted in *New York Dissected,* pp. 167–70.

[17] This review was also printed in the 1856 edition, from which I quote.

of Grass, chose to ridicule the poems twenty years later by comparing them to the poems of James Macpherson and Martin Tupper. Whitman, he said then, "has about as much gift of song as his precursors and apparent models in rhythmic structure and style, Mr. James Macpherson and Mr. Martin Tupper," and in his "capacity for creation" is "rather like the later than the earlier of his masters."[18] Yet Swinburne still praised some of Whitman's themes and his treatment of them. He was probably provoked to scorn by some of Whitman's too ardent admirers in the late 1880's, whom he called "Whitmaniacs," and whose worshipful attitude toward him did him more harm than good. In March 1888, only a few months after the *Fortnightly* article, Oscar Wilde, then in America, wrote Whitman a letter in which he quoted passages from a recent letter to him from Swinburne in which the latter reaffirmed his admiration for much, or most, of Whitman's poetry without, however, denying anything he had said in the article.[19]

On June 22, 1889, Traubel told Whitman of hearing a sermon by the Unitarian minister Minot Judson Savage, which contrasted Shakespeare at the upper extreme of poetic worth with Whitman and Tupper at the other extreme, calling Shakespeare natural and Whitman and Tupper artificial. Knowing Traubel's bias, I suspect he slanted the minister's statement to suit his own purposes. In any case, only five years later, Savage published an article in the *Arena* in which he praised Whitman's poetry. "Whitman," he wrote, "has a rhythm which is all his own, as much as the waves and the surf-beat belong to the sea. . . . Some of his passages need not fear comparison with the finest in the Old Testament."[20] In his biography in 1906, Bliss Perry cited several passages from *Proverbial Philosophy* in which he found "interesting parallelisms with Whitman's methods."[21]

No competent critic who wished to be fair to Whitman has ever said that *Leaves of Grass* is not incomparably better as poetry than Tupper's *Proverbial Philosophy,* and I am sure no competent critic ever will say it. Nevertheless, it is no disparagement of Whitman or his poetry to say that he probably got ideas for both the form and the substance of *Leaves of Grass* from Tupper. Undoubtedly, he learned much from sources of even less distinction, such as Andrew Jackson Davis and the contributors to the *American Phrenological Journal.* After all, Whitman wanted, at first, to be such a popular poet as was

18 "Whitmania," in the *Fortnightly Review,* XLVIII (Aug. 1887), 170–76.
19 *WWC,* II, 288.
20 "The Religion of Walt Whitman's Poems," *The Arena,* X (Sept. 1894), 433–52.
21 *Walt Whitman,* pp. 91–92 and note 1.

Tupper in the 1850's, and for a short while after the publication of his first edition he thought he would be. The last sentence in the 1855 Preface is, "The proof of a poet is that his country absorbs him as affectionately as he has absorbed it." Without admiring or imitating *Proverbial Philosophy*, he might have been encouraged to believe that his own unconventional form would be as readily accepted by readers as Tupper's. What he did not foresee, apparently, was that his subject matter, which, unlike Tupper's, was also unconventional, would prove unacceptable to the masses. Actually Whitman's critical sense developed more slowly than his intellect and his imagination. It is also true, in my judgment, that his feeling for the musical quality of poetry, even his own, was less discriminating than his judgment of its thought content. Such poems as "Out of the Cradle Endlessly Rocking" and "When Lilacs Last in the Dooryard Bloom'd" were the products of deep feeling, half unconscious, rather than conscious artistic skill. Some of his modern critics may be right in saying those poems, in their greater conventionality, are less characteristic of Whitman than "Song of Myself" because they have been more influenced by the musical qualities of poets like Shelley and Tennyson.

I do not mean to say that major nineteenth-century British poets had no influence on Whitman's early poems, but only that the influence, such as it was, was more on the substance of his poems than on their verse form. Even for the substance of *Leaves of Grass* Whitman's debt was almost wholly to prose works—to those of Carlyle and Emerson among others—and to the social and political thought developed in America from Revolutionary sources before 1850. I have said that Tennyson was the only major British poet of the nineteenth century who made a lasting impression on Whitman. It came late, however, and had no appreciable influence on his poetry or his literary opinions before 1870, and but little after that time. His early interest was in Tennyson as a successful contemporary poet whose success he might hope to emulate. He is not mentioned in Whitman's acknowledged published writings, so far as I have found, until 1876, when his name appeared in *Two Rivulets*.[22] Whitman sent his poems to Tennyson by Cyril Flower, who visited Whitman in December 1870, and Tennyson acknowledged the gift in a letter to Whitman dated July 12, 1871.[23] On May 24, 1874, Whitman wrote Tennyson about

---

[22] *Prose Works 1892*, II, 533. His anonymous review of *Maud and Other Poems* along with the 1855 *Leaves of Grass* will be discussed later.

[23] *Correspondence*, II, 125–26 and note 31. I presume the "books" referred to by Tennyson, included the 1860 edition and the 1867 edition of *Leaves of Grass*, for on April 27, 1872, Whitman wrote Tennyson, "I send you by same mail with this, a more neatly printed copy of my 'Leaves'; also 'Dem. Vistas.'" (*Correspondence*,

his paralysis and Tennyson replied on July 8, wishing him a rapid recovery and apologizing for not acknowledging receipt of *Democratic Vistas.* Apparently Tennyson never wrote to Whitman except to acknowledge receipt of one of Whitman's books, or the promise of one, and he never, so far as I can discover, sent Whitman any of his publications. The enthusiasm was all on Whitman's side; Tennyson was polite, but his letters show little warmth of feeling. The nearest thing to a critical appreciation of *Leaves of Grass* in his letters was this sentence in his letter of July 12, 1871: "I discovered great 'go' in your writings and am not surprised at the hold they have taken on your fellow countrymen."[24] Whitman was elated to have received letters from Tennyson, and mentioned the fact in many letters to friends and acquaintances.[25] In 1885 he suggested to his friend W. S. Kennedy that he write a criticism on "Tennyson and Walt Whitman," or "Victor Hugo, Tennyson, and Walt Whitman."[26] When Tennyson's play *Queen Mary* was published in 1875 he made some notes on it, clipped reviews, and wrote the author on July 24: "I have been reading your Queen Mary, & think you have excelled yourself in it. I did not know till I read it, how much eligibility to passion, character and art arousings was still left to me in my sickness & old age. Though I am Democrat enough to realize the deep criticism of Jefferson on Walter Scott's writings, (& many of the finest plays, poems & romances) that they fail to give at all the life of the great mass of the people then & there."[27] By "eligibility" Whitman means something like "responsiveness"; but feeling that this responsiveness was out of keeping with his role as the poet of democracy, he makes

---

II, 174.) John M. Ditsky's article, "Whitman-Tennyson Correspondence: A Summary and Commentary," was published in the *Walt Whitman Review*, XVIII (Sept. 1972), 75–82, after this chapter was written.

24 *Correspondence*, II, 126. Whitman must have been surprised to learn that his writings in 1871 had taken a "hold" on his countrymen, for about that time he told friends that he was discouraged about his "poetic mission." See Rufus A. Coleman, "Trowbridge and Whitman," *PMLA*, LXIII (March 1948), 268; cited in the editor's footnote, p. 126.

25 See *Correspondence*, II, 152, 155, 158, 161, 164, 270. He also sent Tennyson letters to John Burroughs and Mrs. Gilchrist, asking that they be returned.

26 *Ibid.*, III, 391.

27 *Ibid.*, II, 335. Among Whitman's manuscripts on *Queen Mary* and the English sixteenth century (see Library of Congress Whitman Catalog, items 60 and 118) is the following: "Queen Mary, like so many fine plays, poems, romances, &c., is undoubtedly open to the severe criticism of Jefferson on the general scope of Walter Scott, namely, that while it fails to give at all the life of the great mass of the people then and there it picks out the life of a few great persons, & gives that life falsely. [above "falsely," in pencil, "deceptively"] The same criticism can be made, from our point of view, against Shakspere."

a kind of apology for it, anticipating, as it were, Tennyson's reply on August 11th, saying: "I am glad . . . that you find something to approve in a work so utterly unlike your own as my Queen Mary."[28] There is no doubt that Whitman liked Tennyson's poetry, or much of it, for he classed him with Walter Scott, whose works he had loved from boyhood, as a follower of Shakespeare and a belated representative of English feudalism. He tries to explain in many places, but most extensively in the essay "Poetry To-day in America—Shakspere—The Future," why it is proper for a democrat to love the literature of feudalism, but his logic leaves something to be desired. "From first to last," he says, "Walter Scott and Tennyson, like Shakspere, exhale that principle of caste which we Americans have come on earth to destroy."[29] Yet he admits that feudalism in Europe, and also even the system of slavery in the antebellum South, has produced "types of tallest, noblest personal character yet—strength and devotion and love better than elsewhere—invincible courage, generosity, aspiration, the spines of all. Here is where Shakspere and the others I have named perform a service incalculably precious to our America."[30] What he can hardly explain is how the "principle of caste," which has produced these excellent results, can be destroyed without destroying also the results. It would seem that he wished to eat his cake and have it too.

He had always had an innate love of the pageantry of what he called "feudalism," especially as represented in the historical plays of Shakespeare and the novels and narrative poems of Scott, but it was not until after he had established himself as the poet of democracy that he accepted their aristocratic heroes as examples of "noblest personal character" to be emulated in a democratic society. In 1847 he felt, by contrast, that the "turbulence and destructiveness" that are the accompaniments of democracy are good because "they evince that *the people act*; they are the discipline of the young giant, getting his maturer strength."[31] A few days later Whitman wrote another article, "Anti-Democratic Bearing of Scott's Novels," in which he condemns Scott for representing Cromwell as a "blood-seeking hypocrite" and King Charles "a good-natured pleasant gentleman." He also says, "In the long line of these warriors for liberty, and these

---

28 *Correspondence*, II, 339.

29 *Prose Works 1892*, II, 476.

30 *Ibid.*

31 From an editorial on the democratic spirit in the *Eagle*, April 20, 1847 (reprinted in *UPP*, I, 159–60; *GF*, I, 3–6). The editorial is without title in the *Eagle*; Holloway gives it the title "The Democratic Spirit," and the editors of *GF* call it simply "American Democracy."

large-hearted lovers of *men* before *classes* of men, which English history has recorded upon its annals, and which form for the fast-anchored isle a far greater glory than her first Richard, or her tyrannical Stuarts, Scott has not thought one fit to be illustrated by his pen." His way, like Shakespeare's, of describing kings, as "more than mortal . . . is poisonous for freemen."[32] As late as 1856 Whitman had not changed the opinions expressed in 1847. In his essay on Voltaire he said of earlier writers: "Racine, Boileau, Corneille, Molière, La Bruyere, Fenelon—what had they to eat or drink but the shadows of royalty or the aristocracy? Was it not in England the same? Had it not been with Shakespeare the same? . . . Among the profuse shoals of the writers of those times, not one appeared to speak for man, for mind, for freedom, against superstition and caste."[33] In the articles reprinted from Whitman's Brooklyn *Daily Times*, 1857–59, in *I Sit and Look Out*, he does not notice Shakespeare except to quote a few brief phrases and write a short paragraph on Shakespeare's women characters. He does not mention Walter Scott at all. There is in this newspaper a good deal about the Democratic Party, but very little about democracy. For the first time, so far as I have found, in *Democratic Vistas*, he suggests that Shakespeare and other poets of the old world might have something of value for the new world democracy: "Yet could ye, indeed, but breathe your breath of life into our New World's nostrils—not to enslave us, as now, but, for our needs, to breed a spirit like your own—perhaps, (dare we to say it?) to dominate, even destroy, what you yourselves have left!"[34]

Whitman clipped five reviews of Tennyson's poems from British and American magazines published in the late 1840's and early 1850's, and he discussed Tennyson's *"Maud"* in his review of his first edition of *Leaves of Grass* in 1855.[35] The earliest of the reviews clipped was from the *North British Review* (American edition, IX, 25–40) for May 1848 and has the title "Tennyson's Poems—The Princess." This review, which was written by Coventry Patmore, contains marks by Whitman only on the first twelve pages, which are wholly concerned with general principles of art. The rest, which is devoted to a criticism of *The Princess*, is unmarked. Since Whitman's interest was obviously in what Patmore said about poetic art, not in his criticism of *The Princess*, I reserve comment on the passages marked until later,

[32] From the *Eagle*, April 26, 1847 (reprinted in *UPP*, I, 163–64; *GF*, II, 264–66).
[33] From *Life Illustrated*, May 10, 1856 (reprinted in *New York Dissected*, pp. 70–74).
[34] *Prose Works 1892*, II, 407.
[35] Four of these reviews are listed by Bucke in *Notes and Fragments* (*Complete Writings*, X, 66–68), Nos. 37, 45, 52, and 53. All are in the Trent Collection.

when other articles on the art of poetry will be discussed. It is probable that most of the marks were made just before or just after the publication of the first *Leaves of Grass*.

Next, in point of date, is the clipping of William Henry Smith's review of "Tennyson's Poems" in *Blackwood's Magazine* for April 1849. Whitman underlines the following sentence and places a question mark beside it: "Every man of original genius has his mannerism more or less disagreeable; once thoroughly understood, it becomes our only care to forget it." This remark is followed immediately by statements about Wordsworth's being prosaic, about Milton's divinity, and about Shakespeare's "tangled sentences," which presumably illustrate the "disagreeable mannerisms" noted. Following that in the review is a passage on Thomas Moore describing him as having "dwindled down to the most delightful of minstrel-pages that ever brought song and music into a lady's chamber." The reviewer goes on to say that Moore's fame has shrunk to a little point, but that point "is bright as the diamond, and as imperishable." Whitman underlines the last three words and in the margin pencils "bah!" Several other passages suggesting minor faults in Tennyson's poetry are underlined or bracketed, and near the end the poem "Ulysses" is quoted. The poem has been cut out of the review, but beside it, written apparently before it was clipped, is this in the margin: "This redeems a hundred 'Princesses' and 'Mauds,' and shows the Great Master." At the end of the article, at the bottom of page 467, Whitman wrote: "I have read 'Maud'—It will not live long." Since *Maud* was not published until 1855, Whitman must have made the notes in which it is mentioned during that year or later. Pasted to the clipping are two brief newspaper clippings, both dating from 1857.

In the *American Phrenological Journal* for October 1855 appeared a review with the title "An English and an American Poet," anonymous in the *Journal* but written by Whitman, ostensibly a comparison of Tennyson's *Maud* with *Leaves of Grass*, but in the section on Tennyson embracing his work as a whole, apparently, as representing the best poetry of the period in England and America. He writes, in part:

The spirit of burnished society of upper-class England fills this writer and his effusions from top to toe. Like that, he does not ignore courage and the superior qualities of men, but all is to show forth through dandified forms. He meets the nobility and gentry half-way. The models are the same both to the poet and the parlors. Both have the same supercilious elegance, both love the reminiscences which extol caste, both agree on the topics proper for mention and discussion, both hold the same undertone of church and state, both have the same languishing melancholy and irony, both indulge largely in persiflage, both are marked by the contour of high blood and a constitutional aversion to anything cowardly and mean, both accept the love depicted in romances as the great business of a life or a poem, both seem unconscious of the mighty truths of eternity and immortality, both are silent on the presumptions of liberty and equality, and both devour themselves in solitary lassitude.

He admits, however, "that this man is a real first-class poet, infused amid all that ennui and aristocracy."[36] This criticism obviously is a part of Whitman's thinking at the time he made the notes on the *Blackwood* article quoted in the preceding paragraph. I suspect he found the "real first-class poet" in the short poems, especially "Ulysses," not in the longer ones. He was, according to Bucke, in the habit of reciting "Ulysses" along with favorite passages from Homer, Shakespeare, Bryant, and others.[37]

One article that Whitman clipped is not listed by Bucke. It is a review of "Poems of Alfred Tennyson," signed "Is. Io.," in the *Westminster Review* for July 1849. Possibly Bucke failed to list it because Whitman made no marks on it. For the same reason, it requires no discussion here. Moreover, it is not a very good article and would have added little to Whitman's store of notes.

The clipping of Aubrey De Vere's review of the poems of Tennyson, Shelley, and Keats, with the title "Modern Poetry and Poets," from the *Edinburgh Review* for October 1849 (American Edition, XC, 203–27), should have helped Whitman to take a favorable view of Tennyson, since the reviewer was a personal friend of the poet laureate and an admirer of his poetry. At the top of page 205 Whitman wrote in pencil: "Tennyson is the imitation of Shakespeare, through a refined, educated, traveled, modern English dandy." From the beginning of English literature, De Vere said, there have been two schools of poetry, the national and the ideal, culminating in Shakespeare and Milton. He classes Keats and Shelley as poets of the ideal, and says that in his early work Tennyson is of their school, although he has much in common with both schools. He had not yet produced a great national poem, but his progress has been from the ideal to the national. "He has a Shakspearean enjoyment in whatever is human, and a Shakspearean indulgence for the frailties of hu-

---

[36] Quoted from *In Re*, pp. 29–30. Cf. Chapter I, pp. 3–4.

[37] *Walt Whitman* (Philadelphia, 1883), p. 53. In 1876 Whitman recited "Ulysses" to Edward Carpenter and said it was Tennyson's best poem. (Edward Carpenter, *Days with Walt Whitman* [London, 1906], p. 25.) In the MS book "Oratory" in the Library of Congress there is a sheet headed "As Prefatory to Reading Ulysses' Address," followed by instructions to himself and explanatory words for the benefit of his hearers. This may have referred to his reading of Tennyson's "Ulysses."

manity." It was probably this statement in particular, which provoked Whitman's comment.

The opinion of Tennyson expressed in the anonymous article "Recollections of Poets Laureate. Wordsworth: Tennyson," from the *American Whig Review* for June 1852, probably pleased Whitman more than the more favorable opinions of the English reviewers discussed above. Whitman brackets a paragraph in which the author says, "Tennyson is not a great poet, except in a limited range," and calls him the "Laureate of the aristocracy," whose "strength lies in his sweetness." Among other passages marked are the following: "Every one of these poems displays a perfect mastery over the lute strings of language . . . but they resemble the opium state of a gorgeous and subtle mind, rather than that fine, healthy, breezy, sinewy, active, large-hearted thoughtfulness, so characteristic of the Shakespearian and Homeric muse." Referring especially to "In Memoriam," he says Tennyson "treats every thing not philosophically, but *"skeptically,"* and he expresses "doubt of the sincerity of these lachrymal verses." In the margin of the last page appear the following notes, not based on the review: "Tennyson has a pension £200 a year, conferred by the Queen, some years since. . . . Age now (1856) 48 years. . . . Sept. 1855—Tennyson published 'Maud, & other Poems.' It is a love-story, rather tedious and affected, with some sweet passages."[38] It is not improbable that this review had some influence on the opinion of Tennyson expressed in Whitman's "An English and an American Poet."

[38] These annotations are reprinted in *Complete Writings*, IX, 123, 127. Portions of the *American Whig Review* clipping are discussed previously, pp. 239–40.

XVI. *Ideas on Poetic Art*

S EVERAL of the reviews discussed previously contain ideas on poetic art that might have influenced Whitman in the formation of
his own ideas on the subject. Usually when these are intimately connected with the poet reviewed, they are discussed along with discussion of the poet; but if they are ideas of general application they have
been reserved for this chapter, in which I will attempt to relate them
to *Leaves of Grass* and the theory on which it is based. It is worth
noting that the ideas marked in one review are not usually repeated
in any other review clipped. This may be accidental, or, more probably, it is the result of deliberate selection by Whitman at the time
he was formulating his own theory of poetry. This being the case, the
simplest way of representing these ideas is to take up the clipped articles in the order in which they were published. This, of course, is
not necessarily the order in which they were clipped, nor the order
in which they were read. As I have said earlier, an article clipped in
a given year may have been read and annotated several times at wide
intervals of time, although in most cases the differences in the markings are sufficient to justify the conjecture that the more significant
part of them belong to the years just before or just after he wrote the
poems published in the 1855 edition. This would be especially true
of notes on poetic art, whereas biographical notes, as we know, were
more often made in 1856 and 1857, when he was preparing to deliver
lectures, some of them on literature. Through 1845 he was a fairly
regular contributor to the *Democratic Review*, and he also contributed to the *American Whig Review* that year, the first of its publication. For political and other reasons he pretty certainly read both of
these magazines during the next three or four years, during two of
which he was editor of the Brooklyn *Daily Eagle*, an organ of the
local Democratic organization. The *Democratic Review* published
few articles or reviews that contained important literary criticism;
the *American Whig Review* published more and perhaps better literary reviews. Whitman preserved no clippings from the former after
1847 and none from the latter during the years 1848–50.[1]

[1] See Chapter VIII, pp. 145–48.

The only literary article that Whitman clipped from the *Demo-cratic Review* in 1845 was a review of *Festus, A Poem*, by Philip James Bailey (first American edition, 1845), and of this he kept only the first page. This is at present in the Trent Collection, bound with a clipping of a review of Mrs. Browning's *Drama of Exile*, from the *American Whig Review*. The reviewer of *Festus* begins by saying that few modern books are worth careful reading. He says *Festus*, understandably, has been both praised and condemned, for it "is ill-constructed, elaborate, sometimes to weariness, and quite fails in producing an entire and lucid impression"; yet it contains passages "alive with the very soul of poetry . . . worthy of the masters of song." The intended moral is "the triumph of good through evil." This page contains the gist of the reviewer's criticism, and that is probably why Whitman preserved no more of it. If he read through the review, as he probably did, he might have been interested in the reviewer's statement that Bailey's poem teaches "the same doctrine which inspires Carlyle—warfare upon all sham, cordial recognition of the actual."[2]

Whitman clipped six items from the *American Whig Review* for 1845. Two of these, in the January number, I have seen, and they are unmarked; they are the "Hymn of Callimachus" and a review of Elizabeth Barrett's *A Drama of Exile and Other Poems*. The reviewer names Miss Barrett and Tennyson as the most important contemporary poets. Whitman may have found in *A Drama of Exile* his first interest in literary treatments of the fall and of Lucifer. Some collector may have bound the clipping of this review with the clipping of *Festus* in the *Democratic Review* because it had been attached by Whitman himself. A brief article on "Words" by E. P. Whipple was clipped from the February number (No. 144 of Bucke's list), which Bucke says is "scored"; since it is not in the Trent Collection I have not seen this clipping. Some passages in the review would certainly have interested Whitman: style should be unshackled by rules, and each writer is his own standard; words are not "the dress of thought," they are "as Wordsworth has happily said, the *incarnation* of thought," and "bear the same relation to ideas that the body bears to the soul"; a thought "embodied and *embrained* in fit words, walks the earth a living being." In the same vein, J. D. Whelpley's article "On Style," in the October number (Bucke's clipping No. 425), contains much that would have caught Whitman's eye even then. Two examples must suffice: "In nature nothing is more obvious than the mix-

---

[2] Whitman did not preserve, though he must have seen, another review of *Festus* in the *American Whig Review*, Feb. 1847, by H. N. Hudson, which was much more thorough and more critical than the one he clipped.

ture of contrasts and discords ... The few who have attained a happy union of art and nature, seem to have trusted with a careless confidence to the worth of their ideas; and used no art but to exclude what was improper. . . . It is his privilege to assume no disguises: a free people delights in a free speech; for our freedom is of the heart as well as of the hands. . . ."

Two articles were clipped from the May issue: "Thoughts on Reading," by H. N. Hudson (I, 483–96, No. 439 of Bucke's list), and "The Laws of Menu," by J. D. Whelpley (I, 510–21, No. 515 of Bucke's list). Reading this and other articles on ancient India by Whelpley may have been the beginning of Whitman's interest in Hindu philosophy and religion.[3] He did not annotate the article, and so far as I can tell the references to Menu (or Manu) in *Notes and Fragments* were based on later reading.

The most important of Whitman's clippings from American magazines of the 1840's was Hudson's "Thoughts on Reading." Whitman attributed the article to Whelpley, although the Index states that Hudson was the author.[4] He undoubtedly possessed and preserved a copy of this and other issues of the *Whig Review* for some time, but whether he clipped the article soon after publication or later cannot be determined. Neither can the dates of the annotations be certainly known, though we can be reasonably sure that they were made on two or three separate occasions and for different reasons.[5] All underlinings and brackets were made with a lead pencil and could have been made at a first reading or at different times. At the top of page 483 this comment is made in ink: "Good article—something on Shakespeare very good." This and probably other comments in ink were, in my judgment, made not at a first reading, but after a second

[3] Whelpley had published "The Hindoos, Their Laws, Customs, and Religion" in the March number, and "Castes and Occupations of India" in the April number. Another article, "The Bhagvat Geeta, and the Doctrine of Immortality," in the September issue, may have been also by Whelpley, though no author is named. Whelpley was one of Whitman's favorite writers for the magazine. "The Laws of Menu" is a review of Sir William Jones's translation of the *Institutes of Menu*.

[4] At the end of the article he wrote in ink, "is this Whelpley's." Presumably he read from the current issue of the magazine, where the author's name is not mentioned. It is strange that Whitman nowhere mentions the name or work of Henry Norman Hudson, although he was one of the principal Shakespearean scholars of his time (1814–86) and editor of a standard edition of Shakespeare's works in 20 vols. in 1880–81 that, with some revision, is still in use.

[5] Three of Whitman's early compositions were published in the *American Whig Review* in 1845: "The Boy Lover" in the May issue, "Tear Down and Build Over Again" in November, and "The Antiquarian's Story," reprinted from *Franklin Evans* with the title "The Death of Wind-Foot," in June.

or third, perhaps several years after the date of publication. Commenting on a passage in the essay speaking of popular literature of poor quality that "keeps people constantly eating, without ever feeding them," Whitman has filled the outside margin of the page with the following, apparently written with an indelible pencil: "Still all kinds of light reading, novels, newspapers, gossip, &c, serve as manure for the few *great productions,* and are indispensable or perhaps are premises to something better.—The whole raff of light reading is also a testimony in honor of the original good reading which preceded it. —The thousands of common poets, romancers, essayists and attempters exist because some twenty or fifty geniuses at intervals led the way long before." [6] This was made earlier than the notes in ink, I think, and well before Whitman conceived of *Leaves of Grass.* It sounds like self-justification for publishing the kind of stories and essays that he was contributing to the magazines of the early and middle 1840's.

On page 487, beside a passage stating that "in the Greek Mythology, Hercules was the impersonation of moral energy, Whitman wrote in the margin: *"no,* of obedience and the divine lustiness of labor."[7] Hudson was a Shakespearean scholar and probably well acquainted with Greek poetry and mythology; certainly his interpretation of Hercules as represented in Greek poetry is correct. Whitman, who knew little of Greek poetry, especially in the 1840's, is probably basing his interpretation on a superficial knowledge of the twelve famous labors of Hercules and on his democratic bias that conceived "labor" in a modern sense different from that of the ancient Greeks. On page 489 Carlyle is quoted as saying "that Shakspeare begins at the heart of a subject, and works outwards towards the surface; while Scott begins at the surface, and works inwards, but never gets at the heart of it at all." These words are underlined, and at the top of the page is written in ink: "an immense saying," with two hands in ink pointing down and in each margin a row of dots leading to the words quoted. On page 490, first column, Whitman brackets a passage asking why Shakespeare and other great poets have such power over us, and underlines the following remark on Shakespeare: "He comes to us, not as our sovereign, to exact our allegiance, but as our smiling brother"; in answering his own question Hudson says such poets have a "mysterious something" whose power and excellence we can all feel, but whose nature we cannot explain, but which "has been baptized into the name of Genius." At the top of the page are the

---

[6] Part of this quotation was used in Chapter IV, p. 53. In *Notes and Fragments* Bucke prints "raft" for what is clearly and correctly "raff" in the MS.

[7] Bucke did not print this note in *Notes and Fragments.*

words, in ink, "a profound suggestion," and a hand drawn in ink pointing down to the passage quoted.

The next paragraph, second column, begins with this sentence, which is bracketed and underlined in pencil: "One important distinction between talent and genius is, that talent gives us information of the objects and agencies that exist and act around us; genius calls up and draws out what is within us; gives life and reality to the slumbering possibilities of our being." Another sentence in the same paragraph is also underlined: "The man of talent triumphs over us in the superiority of his own power; the man of genius causes us to triumph in the new power he awakens within us." At the bottom of the page a hand in ink points up to these passages and above the hand, written in ink, the direction, "read above *once more.*" Continuing the same contrast of genius and talent through page 491, Hudson quotes Coleridge's distinction: "talent combines; genius creates." Whitman underlines the following: "Genius needs no evidence to authenticate its words, but what it *creates* is the tribunal to which it appeals. The message it has to deliver but sleeps within us, and starts up at the sound of its voice. It gives only what it finds in us, but what we could never find without its help." All these, and other passages in the same vein, are so closely parallel to many passages in *Leaves of Grass,* beginning most notably in "Song of the Answerer" but found in many other poems, early and late, and are so well known, that to quote them or even point them out to any reader of Whitman would be an act of supererogation. The tone of Whitman's notes suggests an increasing interest, perhaps through a number of years, in what Hudson has to say of the poet and of the difference between talent and genius. This points to the probability that some of the comments made in ink were inscribed after a rereading of the essay as late as 1854. The brief notations quoted above are not recorded in *Notes and Fragments,* but several short paragraphs just before and just after the one on the value of light reading may have been suggested by "Thoughts on Reading."[8]

The clippings dating from 1846 have little of importance on the art of poetry. Whitman clipped James Hadley's review of Longfellow's *Poets and Poetry of Europe* from the *American Whig Review* for December, and bracketed and underlined these lines: "The cardinal doctrine of the Goethean philosophy, that an artist may live in art alone, may hold himself aloof from the world of action, neglect the momentous questions that agitate society, refuse to take part by

[8] See paragraphs numbered 166, 167, 169, 170, 171; *Complete Writings,* IX, 161–62.

word or deed in the great events that are going on round him, is a doctrine which could not well be entertained by any but a cold and selfish spirit."[9] Whitman's lifelong interest in Goethe and other German writers could have been stimulated by this essay, though he may have become acquainted with Carlyle's essay earlier.[10] Another brief comment may be worth mentioning. This is written in the margin beside C. A. Bristed's essay "Translators of Homer," clipped from the October number, where the author says (citing Pope, Byron, Shelley, and Coleridge) that "Great poets are usually great translators." Whitman drew a hand pointing to the margin where he wrote: "The *greatest poets* can never be translators of the poetry of others—that is in any other way than Shakespeare translated—which was to take the poor or tolerable stuff of others and make it incomparable." Bucke seems to attribute Whitman's notes on this clipping to the year 1857, but gives no reason. They are printed in *Notes and Fragments* (*Complete Writings*, IX, 222) with notes on Leigh Hunt that were dated, originally, 1857, but the notes on Hunt were from a totally unrelated source. Whitman undoubtedly saw the review of Margaret Fuller's *Papers on Literature and Art* in the November issue, but since the review was unfavorable and obviously prejudiced, he would not have liked it and did not clip it.

The only literary clippings from the year 1847 that could have had an effect on Whitman's theory of poetry were three, all published in American magazines. One of these, the first section of "Nationality in Literature," appeared in the *Democratic Review* for March.[11] There are no marks on this clipping. The essay represents the nationalistic views of the group generally known as "Young America," the most active member of which was Cornelius Mathews. Whitman was not one of this group and did not contribute to the magazine *Arcturus* founded by its leaders, Cornelius Mathews and E. A. Duyckinck, in 1840, and continuing until May 1842, although he contributed several pieces to the friendly *Democratic Review* in 1841 and 1842. He clipped two portions of William Gilmore Simms's essay "The Humorous in American and British Literature," reprinted in the Second Series of Simms's *Views and Reviews*, pp. 142–84. The

[9] At the time he wrote this review James Hadley was twenty-five years old and a tutor in Greek at Yale University. This article is the second part of the review; the first part was published in the November issue and not clipped.
[10] For more on Whitman's interest in Goethe, see Chapter VII, pp. 29–37.
[11] John Stafford says (*The Literary Criticism of "Young America"* [Berkeley, Calif., 1952], p. 87) that E. A. Duyckinck "almost certainly" wrote this article, as well as a second article by the same title in the April number that Whitman did not clip. This is Bucke's No. 519.

first portion included pages 143–46 and is part of Simms's discussion of the general problems of the American writer. He marked a sentence on page 145 advising the young writer to avoid attempting "numerous kinds of composition," lest he succeed in none. The second clipping includes pages 169–84, concluding the essay and the book. This part reviews British humorous literature from Chaucer to Dickens and emphasizes the fact that most of the best humorous writers were not English at all. The middle portion of Simms's long essay, pages 150–68, is a criticism of the humorous writing of Cornelius Mathews, especially the comedy "The Politicians" and the narrative satire, "The Career of Puffer Hopkins." The running title of the essay is "The Writings of Cornelius Mathews," and Bucke lists the clipping (No. 431) by that title, but neither of Whitman's clippings contains a word about Mathews or his writing. Obviously Whitman's interest in clipping the essay was not in Mathews or his work.[12] Whitman endorsed the clipping "Very fine," referring, I suspect, to Simms's criticism of British writers.

A review of several volumes of poetry, including the 1847 edition of Emerson's poems, was published in the *Democratic Review* in 1847, in two installments, one in May and the other in October. Whitman clipped only the first installment (Bucke's No. 434), which is concerned exclusively with Emerson's poems. This review will be discussed in the next chapter among other evidences of Whitman's early interest in Emerson.

The clippings from 1848 publications reveal little or no advance in Whitman's interest in the art of poetry. I have already mentioned De Quincey's review of the 1847 edition of the *Works of Alexander Pope* and suggested it was clipped and marked because of the reviewer's ideas on poetry in general.[13] One of the main features of this review is De Quincey's famous distinction between the literature of knowledge and the literature of power. Whitman bracketed and underlined not only the lines where this distinction is made but also the following passage and drew a hand pointing to it: "Human works of immortal beauty and works of nature in one respect stand on the same footing; they never absolutely repeat each other: never approach so near as not to differ; and they differ not as better and worse, or simply by more and less: they differ by undecipherable and incommunicable differences, that cannot be caught by mimicries, not be reflected in the mirror of copies, nor become ponderable in the scales of vulgar

[12] Simm's *Views and Reviews*, First Series, was actually published in 1846 by Wiley & Putnam, but dated 1845; the Second Series, actually published in 1847, was also dated 1845.

[13] See p. 237.

comparison." Beside a passage saying the poetry of the early eighteenth century exposes "an immoderate craving for glittering effects
from contrasts too harsh to be natural, too sudden to be durable, and
too fantastic to be harmonious," Whitman wrote in the margin in
pencil: "It is the same now." This is the kind of remark that he was
most likely to make in the late 1840's, not after he began writing
Leaves of Grass. The following sentence near the end of the review
is heavily underlined and emphasized by a hand pointing: "To address the *insulated* understanding is to lay aside the Prospero's robe
of poetry." De Quincey's ideas of poetry probably had some influence
in the shaping of Whitman's own views, but probably before the
actual composition of any of the poems of *Leaves of Grass.*

Coventry Patmore's review of "Tennyson's Poems—The Princess,"
clipped from the May issue of the *North British Review,* contained
ideas on poetry which Whitman marked, although he did not mark
Patmore's criticism of *The Princess* itself.[14] I take these ideas up in
the order in which they appear in the review. Whitman underlined
the passage near the beginning of the review stating that early art of
every kind was at its best in the area of religion, and that "the soul of
art is gone, when religion has finally taken her departure." Art
teaches, but not overtly; it is most effective when it depends upon "its
power to force the mind which would appreciate it to self-exertion."
The following sentence is triple-bracketed and underlined twice, once
with a straight line and once with a wavy line: ". . . the highest art,
which is chiefly dependent for its effect upon suggestion, is by no
means universally appreciated, as mere skilful imitation is." Whitman also brackets the rest of the paragraph, which develops this idea,
and draws three hands pointing to the part bracketed; and the following lines are also underlined: ". . . truly original works of art have generally been unfavourably received by critics, who often come passively
to the contemplation of that, which, for its comprehension, requires
activity, and a desire to discover significance. The striking assertion of
Mr. Wordsworth, that a great poet must form the taste by which he is
to be appreciated, derives its truthfulness from what has now been
stated. He must first find a few readers, who will be led by the mere
superficial merits of his productions, to give him credit for meaning
something by forms, which, on account of their unprecedented character, at first convey no significance."[15] One of the most Whitman-

14 See p. 261. Patmore has been identified as the author; see Edgar F. Shannon,
Jr., *Tennyson and the Reviewers* (Cambridge, Mass., 1952), note p. 208. The clipping is from the American edition, IX, 25–40. The criticism of *The Princess* is
chiefly on pp. 37–40.

15 It is hardly necessary to call attention to the many passages in *Leaves of*

like passages underlined and bracketed is the sentence: "A great artist is always best satisfied when he thinks he has succeeded best in concealing his art from all eyes but his own."[16] In a passage developing the idea that art concerns itself with the life of truth, "which none, save those who have lived it, can imagine and depict," and which Whitman has underlined and bracketed with heavy wavy lines, and pointed to with two drawn hands, appears this very interesting sentence: "A work of art is the externalization of the artist's character; it does much of good by the almost irresistible power of example; and influences us, in this respect, exactly as character does; namely, less by a few great and striking features, than by innumerable and minute glimpses and hints of an essential and unobtrusive nobility." With this compare Whitman's well-known lines in "So Long!" (1860): "Camerado, this is no book, / Who touches this touches a man." Some of these marks were undoubtedly made in the late 1840's or early 1850's; others possibly after 1855. One of the latter must be Whitman's bracketing of this sentence in a footnote on page 36: "Mr. Tennyson has been taught, by the reception of his first edition, a little of the wisdom which is commonly the last at which great writers arrive, namely, that of giving the 'reading public' sufficient credit for obtuseness."

Whitman's marks on his clipping of "The Vanity and the Glory of Literature" from the *Edinburgh Review* for April 1849 do not relate to poetic art, but are worth a brief examination for other reasons.[17] At the top of the first page, in pencil, is written "Walter Whitman," and below that, also in pencil, the date 1854. To the right of the date, in brackets, is this note by Whitman evidently referring to the year 1854: "10,000 new books were published in Germany—2025 journals, of which 403 political."[18] There is nothing on the clipping to indicate

---

Grass which reflect the same ideas as expressed here; a single reference should suffice, for example, section 46 of "Song of Myself" (1855 edition, p. 52).

16 Cf. "The greatest poems may not be immediately, fully understood by outsiders any more than astronomy or engineering may" (*Notes and Fragments* in *Complete Writings*, X, 10); "In art originality is an effect just as much as a cause" (*ibid.*, p. 155); and also, "The art of art, the glory of expression and the sunshine of the light of letters is simplicity" (*Preface*, 1855 ed., p. vi). In old age he quoted Taine with approval: "All original art is self-regulated, and no original art can be regulated from without" (*Prose Works 1892*, II, 730).

17 This is a review of *The London Catalogue of Books Published in Great Britain . . . from 1814 to 1846*, beginning on p. 149 and ending on p. 168 (American edition).

18 Printed in *Notes and Fragments* (*Complete Writings*, IX, 221). Bucke prints with this a list of seven of Whitman's clippings as if they were also annotations on the *Edinburgh Review* clipping, but they are not on the clipping.

where he got this information. The penciled name "Walter Whitman" possibly has no relation to the date, though it might have been written there in early 1855, before he adopted the form "Walt Whitman." At the top of page 155 Whitman wrote in pencil: "a good word 'scantlings,' " and drew a hand pointing to these words. The word "scantling" is used in the review in the sense of "a small or scanty portion or amount"—a sense that, according to the *Oxford English Dictionary*, goes back to the sixteenth century. Presumably Whitman understood the meaning of the word as used by the reviewer, but in an uncollected poem published in *Notes and Fragments* he obviously used it in the carpenter's sense of "a small beam or piece of wood; specifically one less than 5 inches square," to quote another definition in the *Oxford English Dictionary*.[19] Like some passages in "Song of Myself," it satirizes a type of American man, "soft-fleshed," "scant of muscle," "scant of gnarl and knot," that seems an anomaly in the "strong growth of America." Some of the notes are in ink, some in pencil, and it is uncertain whether they represent two readings at different times. Commenting on the statement that "the greater part of the masterpieces of antiquity have been secured to us," Whitman wrote in ink: "My own opinion is that myriads of superior works have been lost—superior to existing works in every department, except law, physics, and the exact sciences.—1856." The word "guess" is written in pencil above "opinion."[20]

Another clipping from the April issue of the *Edinburgh Review*, and a more important one, is Aubrey De Vere's review of Henry Taylor's *Eve of the Conquest, and Other Poems*. Although De Vere was a close friend of Taylor, he has comparatively little to say of the poems, but a great deal to say of poets and poetry in general. It would be tedious to quote all the significant passages that Whitman marked, and yet to understand his comments some quotations and paraphrases are necessary. Commenting on excerpts from Taylor's "Lines written in remembrance of the Hon. Edward Ernest Villiers" Whitman wrote in pencil: "Surely these poems are Shakesperean attempts—and not well done—none of the heart of Shakespeare." The reviewer speaks of Taylor's "masterly characterization," and though Shakespeare's name is not mentioned in this connection, Whitman wrote in the margin:

19 *Notes and Fragments*, item 20 (p. 13), in the first section that was not reprinted in *Complete Writings*. This poem, which must have been written about 1854 or 1855, is printed from the manuscript in the Trent Collection in the *Comprehensive Reader's Edition of Leaves of Grass*, pp. 654–55. The text is slightly different from Bucke's in *Notes and Fragments*.

20 In *Notes and Fragments* the pencilled word "guess" does not appear. (See *Complete Writings*, IX, 69.)

"Surely Shakespeare is unapproachable in character." Much of page 186 is devoted to the discussion of how the shield of law, industrialism, and other conditions have enfeebled the modern man so that in literature as in life he is less robust than he was in ruder times. At the top of this page Whitman wrote the word "Character," and at the bottom: "But I will take all these things that produce this condition, and make them produce as great characters as any." On pages 187–88 almost every line has been underlined in a paragraph of nearly two columns of the magazine. This paragraph begins with the statement that the opinion that "a close observation of outward things is unworthy of poetry proceeds, not from too exalted a theory of Art, but from an unworthy estimate of Nature." In developing this idea the critic says, "Truth of fact is worthy of reverence . . . because Nature itself has been modelled upon a frame-work of moral truth; while the kindred world of Circumstance is ruled by Providence. The most common events of human life are instinct with latent principles, which, if at all times detected . . . would at all times approve themselves divine." At the top of page 188 Whitman wrote "Materialism as the foundation of poetry." On page 188 Whitman underlined and drew a hand pointing to this sentence: "It is by the inspiration of genius and of a right mind that a poet is drawn toward the true thought, and warned away from the rest." At the bottom of the page, evidently referring to this sentence but adding something of his own, Whitman commented: "The superior sight, greater breadth, depth, height of vision."

The last seven pages (190–96), which were evidently of great interest to Whitman, concern poetic art, especially as it relates to self control in the use of language and the rule of "just keeping" in the imaginative treatment of nature. On page 190 the critic praises a poem of Wordsworth in which, he says, "so little is expressed, and so much implied." Whitman copied these words at the bottom of the page and underlined them. On page 191 he underlined a passage containing the sentence, "With the merely technical rules of style poetry has indeed little concern." He also underlined and bracketed the following sentence and drew two hands pointing to it: "Without a pure and masterly style, a poet may be popular, but he will never become classical." In warning against overstrained effort in revising until "all freshness has been dissipated," the critic says "Any excessive tension of the faculties precludes the highest species of art—art which hides itself." Figures of speech "brought in to make plainer what is already plain" divert the attention, and "over-vivacious expressions which, as it were, admire themselves" are a defect. Citing examples from Shelley and Byron he added: "But would Homer, or Dante, or Shak-

speare, have variegated their poetic robes with such purple patches?"
At the bottom of page 189 Whitman wrote: "The substance is always
wanted perfect—after that attend to costumes—but mind, attend to
costumes." This seems to be self-advice based on his reading of the
author's comments on style and truth to nature, in which the word
"costume" does not occur; but back on page 185 he had marked a passage saying that in the narrative poetry of Scott and Southey "the predominant elements are those of costume, manners, and incident."
Probably the word "costumes" in Whitman's note does not mean the
same as in the passage on Scott and Southey, but pertains rather to
figures of speech and other stylistic "ornaments," and therefore means
the same as he meant by the word "over-coloring," which is written
in the margin beside the passage cited above on figures of speech and
other ornaments of style. It may be worth while to compare what
Whitman said, in another place, of "over-coloring" in Shakespeare:
"The features of beloved women, compliments, the descriptions of
moderately brave actions, professions of service, and hundreds more,
are painted too intensely. . . . Immensely too much is unnaturally
colored—the sentiment is piled on, similes, comparisons, defiances, ex-
altations, immortalities, bestowed upon themes certainly not worthy
the same, thus losing proportion. . . . Yet on great occasions the character and action are perfect."[21] On page 193 Whitman underlined a
passage saying that art "selects one meaning from nature's countless
meanings, isolates it, and places it before us with a luminous precision
and permanence. Thus to interpret nature, is not to improve nature;
but to bring one of her simpler harmonies within the ken of inferior
intelligences, which, in the infinitude of her complex harmonies,
would otherwise have found there nothing but confusion." The lines
I have quoted are underlined, and at top of page 193 appears the
word "Art," and below it a hand pointing to the passage and this
notation: "(a perfect passage)." On page 194 Whitman wrote, partly
summarizing and slightly adding to the text of the review: "The perfect poem is simple, healthy, natural—no griffins, angels, centaurs,—

[21] From a paragraph which Bucke prints at the end of Whitman's biographical
notes on Shakespeare (see *Complete Writings*, IX, 77–78). Most of p. 192 of the
review is devoted to words, especially words of Anglo-Saxon origin; at two points
in the margin Whitman writes "for Poem of Language." This suggests the date
1855 or 1856, since the 1855 Preface has much to say about language, and because
a passage about language originally appearing in "By Blue Ontario's Shore" and
not reprinted belongs to 1856. In *Notes and Fragments* (*Complete Writings*,
X, 35) is a brief undated paragraph headed "Poem of Language." Since in the
1856 edition a number of poems have titles beginning "Poem of —" it seems probable that 1856, or late 1855, was the time of some of the notes recorded.

no hysterics or blue fire—no dyspepsia, no suicidal intentions." On page 195 the following sentence is doubly and heavily underlined with straight and wavy lines, and at the top of the page Whitman wrote: "Every first-rate poet is felt to be the regent of a separate sphere, and the master of a complete poetic world of his own." Also on page 195 the reviewer stresses self-possession and moderation in poetry. Whitman copied this sentence at the top of the page: "Dante's unshaken self-possession in the midst of the marvels around him, is itself a proof that his vision was true." The following sentence is underlined and bracketed: "Closely allied to self-possession is that rare attribute—poetic Moderation—which excludes such exaggerated admiration of one especial excellence as might lead to the neglect of others. The highest poetry rests upon a right adjustment of contending claims." At the bottom of page 195 Whitman wrote and underlined: "Poetic Moderation." At the top of page 196, the last of the review, Whiman wrote in pencil: "To be re-read and studied."

I have discussed this review at some length because I am convinced that it had a definite influence on Whitman, especially the latter part that is concerned with "over-coloring," self-possession, and moderation in poetic art. I suspect his notes on this part of the review were made in 1856 or late in 1855, after the poems of 1855 and many of the poems of 1856 had been written. Later poems, not published until 1860, seem to reflect the studied rereading of the essay which he advised himself to do. However, he surely had read the essay earlier, perhaps in 1854–55, when he was first writing out the poems of the 1855 edition. His comments on characterization in Shakespeare's plays and on materialism as the basis of poetry may well have been made early. Also his notes on the meaning of "a priori" and "marmoreal" were probably made on his first reading of the review. Gay W. Allen discusses several of Whitman's clippings in the Trent Collection, including "Eve of the Conquest" and the review of Tennyson's *The Princess* in the article Whitman calls "Modern Poetry and Poets," and suggests the possibility they had an influence on the making of *Leaves of Grass*, but he did not undertake to distinguish the probable dates of the several annotations, and he did not identify the reviewers.[22] It would be quite a shock to many admirers and some

---

[22] Gay Wilson Allen, *The Solitary Singer* (New York, 1955), pp. 131–34. Aubrey De Vere is named as the author of the review of *The Princess* published in the *Edinburgh Review*, 1849, by Lord Hallam Tennyson in *Alfred Lord Tennyson: A Memoir, by His Son*, 2 vols. (London, 1897), I, 256. In that review De Vere refers to "our recent notices" of Taylor's *Eve of the Conquest* and Bulwer-Lytton's *King Arthur*; evidently, then, he was the author of these notices.

critics of *Leaves of Grass* if it should turn out indeed that the wealthy and conventional Aubrey De Vere was an influence on Whitman only less powerful than Carlyle and Emerson![23]

There are no surviving clippings that I have seen from magazines published in 1850, and of those from 1851, only two contribute anything to the subject of poetic art. The first of these was a review by J. D. Whelpley, whose opinions Whitman always respected, of an English translation by William Ross of G. E. Lessing's *Laocoön, or the Secret of Classic Composition in Poetry, Painting, and Statuary,* in the *American Whig Review* for January 1851.[24] Some of Whitman's marks are in pencil and some in ink. I cannot be sure which were made first. On page 23, first column, Whelpley says the writers of the seventeenth and eighteenth century did not understand the true principles of classic art, discovered or revived by Lessing. "Impressed with the idea that unity was necessary to a work of art, they conceived of it as an artificial band, holding the parts of the work together, as the tire of a wheel gives unity, and not as the specific or vital principle of an animal gives unity to it." Whitman underlined in ink the last part of this sentence, beginning with "as the tire." On the same page he bracketed all of the second column in ink, and double-bracketed the first half. A pencilled hand at the top and three hands, spaced on the right, point to this double-bracketed portion, which begins as follows: "The purposes of art are simple, and not speculative; its materials derive from nature and tradition, and not from excogitation and analysis; and perhaps it is impossible for any but a people whose actions are free and unrestrained, who have great and national purposes, simple and heroic views, and an experience of life, varied upon sea and land, in peace and war, and through the vicissitudes of calamity and brilliant fortune, to produce an original and classic school of poetry,—a people who believe, or incline to be-

---

[23] Aubrey De Vere, son of a baronet, was born in Ireland in 1814. Privately educated, he was a friend of Tennyson, a follower of Wordsworth in poetry and of Cardinal Newman in religion, and a poet and critic of some stature; he was never well known outside his circle of friends, however, and is now rarely remembered at all. He was a close personal friend of Coventry Patmore and Sir Henry Taylor. Emerson first met Tennyson at dinner at the home of Coventry Patmore, of whom he wrote to his wife May 14, 1848: "Coventry Patmore is a poet who interests me much, not by his poetry, which is three years old & very Tennysonian, but by his ideas on poetry." (See *Letters of Ralph Waldo Emerson,* ed. Ralph L. Rusk [New York, 1939], IV, 66.)

[24] In XIII, 17–26, but Whitman clipped only pp. 21–26, probably because the first four pages are concerned primarily with painting and statuary. Ross's translation was first published in London in 1836. I do not know whether it was reprinted or not.

lieve, that what they think and can do is the best. . . ." Whitman underlined in pencil the portion of this passage beginning with the
words "it is impossible." Later in the paragraph Whelpley warns the
young American poet, and whoever wishes to excel as a writer or
speaker, to beware of the debilitating influence of the "sweet and
sickly literature of French libertinism and English servilism."

On page 24 he underlined a phrase speaking of Milton as "greatest
of all inventors" and wrote in pencil in the margin: "No, no *inventor*
was Milton." On page 25, in a long excerpt from the book, Lessing is
quoted as saying the idea of indignity attached to mechanical labor
was unknown in classical literature; "of all descriptions in the ancient
poets, those of mechanical and agricultural labor are the most interesting and exquisitely wrought." The words here quoted are bracketed and underlined by Whitman. Farther down in the passage
quoted from Lessing is the following passage, to which two hands
drawn in the margin point, one in pencil and one in ink: ". . . in the
day when toil is honored and men are free, when they have ceased to
'love a lord,' perhaps we shall have other heroes and poets, it may be,
even greater than those of antiquity—but not while we are cursed with
a servile literature, and a more servile art." On the last page of the
article, devoted to the classical way of describing beauty in general
terms only, the following sentence is bracketed in pencil on one side
and in ink on the other: "Beauty should be described in poetry by
its effects alone, by the grace of its actions, and by the admiration and
the ardor which it excites."

I have already discussed portions of J. D. Whelpley's article on
"The Hyperion of John Keats" in the October number of the *Whig
Review*,[25] and have suggested that Keats had some influence on the
making of *Leaves of Grass*. Perhaps I should have added that, on the
basis of the article on "Hyperion," it may have been more Whelpley's
influence than Keats's. I need add only one or two notes to what I
said before of this article. On page 320 of the article Whelpley says
that the pleasure of the Sublime is most felt by superior natures, and
is akin to pride. The next sentence is underlined and bracketed by
Whitman: "As a proof, let us observe that poets of the Sublime have
been remarkable for pride." In view of what Whitman says of pride
in *Leaves of Grass*, it may be recognized as, in his view, one of the
sources of the sublime in poetry. He underlined and double-bracketed
the passage where Whelpley says that he affirms "with lord Byron,
that passion is the soul of poetry." But Whitman agrees with Whelpley that the passions, including pride, must be regulated by the moral

[25] See pp. 250–51.

powers. Whelpley also says that it is through feeling more than the intellect that we recognize the poetic. "The idea must be in us, or the image, when presented, will not remind us of any thing real." This is in keeping with Whitman's theory that ideas pre-exist in the mind, though latent, and are evoked by real things or images of them.

From the December issue Whitman clipped an article signed "J. B." on "Theories of Evil." This is No. 412 on Bucke's list, and he says it is "much scored and annotated." I have not seen the clipping and therefore cannot identify the passages marked, but I am sure he would have noticed these lines: "The author believes that Evil is a phantasm, not a reality; or we may say with more accuracy, he believes that, if it does exist, it is but the mask which conceals the features of Good. He regards it as a necessary shadow of the highest throne, darkening the world momentarily, but not disfiguring it. It is a necessity, like the mountains or the atmosphere; it is the complement of Good. Therefore Good, in his opinion, necessitates that shadow which is called Evil."[26] The book here cited is the long poem *Festus*; the author is Philip J. Bailey. The character Festus is compared with Carlyle's Sartor, and the Lucifer of the poem *Festus* is compared with Milton's Satan, Goethe's Mephistopheles and other representatives of the evil principle in literature, including that in the Book of Job. Obviously there is much in Whitman's concept of evil and its function in the world of man that could have been suggested by his reading this essay, and perhaps also the poem. It is likely, however, that he was already familiar with this and other kindred ideas of evil before he read either.

Whitman clipped an article entitled "Imagination and Fact," by an unidentified "new contributor," from *Graham's Magazine* for January 1852. This is obviously a revised reprint, or copying, of the article by the same title published in the *American Whig Review* for November 1851 and signed "W. D."[27] The purpose of the essay seems to be to argue that histories, presumably factual, are scarcely more reliable than works of the imagination. An interesting example is made of how the histories—and in this case Shakespeare's plays based on histories—have wronged Jack Cade and Wat Tyler, who "were animated by the same kind of blood which boiled in the face of a tyrant at Naseby, Marston Moor, Dunbar, and elsewhere—which warmed the hearts of the exiles on the cold rock of Plymouth, and flowed so freely at Lexington and Bunker Hill. We should honor

[26] *American Whig Review*, XIV, 520. I have not identified "J. B."
[27] I have not identified "W. D." and cannot tell whether he was the "new contributor" for *Graham's Magazine*. The revisions in *Graham's* are numerous, but pertain to the style rather than to the substance.

these English rebels—in spite of history, and in spite of Shakspeare."
The excuse for Shakespeare is that he was a man of his time and
obliged chronology and human nature to conform to its standards.
The following sentence, which Whitman bracketed and underlined
and pointed to with a hand drawn in ink, seems to have most impressed him: "The mountains, rivers, forests, and the elements that
gird them round about, would be only blank conditions of matter,
if the mind did not fling its own divinity around them." He drew a
line to the bottom of the page where he wrote in ink: "This I think
is one of the most indicative sentences I ever read." [28] This sentence
must have been marked early, probably soon after the article was
published, since the idea expressed in it seemed then to be new to
Whitman; it would not have been three or four years later. No other
articles from 1852 need be noticed here, since they have already been
discussed or else have nothing to contribute to Whitman's theory
of art.

[28] *Graham's Magazine*, XL, 42.

XVII. *Emerson and Whitman*

N O AMERICAN literary writer except Emerson had any appreciable influence on the composition of the poems of the 1855 edition of *Leaves of Grass*. Whitman admired William Cullen Bryant as an editorial writer and in 1846 called him "one of the best poets in the world."[1] In his early verse, 1838–43, Whitman, like many of the newspaper poets of the time, imitated Bryant as well as some inferior though more popular English and American poets. The poems of *Leaves of Grass* are totally unlike Bryant's poems, yet Whitman retained his high opinion of them to the end of his life.[2] Only Emerson, whose poetry he did not know in 1846, was ever a rival in Whitman's regard as the first-ranking American poet.[3] Next to Bryant, among American poets, Whitman ranked Henry W. Longfellow in the late 1840's. In a review of Harper's "handsome fifty cent edition" of Longfellow's poems in the *Eagle* October 12, 1846, he said this poet deserved "to stand on the same platform with Bryant and Wordsworth," and quoted ten lines from the poem "Rain in Summer" which he said "could never have sprung in the mind of any but a genuine Converser with the Ideal."[4] When Longfellow died he wrote a tribute to him, published in the *Critic*, April 8, 1882, and reprinted in *Specimen Days*. His view of Longfellow had ripened considerably but essentially remained the same as it was in 1846. He said in the *Critic*, "He is certainly the sort of bard and counteractant most needed for our materialistic, self-assertive, money-worshipping, Anglo-Saxon races,

[1] In the *Eagle*, Sept. 1, 1846 (reprinted in *GF*, II, 260–61). In this article Whitman also wrote: "It is an honor and a pride to the Democratic party that it has such a man to conduct one of its principal newspapers—to be an expounder of its doctrines, and act as one of the warders to watch the safety of the citadel." (Part of the article was also reprinted in *UPP*, I, 128–29.) Bryant was very friendly toward his fellow editor of the *Eagle*, defended him when he was dismissed in January 1848, and helped to secure for him a good position with the New Orleans *Crescent*, then just established. (See *UPP*, I, 160–61, note 2.)

[2] For more on Bryant, see pp. 121–22, 232.

[3] In 1888 he told Traubel, "I sometimes waver in opinion as between Emerson and Bryant. . . . But after every heresy I go back to Emerson." (*WWC*, I, 56.)

[4] Reprinted in *GF*, II, 297–98. Whitman calls the title of this poem "Rain" for no reason that is apparent. He reviewed *Evangeline* Nov. 20, 1847.

and especially for the present age in America. . . ."[5] Whittier was
mentioned only once in the *Eagle* and then only to report that he had
been accidentally shot. He quoted Whittier six times, but Longfellow
twenty-two times. Yet in later life he rated Whittier along with Bryant, Longfellow, and Emerson, calling them "unmistakably" the four
best American poets, and said the zeal and moral energy that founded
New England lived on in him.[6] Of Lowell and Holmes, Whitman
said nothing, or almost nothing, and in old age he never spoke of
them in favorable terms. In turn, they had no compliments for *Leaves
of Grass*. There is no way to account for Whitman's love of the poetry
of Bryant and Longfellow long after he had won fame as the author
of *Leaves of Grass* except by recognizing that there was a residue of
conventionalism in his nature that he never lost.

So much has been written about Whitman's indebtedness, or lack
of indebtedness, to Emerson that to go over the evidence again might
seem to be an act of supererogation. The question is not indisputably
settled, however, and probably never will be. All the evidence has
never been assembled in one publication and judiciously evaluated.[7]
I do not propose in this place to review the question in its entirety,
but certainly in a study of the "foreground" of *Leaves of Grass* it cannot be ignored. Whitman himself provided the first objective testimony in his belated reply to Emerson's letter of 1855, which he published, together with that letter, as an appendix to the 1856 edition
of the poems.[8] Whitman's "Letter to Ralph Waldo Emerson," so
called, dated August 1856, was in effect a preface to the 1856 edition
and a sequel to the Preface of 1855. In this "letter" he addresses Emerson as "master," and after considerable brag about the success of his
first edition and what he proposes for the future, he announces a new

[5] *Prose Works 1892*, I, 285.
[6] "My Tribute to Four Poets," originally published in the *Critic*, May 7, 1881,
and reprinted in *Specimen Days* (*Prose Works 1892*, I, 267).
[7] Much of the objective evidence is reviewed by Esther Shephard in *Walt Whitman's Pose* (New York, 1936, pp. 99–106 and 323–97); but her contention that
Whitman found the inspiration of *Leaves of Grass* in the Epilogue to George
Sand's *The Countess of Rudolstadt* leads her, seemingly, to underestimate and
misjudge the evidence she presents. Among other useful studies, two deserve mention here: "The Master of Whitman," by John B. Moore, in *Studies in Philology*,
XXIII (Jan. 1926), 77–99, and "Whitman and Emerson," by Clarence Gohdes, in
the *Sewanee Review*, XXXVII (Jan. 1929), 79–93.
[8] If Whitman wrote Emerson personally to thank him for his letter of praise
there is no record of the letter. However, this does not mean that he did not express
his thanks personally. Emerson was in New York for a lecture on Dec. 11, 1855,
and took Whitman to dinner at his hotel. Doubtless Emerson's letter and *Leaves
of Grass* were important subjects discussed at that meeting.

American literature totally different from the literatures of the past, whether in America or the old world, a literature in which the body, "unabashed" sex, and "passionate friendliness" are to be fully expressed, and out of which a "new moral American continent" will emerge, "with ever-satisfying and ever-unsurveyable seas and shores." Then he continues: "These shores you found. I say you have led The States there—have led Me there." He concludes by assuring Emerson, on behalf of "all the young men," that "we demand to take your name into our keeping, and that we understand what you have indicated, and find the same indicated in ourselves, and that we will stick to it and enlarge upon it through These States." If Emerson was shocked and dismayed at the thought of having his name taken into the keeping of the author of "Children of Adam" it is small wonder. His private letter approving a first volume of poems that he had seen was printed without his permission and exploited in a way to make him seem to approve a second volume that he had not seen and to embrace opinions that he had nowhere expressed. The question whether Emerson retracted his approval of *Leaves of Grass* exercised Whitman and his friends greatly in his later years, but it need not concern us here.[9]

It is virtually impossible to say positively when Whitman first became acquainted with Emerson's work, either by reading or hearing him lecture. Emerson delivered three lectures, two of them chosen from the series titled "The Present Age," at the Mercantile Library in New York on March 10, 13, and 17, 1840.[10] It is unlikely that Whitman heard any of these, since he was teaching "in February and spring of '40 at Triming Square," which was on Long Island, near West Hills.[11] The *Dial*, a Transcendental quarterly, first issued in July 1840, might conceivably have been available to Whitman, and if he read it with some regularity he would have become acquainted with several of Emerson's lectures and essays in 1841 and 1842. In December 1841 and January 1842 Emerson delivered eight lectures on "the Times" in Boston. Six of these lectures were repeated in New York: "Introduction" (or "The Times") on March 3, "The Poet" on March 5, "The Conservative" on March 7, "The Transcendentalist"

9 Horace Traubel recorded Whitman's conversation night after night during the years 1888 and 1889, supposedly for an eventual biography of Whitman, who told Traubel on June 12, 1888, when Emerson's 1855 letter was being discussed: "You will have twenty chapters to your Emerson story by and by." (*WWC*, I, 309.)

10 *The Early Lectures of Ralph Waldo Emerson*, ed. Robert E. Spiller and Wallace E. Williams (Cambridge, Mass., 1972), III, p. 175. See also Rusk's biography, p. 285.

11 Manuscript notebook (*UPP*, pp. 86–88), giving autobiographical data.

on March 9, "Manners" on March 12, and "Prospects" on March 14. The New York *Aurora* on March 7 carried a two-paragraph review of the second of these lectures, and described it as being on the "Poetry of the Times." The editors of *Walt Whitman and the New York Aurora* think that Whitman was then writing for the *Aurora* and that he wrote this review and two or three other comments on Emerson's lectures in New York.[12] The reviewer did not attempt to summarize the lecture, and perhaps did not fully understand it, but if the reviewer was Whitman he could hardly have forgotten it soon, though he might have before he was old. Emerson delivered five lectures in New York in February 1843 on the general subject "New England." I do not know whether Whitman heard any of these or not; if he did he left no record. Some of them would certainly have interested him. In Cabot's summary of them we find this passage: "Our genius is tame: our poems are chaste, faultless, but uncharacterized. So of art and eloquence. We are receptive, not creative. We go to school to Europe. The influence of Wordsworth, Coleridge, and Carlyle found readier reception here than at home. It is remarkable that we have our intellectual culture from one country and our duties from another. . . . We are sent to a feudal school to learn democracy."[13] Whitman's training in Jeffersonian politics would certainly have made him receptive to such ideas, even as early as 1843. It is not likely that he could have heard Emerson lecture again until after his return from England; but during the winter and spring of 1850 Emerson delivered a number of lectures in New York, three of which were repeated in Brooklyn; all were largely attended.[14] Emerson was now famous, and it would have been strange if Whitman did not hear some of these lectures, and he probably read the reviews of them in the New York papers.

After 1844 Emerson's ideas were readily accessible both in his own published essays and in reviews and critical articles, many of them in magazines that Whitman read regularly. In the *Democratic Review* for June 1845 he certainly saw and probably read an article on Emerson's essays "by a Disciple," in which Emerson was praised and many of his most characteristic ideas briefly summarized. Replying to critics

---

[12] See *Early Lectures of Emerson*, III, 341–42, and *Walt Whitman and the New York* Aurora (State College, Pa., 1950), pp. 10–11, 105, and 144. Long reports on all these lectures were printed in the New York *Tribune*. Some of the lectures were printed in the *Dial*, in whole or in part.

[13] James Eliot Cabot: *A Memoir of Ralph Waldo Emerson* (Boston, 1890), II, 749–50.

[14] Ralph L. Rusk, *The Life of Ralph Waldo Emerson* (New York, 1949), pp. 379–80.

claiming the essays were devoid of unity, the author stated, "They have the unity of nature, where the whole reappears in all its parts." "The great truth to which all Emerson's affirmations point," he declares, "is Absolute Identity—the unity of all things in God." Schelling's doctrine of identity, he thinks, is nowhere better expressed than in these essays.[15] Whitman had been a frequent contributor to the *Democratic Review* during the early 1840's, and a story of his appeared in the issue of July–August 1845. He did not clip the article on Emerson, or at least did not preserve a clipping, either because he had not yet developed a genuine interest in Emerson or because he was a regular reader of the magazine and preserved a file of all issues as long as he needed them.

He did clip an article entitled "New Poetry in New England" from the issue of May 1847. This is the first part of a two-part article, the second part of which was published in October. Whitman clipped only the first part; this was almost entirely about Emerson's poetry, which had been published in December 1846, though the volume was dated 1847.[16] Whitman made two annotations on specific passages in this review. On page 396 the reviewer says of Emerson's conception of art: "In poetry, he seems to desire not art, but undisciplined, untrimmed nature. He does not appear practically to apprehend that art is not artificiality, is only nature raised to higher and more perfect degree. To an unfinished, off-hand composition, provided it has some gleams of sense, he will incline to give more praise than to one wrought into fine simplicity and perfect expression." In the margin next to these statements Whitman wrote: "This is as one feels. One feels better satisfied with the garden trimly cut and laid out, and another (I too) enjoys the natural landscape, even barrens and shores and sterile hills above all gardens."[17] On page 397 the reviewer says that Emerson perceives the several aspects of truth but dwells on one aspect at a time, hinting that it is the only one. "Tomorrow we shall receive other hints; it may be in apparent contradiction to those of today, urged likewise as if they were the sole and central truth. . . . Thus, there is hardly a proposition in his poems, or his prose either for that matter, which you cannot find the opposite of in some other place." In the margin beside the last sentence here quoted Whitman

---

[15] XVI, 594–99.

[16] XX, 392–98. The second part reviewed poems published in 1847 by William Ellery Channing, William W. Story, and others. The reviewer is not named. This is Bucke's No. 434. Whitman also clipped the review of Griswold's *Prose Writers of America* (Bucke's No. 433) that preceded the Emerson review (pp. 384–91). He made no marks on this clipping, and Emerson is barely mentioned in it.

[17] *Notes and Fragments* (*Complete Writings*, IX, 158–59).

wrote: "Still if this be so in spirit as well as form it were a fatal defect." [18] Another marginal comment, printed in *Notes and Fragments* on the same page, refers to the statement that Emerson seems to desire not art but undisciplined nature: "The perfect poet must be unimpeachable in *manner* as well as matter." These comments on art and nature seem to have been made before Whitman had fully developed the theory out of which *Leaves of Grass* arose, probably soon after he read the review and as early as 1847 or 1848.

The long comment which Bucke inserts between the first and the third of these short ones was not written on the clipping but on a separate sheet of paper, which he thought, judging from the paper and the handwriting, might belong to the early 1850's. I doubt if the paper or handwriting is a dependable ground for exact dating, but the nature of the comment itself and the fact that it was not written on the clipping suggest to me that it was of later date than the others quoted. I have a notion that the review interested him so much that he got Emerson's volume of poems, and perhaps the essays also, and from reading them developed the ideas set down in *Notes and Fragments*. The note containing these ideas, though rather long, is therefore worth quoting in full:

The superiority of Emerson's writings is in their character—they mean something. He may be obscure, but he is certain. Any other of the best American writers has in general a clearer style, has more of the received grace and ease, is less questioned and forbidden than he, makes a handsomer appearance in the society of books, sells better, passes his time more apparently in the popular understanding; yet there is something in the solitary specimen of New England that outvies them all. He has what none else has; he does what none else does. He pierces the crusts that envelope the secrets of life. He joins on equal terms the few great sages and original seers. He represents the freeman, America, the individual. He represents the gentleman. No teacher or poet of old times or modern times has made a better report of manly and womanly qualities, heroism, chastity, temperance, friendship, fortitude. None has given more beautiful accounts of truth and justice. His words shed light to the best souls; they do not admit of argument. As a sprig from the pine tree or a glimpse anywhere into the daylight belittles all artificial flower work and all the painted scenery of theatres, so are live words in a book compared to cunningly composed words. A few among men (soon perhaps to become many) will enter easily into Emerson's meanings; by those he will be well-beloved. The flippant writer, the orthodox critic, the numbers of good or indifferent imita-

---

18 *Ibid.*, p. 160. This last comment was certainly written much earlier than "Song of Myself," in which he says complacently: "Do I contradict myself? / Very well then I contradict myself."

tors, will not comprehend him; to them he will indeed be a transcendentalist, a writer of sunbeams and moonbeams, a strange and unapproachable
person.[19]

   This opinion of Emerson is unquestionably original and could not
have been formulated solely from reading reviews. It was common
for critics to charge him with obscurity. Some found his style obscure;
others, like a critic of his essays in *Blackwood's Magazine*, found the
obscurity not in his style but in his thought, in what the *Blackwood*
critic called his "mysticism" growing out of his dependence on intui-
tion.[20] Emerson's severest critics were American. A review not clipped
by Whitman but almost certainly read by him, of Emerson's poems in
the *American Whig Review* for August 1847, seems to have had no
purpose other than to ridicule Emerson. No wonder Whitman did
not clip it! A review of Emerson and other American poets ("Nine
New Poets") in the *North American Review* for April 1847 praises
Emerson's prose as poetic but adds that "this volume of professed
poetry contains the most prosaic and unintelligible stuff that it has
ever been our fortune to encounter."[21] Whitman does not admit
that Emerson is obscure; on the contrary, he says, "his words shed
light to the best of souls;" and the few who now understand him may
soon be many. Most, if not all, of what Whitman says of Emerson was
drawn from the essays, not the poems. The qualities he finds in Emerson's essays—heroism, chastity, temperance, friendship, and fortitude—suggest the essays "Heroism," "Love," "Prudence," "Friendship," and perhaps "Compensation." In saying Emerson represents
"the freeman, America, the individual," he may be recalling such essays as "The Young American" from the first series and "Politics"
from the second. In saying he represents the gentleman he could have
had in mind the essay on "Manners," where the following sentence
occurs: "The word *gentleman*, which, like the word *Christian*, must
hereafter characterize the present and a few preceding centuries by
the importance attached to it, is a homage to personal and incommunicable properties."[22]
   In my opinion this paragraph from *Notes and Fragments* comes
closer to an understanding and appreciation of Emerson's essays than

[19] *Ibid.*, pp. 159–60. I have not seen the manuscript from which this was printed.
[20] LXII (Dec. 1847), 643–57. This review was in general very favorable, though
the reviewer found some faults in addition to mysticism.
[21] LXIV, 407.
[22] Whitman must have read this essay in *Essays, Second Series* (first published
in 1844), and he might have heard it, substantially as published, in Emerson's
lecture "Manners and Customs of New England," delivered in New York in February 1843.

Whitman's published criticism of the 1870's and 1880's. For example, in "A Christmas Garland," published in the Christmas number, 1874, of the New York *Daily Graphic*, he complains of Emerson's "too great prudence, too rigid caution," and suggests that his "constitutional distrust and doubt," though they have not stopped him short of genius, "have certainly clipped and pruned that free luxuriance of it which only satiates the soul at last."[23] In "Emerson's Books, (The Shadows of Them)," first published in the *Boston Literary World* May 22, 1880, Whitman wrote that though Emerson "has much to say of freedom and wildness and simplicity and spontaneity, no performance was ever more based on artificial scholarships and decorums at third or fourth removes, (he calls it culture,) and built up from them." Again in this essay he says: "At times it has been doubtful to me if Emerson really knows or feels what Poetry is at its highest, as in the Bible, for instance, or Homer or Shakspere. . . . Of *power* he seems to have a gentleman's admiration—but in his inmost heart the grandest attribute of God and Poets is always subordinate to the octaves, conceits, polite kinks, and verbs." This immediately precedes Whitman's confession that years before he had "a touch of Emerson-on-the-brain," but only for a month or so, and is pretty obviously designed to counteract the opinion, held then as now by many, that he owed a great deal to Emerson's influence.[24]

In the *Eagle* of December 15, 1847, Whitman quotes the beginning sentences of the essay "Spiritual Laws," almost half the paragraph, and introduces them with this comment: "In one of Ralph Waldo Emerson's inimitable lectures, occurs the following striking paragraph, which every heart will acknowledge to be as truthful as it is beautiful." In the third sentence, which in Emerson's text reads, "Not only things familiar and stale, but even the tragic and terrible, are comely as they take their place in the pictures of memory," Whitman substitutes "lures of memory" for the last eleven words of the sentence. This was not just careless copying, but, apparently, an attempt to improve on the text. A half dozen minor changes were presumably due to carelessness.[25] Whitman was wrong, of course, in saying the lines were from one of Emerson's lectures, since "Spiritual Laws" was

---

[23] Whitman deleted this paragraph on Emerson and the paragraphs on Victor Hugo and George Sand when he prepared *Specimen Days & Collect* for publication in 1882; they are reprinted in *Prose Works 1892*, II, 789.

[24] *Prose Works 1892*, II, 515–17. I suspect that Whitman was still smarting from Emerson's slight in printing no selection from *Leaves of Grass* in his anthology, *Parnassus* (published in 1874 and several times reprinted), while including eight of Ellery Channing's poems.

[25] Whitman's quotation is reprinted in *GF*, II, 270–71.

never delivered as a lecture, but there was no way he could have known that. It was the fourth essay in *Essays, First Series*, a new edition of which Emerson saw through the press in Boston just before he embarked for England on October 5, 1847.[26] The paragraph is not reprinted by Holloway in *UPP*, but both there and in *GF*, where it is reprinted, it is presumed to be a review. It was not really a review, only a notice, but Whitman must have had a copy of the book, which may have been secured for the purpose of reviewing. If he did have a copy of this edition, he almost certainly read more than one essay in it. How long he kept the book, of course, is unknown.

In the Berg Collection of the New York Public Library there is a page of Whitman manuscript, written in pencil, that was given to J. H. Johnston in 1892 by Whitman's housekeeper, Mary Davis. It is about Emerson's essays, but it is not dated, and there is nothing I have found by which the date of composition might be determined. I copy it in full because I think it might possibly have been intended for a review of Emerson's essays in the *Eagle* that was not completed, or at least not published, except in the brief extract from "Spiritual Laws." It also may be related to the passage quoted earlier (pp. 429–30) from *Notes and Fragments*.

Essays—1st series—copyrighted 1847. Shrewd & wise reflections, tinged with the library, smacking of Epictetus and Marcus Antoninus and Montaigne and the other old experts—largely metaphysical, with near or distant suspicions of German Fichte and Schelling—but Hegel seems hardly to appear at all; plentiful flowing rivulets of fine thought epigrammatic expressions of the first water, on Self-Reliance, the Over-Soul, Compensation, (these are perhaps the best,) Spiritual Laws, Heroism, Intellect and Art. Those on Friendship and Love are the least good in the volume. Indeed Pure gold, nay diamonds themselves, may be found—nuggets & first class gems in the volume, and not stingily bestowed. [The words "Indeed" and "nuggets & first class gems" are inserted in ink.] What can be superber than this portrait of that curious and baffling element of character we may call *soul-greatness*, eligible to almost every man & woman, high or low. p. 263 & 4 Essays first series.

On the pages cited, from "The Over-Soul," Emerson says that "the inspiration which uttered itself in Hamlet and Lear could utter things as good from day to day, for ever," and that it "comes to the lowly and simple . . . it comes as insight; it comes as serenity and grandeur"; and when we see "those whom it inhabits, we are apprised

[26] Emerson's inscription in a gift copy made to Sophia Foord, formerly the teacher of his children, is dated "1 Oct. 1847." This copy is in the Barrett Collection at the University of Virginia.

of new degrees of greatness." This 1847 edition of *Essays, First Series* was reprinted unchanged in 1850, 1854, 1858, and even as late as the 1870's, but since Whitman pretty certainly owned the 1847 edition, I think it probable that the manuscript is early, perhaps as early as 1847.

From that time on there can scarcely be any question that Whitman was acquainted with Emerson's lectures and essays, but of what he thought of them we know no more than what we read in this early note and in the paragraph quoted from *Notes and Fragments*. Emerson lectured in New York with some frequency, and in March 1850 repeated there his lecture on "Natural Aristocracy," first delivered in England. The lecture-essays on "Representative Men" would have attracted Whitman's attention, especially those on Shakespeare and Swedenborg, and they were available for reading early in 1850. The title "Representative Men" would surely have attracted his attention, since he had reviewed Carlyle's *Heroes and Hero Worship* in the *Eagle* in October 1846 and was certainly aware of the close relationship of the two men. In his notes on Shakespeare, he has, among the notes not based on Collier, this brief paragraph: "Shakespeare is much indebted to the ancients. Hamlet's soliloquy, 'To be, or not to be,' is taken almost verbatim from Plato. To the *Iliad* everyone of his best plays is largely indebted." [27] Whitman's sentence about Hamlet's soliloquy is in the exact words of the Preface to John and William Langhorne's edition of *Plutarch's Lives*, which was reprinted by Harper in 1844. [28] In a marginal note to this, Whitman has written in pencil, "Is this so?" Just below the sentence about Hamlet's soliloquy he has this direction to himself: "See Emerson's Shakespeare," apparently to check against the sentence drawn from the Langhorne *Plutarch*. He undoubtedly read Emerson's "Plato," where Hamlet is called "a pure Platonist." There is nothing in Whitman's notes on Swedenborg to suggest he had read Emerson's essay on him, but he knew a good deal about the life of Swedenborg and his work from other sources. [29]

[27] *Complete Writings*, IX, 75.

[28] See my "Notes on Whitman's Reading," in *American Literature*, XXVI (Nov. 1954), 342.

[29] There were too many books, essays, and newspaper articles on Swedenborg during the 1840's to make it worth while to look for specific sources of Whitman's sketchy notes. With the yellow sheet on which the notes were written in pencil is a long newspaper clipping on Swedenborg entitled "The New Jerusalem." Part of this clipping is pasted on a sheet of the magazine article "Shakspeare vs. Sand," which was clipped from the *American Whig Review*, May 1847, suggesting that the newspaper article was of later date. In a humorous item published in the New Orleans *Daily Crescent* on March 10, 1848, he describes a character as possibly thinking of "some beautiful idea collated from the philosophy of Emanuel Sweden-

Whitman might have heard Emerson lecture on "The Conduct of Life" in 1852, but it is of little significance whether he did or not, since by that time he was undoubtedly acquainted with Emerson's published work, though how well acquainted there is no way of determining. Moreover, he could have gathered a good deal of information from newspaper reports of the lectures, which, though often inaccurate, were so full that Emerson was annoyed, knowing that these reports might cut down attendance at his lectures.[30]

I have earlier indicated some of the items in the *American Phrenological Journal* during the early 1850's that might have influenced Whitman. Although, as I have noted, Whitman must have read Emerson's own works by 1852 and also had available many sources of information about Emerson's principal ideas, it is by no means improbable that he read with attention the long article on Emerson in the *Phrenological Journal* for March 1854 with the title: "Ralph Waldo Emerson. Phrenology, Physiology, Biography, and Portrait." On the basis of the portrait, presumably, the writer characterizes him in phrenological terms thus: "Comparison: unmistakably prominent. Causality: He has less than of lucid, logical. Language: Exactness of expression. Of Order: A large share. Of Agreeableness: Less than we supposed belonged to him. Benevolence, Veneration, Firmness are large. Combativeness seems large. Destructiveness is full. Idealism and sublimity fully developed. Money does not seem to be his idol. Ambition and the love of criticism seem to be his paramount characteristics."

Following this there is a biographical sketch from which I extract a few phrases:

In his view the material creation is but an emblem of spiritual life. . . . To trace the operations of a subtle divine Presence in the mysteries of being—to ascend from the visible phenomena to universal laws—to embody the absolute, the unchanging, the perfect in the expressive forms of poetry—these are the problems which have challenged his warmest interest, and made him a retired and meditative sage, instead of a man of affairs. . . . Relying on certain mystic revelations to the soul of the individual, he shows scarcely any trace of the logical faculty. . . . You look in vain for any consecutive order in the array of his thoughts. . . . Mr. Emerson's predominant individualism leads him to ignore the past, and live in the present. . . . He believes in the perennial influence of inspiration. . . . The individual

---

borg," but he could have said that with but little specific knowledge of the famous mystic. (See *UPP*, I, 194.)

[30] See Rusk, pp. 382–83. The lectures on "The Conduct of Life" were announced in many periodicals, including the *American Phrenological Journal*, April 1852.

soul now conceals the elements of poetry, and prophecy, and the vision of God, as in the days of yore. . . . With this faith, Mr. Emerson attaches no importance to traditional opinion. . . . No school of philosophy or religion can hold this broad, untrammelled thinker within its walls. Even the great teachers of humanity do not win his fealty. Hints and monitions he may receive from their works, but authority never. . . . Mr. Emerson, although a rigid observer of the conventional proprieties of life, has little respect for a formal, imitative, stereotyped virtue. The stamp of nature and originality, in his view, would sanction almost any episode from the regular highway of ethics. He judges of character not by its accordance with any artificial code, but by the test of genuineness and native individuality. He rejects no coin that has the true ring, for want of the sign of some approved mint. An idealist in theory . . . he cherishes a most persistent and unrelenting attachment to reality. . . . He unites the dreamy mystical contemplation of an Oriental sage with the hard, robust, practical sense of a Yankee adventurer.

If Whitman read this characterization of Emerson and remembered it in 1855, he would probably have assumed that the approval in Emerson's letter about *Leaves of Grass* was without condition. Of course he would have found better authorities on Emerson's philosophy than the *Phrenological Journal*, but he would not have ignored it as negligible, and indeed it is more accurate than many of the criticisms published at the time in more highly respected journals.

In view of these and other evidences that could be cited, I am sure that Whitman knew a good deal about Emerson and his writings before the first *Leaves of Grass* poems were written, although in his later years he sometimes insisted that he did not. My own opinion is that the statement made by Whitman in conversation with J. T. Trowbridge in Boston in 1860, and published by Trowbridge in 1902, is substantially accurate, that he "became acquainted" with Emerson's essays in the summer of 1854, and that he began *Leaves of Grass* that summer.[31] Trowbridge does not say specifically that Whitman read Emerson's essays for the first time in 1854; what he did say specifically Trowbridge may have forgotten by 1902, but in using the phrase "became acquainted" I assume he meant that Whitman told him he had not read the essays carefully enough to know Emerson's mind before 1854. Trowbridge also says Whitman told him that he began *Leaves of Grass* in the summer of 1854, and that he "wrote, rewrote, and re-rewote" before printing. A portion of this writing, or rewriting, is doubtless what is preserved in one of the notebooks (item 80 of the catalog of the Whitman collection in the

[31] Trowbridge's "Reminiscences of Walt Whitman" was published in the *Atlantic Monthly*, LXXXIX (Feb. 1902), 163–75; see also Trowbridge, *My Own Story* (Boston, 1903), pp. 365–68.

Library of Congress) reprinted in *Uncollected Poetry and Prose* and
termed by Holloway Whitman's earliest notebook. Though Holloway, and others following his lead, date this notebook from 1847,
internal evidence suggests that it was written, in part at least, in
1854.[32] Whitman himself, in the Preface to the separate publication
of "As a Strong Bird on Pinions Free" (1872), said that he commenced
"elaborating the plan" of his poems as early as 1847, and continued
till 1854, "(from the age of twenty-eight to thirty-five)," but that the
final formulation took a "far different shape from what I at first supposed."[33] In the Preface to the 1876 edition of *Leaves of Grass* and
Two Rivulets, he said that the poems of his earlier volumes were
"composed in the flush of my health and strength, from the age of
30 to 50 years," which would have been from 1849 to 1869.[34] Bucke
stated in his biography, which Whitman read and approved before
its publication, that "the first definite conception" of *Leaves of Grass*
was in 1853–54. Although Whitman was notoriously undependable
about dates, we may be fairly sure that Bucke reported the dates as
Whitman gave them to him, and that Whitman would have made an
effort to remember them accurately.[35] The statement in the 1872
Preface is irrelevant so far as the beginning date is concerned, since
his first plan was confessedly not the plan of *Leaves of Grass*. The
dates in the 1876 Preface are only approximate because the 1872 edition included poems written between 1869 and 1872, though only
three or four of the longer and more important ones. The most dependable evidence, therefore, in my judgment, supports the year
1854, or possibly 1853, as the date of the commencement of *Leaves of
Grass* as we know the early poems in it.

That Whitman was indebted to Emerson to some extent in writing *Leaves of Grass* no one has ever denied, not even Whitman himself, as we have seen. How much he was influenced, and in what
particulars, it is not easy to determine. Obviously he was not influenced by the metrical form of Emerson's poetry. It could be argued
that Emerson's prose style is sometimes reflected in the style of *Leaves
of Grass*; but if, as has sometimes been said, "style is the man," we
should expect no greater similarity between the styles of Emerson and
Whitman than between the personalities of the two men, and that
was little indeed. But ideas are another matter. Two men may be per-

---

[32] See my article "Early Notebooks of Walt Whitman," *Studies in Bibliography*,
XXIV (1971), 197–204.

[33] See *Prose Works 1892*, II, 461–62.

[34] *Ibid.*, II, 468.

[35] *Walt Whitman*, p. 135.

sonally very unlike and yet have many ideas in common, as we know to be true, for example, of Emerson and Carlyle, or Emerson and Thoreau.

The earliest attempt to record parallels between Emerson's ideas in the essays and Whitman's in *Leaves of Grass* was made by William Sloane Kennedy, whose article "Identities of Thought and Phrase in Emerson and Whitman" was published in the *Conservator*, a periodical of limited circulation largely devoted to favorable studies of Whitman, in August, 1897.[36] Kennedy selected thirty-four passages from *Leaves of Grass*: twelve from the 1855 edition, eight from 1856, ten from 1860, and four from later editions, and matched them with an equal number of passages from Emerson's essays, chiefly from the first and second series, originally published in 1841 and 1844 respectively. The ideas are usually identical, or nearly so, and the phrasing is similar though rarely identical in more than a few significant words. The article could justifiably be used to prove that Whitman borrowed the ideas from Emerson, and yet Kennedy's expressed purpose was quite different. He was trying to demonstrate that those who found evidence of identity of thought and phrase in Bacon and Shakespeare and used that evidence to argue that Bacon wrote the plays attributed to Shakespeare, proved nothing, since two writers of the same period often had identical or similar ideas, and he cited the parallel case of Emerson and Whitman. He was challenged to find a dozen such passages in these two writers, and came up with thirty-four, and claimed he could have found a great many more. This proved nothing, he said, "for in the case of Walt Whitman and Emerson we of course know that the writings of each was by each. Whitman had not even read Emerson's books when he published his first quarto. As for his ethical poems published in 1856 (he first read the essays of Emerson in that year) they show just about the influence of Emerson that Bacon's writings show the influence of Shakespeare or Shakespeare's of Bacon—no more." I will quote a few of Kennedy's parallels to illustrate their character.

Emerson, "Self-Reliance"	Whitman, "Song of Myself"
Suppose you should contradict yourself; what then?	Do I contradict myself? Very well then I contradict myself.
In every work of genius we recognize our own rejected thoughts.	These are the thoughts of all men I act as the tongue of you.

[36] VIII, 88–91. This article was reprinted with the title "Walt Whitman's Indebtedness to Emerson," in Kennedy's *An Autolycus Pack or What You Will* (West Yarmouth, Mass.: Stonecroft Press, 1927).

Let us never bow and apologize more.	I do not trouble my spirit to vindicate itself or be understood, I see that the elementary laws never apologize.
Trust thyself; every heart vibrates to that iron string.	And nothing, not God, is greater to one than one's self is.

It would take up too much space to quote anything like all the parallels of this kind readily identifiable in *Leaves of Grass* and in Emerson's essays. I could cite twenty from "Self-Reliance" alone, a dozen from "Compensation," an equal number from "History," and several each from "Spiritual Laws," "Heroism," "Prudence," the essay on Plato in *Representative Men,* and perhaps others. Kennedy cited only one parallel from Emerson's "The Poet," an oversight I cannot account for unless he became aware of the danger of making Whitman's indebtedness to Emerson too obvious. I have no doubt that Whitman read the essay with great care in 1854 and perhaps also earlier and that it had a marked influence in shaping his image of himself as the new American poet that Emerson said he had looked for in vain. In Emerson's letter to Whitman greeting him "at the beginning of a great career" there is a strong implication that he recognized in the first edition of *Leaves of Grass* the promise of such a poet. To feel the full impact that the essay had on Whitman one must read it carefully in the light of a detailed knowledge of Whitman's work, especially the Preface and poems of the 1855 edition. It would be tedious to try, at this point, to list all the ideas in "The Poet" that might have had an influence on Whitman, but I will quote a number of passages, citing by page numbers the text of "The Poet" in Volume III of the Centenary Edition of Emerson's works, and follow each passage with at least one parallel from Whitman's works, especially from the Preface and poems of the first edition of *Leaves of Grass.* These will be parallels, chiefly, in ideas, though some similarity in phrasing may be noted. Sometimes the parallel will be one of Whitman's practice instead of his idea of poetry.

1. Page 5: ". . . the poet is representative. He stands among partial men for the complete man, and apprises us not of his wealth, but of the common wealth. The young man reveres men of genius, because, to speak truly, they are more himself than he is. They receive of the soul as he also receives, but they more."

1. Preface, two passages. Page vii: "The messages of great poets to each man and woman are, Come to us on equal terms, Only then can

you understand us, We are no better than you, What we enclose you enclose, What we enjoy you may enjoy." Page xi: "The direct trial of him who would be the greatest poet is today. If he does not flood himself with the immediate age as with vast oceanic tides . . . and if he be not himself the age transfigured . . . let him merge in the general run and wait his development." "Song of Myself," lines 401–402: "In all people I see myself, none more and not one a barleycorn less, / And the good or bad I say of myself I say of them." (For other parallels, see lines 137–38, 330–48, 354–57, and *passim*.) "Song of the Answerer": "He is the answerer, / What can be answered he answers, and what cannot be answered he shows how it cannot be answered / . . . the mechanics take him for a mechanic, / And the soldiers suppose him to be a captain . . . / No matter what the work is, that he is one to follow it or has followed it. . . . / The English believe he comes of their English stock, / Whoever he looks at in the traveler's coffeehouse claims him, / The Italian or Frenchman is sure, and the German is sure, and the Spaniard is sure. . . ."[37]

2. Page 6. "The poet is the person in whom these powers [i.e., the power as an artist to feel the impressions of nature and the power to express them] are in balance, the man without impediment, who sees and handles that which others dream of, traverses the whole scale of experience, and is representative of man, in virtue of being the largest power to receive and to impart."

2. Preface, 1855, p. vi: "The known universe has one complete lover and that is the greatest poet. . . . What balks or breaks others is fuel for his burning progress to contact and amorous joy. . . . The fruition of beauty is no chance of hit or miss. . . . This is the reason that about the proper expression of beauty there is precision and balance."

Emerson's phrase, "traverses the whole scale of experience," is exemplified in the poet of *Leaves of Grass*, especially in the catalogues of "Song of Myself," and might be illustrated by a hundred passages in this and other poems. Emerson's statement that the poet has "the largest power to receive and to impart" suggests Whitman's image of the "swallowing soul" in "Song of Myself" (lines 800 and 831–32) and the lines, "I act as the tongue of you, / It was tied in your mouth . . . in mine it begins to be loosened" (1248–50).

[37] In his essay on Plato in *Representative Men* (IV, 41) Emerson says: "An Englishman reads and says, 'how English!' a German,—'how Teutonic!' an Italian,—'how Roman and how Greek! . . . so Plato seems to a reader in New England an American genius. His broad humanity transcends all sectional lines."

3. Page 7. "The poet is the sayer, the namer, and represents beauty. He is a sovereign . . . is emperor in his own right."

3. This might almost be the statement of Whitman's central theme in the second section of "Song of the Answerer" (first published in 1856). Here the word "sayer" is not used, but it is clearly the function of the true poet to "say" or create ("beget"), as distinguished from that of the "singer," who does not "beget." In the same poem Whitman says that "The true poets are not followers of beauty, but the august masters of beauty." In "Song of the Rolling Earth" the line, "Say on, sayers! sing on, singers!" shows Whitman's distinction between the true poet, the sayer, and the lesser poet, the singer.

4. Pages 8–9. "For we do not speak now of men of poetical talents, or of industry and skill in metre, but of the true poet."

5. Pages 9–10. "For it is not metres, but a metre-making argument that makes a poem,—a thought so passionate and alive that like the spirit of a plant or an animal it has an architecture of its own, and adorns nature with a new thing. The thought and the form are equal in the order of time, but in the order of genesis the thought is prior to the form. The poet has a new thought; he has a whole new experience to unfold . . ."

4 and 5. Preface, 1855, p. v, has the closest parallel to both of these: "The poetic quality is not marshalled in rhyme or uniformity or abstract addresses to things nor in melancholy complaints or good precepts, but is the life of these and much else and is in the soul. The profit of rhyme is that it drops seeds of a sweeter and more luxuriant rhyme, and of uniformity that it conveys itself into its own roots in the ground out of sight. The rhyme and uniformity of perfect poems show the free growth of metrical laws and bud from them as unerringly and loosely as lilacs or roses on a bush, and take shapes as compact as the shapes of chestnuts and oranges and melons and pears, and shed the perfume impalpable to form. The fluency and ornaments of the finest poems or music or orations or recitations are not independent but dependent. All beauty comes from beautiful blood and a beautiful brain."

6. Page 10. ". . . the experience of each new age requires a new confession, and the world seems always waiting for its poet."

6. I find nothing in Whitman's early writings that corresponds exactly to Emerson's idea that each new age requires a new poet, but several passages in the poems approximate the idea. I need cite only one example out of many. In the 1855 Preface he says: "The Ameri-

can poets are to enclose old and new for America is the race of races. Of them a bard is to be commensurate with a people. . . . His spirit responds to his country's spirit. . . . he incarnates its geography and natural life and rivers and lakes." In the last sentence of the Preface he boasts that "the proof of a poet is that his country absorbs him as affectionately as he has absorbed it."

7. Page 11. "Man, never so often deceived, still watches for the arrival of a brother who can hold him steady to a truth until he has made it his own."

7. This statement has its parallels in "Song of Myself," sections 46 and 47, where Whitman says he has no chair, no church, no philosophy, but leads each man or woman to a knoll and points to the public road: "Not I, not any one else can travel that road for you, / You must travel it for yourself." Also the lines: "I am the teacher of athletes, / He that by me spreads a wider breast than my own proves the width of my own, / He most honors my style who learns under it to destroy the teacher."

8. Page 14. "The Universe is the externalization of the soul."

8. This idea is everywhere apparent in *Leaves of Grass*, though not expressed precisely as Emerson expresses it. In "Song of Myself" (lines 52–54): "Clear and sweet is my soul . . . . and clear and sweet is all that is not my soul. / Lack one lacks both . . . . and the unseen is proved by the seen, / Till that becomes unseen and receives proof in its turn." In an early notebook (item 80 in the catalogue of the Whitman Collection in the Library of Congress) he wrote, probably in 1854 or 1855: "The soul or spirit transmits itself into all matter . . . into the earth—into the motions of the suns and stars. . . . It makes itself visible only through matter." (This was printed in *UPP*, II, 64–65.)

9. Page 15. "Since every thing in nature answers to a moral power, if any phenomenon remains brute and dark it is because the corresponding faculty in the observer is not yet active."

9. Perhaps the closest parallel to this sentence is to be found in "A Song of the Rolling Earth" (1856), particularly in these lines: "I swear the earth shall surely be complete to him or her who shall be complete, / The earth remains jagged and broken only to him or her who remains jagged and broken."

10. Page 15. ". . . every man is so far a poet as to be susceptible of

these enchantments of nature; for all men have the thoughts whereof the universe is the celebration."

10. This has many parallels, more or less close, in "Song of Myself" and elsewhere. In section 30 (line 648) we read: "All truths wait in all things." In "Song of the Open Road" (1856): "You objects that call from diffusion my meanings and give them shape."

11. Page 17. "Thought makes everything fit for use. The vocabulary of an omniscient man would embrace words and images excluded from polite conversation. What would be base, or even obscene, to the obscene, becomes illustrious, spoken in a new connection of thought. The piety of the Hebrew prophets purges their grossness."

11. There is no doubt in my mind that Whitman read and remembered this statement and that in it he found justification for the occasional grossness and for the sexual imagery of the 1855 and 1856 editions.

12. Pages 17–18. "Bare lists of words are found suggestive to an imaginative and excited mind."

12. I would not go so far as to claim that Whitman's catalogues were developments from this idea, but they were certainly supported by it.

13. Page 18. "For as it is dislocation and detachment from the life of God that makes things ugly, the poet, who re-attaches things to nature and the Whole . . . disposes very easily of the most disagreeable facts."

13. With this compare "Song of the Answerer," Part I (1855), describing the poet: "He puts things in their attitudes. . . . He resolves all tongues into his own. . . . He is the joiner." For the closest parallel see "Passage to India" (1868), section 5: "Finally shall come the poet worthy of that name, / The true son of God shall come singing his songs. / . . . Nature and Man shall be disjoin'd and diffused no more, / The true son of God shall absolutely fuse them."

14. Page 20. "The world being thus put under the mind for verb and noun, the poet is he who can articulate it. For though life is great, and fascinates and absorbs; and though all men are intelligent of the symbols through which it is named; yet they cannot originally use them."

14. The idea that the poet articulates thoughts that others have but cannot find words for has a parallel in Whitman's "Song of Myself," lines 1248–50, quoted in connection with No. 2.

15. Page 21. "All the facts of the animal economy, sex, nutriment, gestation, birth, growth, are symbols of the passage of the world into the soul of man, to suffer there a change and reappear a new and higher fact. He uses forms according to the life, and not according to the form. This is true science. . . . By virtue of this science the poet is the namer or Language-maker."

15. This statement, like that in No. 11, is surely related to Whitman's practice in "I Sing the Body Electric" and in other poems, particularly in some of the poems of "Children of Adam."

16. Page 27. "The poet knows that he speaks adequately then only when he speaks somewhat wildly. . . . Not with the intellect used as an organ, but . . . suffered to take its direction from its celestial life. . . ."

16. This statement is roughly paralleled in "Song of Myself" (line 638): "I talk wildly. . . . I have lost my wits . . ." This is not as close a parallel, however, as that in lines 1332–33: "I too am not a bit tamed . . . I too am untranslatable, / I sound my barbaric yawp over the roofs of the world."

17. Page 29. "So the poet's habit of living should be set on a key so low that the common influences should delight him. His cheerfulness should be the gift of the sunlight; the air should suffice for his inspiration, and he should be tipsy with water."

17. These ideas are everywhere exemplified in *Leaves of Grass*, though parallels in phrasing are comparatively few. Perhaps the closest is in "Song of Myself" (line 259, text of 1855): "What is commonest and cheapest and nearest is Me." The idea of cheerfulness is common in "Song of Myself": "And whether I come into my own to-day or in ten thousand or ten million years, / I can cheerfully take it now, or with equal cheerfulness I can wait." (Lines 417–18.) The word "inspiration," as here used, does not occur in the poems, but in the 1855 Preface we read that "the new breed of poets . . . shall find their inspiration in real objects today" (p. xi). The closest parallels are to be found in *Democratic Vistas*.

18. Page 30. "If the imagination intoxicates the poet, it is not inactive in other men. . . . The use of symbols has a certain power of emancipation and exhilaration for all men. . . . Poets are thus liberating gods."

18. Though he is a richly imaginative poet, Whitman never used the word "imagination" or "imaginative" in *Leaves of Grass*. However, there can be little doubt that he was often "intoxicated," in

Emerson's intended sense, by the imagination. An example of such intoxication is described in the passage in "Song of Myself (section 5) that is sometimes considered a record of a genuine mystical experience. But the only "mysticism" in *Leaves of Grass* is the work of the poet's imagination. The word "symbol" is used only once in the poems signifying a literary device, and that is in "Song of Myself" (line 1313). The idea that poets are liberating gods, or god-like men, is implicit in *Leaves of Grass* and often explicit in *Democratic Vistas*. The closest parallels in the poems are in the second part of "Song of the Answerer."

19. Page 34. "The religions of the world are the ejaculations of a few imaginative men."

19. In "Song of Myself" (section 38) Whitman seems to have had a vicarious or imaginative experience comparable to the resurrection of Jesus, so that in the remaining portion of the poem he seems to be inaugurating, or announcing, a new religion. He does not use the word "ejaculate" here, but the style of the poem is certainly ejaculative. In "By Broad Potomac's Shore" (1872), speaking of himself he has the line: "(Still uttering, still ejaculating, canst never cease this babble?)" (See also "Thou Mother with Thy Equal Brood" (1872): "I merely thee ejaculate!").

20. Page 34. "For all symbols are fluxional. . . ."

20. Whitman has little to say about symbols, but he used them often, and he showed by his practice that he agreed with Emerson that they are "fluxional"—that is, a given symbol may mean different things in different contexts.

21. Page 37. "I look in vain for the poet whom I describe. . . . Time and nature yield us many gifts, but not yet the timely man, the new religion, the reconciler, whom all await."

21. In the first part of "Song of the Answerer," speaking of the poet, Whitman says: "Him all wait for . . . His welcome is universal." In "Starting from Paumanok" (1860) he said (section 7): "I too, following many and followed by many, inaugurate a religion . . ." He does not use the term "reconciler," but his description of the poet makes him that, both in "Song of Myself" and in "Passage to India," where he is said to reunite man and nature.

22. Pages 37–38. "Our log-rolling, our stumps and their politics, our fisheries, our Negroes and Indians, our boasts and our repudiations, the wrath of rogues and the pusillanimity of honest men, the

northern trade, the southern planting, the western clearing, Oregon and Texas, are yet unsung. Yet America is a poem in our eyes, its ample geography dazzles the imagination, and it will not wait long for metres."

22. This passage would have been a challenge to Whitman, and it looks as if he attempted in his poems to fulfill Emerson's promise. In the 1855 Preface he said, "The United States themselves are essentially the greatest poem." See also "Song of the Rolling Earth." Whitman's geographical poems, especially, seem to be such as Emerson called for.

23. Page 40. "Doubt not, O poet, but persist. Say 'It is in me, and shall out.' "

23. "Song of Myself (lines 586–88): "Speech is the twin of my vision . . . / It provokes me forever, / It says sarcastically, Walt, you understand enough . . . . why don't you let it out then?" (Later texts have "contain" instead of "understand.")

24. Page 41. "The conditions are hard, but equal. Thou shalt leave the world, and know the muse only. Thou shalt not know any longer the times, customs, politics, or opinions of men, but shalt take all from the muse. . . . Thou shalt lie close hid with nature, and canst not be afforded to the Capitol or the Exchange. The world is full of renunciations and apprenticeships, and this is thine; thou must pass for a fool and a churl for a long season."

24. This passage describes rather well Whitman's dedication to his task of writing *Leaves of Grass*. In the Preface of 1855 he has a somewhat similar requirement of the poet: "This is what you shall do: Love the earth and sun and the animals, despise riches, give alms to every one that asks, stand up for the stupid and crazy, devote your income and labor to others, hate tyrants, argue not concerning God, have patience and indulgence toward the people, take off your hat to nothing known or unknown or to any man or number of men . . ." (pp. v–vi). Actually Whitman is addressing all those who undertake to follow him, but presumably he was thinking primarily of poets who would follow him.

25. Page 42. "And this is the reward; that the ideal shall be real to thee, and the impressions of the actual world shall fall like summer rain, copious, but not troublesome to thy invulnerable essence."

25. This passage suggests the aspect of idealism in Whitman and his poems, although it does not account for Whitman's insistence on reality.

Allowing that Emerson influenced Whitman's concept of the poet and his practice of poetry in all these ways, and more, there remains a great deal in Whitman that was highly individual and that Emerson did not influence. I will merely mention some of these individual characteristics revealed through *Leaves of Grass* without going into detail. They will be evident to all who have read the poems.

1. The verse form of *Leaves of Grass*—perhaps the most obvious difference in the practice of the two poets.

2. Whitman's realism, accepted both as a philosophical principle and as a basis for poetic style.

3. Whitman's stress on the life in cities contrasted with Emerson's stress on life in the country.

4. Crudeness in imagery and language in *Leaves of Grass* (though not in his personal manner or his prose usually), showing at best a lack of taste.

5. Emphasis on sex as the basic principle of creativity, but especially the free treatment of sexuality in the animal body.

6. Love and appreciation of music in all forms, and a fondness for the theater.

7. Belief, frequently stressed in the poems, in the immortality of the individual self without, however, pretending to understand it. There is some question whether Emerson, especially in his middle years, firmly believed in individual immortality.

The fundamental difference between Emerson and Whitman was in their personalities. Emerson was a somewhat over-refined product of New England Puritanism, overlaid but not obscured by philosophical idealism drawn from many sources. Whitman was a comparatively unrefined product of working class country and small-town democracy, overlaid with a thin coating of Quaker and Evangelical piety and a thick coating of big-city worldliness, including the refinements of the theater along with the crudeness of the life of the streets. Emerson was an intellectual, Whitman a man of feeling. Emerson was, by temperament, an aristocrat, Whitman a democrat. Emerson broke away from his formal education and moved in the direction of piety and democracy, while Whitman, with but little formal education, undertook to educate himself and move in the direction of Emerson. Their degree of identity is to be discovered in some measure in the books they read, Emerson thoroughly, Whitman casually or at second hand in reviews. If Whitman was considerably influenced by Emerson, and I think he was, that influence was made possible by the common ground on which they met that had been prepared ahead of them by the literary interpreters of philosophy in Europe and England in the late eighteenth and early nineteenth century. If, therefore, Whitman was "simmering," as he told Trowbridge, in 1854, it was not merely internal heat that made him simmer, nor the limited knowledge of Emerson that he had picked up before 1854, but all the experiences that I have described in the preceding pages. That it was indeed the thorough reading of Emerson's essays in the summer of 1854 that brought him "to a boil," I have no doubt. It must be remembered, however, that Whitman's reading of Emerson's essays was at the end, not the beginning, of the long "foreground" of *Leaves of Grass*.

Index

peasants had moved to larger cities to work in factories.

To make matters worse, Jewish craftsmen found that they could no longer compete with the increasing number of factory-made products. One small business after another failed and all hope of earning a decent livelihood vanished. The dream of finding a better parnosseh in America replaced it. Hesitation about leaving the familiar streets of Polotsk was overcome by the terrorism of pogroms. For innumerable Russian Jews, America took on the image of the Promised Land.

> Businessmen talked of it over their accounts; the market women made up their quarrels that they might discuss it from stall to stall; people who had relatives in the famous land went around reading their letters for the enlightenment of less fortunate folks; the one letter-carrier informed the public how many letters arrived from America and who were the recipients; children played at emigration; old folks shook their sage heads over the evening fire, and prophesied no good for those who braved the terrors of the sea and the foreign goal beyond it. [7]

German steamship companies advertised cheap transatlantic passage, and letters from America reported that America needed laborers and paid them well. According to these letters, from the moment they arrived Jewish newcomers would have as many rights as everyone else; they could live where they pleased and do whatever work they wanted with hope of saving enough money to bring friends and relatives across; there was free education

---

FROM PEONAGE

Hacienda Buenavista, Mexico, 1920's

AND KITCHENS

re dawn, the sound of women slapping tor-
be heard in each of the villages on the lands
a Buenavista. Women got up first to make the
rncakes that their husbands and sons ate for
nd carried to the fields for lunch. After soften-
rn kernels in warm lime water and boiling
n earthenware pot to remove their husks, a
bed the pulp against a grinding stone with a
e to smooth it into dough. She rolled a bit of
a ball, slapped it quickly into a pancake
threw it down on the earthen or iron griddle
charcoal fire. The hearth at which she knelt
imply of three stones to support the griddle.
at least a hundred tortillas every morning
later. Each working man in the family ate
ty-five a day, the women of the household ate
ozen apiece, and the small children somewha

and no compulsory military service; and they need not fear persecution for their religious customs.

Family after family in Polotsk and throughout the Pale resolved to begin life over again in the New World. They dismantled their homes, selling furniture, books, and boxes of belongings, but they kept their Bibles and prayerbooks, the precious bedding which was an important part of every dowry, their samovars, and some pots and pans. Having been warned of border guards and ticket agents who might swindle them, they sewed into the linings of their jackets the few rubles they had managed to save or the dollars sent to them from America.

On the day of a family's departure, it seemed that over half the town appeared at the railroad station to wish them a good journey. Uncertainty, desolation, and homesickness filled the hearts of the emigrants as their train pulled out of the station, carrying them away from the only life they had ever known. They were embarking on an enormous journey with very little experience in traveling, not enough money, no knowledge of the conditions, customs, and language of the place to which they were going, and only a vague idea of their route, future plans, and final destination. But the changing world of the shtetl had helped prepare them for the modern country to which they were going.

Trains, thickly packed with refugees, moved across western Russia and Germany to the ports of Hamburg and Bremen where the emigrants would board a ship. Jews who were evading conscription or who had been leaders of the anti-tsarist movement had no passports and were forced to steal through the woods across the

border and out of
were part of a migra
eastern Europe betw
ing to Canada and
various other count
to New York. And
remained, though s
lantic coast and in t
copies of the Torah

TO FIELD

Even befo
tillas coul
of Hacien
thin flat c
breakfast
ing the c
them in a
woman ru
second sto
dough int
shape, and
set over a
consisted
She made
and more
about twe
at least a
fewer.

The early morning light revealed calendars, religious pictures and a few postcards on the earth-colored walls of the windowless, one-room adobe house made smoky by the charcoal fire. A fortunate family had a separate kitchen built into a lean-to outside. Extra clothes and sombreros hung from nails driven into the walls. The family's best clothes and the trinkets worn for fiestas, important papers, and other valuables were stowed in a wooden storage chest. In one corner, a small table with candles and flowers on it was placed under a carved wooden figure of Jesus Christ or the Virgin Mary or a picture of a Catholic saint.

As the girls of the family awoke, they smoothed out the cotton dresses or the skirts and blouses they had slept in and combed and braided their long dark hair. The father and sons got up from their straw mats and put on homemade, loose-fitting white cotton pants called *calzones*. Then they added a patched collarless shirt knotted together at the front, and heavy huaraches, or sandals. On Sundays, they would don clean sets of clothes to go to Mass.

One by one the boys and girls threw a little cold water across their faces from the big clay water jug in the corner and dried themselves with shirttails or a skirt. One of the sons shouldered the wooden yoke to which two water cans were attached and set out for the nearest fountain. It might take ten trips for him to fetch enough water for the day's washing and cooking, for watering the animals and the flowers that brightened the yard, the doorway, and the inside of the house.

In most households, there were not enough earthenware plates and cups to allow everyone in the family to eat at once. Father and grown sons sat down first on stools, benches, or crates around the low homemade table to eat the tortillas and chile (hot red or green peppers usually made into a sauce) that had been prepared for breakfast. Meanwhile, one of the daughters put similar food into fiber shoulder bags for the men's lunch and filled gourds with water. The women and younger children waited until later to eat their breakfast.

Around six o'clock, when the men were ready to leave for the fields, each took the colorful wool serape from the mat on which he had slept, folded it lengthwise, and draped it over one shoulder. Woven on handmade looms, these blankets were among a family's most valuable possessions, covering them at night and protecting them from cold and rain during the day. The men took their wide-brimmed straw sombreros from the nails on the wall; these would shield them from the sun. Each also took along the long steel knife with curved tip, called a machete, which he used for hoeing and for cutting crops.

As the men left their houses and headed toward the fields, they walked along the unpaved main street of the village with its deep gulleys filled with large stones. Chickens and pigs ran off the street into nearby yards as the men approached. There usually were less than twenty houses in each village, and because they were built on the poorest and stoniest land, the vegetable gardens beside them yielded poorly.

The men walked up and down hills for over an hour to get to the wide fields of the flat valley where they worked. The countryside for miles around was all part

In the morning mist, men wait at market to sell their wood.

of one hacienda or giant plantation. Spreading over a hundred thousand or more acres of Mexico's high central plateau, Buenavista was among the largest of the 380 haciendas in the state of Michoacán. Wheat, corn, and beans were raised on the plains, and cattle, horses, sheep, and goats grazed on the less fertile hillsides. Fuel came from the forests, and from the wastelands came lime, stone, and clay for building the adobe houses, coarse grass for thatching the roofs, and herbs for curing illnesses.

Fifteen or twenty villages were scattered over the land belonging to Hacienda Buenavista, most with fewer than a hundred inhabitants. The families living in villages on

This family's house has walls of adobe and a roof of grass.

the hacienda were descended from the Indians who had once owned the land and had farmed it communally, each man taking home a share of the crop. After the Spanish conquest of Mexico in 1521, Spaniards had become owners of enormous tracts of land and through the years, right up to the early 1900's, their descendants absorbed more and more village land, leaving the Indian

villagers with none. By the 1920's, the majority of the
families on the hacienda did not even own their adobe
houses or the gardens beside them.

Throughout Michoacán, most of the land belonged to a
few hundred *hacendados,* men of direct Spanish descent.
A hacendado lived most of the time in Mexico City and
often traveled in Europe, seldom visiting his estate. He
left his lands under the management of an administrator
who, with the help of several assistants and a number of
foremen, worked the villagers hard. In various haciendas
throughout the state, the foremen treated their men so
badly that it seemed as if the villagers actually belonged
to the hacendado—which in a way they did, since no
matter how hard they worked they never earned enough
money to be free of the debts they owed their master.
The very word peon came to mean a worker who lives
in virtual slavery based on debt.

When the hacendado did come to the hacienda, he rode
in a leisurely fashion around the estate on a fine white
horse, inspecting the fields and cattle. He stayed in his
big stone house with its red-tile roof. Iron bars over the
windows and doors and a high thick wall around the
grounds provided defense against any uprising of
the peons or an attack by bandits who lived in the hills.
The walls enclosed flower and vegetable gardens, orchards, workshops, stables, tool sheds, and granaries.

Some of the peons tended the gardens and orchards
near the main house, while others cut trees from the forests and hauled firewood. Peons cleared stubble from the
land and guided crude wooden plows pulled by oxen
across the fields. They sowed the wheat and planted the

corn by hand, weeded the rows, and finally cut the crops.

The faces and necks of the peons were often sunburned and their hands and feet always scratched and calloused from working in the fields. As one worker recalled, the hardest time was during the summer:

> At about eleven o'clock it would begin to get hot. Then the body starts to sweat and one drinks water and more and more water. We ate at about two. A few neighbors would come together, build a fire and heat the *tortillas*.[1]

After a short siesta the peons worked and drank more water until they left for home in the late afternoon. The regular rains that brought relief from the heat between May and October did not fall until late afternoon or early evening.

When there was no work for the peons in the fields, they spent their days twisting maguey fiber into rope, gathering wood in the hills and selling it, cutting hay for animals, picking fruit and vegetables from their own gardens, or making tools. If they had a donkey or a mule, they used it to haul corn after the harvest and later corn stalks and firewood. They might make some extra money by loading such goods as eggs or wood on the donkey and walking to a market town to sell them.

Everyone in the family worked hard—the men in the fields and the women in their kitchens. By the age of twelve, most children were working full time with their fathers or mothers. Few boys or girls went to school for more than a couple of years. A peon knew what his son learned from him in the fields was more useful than what

Men work the fields by hand, cutting stalks with machetes.

he would learn in school. The hacendados, afraid that better educated laborers would demand more wages and benefits, did not encourage the peons to educate their children. In the 1920's, three out of four adults could neither read nor write.

When the men and boys were away in the fields, the women and girls fed the pig and chickens and watered

or weeded the flower and vegetable gardens. Boys too
young to go to the fields could help with these jobs and
pick any fruit that was ripe on the trees in the yard.
While one of the daughters folded serapes, rolled the
straw mats in a corner, and washed the breakfast dishes,
another swept the dirt floor with a twig broom. The
mother kept her eye on any small children as she continued to shell and grind corn; she spent about six hours
a day kneeling at the grinding stone. There was always
washing and sewing to be done. The housewife might
carry her basket to the hacienda store to buy small quan-

A woman weaves a serape in a room built of cane stalks.

tities of kerosene, matches, and candles, rice, lard, and chile. By slinging her baby in the blue cotton shawl, or *rebozo*, that covered her head and shoulders, she kept her hands free. As she walked along, she modestly fixed her eyes on the ground in front of her. To smile was considered flirtatious.

A woman served the men of the family a hot meal when they returned from the fields. The men and boys helped themselves to tortillas from the pile in the middle of the table and used them to scoop the fried beans and chile from their plates. The wife often served pulque, a thin whitish beverage fermented from the juices of the giant maguey plant. Coffee was a luxury, but tea made from orange leaves, lemon-grass, or cinnamon was common. For months at a time, there would be no milk, butter, cheese, eggs, fresh vegetables, or meat on the table. Bread appeared only on special occasions, such as fiesta days when every family managed to eat a more elaborate meal than usual.

Although the villagers had been converted to the Roman Catholic religion after the Spaniards conquered Mexico, they still retained many of their Indian traditions. Most of the local gods had been transformed into Catholic saints. Each village had a patron saint who protected it and sent the rain. Villagers honored the saint once a year with an elaborate fiesta; they offered prayers, displayed flowers, lit candles, burned incense, set off fireworks, ate and drank heartily, and performed religious dances to the music of reed flutes, armadillo-shell mandolins, and more modern instruments.

The saints seemed closer to the people than did God,

who was always punishing them with illness, accidents, storms, and crop failures. Villagers tried to please the saints and gain their favor so the saints would ask God's protection for them. If a family invoked no other saint, they at least prayed to the Virgin of Guadalupe, patron saint of Mexico, on her fiesta day. Some Mexicans carried an amulet with the Virgin of Guadalupe on it in the belief that she always watched over the bearer.

Peons inherited a belief in many spirits from their Indian past. To guard against illness, they tried to please *los aires,* spirits who, taking the form of wind, demons, or "little people," could cause pimples, sores, and more serious diseases. Most people also believed in witches who turned themselves into pigs or dogs and did harm in the night. In some localities, villagers buried ancient idols in their fields to guard the corn against evil. Believing that the color red obscured a witch's eyesight, many Indian women tied red thread around the wrists and ankles of their children and placed the red feather of a woodpecker in their young ones' hair to ward off the "evil eye" which brought sickness. They treated illnesses with mixtures of herbs, reptile skins, alcohol rubs, and a variety of other home remedies. Not everyone recovered from disease, and the funerals that followed deaths were elaborate.

> The celebration lasts about three days, during which the Indians dance all night and part of the day beside the corpse stretched out between four candles. Violins and guitars are played and songs sung in honor of the dead man. [2]

A NEW CONSTITUTION FAILS

For years the peons had been bound to the haciendas by debt. They had been paid in corn, pulque, candles, and coffee and in coins that could be spent only at the hacienda store. They had to buy everything they needed there. The hacendado kept them in permanent debt by advancing more money and goods than they were ever able to repay. Sons inherited their fathers' debts. Until all debts were paid, a man was not free to leave the estate to look for work somewhere else; his future seemed dim.

A revolution had begun elsewhere in Mexico in 1910, and the revolt continued as peons rose up unsuccessfully against hacendados. They hoped to overthrow the descendants of the Spanish conquistadors and regain the land they had lost. A new constitution in 1917 promised that communal lands taken from the villages would be returned, and it forbade hacendados to pay a peon in any form but money or to force him to work off a debt. Workers in the cities and towns were guaranteed higher wages, an eight-hour working day, an end to child labor, and new houses and schools. The promises aroused hopes but the government did little during the 1920's to put the reforms into effect. Peons and urban workers became disillusioned.

The system of peonage continued despite the fact that hacendados canceled the past debts of their peons and began to pay them in coins that could be spent anywhere. This meant the peons should be free to leave haciendas like Buenavista to look for work at better pay on other haciendas or in the cities. Most peons, however, had so little money that they fell quickly back into debt and

could not leave home. Few really wanted to leave the
land their forefathers had tilled. A peon had been born
and married and expected to die in his village; his fellow villagers were his trusted friends. He worked in the
fields with men from nearby villages, but he would not
invite them into his home.

Though temporarily freed from past debts, an uneducated peon who had always been told what to do lacked
the technical know-how and ambition to begin farming
on his own. Besides, he had no tools, animals, seeds, or
savings to equip a farm even if there had been unoccu-
pied land for him. As long as he remained on the hacienda, he received seeds and tools, oxen for plowing,
and supplies for his family. He did not have to pay rent
on the site that his house occupied or on his garden. He
could graze his donkey or mule, if he had one, on hacienda land, and when the crops failed, he could still
get food on credit at the hacienda store.

Many peons hopefully awaited the day when they
would be able to work for themselves on communal village lands; this day would not arrive during the 1920's.
A village needed twenty farming families residing in
it before it could apply to the government for a grant
of land. Most of the villages on Buenavista were too small
to qualify. The peons of larger villages hesitated to apply,
fearing that the hacendado would punish them. Other
hacendados in Mexico had threatened to burn the houses
of villagers who applied. Where villagers did make re-
quests for land, their applications were held up for years
in legal red tape and sometimes ignored.

It was difficult for a young man to break away from

the life of a peon. In his mid-teens, he married a girl his parents approved of and brought her home to live. The son continued to work with his father on the hacienda and to add his earnings to the family income. Every young man knew that he could not do better unless he went to work as a laborer in a city or left Mexico altogether. His first step away from the hacienda was usually taken during the seasons when there was no farm work. A youth who was free from debt would take a rickety bus at the main gate of the hacienda into the town of Morelia, capital of Michoacán. There he might apprentice himself to a baker or a shoemaker until spring when he returned to the hacienda. If he could earn enough money in Morelia he often did not go back to the hacienda at all. Sooner or later, he might go to Mexico City to work as a delivery boy for a butcher or as a streetcar conductor. In the city, he shared a one-room apartment with his wife and children or with friends from his village and gave up his white calzones for the dark overalls of the city worker.

TEXAS, CALIFORNIA, AND ARIZONA

In Morelia or Mexico City, young men heard from fellow Mexicans who had been across the United States border, or from American recruiters, about the need for farm laborers in Texas, California, and Arizona. Mexicans would be paid five or six times what they had earned on the hacienda to pick cotton, fruit, and vegetables in the United States. This meant plenty to eat and money to send back home. When these young men returned to the villages on Hacienda Buenavista, they spoke enthusiastically of the money and clothes that could be had in the United States.

An increasing number of young men were tempted by the higher wages that America offered. More Mexicans left their country during the 1920's than during any other decade; in the decades that followed, more land was returned to the farmers. Mexicans left in greatest numbers from states, like Michoacán, on the high central plateau where the hacienda system seemed indestructible.

Crossing the United States border meant not only an escape from low wages but also from the hopelessness of peonage and the uncertainties of the post-revolutionary years in Mexico. During the 1920's, the demand for unskilled Mexican workers increased rapidly in the United States. Laws passed here in 1921 and thereafter restricted the number of European immigrants, at the same time postwar prosperity stimulated the expansion of American farming and industry and thus intensified the need for unskilled laborers. Recruiters for American mines, ranches, and railroad companies offered Mexican peons who had never earned more than twenty-five cents a day as much as $1.25 to $1.50 a day. Many were also drawn by the excitement of a new experience:

Once when I was with a number of boys we got some letters from some friends we had here [in America] and we got a desire to come and know the famous country.[3]

Young men from Buenavista and other haciendas usually departed in the company of a few friends. They traveled by freight train or by bus, sometimes walking part

Youths first left haciendas for jobs in Mexican cities.

of the way, begging for food and sleeping outdoors under the serapes they carried over their shoulders. The emigrants headed toward Nuevo Laredo, Ciudad Juárez, Nogales, or Mexicali on the Mexican side of the border.

Arriving at one of these towns, a migrant found a bed in a boardinghouse or a hotel. It sometimes took three or four days for him to obtain a passport from the Mexican Migration Office in town, because so many other men were there for the same purpose. Once a man secured a passport he took it to the American consulate nearby to apply for a visa, which also took several days to obtain and cost him $10. Later he would have to pay an $8 head tax. Finally he was given a literacy test and a medical examination, and if he passed these he was allowed to cross the border into Laredo or El Paso, Texas, into Nogales, Arizona, or into Calexico, California. Nearly half a million Mexicans followed this procedure during the 1920's and came to the United States; probably about a hundred thousand came from the state of Michoacán alone.

Large numbers of migrants, however, did not have enough money to pay the cost of the visa, the head tax, and a week or more in a boardinghouse. Others could not read enough Spanish to pass the literacy test. Some had already contracted through a recruiter to work for an American farmer even though it was against American law to do so while still in Mexico. All these men were determined to go to the United States, but they could not enter legally.

There were many ways of crossing the border illegally, though:

> Most of them [are] engineered by professional
> smugglers, called "coyotes," who hang around the
> *plaza*, hotels, restaurants, and even offices where
> the laborers must go, and suggest that for a lower
> price—from five to ten dollars—and less trouble,
> they can go over the border. Sometimes they take
> them in automobiles across the shallow places in the
> river, or in carts and trucks. Others are taken in
> boats, and some even swim across, a dangerous
> thing to do because the river [the Rio Grande] is
> treacherous.[4]

Frequently after dark the men simply climbed over the
barbed wire fence that marked the border in some small
town where the line was not carefully guarded. Since no
record could be kept of Mexicans who entered the United
States illegally, it is impossible to know how many did;
but it is probable that there were four illegal immigrants
for every legal one. The percentage of legal crossings
was much higher from the states like Michoacán that
were farther from the United States border. Mexicans
from the border states could easily tell an immigration
officer that they were crossing over to shop. Once beyond
the border, they disappeared into the Spanish-speaking
population and their departure went unrecorded.

Whether they crossed into the United States legally or
not, half the migrants ended up in Texas. Most of the
rest went to California or Arizona, fewer to New Mexico.
Smaller numbers—but a relatively high percentage from
Michoacán—headed north to the industrial jobs offered
in Chicago, Gary, Detroit, and Kansas City.

Most Mexicans who entered the United States, legally or illegally, had no intention of staying indefinitely. Unlike immigrants from across the ocean, they knew they could go home without saving a lot of money for passage. They were seeking temporary work—planting and harvesting cotton or sugar beets; picking oranges, peaches, tomatoes, or cherries; cleaning stockyards, repairing railroad tracks, or working in brickyards or factories. After a year or two, many of them would return to Mexico, but in the meantime, they sent postal money orders back to their families. When they did return home, they took back American dollars, mechanical skills and techniques, and even some cars, although Mexican village roads were not fit to drive on. They brought back to the villages, like those on Hacienda Buenavista, memories of a higher standard of living in the United States. Their reports inspired others to work for a year or two north of the border. Some immigrants never went home to Mexico, and many who did found life on the haciendas so miserable that they returned to the States for good. Their sons and daughters were born as citizens of the United States, but the generation of Mexicans who had crossed the border themselves kept their homeland close to their hearts:

> I will never change my citizenship, for that would be to deny the mother who has brought me into the world. That is the way one's country is. We were born there and it is for us to love her always.[5]

IMMIGRATION FACTS AND FIGURES

All Americans are immigrants or descendants of immigrants. Even the American Indians are believed to have traversed a land bridge from Asia to North America thousands of years ago. Since the time when European colonies were first established in the American wilderness, more than 44 million people have crossed the Atlantic or Pacific Oceans or the Mexican or Canadian borders to this country.

No immigration statistics were kept before 1820, but it has been estimated that some 200,000 European colonists arrived between 1689 and 1754[1] and that 250,000 people came between the end of the Revolutionary War and 1820.[2] No figures exist for the number of Africans brought to this country as slaves, but it was certainly less than a million.[3] The following charts show the total number of immigrants from all countries between 1820 and 1967.

IMMIGRATION BY COUNTRY,
1820-1967†

Europe	35,350,575	Sweden[4]	1,263,590
Albania[12]	2,257	Switzerland	338,097
Austria and Hungary[2]	4,289,215	Turkey in Europe	163,089
Belgium	196,181	U.S.S.R.[6]	3,345,909
Bulgaria[11]	66,832	Yugoslavia[11]	76,347
Czechoslovakia[12]	130,866	Other Europe	50,791
Denmark	358,333		
Estonia[12]	1,038	Asia	1,299,763
Finland[12]	30,008	China[18]	426,761
France	718,436	India	22,631
Germany[2]	6,879,495	Japan[7]	352,748
Great Britain:		Turkey in Asia[8]	208,906
England	3,034,619	Other Asia	288,717
Scotland	807,373		
Wales	93,738	America	6,881,081
Not specified[3]	799,759	Canada & Newfoundland[9]	3,870,839
Greece	528,894	Mexico[10]	1,457,307
Ireland	4,708,845	West Indies	839,369
Italy	5,096,204	Central America	186,503
Latvia[12]	2,295	South America	419,488
Lithuania[12]	3,582	Other America[14]	107,575
Luxembourg[16]	2,481		
Netherlands	346,822	Africa	61,694
Norway[4]	851,093	Australia & New Zealand	92,056
Poland[5]	478,026	Pacific Islands[17]	22,454
Portugal	319,244	Not specified[15]	268,662
Rumania[13]	160,638		
Spain	206,478	**ALL COUNTRIES**	43,976,285

[1]Data for fiscal years ended June 30, except 1820 to 1831 inclusive and 1844 to 1849 inclusive fiscal years ended September 30; 1833 to 1842 inclusive and 1851 to 1867 inclusive years ended December 31; 1832 covers 15 months ended December 31; 1843 nine months ended September 30; 1850 15 months ended December 31; and 1868 six months ended June 30.

†U.S. Bureau of the Census, *Statistical Abstract of the United States, 1968* (Washington, D.C., 1968), p. 60.

[2]Data for Austria-Hungary were not reported until 1861. Austria and Hungary have been recorded separately since 1905. In the years 1938 to 1945 inclusive Austria was included with Germany.

[3]Great Britain not specified. In the years 1901 to 1951, included in other Europe.

[4]From 1820 to 1868 the figures for Norway and Sweden were combined.

[5]Poland was recorded as a separate country from 1820 to 1898 and since 1920. Between 1899 and 1919, Poland was included with Austria-Hungary, Germany, and Russia.

[6]Between 1931 and 1963 U.S.S.R. was broken down into European U.S.S.R. and Asian U.S.S.R. Since 1964 total U.S.S.R. has been reported in Europe.

[7]No record of immigration from Japan until 1861.

[8]No record of immigration from Turkey in Asia until 1869.

[9]Prior to 1920 Canada and Newfoundland were recorded as British North America. From 1820 to 1898 the figures included all British North American possessions.

[10]No record of immigration from Mexico from 1886 to 1893.

[11]Bulgaria, Serbia, and Montenegro were first reported in 1899. Bulgaria has been reported separately since 1920 and in 1920 also a separate enumeration was made for the Kingdom of Serbs, Croats, and Slovens. Since 1922 the Serb, Croat, and Slovene Kingdom has been recorded as Yugoslavia.

[12]Countries added to the list since the beginning of World War I are theretofore included with the countries to which they belonged. Figures are available since 1920 for Czechoslovakia and Finland and since 1924 for Albania, Estonia, Latvia, and Lithuania.

[13]No record of immigration from Rumania until 1880.

[14]Included with countries not specified prior to 1925.

[15]The figure 33,523 in column headed 1901-1910, includes 32,897 persons returning in 1906 to their homes in the United States.

[16]Figures for Luxembourg are available since 1925.

[17]Beginning with the year 1952, Asia includes Philippines. From 1934 to 1951 the Philippines were included in the Pacific Islands. Prior to 1934 the Philippines were recorded in separate tables as insular travel.

[18]Beginning in 1957 China includes Taiwan.

NATIONAL ORIGINS OF IMMIGRATION TO
THE UNITED STATES, 1820-1967†

IN MILLIONS

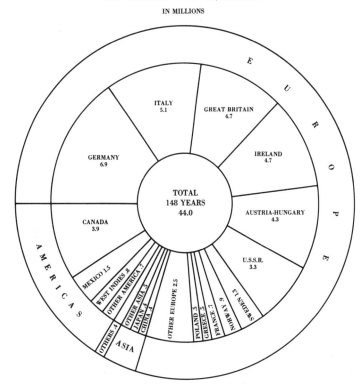

Over 32 million of these immigrants, largely from Europe, arrived in the single century between 1815 and 1914. They came in three great waves, each larger than the one before. The first wave (1830-1860) brought northern Europeans mainly from Great Britain, Ireland, and Germany. The second wave (1860-1890) was made up of British, Scandinavians, Germans, and Austrians,

†Based on *Annual Report* of the U.S. Immigration and Naturalization Service, 1967.

also primarily from northern Europe. The source of the third wave (1890-1914) shifted from the north and west of Europe to the south and east, bringing Slavs and Jews from eastern Europe and Mediterranean peoples from Italy and Greece.

WAVES OF IMMIGRATION†

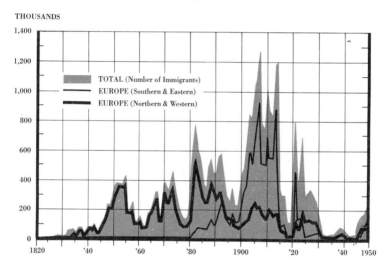

THOUSANDS

Throughout most of the 1800's, Americans regarded their country as a refuge for the poor people of Europe and looked to these immigrants as suppliers of much needed population and cheap labor. Until the 1880's, almost anyone who wanted to come here could. Thereafter various categories of immigrants were excluded. The first people to be rejected were those who had certain diseases or criminal tendencies or who would be unable

†Reproduced by permission of the publishers from Francis J. Brown and Joseph S. Roucek, *One America* (Englewood Cliffs, N.J.: Prentice-Hall, Inc., 1946), pp. 6, 7, 636.

to support themselves. In 1882, the Chinese exclusion law barred the further immigration of Chinese in response to the claim of workers in California that Chinese laborers were taking jobs away from native workers. (This law remained in effect until 1943.) When labor unions complained that European immigrants, working for lower wages, were depriving native Americans of jobs, Congress passed the contract labor law in 1885. This law prohibited American employers from hiring workers in Europe and financing their passage to this country.

Agitation for further restriction increased during the 1890's and the first two decades of the 1900's. These were the years when tremendous numbers of "new immigrants" were arriving from southern and eastern Europe, bringing ways of life that were noticeably different from those of previous groups already settled in the United States. Their arrival coincided with a depression in the 1890's and with the realization on the part of native Americans that the once endless supply of land was running out. After World War I came the added fear that hoards of Europeans, fleeing their war-torn countries, would descend on the United States and change the way of life here. People argued that the influx of a variety of races and cultures would threaten national unity.

Responding to the demand for immigration restriction, Congress rejected the old principle of America as an asylum for the oppressed. After several unsuccessful attempts, it enacted a law in 1917, over President Wilson's veto, requiring all immigrants to pass a simple literacy test. This was intended to keep out the poor and uneducated "new immigrants," but so many of them passed the test that it really did not work. During the 1920's, Congress set a ceiling on the total number of immigrants who could enter the United States each year from Europe. At the same time, it inaugurated the national origins quota system which attempted to maintain the ethnic balance then existing in America. Northern and western European countries that had sent the most immigrants to America in the past could continue to send the most, but southern and eastern European countries that had more recently begun to send immigrants would have much lower quotas. The law virtually excluded Asians but placed no numerical limitation on immigrants from Canada and Latin America. This policy was preserved in the immigration law of 1952, except that Asians were made eligible for admission.

The most recent immigration law, passed in 1965, has phased out the ethnically-oriented quota system and admits immigrants from all countries on a first-come, first-served basis with preferences given to those who have relatives in the United States or skills that are particularly needed here. A total of 170,000 immigrant visas a year are allotted to all nations outside of North and South America, but no one of these nations can use more than 20,000. For the first time a limit of 120,000 immigrant visas a year has been imposed on the nations of North and South America. People from Italy, Greece, Portugal, China, and the Philippines, whose countries had very small quotas before 1965, are now coming to the United States in much larger numbers.

REFERENCE NOTES

FROM AUTHORITY (pp. 1–24)

1. *An Answere for the tyme to the examination put in print, without the authour's name, pretending to mayntayne the apparrell prescribed against the declaration of the mynisters of London* (1566), in Henry Martyn Dexter and Morton Dexter, *The England and Holland of the Pilgrims* (Boston: Houghton Mifflin and Co., 1905), p. 117.

2. Old Ballad. Mildred Campbell, *The English Yeoman under Elizabeth and the Early Stuarts* (New Haven: Yale University Press, 1942), p. 221.

3. E. C. E. Bourne, *The Anglicanism of William Laud* (London: Society for Promoting Christian Knowledge, 1947), p. 55.

FROM FREEDOM (pp. 25–46)

1. R. S. Rattray, *Ashanti* (Oxford: The Clarendon Press, 1923), p. 96.

2. Mungo Park, *Travels in the Interior Districts of Africa* (London: W. Bulmer and Co., 1799), Vol. I, p. 47.

3. Rattray, *Ashanti*, p. 215.

4. Basil Davidson, *The African Slave Trade:* Precolonial History 1450 1850 (Boston: An Atlantic Monthly Press Book; published in hardcover as *Black Mother* by Little Brown and Co., 1961), p. 90.

5. Daniel P. Mannix and Malcolm Cowley, *Black Cargoes:* A History of the Atlantic Slave Trade, 1518-1865 (New York: The Viking Press, 1962), pp. 47-48.

6. Captain Thomas Phillips. *A Journal of a Voyage made in the Hannibal of London, 1693-1694,* Vol. VI, in Mannix and Cowley, *Black Cargoes,* p. 48.

FROM FAMINE (pp. 47–71)

1. J. G. Kohl, *Ireland* (New York: Harper & Brothers, 1844), pp. 12–13.

2. Gustave de Beaumont, *Ireland: Social, Political, and Religious,* Vol. 1 (London: Richard Bentley, 1839), p. 268.

3. *Dublin Penny Journal,* I (Aug. 19, 1832), p. 58, in Marcus Lee Hansen, *The Atlantic Migration, 1607-1860: A History of the Continuing Settlement of the United States* (Harper Torchbooks; originally published by the Harvard University Press, 1940), p. 203.

4. Father Mathew to Charles Edward Trevelyn, Assistant Secretary of the Treasury (August 7, 1846), in Cecil Woodham-Smith, *The Great Hunger: Ireland, 1845-1849* (A Signet Book published by the New American Library; originally published by Harper and Row, Publishers, Inc., New York, 1962), p. 86.

5. Extracts from Joseph Crosfield's report of his journey in company with William Forster, made to the London Relief Committee of the Society of Friends, *Transactions of the Central Relief Committee of the Society of Friends during the Famine in Ireland, in 1846 and 1847* (Dublin: Hodges and Smith, 1852), p. 146.

6. Nicholas Cummins, Magistrate of Cork, to the Duke of Wellington and to *The Times* (London, Dec. 24, 1846), in Woodham-Smith, *The Great Hunger,* p. 157.

7. Sir William Butler, in Woodham-Smith, *The Great Hunger,* pp. 365–366.

8. Woodham-Smith, *The Great Hunger,* p. 290.

9. A. C. G. Dobree, Commissariat Officer at Sligo, in Woodham-Smith, *The Great Hunger,* p. 174.

10. David Alfred Chart, *An Economic History of Ireland* (Dublin: Talbot Press, 1920), p. 105.

FROM TYRANNY (pp. 72–95)

1. Charles Loring Brace, *Home-life in Germany* (New York: C. Scribner, 1853), p. 132.

2. Veit Valentin, *1848:* Chapters of German History, translated by Ethel Talbot Scheffauer (London: G. Allen and Unwin, Ltd., 1940), p. 55.

3. Augerstein, *Die Berliner März-Ereignisse im Jahre 1848,* in J. G. Legge, *Rhyme and Revolution in Germany:* A Study in German History, Life, Literature and Character, 1813-1850 (London: Constable and Company, Ltd., 1918), p. 190.

4. *Ibid.*

5. *Ibid.,* pp. 284-285.

6. *Ibid.*, p. 285.

7. *The Reminiscences of Carl Schurz*, Vol. I, 1829-1852 (New York: The McClure Company, 1907), p. 119.

8. Frederick William IV to Baron von Bunsen, Prussian Ambassador at London (Potsdam, Dec. 13, 1848), in Legge, *Rhyme and Revolution in Germany*, p. 517.

FROM DISORDER (pp. 96–118)

1. Hamilton Holt (ed.), "The Life Story of a Chinaman," pp. 281-299, *The Life Stories of Undistinguished Americans As Told by Themselves* (New York: J. Pott and Co., 1906), p. 285.

2. Olga Lang, *Chinese Family and Society* (New Haven: Yale University Press, 1946), pp. 25-26.

3. Mrs. E. T. Williams, "Popular Religious Literature," *Journal of the Royal Asiatic Society*, North China Branch, N. S., XXX (1899-1900), 25-26, in Kung-Chuan Hsiao, *Rural China:* Imperial Control in the Nineteenth Century (Seattle: University of Washington Press, 1960), paperback edition, p. 413.

4. Russell H. Conwell, *Why and How:* Why the Chinese Emigrate and The Means They Adopt for Getting to America (Boston: Lee and Shepard, 1871), pp. 149-150.

5. *Ibid.*, p. 184.

FROM LANDLESSNESS (pp. 119–138)

1. George M. Stephenson, "Typical 'America Letters,'" *Yearbook* of the Swedish Historical Society of America, Vol. 7 (1921-22), p. 78.

2. *Ibid.*, p. 91.

3. Vilhelm Moberg, *The Emigrants*, translated from the Swedish by Gustaf Lannestock (New York: Simon and Schuster, 1951), p. 49.

FROM FUTILITY (pp. 139–161)

1. V. di Somma, "Dell economia rulale nel mezzagiorno," *Nuova Antologia*, March 16, 1906, p. 307, in Robert F. Foerster, *The Italian Emigration of Our Times* (Cambridge: Harvard University Press, 1919), p. 77.

2. Carlo Levi, *Christ Stopped at Eboli*, translated from the Italian by Frances Frenaye (New York: Farrar, Straus, 1963), pp. 121-122.

3. Foerster, *The Italian Emigration of Our Times*, p. 22.

4. U. S. House of Representatives, 50 Cong., 1 sess. H. misc. documents 572 (Washington, 1888), in Rudolph Vecoli, "Chicago's Italians Prior to World War I" (unpublished Ph. D. dissertation, University of Wisconsin, 1962), p. 91.

FROM OPPRESSION (pp. 162–183)

1. Mark Zborowski and Elizabeth Herzog, *Life Is With People:* The Culture of the Shtetl (New York: Schocken Books; originally published by International Universities Press, Inc., 1952), p. 428.

2. *Ibid.*, p. 256.

3. *Ibid.*, p. 222.

4. Maurice Samuel, *The World of Sholom Aleichem* (New York: Schocken Books; originally published by Alfred A. Knopf, Inc., 1943), p. 288.

5. Mary Antin, *The Promised Land* (Boston: Houghton Mifflin Co., 1912), p. 37.

6. Zborowski and Herzog, *Life Is With People*, p. 310.

7. Mary Antin, *From Plotzk to Boston* (Boston: W. B. Clarke and Co., 1899), p. 12.

FROM PEONAGE (pp. 184–202)

1. Oscar Lewis, *Pedro Martínez:* A Mexican Peasant and His Family (New York; Random House, 1964), p. 55.

2. Manuel Gamio, *Mexican Immigration to the United States:* A Study of Human Migration and Adjustment (Chicago: The University of Chicago Press, 1930), p. 223.

3. Manuel Gamio (compiler), *The Mexican Immigrant:* His Life-Story (Chicago: The University of Chicago Press, 1931), p. 25.

4. Gamio, *Mexican Immigration,* pp. 205-206.

5. Gamio, *The Mexican Immigrant,* p. 49.

IMMIGRATION FACTS AND FIGURES (pp. 203–208)

1. Maurice R. Davie, *World Immigration* (New York: The Macmillan Co., 1936), p. 21.

2. William J. Bromwell, *History of Immigration to the United States* (New York: Redfield, 1856), pp. 18-19.

3. Charles Wagley and Marvin Harris, *Minorities in the New World:* Six Case Studies (First published in 1958 by the United Nations Educational, Scientific, and Cultural Organization), Columbia paperback edition, p. 120.

En-p'ing